AMERICAN JURISPRUDENCE,

1870–1970: A HISTORY

JAMES E. HERGET

AMERICAN JURISPRUDENCE,

1870-1970

A HISTORY

Rice University Press   Houston, Texas

Copyright 1990 by
Rice University Press
All rights reserved'
Printed in the USA
1990

Requests for permission to
reproduce material from this work
should be addressed to:
Rice University Press
Rice University
Post Office Box 1892
Houston, Texas 77251

Library of Congress Cataloging-in-Publication Data
Herget, James E.
    American jurisprudence, 1870–1970 : a history / James E. Herget.
       p.   cm.
    Includes bibliographical references and index.
    ISBN 0-89263-305-0 : $35.00
       1. Jurisprudence—United States—History. I. Title.
KF380.H47   1990
349.73—dc20
[347.3]   90-52941
                                                        CIP

TO HELEN

CONTENTS

PREFACE

Jurisprudential activity has alternately thrived and stagnated in response to social change and intellectual trends. The last two decades have seen a flourishing of new scholarship that sometimes appears derivative of earlier writings. Often this work reveals a lack of knowledge of previous relevant scholarship in the history of jurisprudence.

It would be unthinkable for a chemist to pursue a line of experimentation that had been completed and documented in the literature a half century ago. A linguist who set out to record and analyze the language of a traditional society whose language had already been recorded and analyzed by others would be regarded as wasting time. Yet, in jurisprudence, much of the practice, both past and present, seems to arise out of an ignorance of what has gone before.

One of the reasons that previous work in the field is ignored is because the field is ill defined. It is a ragbag, a stepchild of philosophy, social science, history, and law itself. The lack of organization in jurisprudence makes it difficult to know what is significant in past scholarship. A traditionally recognized body of learning does exist, more or less, but, as bibliographies attest, the subject has little coherence, is not easily researched, and often fails to demonstrate any unifying principle.

The reason no unifying principle can be found is because there is no conceptual unity. The various jurisprudential "schools" started from different premises, were influenced by different intellectual climates, sought to answer different questions, and arose at different periods in history. The tie that holds them together is not a principle but a continuity. Although scholars have the benefit of the work of those who went before them, each generation has its own problems and its own new ideas and perspectives. Ahistorical consideration of theories by themselves, while worthwhile, can be less rewarding than a study of the same theories in their historical context. This is the difficulty with textbooks on jurisprudence that present a smorgasbord of legal theories seriatim, each seeming to stand independently, unrelated to the others. Often omitted in such texts, the historical connections between the theories give us an understanding of their relationship to each other and an appreciation of the earlier efforts of scholars.

What is needed, then, is a guide to jurisprudential thought that ties some of the strands together historically. This is what I attempt to provide here.

By showing how and why issues have arisen historically and how they have been dealt with, one can develop a family tree of jurisprudential thought. Of course, to do the whole job one would have to begin with Plato and trace developments to the most recent critical legal scholar. Lacking both time and space to do that, I have narrowed the scope of this project to one century of development in the United States. Much of our significant jurisprudence occurs in this period. Because many of the leading thinkers in this period were not Americans, it will be necessary to point out the impact of foreign work on Americans, although all that can really be done within the scope of this book is to identify briefly some of those influences.

Jurisprudence is, of course, the philosophy of law. It involves speculation and argumentation about the fundamental characteristics of law and legal systems, about the nature of legal obligation, about the explicit and implicit sources of the law, and about the justification of the law, among other subjects. We need not offer a specific definition; indeed, the approach taken here will be to examine what the scholars of the time thought to be the questions and answers of jurisprudence, and to the extent possible we will explain why they thought so.

We shall consequently let history define our subject matter for us. We will look to the legal periodical literature and to books and monographs. In other words we will consider as appropriate subject matter for this book what the community of legal scholars (broadly construed) at any particular time regarded as legal theory or jurisprudence. It is their efforts to deal intellectually with the philosophic aspects of law that will be chronicled here. This is essentially a history, not a philosophic work, and its basic organization is therefore chronological.

A bibliography of both primary and secondary sources is offered for the reader who wishes to pursue a particular subject further. Biographical information about the various theorists has been taken from standard biographical dictionaries, and no attempt has been made to footnote these sources. For further information on the general movements in jurisprudence, philosophy, and law, the reader is referred to the bibliography of secondary sources.

I wish to thank my colleagues, Stephen K. Huber and David R. Dow, for reading a draft of the entire manuscript and offering valuable suggestions. In addition, John Mixon and Joseph Sanders read selected chapters and also made valuable suggestions. I am also indebted to Rice University Press. All errors, of course, are my own. I would like to thank Dean Robert Knauss and the University of Houston Law Center for a semester's leave to work on the book.

INTRODUCTION

This history of jurisprudence tells its own story, but it is appropriate at the outset to consider what motivated scholars to articulate jurisprudential theory and what the main issues were with which they struggled. When one realizes that theorists attempt to do different things with their theories, it becomes clear that the theories are not so much opposed to one another as they are traveling in different directions. This does not necessarily mean that they can be completely reconciled; inevitably there will be points of confrontation where theories lead to specific contradictory conclusions. However, each theory can be better appreciated if one understands the author's objective. Two broad objectives can be identified in the work of jurisprudential writers: to make legal scholarship intellectually respectable and to provide a groundwork for either justification or criticism of specific aspects of the existing law or of the legal system in general.

There is no doubt that from 1870 to 1940 the principal motivation for most theorists was to make scholarly work in law "scientific." That law was a legitimate subject of study at a university was in doubt. The Anglo-American tradition in legal education lagged far behind the Continental. The early American scholars attempted to construct a respectable discipline along two quite different lines. Following the lead of the English positivists, scholars like Henry T. Terry, Wesley N. Hohfeld, and Albert Kocourek sought to ground legal scholarship in an analytic science built on definition and classification. Others like William G. Hammond and James C. Carter, influenced by Henry Maine and Friedrich Carl von Savigny, sought to base legal knowledge on history, with principles of legal evolution as the guide to understanding. In each case the primary purpose of developing theoretical explanations was to demonstrate that the study of law involved much more than mere systemization of professional practices and that it required sophisticated learning and intellectual skill. While some interesting theories were offered, the evolutionists failed to establish a tenable theory that would withstand the test of time. On the other hand, advocates of the expository paradigm, especially the proponents of the *Restatements*, were moderately successful in establishing the legitimacy of the discipline of law, at least until their view of "science" was challenged.

After Roscoe Pound had drawn attention to the importance of extra-legal factors in explaining the legal process, and after the social sciences had become established, many legal scholars rejected the old analytical science and pseudoevolutionary theory in favor of the new social science. Frederick Beutel, Walter Wheeler Cook, Hessel Yntema, Underhill Moore, and Huntington Cairns were among the leading "legal scientists." The new science was usually a form of behaviorism, and a crude philosophical grounding of it was accepted by most theorists. However, the discipline of law itself was not ultimately made into a social science; indeed, to the extent that empirical investigation of legal phenomena succeeded, it was ultimately appropriated by the social scientists into their own disciplines, thereby casting new doubts on the legitimacy of the law professor's vocation. Jurisprudence never quite succeeded in proving law academically worthy. It was half a victory.

Few scholars in the late nineteenth and early twentieth centuries were moved to create jurisprudential theory for the purpose of providing moral or political critiques of law. While specific legal reforms were regularly advanced by progressives—a group that included much of legal academia—general philosophical justification of the law from a moral standpoint received little attention from legal scholars until the late 1930s. The accepted justification of the system tended to be either a reverent restatement of the liberal political doctrines of the founding fathers or an appeal to the mysterious power of the ancient common law to work itself out for the good of all. Even Pound, the foremost expounder of jurisprudence, rather tardily added his program of pragmatic interest-balancing to his sociological jurisprudence, and it did not immediately elicit much criticism or praise in the 1920s.

Many of the realists prided themselves on having no moral dimension to their theory, although they tended to be pragmatists by temperament. The most extreme among them, like Thurman Arnold, preached moral and cultural relativism. This was part of what set the stage for the resurgence of interest in the moral basis of law. From the late 1930s to 1970 much jurisprudential writing was motivated by a desire to justify law on moral grounds, and particularly to justify the democratic American legal system. The world political climate challenged home-grown American legal values. The Neo-Thomists were the leaders in the justificatory movement, although other voices were heard as well. Jerome Hall and Edmond Cahn offered intuitive theories. Filmer Northrop relied on "first-order facts." Felix Cohen advocated utilitarianism. Lon Fuller talked about the morality of law. Ronald Dworkin spoke of traditional principles and policies. Charles Fried and John Rawls advanced a more Kantian perspective. Even Pound's theory of interests still had supporters. None of these specific views became dominant. Although there were some indications that a mainstream consensus might materialize, jurisprudence failed to provide a generally accepted justification for the legal system before 1970.

Dissatisfaction with the existing legal system and the critique of it, the alternative to justification, was a motivating force in producing legal theory in the forty years before 1970. Although both Oliver Wendell Holmes, Jr., and Roscoe Pound had been critical of formalism in law, the American legal realists made negative criticism central to their efforts. Led by scholars like Karl Llewellyn, Jerome Frank, Thurman Arnold, and Hessel Yntema, the realists attacked the premises of the dominant expository paradigm. They cast serious doubts about its validity by demonstrating in individual cases and in specific subject areas of the law that formal rules of law were highly ambiguous, often contradictory, and failed to determine judicial decisions. They looked to social science to develop an alternative theory, but this effort failed. Nevertheless, their critique was never effectively repudiated.

A second wave of criticism against the legal status quo took the form of protest against legal racial discrimination, beginning in the 1950s and later widening into a more general critique in favor of the "rights" of the disadvantaged in American society. Scholars attempted, on the one hand, to justify the innovative decisions of the Warren Court and, on the other, to attack the establishment policies that seemed to disfavor the poor, certain ethnic groups, and women. Dworkin, Rawls, and others formulated theories based on natural rights or on political principles that overrode the rules of the legal system. A theoretical basis was sought that would justify both the overall system of democracy and individual rights, especially the rights of society's disadvantaged.

The negative criticisms of both realists and latter-day moralists were successful. Both movements set jurisprudence to work to find an epistemological and moral grounding for challenging the established system.

A century of jurisprudential history has also witnessed the creation of and struggle with numerous controversial issues. These can, however, be classified into two very general categories: How is law to be understood? And what is the basis for evaluating the law? The first question involves two different, although related, intellectual issues. First, what must be taken into account and what must be excluded in giving an intelligible and useful explanation of law? The advocates of the expository paradigm like Henry T. Terry and Wesley N. Hohfeld (and later Hans Kelsen and H.L.A.

Hart) followed the Austinian example of deliberately limiting the "legal" to authoritative rules. Law was autonomous; it was argued that efforts to explain law by using history, sociology, or politics confuse different types of explanation. A narrow and carefully guarded approach would eliminate confusion, it was thought, and would help judges and lawyers to think clearly. Above all, jurisprudential theory must assure that the individual morality of the judge, the customary morality of society, and the morality of ecclesiastics be carefully distinguished from the law. Clarification of concepts and terminology were the important tasks for legal scholars. The method of isolating law from other social phenomena was achieved by postulation or definition.

The Poundians took almost the opposite approach. Sensing the inherent sterility of the expository perspective, they advocated taking into account the morality, customs, and practices of society in explaining judicial decision. In addition, the insights of psychology and anthropology were to be considered. The realist extremists tended to exclude entirely the very things that the positivists thought central: legal principles, concepts, doctrines, and rules. Also important (at least for Pound himself, Julius Stone, and Morris and Felix Cohen), the moral aspect of law as dictated by a pragmatic moral philosophy must be included in any comprehensive account. Failure to relate these important factors to the overall process of making and applying law would result, it was suggested, in a failure of explanation. The issue of how to account for the law between the expository and the Poundian paradigms was never better pinpointed than in the exchange between Edgar Bodenheimer, H.L.A. Hart, and Ronald Dworkin in the 1960s.

The evolutionists had a different perspective on the question of how law was to be understood. They were eager to explain law as a historical product. Theorists like William G. Hammond, James C. Carter, John Henry Wigmore, and even Holmes (in his historical mode) were fascinated by explanations of the origins of legal artifacts and how they evolved into their current status. They illuminated a perspective that had been totally ignored by the positivists and had been largely disregarded by the Poundians, although historical explanation was not theoretically ruled out in that paradigm. For evolutionists, to account for law was to account historically. Friedrich A. Hayek was the lone supporter of the evolutionary insights in the second half of the twentieth century. It must be noted, however, that the evolutionists failed to see the value of the other approaches, and, regrettably, many theorists of other persuasions failed to see the kernel of truth in the evolutionary paradigm. As a result, no other theory before 1970 incorporated the insights of this school of thought.

The natural-law thinkers and their allies required a moral theory to accompany any legal theory. Their conception of the positive law of a given society could be quite consistent with the expository view, as with most of the Thomists, or it could be consistent with a Poundian view, as with Jerome Hall and Lon Fuller. What was distinctive, of course, was that they insisted on emphasizing the importance of a moral grounding for any legal system. The law received its legitimacy, its authority, and its meaning from its moral source. No understanding of law could be adequate without accounting for this moral dimension. Thus, the several viewpoints differed on what was to be included in accounting for law.

The different schools of thought also suggested different answers to another side of the question, "How is law to be understood?" From an epistemological perspective some theorists asked not what is to be included in our explanation of law, but how we know what we know about law. Advocates of the expository paradigm seemed to come closest to a nineteenth-century philosophy of science. Basic concepts of the "science" were postulated or defined, and empirical data on the operation of actual legal systems were placed within the postulated scheme. Terms and concepts could be modified to adapt to the facts. Unlike theories of natural science, however, the Austinian types of legal theory were not predictive, partly because their basic propositions were analytic (true only by definition) instead of synthetic, and partly because they were normative and not descriptive. While they might prove what law *ought* to be in a particular case, the result could not be empirically verified. Legal positivism was a pseudoscience.

The evolutionists presented an even more obscure idea of how they knew what they knew. The reported events in legal history could be assimilated into an empirical theory, but the explanations offered of historical change were pure speculation. Unlike Darwin's theory, those of the legal evolutionists did not offer any explanatory mechanism. There was no real counterpart to Darwin's reproduction, environment, mutation, and natural selection.

A little more could be said for the Poundians' epistemology. The sociological aspect of the paradigm pointed to real scientific thinking. However, in practice this turned out to require the incorporation of norms or values into the facts; that is, legal scientists could deal with the reality and validity of norms as observed in a particular legal system, but there was no way in which they could evaluate those norms. Yet the full-blown Poundian paradigm purported to have a normative dimension. How one could know the relationship between the facts of legal phenomena, the norms of the legal system, and the pragmatic interest-balancing evaluative scheme was never adequately explained. Certainly a simple empiricism would not explain this theory, nor would a set of definitions.

The Thomists offered the most respectable epistemology; indeed, one of the great attractions of this version of natural law was the fact that it provided a theory of knowledge. This essentially Aristotelian theory, however, was at odds with much of the philosophy of modern science, and, as advanced by Roman Catholic thinkers, it suggested acceptance of theological ideas that were out of the mainstream of western thinking in the twentieth century.

Fuller, Hall, Cahn, and Felix Cohen reasserted the vague but somehow attractive idea that the moral imperatives behind legal precepts were not absolute and immutable but were determined, at least in part, by the context of decision; yet, these moral notions were not subjective to the decision-maker. This was perhaps a variation on the pragmatism of William James and John Dewey (and hence foreshadowed by Poundian theory), but it reflected a characteristic shift in thinking from the first to the second half of the twentieth century. Both Dworkin and Rawls (with his process of reflective equilibrium) suggested that we can have normative knowledge that is contingent on our own experience and culture yet can be empirically objective at the same time. Coming from an entirely different perspective, the critical theorists were approaching a similar conclusion. This epistemology was not fully worked out in the period covered by this book, but the seeds of it were planted.

When the other major issue—evaluation of the law—is raised, theories of natural law immediately come to mind; it is true that natural-law thinkers and others who emphasized the moral aspect of law were very much concerned with measuring or interpreting the positive law according to moral standards, and they constructed theories in which positive law was subordinated to higher moral principles. Nevertheless, the evaluation of law was a concern of others as well.

The advocates of the expository paradigm evaluated the law internally; that is, they evaluated specific rules, doctrines, and concepts in terms of their consistency with other aspects of the system. Court decisions could be labeled right or wrong depending on how closely they used logic to arrive at their conclusions from premises established by official legal precepts. A critique of any area of law could be made through logical analysis with perhaps a little help from analogical reasoning. While no positivist ever insisted that court decisions flowed inexorably from formal premises, this was nevertheless the ideal, and approximation to the ideal was always to be sought. Rigorous terminology, as suggested by Terry,

Hohfeld, and Kocourek, was thought to be indispensable for clear thinking on legal questions. This was consistent with the traditional roles allocated to the judge and the lawyer by liberal democratic theory. Major questions of policy were for the legislature; operation of the legal system was confined to analysis of the law.

The Poundians rejected this view, although skeptical realists and legal scientists offered nothing in the way of evaluative standards. Pound and some of his followers offered pragmatic interest-balancing as the preferred mode of evaluation. This meant going outside the legal system and, especially, evaluating law in terms of its consequences. While the theory showed great promise and was consistent with the temperament of the times in which it was developed, it was never refined into a workable system. Later, Myres McDougal and Harold Lasswell did systematize such evaluation, but their scheme used innovative terminology and concepts that were never accepted by the legal profession or even by legal academia.

Those theorists who had roots in the Poundian paradigm but wanted to develop the moral basis of law—Fuller, Hall, and Cahn—were only partly successful in their efforts. Fuller offered insights but no overall theory. Hall and Cahn fell back upon intuitionism. It remained for Rawls, Fried, and especially Dworkin to develop more positive theories of the moral-legal relationship. However, these developments reached fruition after 1970.

1

THE BACKGROUND OF

EUROPEAN THINKING

As with American cooking, dress, manners, language, law, and general philosophic development, American legal theory started as a European transplant, beginning to grow in the late 1800s and reaching maturity around the third decade of the twentieth century. Even after that, fresh injections of new ideas from Europe continued to affect American thinking. To understand the beginnings of serious American legal philosophy in the late nineteenth century we must first sketch the background of thinking that carried over from Europe. Let us briefly survey the ideas about law, its nature, its justification, its role in society, its place in legitimate academic study, and its relation to other bodies of knowledge that pressed upon the new world from the old.

Classification of philosophical "schools" is somewhat arbitrary, but we can use the conventional categories of thinking that many nineteenth- and early twentieth-century thinkers employed. There were three major schools of thought: natural law, positivism, and historicism. To avoid misleading connotations that these names sometimes generate, I will use the terms "the moral paradigm," "the expository paradigm," and "the evolutionary paradigm," respectively.

The Moral Paradigm

Theories of natural law, also known as the law of nature, natural rights, human rights, the law of reason, divine law, natural justice, and in this book the moral paradigm, were dominant in Europe down to the end of the eighteenth century, although the roots of this type of thinking run back through medieval times to the ancient Greeks and Romans. Kant and Rousseau, however different, were the last of the great thinkers to make a concept of natural rights central to their jurisprudential thinking. In this view morality and law are inseparable.

With the exception of sporadic expositions of the Thomistic version by scholars at Roman Catholic institutions, the old moral paradigm did not really receive any intellectual support in American jurisprudence until around 1940. These developments are discussed in chapter 9. And while the idea has had some impact upon Supreme Court decisions throughout American history, serious theoretical exposition in the natural-law mode did not begin until World War II.

It is important to understand the main theme of the moral paradigm since the evolutionary and expository schools are in part reactions to it. The key to grasping the idea of natural law lies in understanding the kind of explanation of social phenomena that it offers. Modern science explains natural phenomena in terms of cause and effect. Social science also attempts to use this kind of explanation, although there is some doubt that it succeeds. Much historical explanation is essentially similar to that of social science. Another, and older, way of explaining things is in terms of purpose. Such teleological explanations are quite commonplace in ordinary parlance. For example, what is a typewriter? It is a machine used for typing words and numbers on paper. We understand what it is by knowing what it is supposed to do, by knowing its purpose. Human inventions and institutions are, in fact, usually described or explained in terms of their purpose or function.

To take an example of how something can be explained in two ways, consider the question, "What is an airplane?" The answer may take the following form: it is a machine that rises in the air when the lift created by passage of air over the wings exceeds the force of gravity and is propelled forward when the thrust exceeds the drag. This is a technological explanation that depends on certain scientific principles, which in turn assume cause and effect. The question may be answered, however, just as legitimately by saying that an airplane is a machine that enables people to fly; here, the airplane is explained by reference to its purpose.

The latter type of explanation in relation to law leads to the concept of natural law. Human beings have certain characteristics in common. They eat, sleep, procreate, fight, celebrate, and so forth; that is, they have a common nature, a kind of normal functioning. One of the features of common human nature is the necessity of social cooperation. But in order for people to live together in society and thereby accomplish many other natural functions, certain types of conduct must be made mandatory: for example, people cannot generally kill one another; at least some of the people must be economically productive; an agreement must be reached on the allocation of some types of decision-making within the group; and continuing violence within the group must be prevented. Thus, the nature of human beings requires that certain kinds of conduct be prohibited and other kinds of conduct be permitted, or perhaps required. These general principles of human conduct, applicable to all peoples at all places and times (so long as human nature remains the same), are the natural law.

In some versions of the moral paradigm that were articulated in the seventeenth and eighteenth centuries—by Hobbes, Locke, Kant, Rousseau, and others—the social contract became a key feature. Under this view human beings in a hypothetical state of nature would opt for the establishment of a government with lawmaking powers. Although these theories may, on the surface, appear to be empirically based, there is at the foundation of all of them a teleological argument.

Natural laws take the form of deontic statements like "Thou shalt not kill." This statement creates a right on the part of all persons in the society to be free from homicidal acts by others. It also creates a duty on the part of all persons to refrain from killing others. Natural rights, then, are not something different from natural law but refer to the entitlement aspect of the relationship created by a natural law. Thus, to be endowed by one's creator with certain "inalienable rights" is an indirect way of saying that the creator has established a natural law that entails both those rights and corresponding duties in other persons.

Human laws have a role to play in the moral paradigm. They are convenient and sometimes even necessary to limit conduct in certain ways dictated by the context of social intercourse. A simple example would be the law that requires automobile drivers to drive on the righthand side of the road. This is not a natural law, but the natural law dictates that some such rule be adopted and enforced by the authorities in a society in which automobiles are commonplace. The rule may require driving on the left side (as in England and Japan), or on the right side, or it may be more complicated. The absence of such a rule would result in traffic snarls, if not in injury and chaos; hence, in this context some human rule is needed to supplement the natural law. Such rules derive their authority from the fact that they are supplemental to and derivative of the natural law. Human laws (or purported human laws) that are contrary to the dictates of natural law lose their authority and legitimacy for that reason; they are not law but exercises of naked power.

The moral paradigm makes natural law both the legitimator and the authority for all human laws. A legal system that generally conforms to the requirements of natural law is one that deserves respect and obedience. One that does not suggests civil disobedience or even revolution.

The moral paradigm can be used to support radical as well as conservative political causes. It was used by Thomas Aquinas to justify obedience to the medieval political-legal structure and by Thomas Jefferson to justify the revolt against the king of England. The moral paradigm contains its own built-in standards for the critique of positive law. It views such law as a part, and a subordinate part, of the necessary moral relationships between individuals in society.

It is worthwhile in this discussion of the moral paradigm to point out some of its better-known shortcomings. Some critics would say that the idea of natural law makes sense as an abstract generality, but any attempt to apply it to specific legal and ethical issues is impossible. Hence, the idea is useless as a practical matter. This is best illustrated by the efforts of some seventeenth- and eighteenth-century philosophers to list fundamental or natural rights to which all men (and not necessarily women) were supposed to be entitled. No one's list agreed with anyone else's.

Another objection to the moral paradigm is that it assumes agreement on what the human being's "ends" are, or, putting it another way, that the particular theory justifies or prescribes what the ends of a person are. But, in fact, people have all sorts of different ideas about what their ends in life are. What might be a good moral code for a group of altruistic otherworldly monks would not work for a society of cutthroat entrepreneurs. Some people see perfection in the arts, music, or scholarship as the ultimate purpose in life; others prefer the pursuit of wealth. Physical survival is deemed paramount by some, while the martyr and would-be martyr believe self-sacrifice to be a higher good. This disagreement on the priority of purposes undermines any attempt to construct a universal code of conduct even at the most abstract levels.

Knowledge of the natural law is supposed to be within reach of every mature person of ordinary intelligence, but the manner in which such knowledge is obtained has never been satisfactorily explained. Certainly in the context of a particular legal problem or issue good minds seem to differ. If, then, knowledge of the natural law is so problematic, its usefulness is illusory. Perhaps the apparent knowlege claimed for natural law is nothing more than one's set of cultural prejudices. After all, natural law was given credence by both the ancient Greeks and the Romans, two societies in which slavery was commonplace. Finally, some would say that teleological explanations are unacceptable. They are nonempirical, unscientific, and carry with them unwanted metaphysical baggage. In some versions they include a theological basis that is not universally accepted. The moral paradigm smacks of the philosophical discourse of bygone days, discourse in which a priori principles and philosophic universals are used to play games in an abstract world unrelated to reality.

The Expository Paradigm

The expository paradigm became the European jurisprudence initially dominant in late nineteenth-century America. This is partly because it was the most English of jurisprudential views. American law was English; the American language was English; and the American scientific temperament was, like the English, empirical rather than ideal or metaphysical. The term "positivism," another name for the expository paradigm, itself connotes the factual, the real, the concrete. It should be noted, however, that there is an ambiguity in the term. For John Austin, the father of legal positivism, the term is used to denote *position*, that is, a law is a law because it is laid down by a superior to an inferior. As used by Auguste Compte, the father of sociology, the term means empirical, concrete, or factual. Other names for this kind of jurisprudence are analytic jurisprudence and Austinianism. To understand why the expository paradigm has had such an impact on English and American jurisprudential thought, it is necessary to see it against the background of development in legal education in the two countries.[1]

The tradition of legal education on the continent of Europe is coterminous with the tradition of higher education in general. The first subject to be studied in the newly formed universities of the eleventh and twelfth centuries was law, that is, the newly rediscovered law of the *Corpus Juris Civilis* of Emperor Justinian. Roman law continued to be studied in the universities of Europe (including Oxford and Cambridge) from that time to the present. However, in most countries of the Continent the Roman law, through its new forms as civil law or canon law, worked its way into the accepted doctrine and practice of medieval jurisdictions and later into national legal systems. Thus, law as the legitimate object of study in the university was never questioned. In England a different course of events took place.

Because of the early centralization of legal power with the king in England and because of the rise of the peculiar institution of the Inns of

---

1. For the history of legal education in England, see generally T. Plucknett, *A Concise History of the Common Law*, 215-93 (5th ed. 1956). For the history of legal education in the United States, see generally R. Stevens, *Law School: Legal Education in America from the 1850s to the 1980s* (1983).

Court, the development of English law, the English legal profession, and English legal education diverged from the Continental pattern. Roman law continued to be taught at Oxford and Cambridge as canon law and civil law (scholars of the latter are called civilians), but practical legal education in the law of the king's courts was carried on at the Inns of Court from the 1200s to the 1500s; and it is the law of the king's courts that was ultimately to prevail. But from the time printing was introduced in England in the early 1500s, the importance and educational role of the Inns of Court declined. An apprenticeship system eventually replaced the earlier, more rigorous educational experience at the Inns of Court for the barristers (and judges), although the formal requirement of attendance at one of the Inns remains to the present day.

Philosophy in the general sense of theoretical speculation has been an activity of scholars at universities and of occasional unaffiliated free thinkers. It has never been a common activity of lawyers. Even the greatest legal thinkers in the English tradition who wrote scholarly works—Bracton, Coke, Hale—wrote analyses of the law being practiced before the courts. Their concern was practical. Although concepts had to be developed and critically scrutinized and apparent inconsistencies had to be reconciled, theory in any grand sense was beyond the interests of these legal craftsmen.

The application of legal theory to the English legal system itself, as opposed to the long-term academic discussion of natural law and Roman law in all its old and new forms by the civilians (jurists of the Roman-derived law), was precipitated in England by the creation of the Vinerian chair of law at Oxford in 1758, the first vehicle through which English (the king's) law was ever taught to English students at a university. William Blackstone first occupied this chair. By virtue of his mission to present the English law to educated nonlawyers, he was forced to make an organized exposition of what the English law was, to the extent possible in lay terms, and to demonstrate why it was a legitimate "science" or subject fit for academic treatment. Viewed in terms of this basic mission, Blackstone was successful.

Blackstone's efforts to relate the English law to general academic theory about law and to give an organized exposition of that law led to the critical reaction of Jeremy Bentham and the philosophical radicals, and through the legal specialist of the group, John Austin, English legal theory came into flower. In spite of the creation of some additional chairs of law at Cambridge, Oxford, the University of London, and a few American universities, legal education for lawyers in both countries remained a matter of apprenticeship until the second half of the nineteenth century. In 1846 the House of Commons appointed a committee to report on what had come to be regarded as the sad state of legal education in England. This resulted in the establishment of the Council of Legal Education in 1851 and the Royal Commission in 1855. A bar examination was established over great objections, and serious attention was finally given to the subject matter of the examinations and therefore the subject matter of the law courses taught at the Inns of Court and the universities. The remarks of William Markby, a professor at Oxford, written in 1871, describe the situation and the attitude of academics to it.

> Until very lately, the only study of law known in England was that preparation for the actual practice of the profession which was procured by attendance in the chambers of a barrister or pleader. The Universities had almost entirely ceased to teach law; and there was nowhere in England any faculty, or body of learned persons, who made it their business to give instruction in law after a systematic method. . . .
>
> But the only preparation and grounding which a University is either able, or, I suppose, would be desirous to give, is in law considered as a science; or at least, if that is not yet possible, in law considered as a collection of principles capable of being systematically arranged, and resting, not on bare authority, but on sound logical deduction; all departures from which, in the existing system, must be marked and explained. In other words, law must be studied in a University, not merely as it has resulted from the exigencies of society, but in its general relations to the several parts of the same system, and to other systems.[2]

Although further reform was slow, the teaching of law gradually migrated into the hands of professors and away from lawyers' chambers and offices.[3]

After the Civil War a similar phenomenon occurred in the United States, although not because of any government commission. Led by the Harvard Law School under Dean Christopher Columbus Langdell, a sweeping change in legal education arose from a fundamental shift in the role of the university in American life. From a trainer of preachers and priests, the

2. W. Markby, *Elements of Law*, ix–x (1871).
3. For discussion of these developments by contemporaries, see Comment, Legal Education in England, 11 Alb. L. J. 87 (1875).

university in America became the seat of higher learning in all fields, particularly the sciences. This is where the positive philosophy of law, or science of law, as propounded by Bentham and Austin came into play.

Bentham and Austin provided the most important theorizing about the law by English thinkers. Bentham's inspiration, in a negative way, was the exposition of English law given by Blackstone in the third quarter of the eighteenth century, later to be published in four volumes as *Commentaries on the Laws of England*.[4] Blackstone's *Commentaries* was not in substance a work of legal theory. However, two aspects of the *Commentaries* are significant for legal theory. First, Blackstone organized the body of the common law into categories for the purpose of exposition (rights of persons, rights of things, private wrongs, public wrongs). These categories, borrowed and modified from civil law, had never been applied to English law; indeed, the English law had never been completely organized before. Mathew Hale, author of a history of English law,[5] had provided the outline for this organization, drawing on the organization of Justinian's Institutes, and Blackstone amplified and completed it.[6] Thus, Blackstone offered an organizational structure upon which analysis could be undertaken.

Second, Blackstone's famous introductory chapter purported to connect the world of legal theory, that is, academic discourse, to the actual world of English law so that the latter could be viewed in the context of the overall "scientific" study of law as it was understood in the eighteenth century. Actually, no one had ever made any serious connection between English law and legal philosophy, and, indeed, Blackstone failed to do so himself. What he propounded in his introductory chapter was a not very disguised version of Swiss theorist Jean Jacques Burlamaqui's statement of natural law and its relation to positive, or human law.

Bentham was very upset with the conservative, apologetic, and somewhat intellectually dishonest presentation of law given by Blackstone, and he devoted many hours to a critique of Blackstone's exposition. This critique is contained in two of Bentham's earliest works, *A Comment on the Commentaries* and *A Fragment on Government*; only the latter was published in his lifetime (in 1776). Bentham's principal and very creative major work was *Introduction to the Principles of Morals and Legislation*,

---

4. W. Blackstone, *Commentaries on the Laws of England* (4 vols. 1765–69).

5. M. Hale, *History of the Common Law* (1792).

6. See W. Hammond, *Introduction to The Institutes of Justinian* (trans. Sandars), first American edition (1876), for the origins of Blackstone's scheme of organization.

published in 1789, in which he outlined his general philosophy of legislation and law.

Bentham's pupil and colleague, John Austin, was most interested in the implications of Bentham's theories for the law, whereas the other famous members of this group of philosophical radicals, James Mill and John Stuart Mill, focused their attention on the political and ethical side of Benthamite philosophy (utilitarianism) and on its epistemology. Austin completed his seminal work, *The Province of Jurisprudence Determined*, in 1832. It was not enthusiastically received in England, but it was very highly regarded on the Continent. The work was republished posthumously by his widow in 1861 along with his additional "Lectures on Jurisprudence," an extension of the earlier work not previously published.[7] Because of developments in legal education in both England and the United States, the timing of this later publication was probably important in promoting the influence of the work.[8]

It was well known even in America that Roman law had long been taught at the universities in most European countries and that it was regarded as a science or discipline worthy of academic treatment. The common law, on the other hand, had, for the past two or three centuries, been regarded primarily as a practice, an art or trade (albeit prestigious) to be learned by watching, reading, listening, and doing under the guidance of practitioners and judges. Could it be that the common law was nothing more than a highly skilled artisan's practice, like the mortician's or the tanner's? Or was it an intellectual system having its own principles, like astronomy or chemistry—a science? The Romanists had shown the way; it had to be a science.[9] Pride in one's own legal system demanded that the common law be given systematic treatment like the rival civilian systems. Anglo-American law needed to be studied and taught as a science. It sought the legitimacy of an academic discipline.

This presented a challenge to the fledgling universities in the United

7. J. Austin, *Lectures on Jurisprudence* (1861). A reprint of this work in three volumes was published in 1970 by Burt Franklin, New York. Further references to this work will be to that edition and will be designated "Austin."

8. It was the first "scientific" attempt to analyze the law by an English author, and was republished at a time when the scholarly study of law was trying to become scientific. "Experience shows that to establish a study on this [scientific] footing we must have books and teachers specially suited for the purpose. At present, of the first we have scarcely any." W. Markby, *Elements of Law*, x (1871). Markby acknowledged Austin's work as seminal, and he sought to provide a student's version of it in his own book.

9. See Comment, Is Law a Philosophy, a Science or an Art?, 10 Alb. L. J. 371 (1874).

States and to a lesser extent to the two established fortresses of academe in England, Oxford and Cambridge, in which the scholars were absorbed mainly in the study of the classics of the ancients (including the law of Rome). One option was to examine the practice of the most prestigious Continental scholars and to try to imitate their ways. Some Anglo-American scholars were willing to look to the French and Germans, but national pride tended to discourage the importation of foreign methods, at least overtly.[10] Perhaps more important, Anglo-American law had developed in such different ways from civilian systems that it could plausibly be argued that foreign methods were inapplicable. Yet the achievements of the Continentals, primarily the Germans, in the systemization and theoretical development of law challenged the Anglo-Americans to cultivate a serious science of law. The scientific jurisprudence of Austin was offered to the academic world at just the right time.

John Austin outlined a universal theoretical framework that would explain what law was and how it related to the political and social phenomena of any society. Moreover, along with Blackstone, he also provided a basic organizational scheme for the various branches of the law and their subdivisions.[11] In the face of the chaotic historically derived English forms of action, equity, and law merchant with their complex pleadings, precedents, procedures, and convoluted court system, Austin provided a way of conceptualizing and analyzing all of it so that methodical exposition of the whole—scientific treatment—could be accomplished by the scholar. Austin offered the organizational key to the temple of science that the American and English legal scribes sought to enter.

It is important to note that while Austin was a faithful pupil and colleague of Bentham and aimed at the same reform goals, he was also influenced considerably by Continental, particularly German, legal scholarship. He spent a substantial part of his professional life on the Continent, became familiar with civilian legal developments, and mixed with scholars there. Thus, many would contend today that the German influence on the struggle to develop a science of law in England and the United States was much greater than it may superficially appear to have been.

Before reviewing the philosophical approach that Austin's work offered, which was so eagerly welcomed by the Anglo-American "legal

10. The most influential follower of Austin, Professor Thomas E. Holland at Oxford University, did in fact borrow many of his ideas from the Germans, who are cited profusely in his main work, *The Elements of Jurisprudence* (1880).

11. See the tables and notes in Austin, vol. 3, 141ff.

scientists," it will be helpful to outline the difficulty in dealing with law that Bentham and Austin perceived. The problem was twofold: the state of the English legal system at the end of the eighteenth century was chaotic, and the system in light of the accepted morality of the time was unjust.

Bentham was a rationalist reformer. He came to realize better than anyone before him (partly through Blackstone's lectures), that English law was primarily the creation of blind historical accident and that it had no principles, organization, rhyme, or reason. In addition, it was morally corrupt. It often failed to accomplish whatever objectives might be imagined for it; it perpetrated anachronistic rules that made no sense; it ground the poor, fleeced the rich, and gloried in rhetorical nonsense—all in the name of solemn tradition. Bentham's mission in life was to slay this rhetorical dragon. Legislation was to be his sword; indeed, he would be the "Newton of legislation."

Bentham divided the world of legal power conceptually into two parts. On the one side was legislative activity. Laws would be repealed and reformed on the basis of their usefulness to society. The standard by which all laws would be measured was utility, not the utility to any particular individual or individuals but the greatest good for the greatest number. This could be determined through the *felicific calculus* of pleasures and pains. Whatever produced as its consequences more pleasure than pain was good; whatever produced more pain was bad. The ethical theory we know as utilitarianism was Bentham's yardstick to evaluate the law.

But there was a second part to Bentham's approach. The law must be carefully identified and brought into the light of day for evaluation. This may seem obvious to us today, but for people of Bentham's time the task was not so simple. The sources and relative authority of English laws were terribly obscure. They lay hidden in the forms of action, special pleading, bills in Chancery, ancient charters, and occult teachings of precedent. Some said that the Bible was a part of the law of England, perhaps Christian morality generally, along with the king's prerogative, the teachings of the yearbooks, and, of course, the natural law! And above all, the knowledge of this archaic system was the private preserve of lawyers.

How could one attack an iniquitous system that folded itself in the arms of patriotism, morality, and immemorial tradition? It was first necessary to establish a method to determine what counted as law and what did not. Law could never be successfully attacked and reformed if it remained synonymous with goodness and justice. A system had to be devised that would clearly identify law as separate from morality. Bentham set about to do so, and Austin completed the job.

Legislative reform, the first activity of the Benthamite attack on tradition, was to be a science. It was called by its author "censorial" jurisprudence. Much of Bentham's own professional life moved in this direction, including his development of the theory of utilitarianism and his specific reform projects, especially in the field of criminal law. The second thrust of the attack, "expository jurisprudence," consisted in the design of a universal system to describe the law of any country and to distinguish it from the many phenomena that might erroneously appear to have the force of law, such as morality, religion, politics, philosophy, and custom. Once identified, the law would have to be clarified, organized, and carefully analyzed into its fundamental concepts. Systemization was necessary to be sure that there were no inconsistencies that could result in contradictory applications. Indeed, the full application of the law to all situations would need to be known so that the social consequences of the law could be evaluated by the censorial scientist.

With these needs in mind Austin proceeded to develop a system of expository jurisprudence. His method was to give a definition of law that would exclude those competing norms which might be confused with law, such as biblical authority, church doctrine, divine law, customary morality, political dogmas, and so on. Law consisted of the commands of the sovereign, who was that person or persons whom the bulk of any society was in the habit of obeying, a question to be determined empirically in any given society. A true sovereign was not himself or herself in the habit of obedience to anyone else. Thus, while legal authority might be spread throughout a society among various officials, there must be some ultimate lawmaking authority to which all others are subordinate. True legal systems can be found only in societies (nations) where such ultimate authority can be identified.

In Austin's theory the sovereign, acting directly or by delegation to subordinates, issues commands that create rights and duties on the part of individuals in society. These are legal rights and duties that carry the sanction of official force or threat of force. Citizens are expected to comply with their legal obligations under penalty of legal sanction. Conversely, if the violation of a norm is followed by the imposition of a sanction, then it is a legal norm.

In this view it becomes the task of the jurist or legal scholar to reveal and clarify the meaning of the law in various contexts. A common and strictly followed vocabulary and a conceptual structure (preferably one applicable to any legal system) are starting points. An understanding of the relationship between substantive rule, procedure, and remedy is also essential. Austin conceived that there were certain basic ideas common to all legal systems that needed to be carefully analyzed and distinguished. Among these basic concepts, with all their subspecies, were rights, duties, sanctions, persons, acts, forbearances, will, motive, and others.

Although Austin tended to follow the organization of the law that originated with the civilians and that was influenced by Blackstone, he was not especially pleased with it.[12] He favored codification of the law (one of Bentham's favorite reforms), but, unlike Bentham, he appreciated that an intellectually satisfactory codification would have to be preceded by further analytic development along the lines that he had started and that it would require the work of many minds over an extended period of time.

Within this scientifically derived autonomous framework of rules, concepts, and principles the Austinian scholar could engage in analysis and exegesis. She or he draws the perimeters of legal concepts, reconciles conflicting authorities, sometimes introduces new rationale, and critiques doctrine in the light of its consistency with other aspects of the legal system. This internal critique—expository jurisprudence—was regarded as the scientific study of law because it invoked intellectual activity on a clearly defined subject matter in which principles and logic played important roles.

Austin's work presented itself to those officials considering what the proper form and substance should be for the academic teaching of law in England in the third quarter of the nineteenth century. They tended to favor Austin's approach, since it not only provided organization and coherence but could be regarded as genuinely scientific by the standards of the day.[13] As a jurisprudence it had an additional appeal; it avoided political controversy, since it concerned itself solely with the internal critique of the law.

Austin's work was dry and repetitive, written in a style that made reading it truly laborious; it did not long remain the only statement of

12. See W. Hammond, note 6.

13. By 1883 it could be said by a Cambridge professor, "After a life which had so little of the well-deserved success to balance so much disappointment and failure, the work of the dead Austin is achieving results beyond what even he would have anticipated. It is undoubtedly forming a school of English jurists, possibly of English legislators also. It is the staple of jurisprudence in all our systems of legal education." E. Clark, *Practical Jurisprudence: A Comment on Austin*, 4–5 (1883).

English jurisprudence. It was followed by the work of disciples who modified it in directions necessary for academic use by both simplifying and expanding its various themes. Scholars at all of the British universities began to pursue Austinian analysis,[14] and Americans as well began reading Austin and his followers after the Civil War. The analytic influence gradually crept into legal academe as university-affiliated law schools began to proliferate.

A very limited critique of the expository paradigm may be useful by way of conclusion. It could be argued that the original division of the intellectual study of law into censorial and expository sciences was a mistake. First, the division, as it has worked out at least, has placed the two subject matters in the hands of two different sets of thinkers. The expository paradigm has engaged those who deal with the law on an everyday basis—arguing, justifying, advising—the lawyers, law teachers, and judges. The censorial paradigm (or science of legislation) has placed the questions of policy—moral, political, technocratic—in the hands of political scientists, sociologists, clergy, and "experts" of every stripe, many of whom are not legally trained and who may not have a technical understanding of how the legal system really works. One consequence of this division of labor is that lawyers feel no obligation, as lawyers, to be critics—to reform and improve the law.

The division of scientific effort between censorial and expository has also been criticized on the grounds that divorcing law from morality and politics is impossible and results in a false sense of certainty. Law operates

14. Markby's simplification of the Austinian work, *Elements of Law* (1871), was followed by two works by Sheldon Amos, professor at University College, London, one designed for beginning students, the other more sophisticated: *A Systematic View of the Science of Jurisprudence* (1872) and *The Science of Law* (1874). The most influential and important of the revisions of Austin's work was that of Thomas Erskine Holland, professor of law at Oxford, entitled *The Elements of Jurisprudence*, first published in 1880 and followed by twelve editions to 1917. An earlier preliminary work entitled *Essays upon the Form of the Law* was published by Holland in 1870. Two Cambridge scholars followed Holland's lead and published their own versions of the Austinian gospel: E. Clark, *Practical Jurisprudence: A Comment on Austin* (1883), and J. Lightwood, *The Nature of Positive Law* (1883). In the same year Australian W. E. Hearn published *The Theory of Legal Rights and Duties: An Introduction to Analytical Jurisprudence* (1883). In New Zealand the prolific J.W. Salmond published *Essays in Jurisprudence and Legal History* (1891), *First Principles of Jurisprudence* (1893), and *Jurisprudence, or the Theory of Law* (1902, 11th ed. 1966); another Australian, W. Jethro Brown, offered his significant gloss on the master in *The Austinian Theory of Law* (1906).

through language in a cultural context. Decision-making by judges and lawyers necessarily incorporates this moral and political background. Much of what enters into legal decision-making is implicit, that is, not found in the explicit formal rules of the system. Therefore, by confining the study of law to the formal structure, the expository paradigm excludes data and sources that are in fact a part of the process.

A related criticism is that law as a logical system of interrelated rules is an ideal, not an actuality. Judges do not arrive at their conclusions in syllogistic fashion; failure to take into account the nonlegal (from the Austinian viewpoint) factors in legal argumentation results in an inability to understand and predict. Studying law from the standpoint of the expository paradigm is like studying Latin grammar; it exercises the mind but has no practical consequences. Or, worse, it may create and encourage the illusion that the law is a body of objective rules more or less uniformly applied in judicial proceedings, when in fact it is a process strongly influenced by moral and political policy judgments.

Finally, we should note that the expository paradigm does not account for historical change in the law. In the rationalistic view of Bentham and Austin, law can change only through deliberate legislation. This narrow view of the possibilities of change might be expected in a Continental lawyer or anyone unfamiliar with judicial activism, but it is especially curious coming from two scholars who had studied the common law. The kind of understanding that history can provide is excluded from the expository paradigm. Indeed, the entire rationalistic approach to understanding humanity and society seems clumsy and naive.

The Evolutionary Paradigm

We will label the evolutionary paradigm that viewpoint also known as historicism, evolutionary jurisprudence, the historical school, legal evolution, or the Darwinian theory of law. It has played not a dominant but a main supporting role in American legal philosophy. It has two sources in European thinking, both of which have had an impact upon American thought: the German historical school and the work of the English evolutionists Herbert Spencer and Henry Maine.

The German historical school is a part of that monumental and (especially to those oriented to English philosophy) opaque body of learning known as nineteenth-century German idealism. Hegel set the tone and atmosphere for the legal theory; Gustav Hugo and Friedrich Carl von

Savigny were the seminal thinkers. In many ways the historical school was a reaction against the excessive rationalism of the late eighteenth century and the notion of natural law as expressed in its extreme form, the French Revolutionist's "Rights of Man." The nineteenth century is known, of course, as the century of evolution, and legal theory contributed substantially.

Already in the eighteenth century some thought had been given by a group of Scottish theorists, including David Hume, Adam Smith, John Millar, and Bernard Mandeville, to the idea that social institutions, including law, could "develop" in a nonrational way.[15] Sometimes known as the Scottish historical school, they had taken up a train of inquiry suggested by Montesquieu in which social institutions grow in different ways in different societies and in the same society at different times because of different environments. A system of adaptation seemed to be suggested. Borrowing from these Scottish ideas, Englishman Edward Gibbon published the first volumes of his monumental work, *The Decline and Fall of the Roman Empire,* in 1776. A part of that work was devoted to the development of Roman law. Gustav Hugo, a professor at Göttingen, was impressed by Gibbon's approach. He borrowed from Gibbon's work, advocating to his German colleagues a deeper method of historical investigation of the law.

Friedrich Carl von Savigny, ultimately professor of law at Berlin, combined the ideas of Hugo with those of Edmund Burke and Johann Gottfried Herder to produce the definitive statement of the German historical school. Burke, a conservative British politician and writer, emphasized the advantage of the slow organic growth of society as opposed to violent revolution. Herder stressed that the proper foundation for a society was not allegiance to a common political sovereign, something that European politics had demonstrated could be very artificial, but the sharing of a common culture by a people (*Volk*). A common language is the primary identifying feature of the *Volk.* Savigny's first and most important statement of the historical view came in *Zum Beruf unsrer Zeit für Gesetzgebung und Rechtswissenschaft,* published in 1814.[16]

The intellectual atmosphere that led to the development and acceptance of the German historical school cannot be fully appreciated without taking into account the inspiration and analogy provided by the study of com-

15. See P. Stein, *Legal Evolution,* 23–50 (1980).

16. This was translated into English as *On the Vocation of our Time for Legislation and Legal Science* (Hayward trans. 1831).

parative philology. This academic discipline had succeeded in showing the connection between various modern languages. The philologists demonstrated that most languages belonged to "families" and that those families found in the European subcontinent were subgroups of a much older tongue, to be dubbed the Indo-European language. They not only developed a taxonomy of languages but also explained why French and Spanish, or English and German, were now different although they had the same origin. The method of explanation was historical. The rules of speaking had slowly changed over many years as once-common groups had become isolated from each other. Nothing of this change was planned. It did sometimes appear to follow certain patterns or principles (e.g., Grimm's law), but they were not known to the persons doing the speaking. Over time words changed their meaning; new words entered the tongue, others dropped out; rules of grammar changed. Language simply grew.

The philologists offered a type of explanation for an important social institution—language—that was in direct contrast to the rationalist view of the world. Behavior in the form of obedience to rules of grammar and word usage was shown to have "grown," "developed," or "evolved" over long periods of time without conscious human direction. Savigny applied this insight to another rule-oriented social institution, the law.

Savigny completed the analogy between language and law. For him the law consists of the rules and principles that people follow in dealing with others in society. These norms develop unconsciously in tandem with other facets of the culture like family, religion, and the economy. In simple societies these norms are well known to all and are generally followed more or less automatically. As society advances, this popular consciousness of the law becomes imperfect because of its growing complexity. Machinery for promulgation and enforcement becomes necessary. The jurist is called upon to clarify and reformulate. But the basis of the law remains the traditional body of cultural norms.

For Savigny the rules and principles of the law are, like language, a part of the culture of a particular group. They are not universal, and indeed are not capable of application to other peoples and countries. Natural law is a myth. Legislation, while sometimes necessary for the proper re-creation of the law, should be undertaken cautiously if at all. This view of the law, essentially mystical, nationalistic, romantic, and conservative, became widely accepted in varying forms by many scholars in Germany well into the twentieth century.

Following a general world view that paralleled Hegel's, Karl Marx and Friedrich Engels developed a type of evolutionary theory of society in which changes in the economy or technology of production lead to changes in all other aspects of culture, including law.[17] Proceeding through historical stages that correspond to different types of economic systems, society has inevitably moved from slavery to feudalism to capitalism and will move to socialism and communism.

Although Marxist theory itself does not address most of the traditional problems of jurisprudence, it does make a place for law in its general picture of society which has implications for jurisprudence. For example, the type of law that prevails in any society will reflect the economic conditions of that society and the world view of the dominant class. Any significant change in law will not occur without a radical change in the economy or "means of production." Thus, efforts to reform law short of revolution are futile. Also, the prevailing law will always exploit the labor of the working classes, although it may falsely appear to serve all persons in society equally well. While the inevitable march of history and economic determinism loom large in overall Marxist theory, law at any given time is viewed in standard positivist terms as a system of rules emanating from authority which represents the policies of the ruling class. The Marxist way of thinking did not find easy acceptance among American scholars of jurisprudence, but it occasionally appeared.

The other major source of historical or evolutionary thinking that influenced American scholars in the late nineteenth century was the work of Spencer and Maine. These English thinkers grafted the notion of evolution onto the tradition of British empirical science and epistemology. They were greatly influenced by developments in geology and biology (Lyell, Hutton, Lamarck, and Malthus) which suggested that plants, animals, human beings and the earth itself had evolved over long periods of time. The substantial accomplishments of the comparative philologists were also very likely known to them; in addition historians have confirmed that Maine and Spencer had been exposed to German legal historicism.[18] Working in the 1840s and 1850s, these scholars were not originally influenced by Darwin's *Origin of Species*, 1859.[19] Darwin's influence on American legal thinkers, on the other hand, may have been substantial,

17. For a short general introduction to Marxist theory, see C. Mills, *The Marxists* (1962). For excerpts relating to the philosophy of law taken from classic Marxist writings, see D. Lloyd and M. Freeman, *Introduction to Jurisprudence*, 952–1095 (5th ed. 1985).

18. A definitive work in this area is J. Burrow, *Evolution and Society* (1966).

19. For the relationship among the various prophets of evolution in Great Britain see Burrow, ibid.

but only by analogy between the legal and the biological worlds and only after Maine and Spencer had shown the way.

Herbert Spencer is regarded as the founder of sociology in England, although that term and that science were first conceived and advanced a few years earlier by Auguste Compte in France. Spencer was not a lawyer, but his wide-ranging interests in all societal development led him to include law within the province of his "Synthetic Philosophy." His major works were *Social Statics* (1851), *The Study of Sociology* (1873), and *The Principles of Sociology* (1876).

Spencer likened the evolution of society to the evolution of plants and animals. Moving from lower uniform and formless associations of peoples to higher diversified and specialized types, society progressed as time went by to ever higher degrees of development. Spencer accepted the Lamarckian view that human beings acquire characteristics from experience that are then passed on genetically to their offspring. Successful ways of human interaction learned in prior generations are inherited by succeeding generations. The senses of justice and morality thus become instincts.

Spencer also emphasized that society could be improved very little by deliberate means. Ultimate improvement would come as a matter of evolution; hence, efforts at social reform were to be regarded skeptically, since they might actually interfere with the direction of the evolutionary process. For Spencer laissez faire was both a social and an economic creed. This view was subsequently called social Darwinism, although it originated with Spencer and was never endorsed by Darwin.

Spencer's work had a strong impact upon American social thought in general and upon the work of social scientists in particular. It provided a "scientific" reason why the culture of western Europe was superior to others. It explained why the Aryan race had advanced so much farther than others, and it gave a justification for treating "inferior" races, particularly the Negro, differently than the dominant white race. William Graham Sumner, an eminent Yale social scientist and follower of Spencer, could in all seriousness extoll the virtues of poverty; it was, of course, nature's way of eliminating the unfit.[20]

Social Darwinism, mainly in the form of unarticulated assumptions,

20. W. Sumner, *What Social Classes Owe Each Other* (1883). Sumner concluded that they owed each other nothing. Some of the chapter headings in this little book strike an interesting chord: "Poverty is the Best Policy," "It Is Not Wicked To Be Rich," "On the Value of the Rule to Mind One's Own Business."

crept into legal thinking as well. The legalization of racial segregation by the Supreme Court's decision in *Plessy v. Ferguson*[21] has been traced to Spencerian assumptions about the nature of society and race held by the justices of the court.[22] Decisions such as *Lochner v. New York*[23] striking down remedial social legislation that interfered with laissez-faire ideas became notorious and controversial. What is most significant is that the views of Spencer and his followers were regarded as scientific by a wide audience until the advent of "better" social science in the 1920s.[24]

Henry Maine was a lawyer, a professor at both Oxford and Cambridge, and a reader at the Inns of Court. He had a profound knowledge of Roman law and common law and a substantial acquaintance with Hindu law. He was subject to the same intellectual currents that moved Spencer, but he confined his work to the field of law, and it proved more influential with legal scholars. His first and most influential work was *Ancient Law: Its Connection with the Early History of Society, and Its Relation to Modern Ideas* (1861).[25]

Maine advanced the thesis, bolstered by illustrations from Roman and occasionally common law, that law and legal systems develop through stages over long periods of time. Every known society, including contemporary preliterate societies as well as ancient ones known only through history, is in a certain stage of legal development that is related to other facets of its culture like religion, social class, technology, politics, economy, and even language. While some societies remain stuck at a particular stage of development, other more "progressive" societies move on to more advanced stages. Apparently only two progressive societies had emerged at the time of Maine's writing—the ancient Roman and the modern western European; the latter is composed of two separate historical developments, the civilian and common law traditions.

The stages through which each legal system moves exhibit certain characteristics that are not found in the earlier stages. The characteristic of the most rudimentary type of legal development is arbitrary legal

21. 163 U. S. 537 (1896).

22. P. Rosen, *The Supreme Court and Social Science*, 29–36 (1972).

23. 198 U. S. 45 (1905).

24. A newer social science emphasizing environment over heredity was more congenial to the thinking of the progressive reformers. It developed parallel to sociological jurisprudence, as explained in chapters 6, 7, and 8. See Rosen, note 22, 23–45.

25. Maine's other books, widely read throughout Europe and America, were *Village Communities* (1871), *Lectures on the Early History of Institutions* (1875), and *Dissertations on Early Law and Custom* (1883).

judgment. Legal decisions are made by authority figures, and they gain their legality from the fact that they proceed from authority, not because they are the application of some generally recognized norm. This type of isolated judgment is gradually replaced by customary law. The society recognizes certain norms of behavior and insists on their observance and enforcement; such custom is often bound up with religious ideas. It is this stage that most societies have failed to leave.

However, the progressive societies are able to modify their legal rules through the use of fictions. The immutability of the customary law is acknowledged, but in fact it is undermined through the employment of legal fictions. Beyond this stage comes the notion of equity. Equity allows authorities to bend the law where necessary to conform to perceived higher standards that would otherwise be violated by literal and wooden application of the law. Finally, the last stage to which the progressive societies have moved is that of explicit legislation. Law can be deliberately modified for a variety of policy reasons by appropriate legislative authorities.

Maine does not attempt to explain the mechanism or causative factors that propel a society from one stage to another. And although he implies from time to time that "progress" is a good thing, it is clear that he believes that all legal change is not necessarily good (such as the development of democratic government). Maine sees a parallel movement in the history of Rome and of modern western Europe from a legal system that allocates powers, rights, and duties on the basis of family, sexual, or tribal status to one in which the individual is the focus of the system, thereby acquiring more freedom to act and interact with other individuals according to his own desires. As Maine puts it in his most quoted line, "The movement of the progressive societies has hitherto been a movement *from Status to Contract.*"[26]

Maine's ideas have had important consequences. They suggest that the study of legal history is essential to a complete understanding of legal institutions. They suggest that the comparative study of different legal systems can reveal new truths. They open avenues of inquiry for sociologists and anthropologists to explore the connections between law and other cultural institutions and to investigate the mechanisms of social change that modify legal institutions. Most important for jurisprudence, Maine showed that it is possible to gain a kind of understanding of law that is quite different from that provided by the Bentham-Austin exposi-

26. H. Maine, *The Ancient Law*, 165 (American ed. 1864).

tory paradigm. Under the evolutionary paradigm, rules and legal institutions change in nonrational ways of which people are unaware as the changes occur. These changes are related to other phases of culture, and therefore moral, political, and economic factors do influence what the law is. The evolutionary paradigm destroys both the notion of the separation of law and morality and the notion of law as the deliberately created commands of a sovereign.

There are, of course, some commonly observed objections to the evolutionary paradigm. First, while we are told that law evolves as a part of general cultural evolution, we are given no explanatory mechanism. Are there "laws" of legal change? If so, what are they and how do they operate? The historicists and evolutionists have raised this type of question but have furnished no real answers. Similarly, we are told that legal rules and principles derive from or grow out of the morality of the society; but how does this transformation happen? Indeed, how is it possible to know whether a given norm is moral or legal? Does it matter? We are directed to the connection between law and cultural norms, but the differentiation of the former from the latter is not adequately explained. In some versions of the evolutionary paradigm this becomes a matter of metaphysics or mystery.

We are also led to another dilemma. In some versions (usually older, Spencerian ones) the evolution of law and society is seen as progressing to ever "higher" forms. This leads to value judgments about different societies and legal systems that usually acknowledge the western European traditions as the most "advanced" and disparage "primitive" and "savage" societies, both ancient and contemporary. Such moral judgments based on a false notion of evolutionary progress are unacceptable today. Darwin did not need "progress" as a part of his biological theory, and there seems to be no reason to place it in any theory of legal evolution. However, if we refuse to draw moral conclusions from historical change, it is necessary to address the other side of the dilemma, cultural relativism. The evolutionary paradigm in itself cannot give us a standpoint from which to critique a legal rule or a legal system. The Austinians can at least tell us that a rule or doctrine of law is inconsistent with other established parts of the system (and hence illegal), and the natural lawyers can tell us that torture of prisoners is inherently bad (and also illegal). But to the evolutionist one legal institution is of no greater value than another, all being products of their time and place. There is no evolutionary standard to tell us whether a dinosaur is better or worse than a cockroach or a measles virus.

Finally, the evolutionary paradigm is said to be incomplete; it does not tell us how we know what the law is at any given time and place. It ignores the prime question asked by the Austinians: What is the law? It assumes that the scholar will find the answer to that in the historical data of the period. This means that the evolutionary paradigm is not of much practical value to the lawyer or judge who must deal with the law here and now.

We know from the literature of the times that the three major jurisprudential paradigms and the scholarly works that expounded them were known to educated Americans in the latter part of the nineteenth century. No new paradigm indigenous to America had been put forth before 1870. It is, therefore, against the background of these three ways of thinking about law that the Americans began to advance some of their own ideas.

THE BEGINNINGS

1 8 7 0 – 9 0

The twenty years from 1870 to 1890 saw the first original thinking by Americans in the field of jurisprudence. Each of the old-world paradigms competed for acceptance; the moral paradigm was not seriously entertained, and, while the evolutionary paradigm received some support from scholars, the expository paradigm became dominant. Five thinkers made especially significant contributions in this period: C.C. Langdell, O.W. Holmes, Jr., George H. Smith, William G. Hammond, and Henry T. Terry.

The body of the law in 1870 was immensely different from what it would become by 1970. Oliver Wendell Holmes, Jr., was beginning his great legal career. He later recalled, "When I began, the law presented itself as a ragbag of details. . . . The only philosophy within reach was Austin's *Jurisprudence*. It was not without anguish that one asked oneself whether the subject was worthy of the interest of an intelligent man."[1]

The ragbag of law to which Holmes referred consisted principally of (1) the common law, that is, the judge-made law relating to civil and (earlier) criminal law that had been created in countless appellate court opinions in England by the common-law courts and by all the appellate courts in the United States; (2) equity, that is, the special body of law created in the same manner by the court of Chancery in England and by its American counterparts; (3) constitutional law, being the documents of state and national constitutions and the judicial gloss that had been placed on them; (4) a recently codified law of crimes in most states; (5) the law of procedure, which had been a part of the common law (and of equity for equity cases), but which was becoming partially codified; and (6) a large but unorganized body of statutes dealing with a miscellany of topics. The age of heavy statutory regulation at both the state and the national levels

1. *Collected Legal Papers*, 285 (1920), quoted in 44 Harv. L. Rev. 721 (1931).

had not yet arrived, although it was near. The source of American law at this time was strongly weighted toward the cases.

The growth of English law since the thirteenth century through judicial decision created an immense body of legal sources in the reports (and earlier in the yearbooks). These sources were manageable primarily through the use of abridgments and digests that furnished an alphabetical index to the cases and through handbooks and treatises on isolated legal topics. The problem of source management was compounded in the United States by the fact that the number of jurisdictions (and hence bodies of law) had grown to thirty-seven by 1870. Although the common law and equity were often envisioned as a single body of law (unfortunately sometimes interpreted differently by different courts), the common law of each of the states was nevertheless likely to diverge in important respects as lines of interpretation were worked out in successive cases. This meant that the law of the United States was growing increasingly more complicated. Various solutions to the problem were proposed in succeeding years. We will note some of these proposals in this chapter and in chapters 3 and 4 and will observe how jurisprudential views had an impact on the kinds of solutions that were advocated.

While the case-law origins of common law and equity were in themselves unorganized, some help for nineteenth-century lawyers was at hand.[2] American digests and abridgments were prepared and utilized by the bar to obtain access to the reported cases. A number of treatises were written on specific topics. Law journals that reported especially interesting cases and pointed out recent developments appeared from time to time, and, most important, Blackstone's *Commentaries* were printed in the United States in successive editions throughout the century. Virginian St. George Tucker published his own revised edition of the *Commentaries* in his *Tucker's Blackstone* (1803), and New York's Chancellor Kent provided his more Americanized treatise in *Commentaries on American Law* (1826–27). These works, basically following the orientation of Blackstone, also went through numerous editions in the nineteenth century. Blackstone's work did not cover equity, but other authors took up the slack in this area, particularly the eminent Joseph Story, who wrote the substantial volumes *Equity Jurisprudence* (1836) and *Equity Pleading* (1838).

These general treatises were the only form of writing that attempted to present in an organized fashion the whole of the law, and even they fell

2. See L. Friedman, *A History of American Law*, 621–32 (2d ed. 1985).

short since they omitted almost everything statutory. Nor did they give reasons for their systems of organization, which tended to become obsolete as the law changed. Blackstone and his imitators had based the organization of their texts on two fundamentally different principles. The major outlines were borrowed from the civilians, but the more detailed discussions centered around the old English forms of action. The forms of action were, indeed, the organizational framework in which the law had developed. However, since these forms were essentially procedural and remedial, they classified the substantive law into categories of procedure. The irrationality of this scheme gradually became apparent when the forms of action were abolished and law and equity were merged in some American jurisdictions in the second half of the nineteenth century. In addition, as the century passed and the gloss on the original texts grew with each new edition, the usefulness of these books became more and more limited to the function of an abridgment or digest, which would lead the reader to the latest judicial opinions on a subject. This in turn led to the need to update them constantly with annotations containing recent cases. There was a monumental failure to bring organization and a broader rationality to American law.

Until 1870 lawyers in America learned the disjointed body of American law by studying in the offices of experienced practitioners and reading recommended materials such as Blackstone, the various Story treatises, and other books. This was a hit-or-miss proposition, and the truth is that the American bar was not well educated.[3] Some students attended law "schools," but these were little more than efficiently organized apprenticeship systems. Even the few university-affiliated law schools such as those at William and Mary, Harvard, Virginia, and Columbia offered only lectures for those who would pay to attend; there were no examinations, entrance requirements, or degrees.

One response to the overall lack of rationality in law came in the form of a movement for codification.[4] Although other social and political factors can be credited for much of the impetus to the codification movement, it is worth noting here that the proponents of the movement thought that it would supply the law with its missing organizational structure. David Dudley Field, a prominent New York lawyer, led the fight

3. See R. Stevens, *Law School: Legal Education in America from the 1850s to the 1980s*, 1–34 (1983).

4. On codification see ibid., 403–411, and J. Honnold, *The Life of the Law*, 100–144 (1964).

for codification, beginning in 1848; this fight continued to the end of the century. As a general proposition, codification lost; however, the movement did have some practical results, and it left its mark on jurisprudence. The failure of codification left the job of bringing system and logic to law primarily to the post-1870 legal scholars.

The Science of Legal Principles

Christopher Columbus Langdell (1826–1906) introduced his case system of study at Harvard in 1870; it slowly caught on there, and later spread to other schools.[5] Without straying too far into the history of legal education, it is important to note briefly the jurisprudential view that prompted Langdell to initiate his new method of teaching. He had been hired by the new president of Harvard University, Charles Eliot, to take charge of the sleepy law school and turn it into an institution that could be regarded as an honest part of a modern university. The study of law belonged at Harvard only if it were scientific. Langdell's view of the law was scientific to him and apparently to Eliot and others. Unfortunately, Langdell was not given to theorizing much about his method or his notion of science, and what theory we can attribute to him is mostly by inference. Had he spelled out his philosophy of law, he could have become the first significant American legal philosopher.

The most suggestive statement Langdell made about his new scientific method of law study is found in the preface to his casebook on contract law:

> Law, considered as a science, consists of certain principles or doctrines. . . . Each of these doctrines has arrived at its present state by slow degrees; in other words, it is a growth, extending in many cases through centuries. This growth is to be traced in the main through a series of cases; and much the shortest and best, if not the only way of mastering the doctrine effectually is by studying the cases in which it is embodied. . . . It seemed to me, therefore, to be possible to take such a branch of the law as Contracts, for example, and, without exceeding comparatively moderate limits, to select, classify, and arrange all

5. Theodore Dwight at Columbia offered an alternative to both the traditional lecture and Langdell's case method (a combination of lecture, quizzes, and tutorials). One of the main academic debates in the years from 1870 to 1900 was the comparative value of the case method. The case method won.

the cases which had contributed in any important degree to the growth, development, or establishment of any of its essential doctrines; and that such a work could not fail to be of material service to all who desire to study that branch of law systematically and in its original sources.[6]

Inferences from this and a scattering of other Langdell writings[7] suggest that Langdell thought of the common law, including equity for this purpose, as a body of principles governing human relationships that was the product of hundreds of years of development by English and American courts. These principles could become known to the jurist and legal scholar through the study of reported cases that illustrated their application to particular factual situations. All cases were not equal, however; only the cases best reasoned and most consistent with one another could serve as guides. The law was not the multitude of rules one could find stated in the cases, but the principles which the best of these cases demonstrated as illustrations. The efficient and sure means of learning the law was not to read a text like Blackstone or Story, nor to attempt to wade through cases from all jurisdictions dealing with some specific subject, but to be guided step by step through the reasoning of the best-thought-out judicial decisions by one who had mastered the subject.

The key to this was the casebook, a compilation of the leading appellate opinions carefully selected by someone who thoroughly knew the subject. Following the reasoning in these cases, students would be led to a proper understanding of the law of that subject and, furthermore, would be capable of supporting the relevant legal propositions with acceptable and convincing argument. An analogy, however crude, was drawn to the inductive method of chemists who use specific empirical experiments to establish general principles applicable to a wide range of new situations.

6. C. Langdell, *A Selection of Cases on the Law of Contract* (1871), quoted in A. Sutherland, *The Law at Harvard,* 174 (1967). Langdell did not think the number of principles was very numerous. "But the cases which are useful and necessary for this purpose at the present day bear an exceedingly small proportion to all that have been reported. The vast majority are useless, and worse than useless, for any purpose of systematic study. Moreover the number of fundamental legal doctrines is much less than commonly supposed; the many different guises in which the same doctrine is constantly making its appearance, and the great extent to which legal treatises are a repetition of each other, being the cause of much misapprehension. If these doctrines could be so classified and arranged that each should be found in its proper place, and nowhere else, they would cease to be formidable from their number."

7. See especially his speech given at the 250th anniversary celebration of Harvard University reprinted in Celebration Speeches, 3 L. Q. Rev. 118 (1897).

Langdell's method took care of the problem of the proliferation of the law, the multitude of cases, and the confusion of sources. For Langdell there were right and wrong answers to questions of legal doctrine. Some cases were decided incorrectly when weighed against arguments based on principle and consistency. The common law was not fragmented into the laws of many jurisdictions, but remained as a single line of development from the ancient English decisions to the latest appellate cases in Delaware or Kentucky. This is not to say, of course, that all novel legal questions could be easily resolved; but the case law would develop, and the correct answers would eventually emerge. Statutes that differed from state to state provided a problem for Langdell; he never offered any solution to this proliferation of legislative variations. But there could be a national jurisprudence for common law and equity, and, as a result, there could be national law schools suitable for training lawyers for practice in any common-law jurisdiction. Harvard would be the leader.

Langdell's approach did not, however, address the problem of the overall organization of the law or the rationalization of it into its most general principles. His own subject was "contracts," a subject that had not existed a century before. Blackstone treated it as a small subspecies of the law of property. It was concealed in the actions of debt, covenant, assumpsit, the common counts, and certain remedies available only in equity. What was the relationship of contract to tort, to property, to civil proceedings generally? Did it have any concepts in common with these other areas? Were contracts in the fields of telegraphs or railroads a subspecies of the main doctrines of contract as Langdell expounded them, or were they different? Probably for Langdell these kinds of questions were of no consequence; but we don't know.

Rather than being analogous to the inductive work of chemists, Langdell's idea of law is closer to the notions of Savigny. As noted in chapter 1, this view saw law arising from the custom or spirit of the people, which varies at any given time in history and is largely unknown to jurists. It is worked into the logical structure of the official law by judges (jurists in the civilian legal systems) as they decide new cases. Given the basic understructure worked out in early years, contemporary courts must adapt the law to new situations through careful analysis (or more accurately, reanalysis) and application of the underlying principles, which themselves must be inferred from prior case law. This means that there can be a science of law, a way of knowing law above and beyond the face value of any specific judicial opinion or set of stated rules. The law (at least judge-made law for Langdell) consists of this body of interrelated principles and perhaps includes the logical technique for applying these principles to new (as well as hypothetical) cases.

We have no evidence that Savigny's work was known to Langdell or was an influence on his thinking. Langdell's later development along the lines of the expository paradigm (see chapter 4) suggests that perhaps the similarity of this justification for the case method to the theory of Savigny was coincidental, or perhaps that he shared with most of the intellectuals of his time the same general awe of the idea of evolution. Langdell's view of the law may well have been typical of the intellectual lawyer of his day. Although his philosophy remained inchoate, it contained the seeds of some of the major jurisprudential ideas that would dominate thought for the next half century: that the law consists of principles, something apart from the cases themselves; that these principles are the proper object of intellectual study; that the law changes over time in ways unplanned, yet such change is aided by judges; and that rigorous legal analysis is the only rational way of understanding the law and making it applicable to new situations.

These notions, grounded on the firm belief that law could be a science, permeated legal intellectual activity in the last quarter of the nineteenth century.[8] Yet they were notions that potentially conflicted with one another; they did not constitute a consistent, well-thought-out philosophy. Nevertheless, in instituting the case method with all its implications, Langdell gave the study of law respectability as a "science" and also opened up lines of inquiry that others, and, as it turns out, he himself, would explore.

The Amazing Holmes:
Analyst, Evolutionist, Skeptic

Oliver Wendell Holmes, Jr. (1841–1935), offered a clearer and fuller expression of some new jurisprudential ideas. It was in 1870 that Holmes, as the newly appointed editor of the *American Law Review*, a fledgling legal periodical published in Boston, wrote his first jurispruden-

8. See, for example, Comment, The Philosophy of Law, 6 Alb. L. J. 179 (1872); Comment, The Scientific Basis of Law, 7 Alb. L. J. 321 (1873); S. Amos, *The Science of Law*, vi–x (1874); Comment, Case Law and Inductive Science, 10 Alb. L. J. 301 (1874); J. Lightwood, *The Nature of Positive Law*, 1–24 (1883); Platt, The Proposed Civil Code of New York, 20 Am. L. Rev. 713 (1886); Smith, The English Analytical Jurists, 21 Am. L. Rev. 270 (1887).

tial article.[9] This was the first in a series of three articles in which Holmes wrestled with the essentially irrational and amorphous condition of American law.[10]

Holmes' concern at this time was with the principles of organization that one should use to codify or otherwise arrange the body of the law. His point of departure was Austin. Holmes agreed with Austin's objectives but disagreed with most of his specifics. Austin and others had used the concept of "rights" as an organizing principle. Holmes thought that "duties" would serve better because that concept was more fundamental; he regarded rights as derivative of duties. The next steps in the organizational scheme were to identify to whom the duties were owed and to identify who owed them. These duty-owing or duty-owed persons (or entities, in the abstract) were apparently regarded as fundamental parts of the model, a view that did not differ substantially from Austin's. The fundamental relationships thus established were explained in Holmes' text and diagrammed in a chart accompanying the article (see appendix A).

Although Holmes gives some explanation of why he regarded this classificatory scheme as more scientific or philosophical than its alternatives, his ultimate criterion still remains obscure. In view of his pragmatic orientation, it seems certain that his scheme of relationships was not based on any Kantian, Hegelian, or other metaphysical notion. He tells us in his follow-up article:

> It suffices to say in opposition to so-called practical schemes, which are sometimes formally suggested, and always implicitly by books on such subjects as telegraphs, railroads, &c., that the end of all classification should be to make the law *knowable*; and that the system best accomplishes that purpose which proceeds from the most general conception to the most specific proposition or exception in the order of logical subordination.[11]

One of the corollaries of setting up a classificatory system based on the concepts of the classifier, as opposed to concepts already found in juridical literature (especially the cases themselves), is that the new classification

9. Holmes, Codes, And the Arrangement of the Law, 5 Am. L. Rev. 1 (1870), reprinted in 44 Harv. L. Rev. 725 (1931). The biographical literature on Holmes is overwhelming. See the bibliography of secondary sources in this book.

10. The others were The Arrangement of the Law—Privity, 7 Am. L. Rev. 46 (1872), and The Theory of Torts, 7 Am. L. Rev. 652 (1873), reprinted respectively in 44 Harv. L. Rev. 738, 773 (1931).

11. Holmes, The Arrangement of the Law—Privity, note 10, 738, fn. 2.

makes some old terms appear irrational and suggests that some old classifications are wrong. As an example, Holmes says that the term "bailment"
is no longer useful, although there are historical reasons, no longer relevant, why it came into use. Likewise, he tells us that express contracts and
implied (in law) contracts do not both belong under the larger conceptual
category of contracts, the latter having been included there because the
duty (of restitution) that the law recognized had to be enforced through
the form of action appropriate for the enforcement of contracts. Again, he
says that various types of transfers of property (by will, by marriage, by
deed, and so forth) can be encompassed under the larger conceptual
category of privity. In contrast, other types of property transfer (by adverse possession, by finding, by operation of the law of admiralty) do not
fit under privity but under another principle.

Privity, in this new and broader sense, is a deliberately constructed
jurisprudential concept, more abstract than familiar legal concepts but
necessary (or convenient) to provide organizational coherence to the
system so that the relationships of all parts to all other parts can be
knowable. Holmes also gives us a chart explaining how various kinds of
property transfers fit under the idea of privity (see appendix B); and he
borrows the old civilian concept of persona to explain privity. Personae
are the "objects of succession in privity." By this he means the abstract
notion of a person into whose shoes someone else can step, or to whose
rights and duties another can succeed. A corporation is the archetypal
persona.

Holmes also gives a thumbnail classification for the law of torts,[12]
heretofore erroneously classified according to the form of action appropriate for each class of wrong. His scheme matches duties, according to
whom owed, against states of mind or lack thereof. Apart from these
specifics relating to torts and succession to property, and his general idea
of classifying according to duties, Holmes does not give us a complete
classificatory system for the law but characterizes his proposals as suggestive. He also realizes, as did Austin, that the creation of such a system
would be a very major undertaking.

In addition to differing on the arrangement of the law, Holmes also
departed from Austin over the definition of law, perhaps exposing the
shortcomings of Austin's German orientation.[13] The idea that all laws

12. Holmes, The Theory of Torts, note 10. This is also complete with chart (see
appendix C).

13. Most of the discussion of Holmes' disagreement with Austin can be found in a

could be subsumed under the notion of commands of the sovereign was, to Holmes, too unfaithful to reality and stretched the concept of a "command" beyond the elasticity that language permitted. The sources of law were too varied and differing (including custom, mercantile usage, judicial precedent, and simple societal expectations) to be squeezed into the model of a command. The idea of sanction, as used by Austin, was also untenable according to Holmes. It was wooden and smacked of crude penalties; it did not allow for all of the many consequences that can follow from legally relevant behavior. "Austin . . . looked at the law too much as a criminal lawyer." Holmes did not propose a definition of the word "law" per se but rather chose to characterize the subject matter of juristic concern in the following way: "The only question for the lawyer is, how will the judges act? Any motive for their action, be it constitution, statute, custom, or precedent, which can be relied upon as likely in the generality of cases to prevail, is worthy of consideration as one of the sources of law, in a treatise on jurisprudence."[14]

The contemporary treatises on jurisprudence, did not, however, pursue Holmes' suggestion; and unfortunately Holmes himself never bothered to write a treatise on jurisprudence. His keen insight on the central role of courts was eventually followed up and elaborated upon by John Chipman Gray in a creative development that we will examine in chapter 6. But it is important to note that in the early 1870s Holmes was trying to follow the expository paradigm, seeking to improve on Austin but differing from Austin in many particulars.

It is significant also that Holmes in this period touched on all of the major themes that American jurisprudence would follow in the succeeding half century or so. His original 1870 essay began with these amazingly insightful observations:

> It is the merit of the Common Law that it decides the case first and determines the principle afterwards. Looking at the forms of logic it might be inferred that when you have a minor premise and a conclusion, there must be a major, which you are also prepared then and there to assert. But in fact lawyers, like other men, frequently see well enough how they ought to decide on a given state of facts without being very clear as to the *ratio decidendi.* . . . It is only after a series of determinations on the same subject matter, that it becomes necessary

---

notice of articles in The Law Magazine and Review, 6 Am. L. Rev. 593 (1872), reprinted in 44 Harv. L. Rev. 788 (1931).

14. Ibid., note 13, 790.

to "reconcile the cases," as it is called, that is, by a true induction to state the principle which has until then been obscurely felt. And this statement is often modified more than once by new decisions before the abstracted general rule takes its final shape. A well settled legal doctrine embodies the work of many minds, and has been tested in form as well as substance by trained critics whose practical interest it is to resist it at every step.[15]

Is it any wonder that a scholar who understood the common law so subtly could ever be hemmed in by the Austinian strictures of an autonomous system of logically interrelated rules?

Indeed, even in his first writings Holmes rejected the idea of adopting codes in the forms then proposed. Codes could not be short as then advocated, because they would oversimplify. Codes could not assume the organization of the law prevalent in current treatises and texts because they would be repetitive and contradictory. The theoretical basis had not yet been laid; the truly fundamental concepts had not yet been worked out. The amount of careful legal analysis and comparison that would have to be done to arrive at an adequate code was seriously underestimated by current proponents. A code could, however, in Holmes' view, serve the purposes of organizing, clearly identifying, and clarifying the law (Austin's objectives), if properly done. He saw that such a project would require in-depth reanalysis of the whole of the law and that it would necessarily be a long-term project.

But Holmes' flirtation with the expository tradition was short-lived. He became convinced in the latter part of the 1870s that the pursuit of jurisprudence in this direction would lead to deadends, or worse, to false learning. A perceptive biographer of Holmes, Mark DeWolf Howe, suggests that Holmes perceived the mystical hand of German metaphysics behind the expository paradigm, and this ran counter to his empiricist and pragmatic leanings.[16] He refused to search for the ultimate principles, categories, and concepts behind the law; he thought there were none. Never the prisoner of any insight, however powerful, Holmes began to pursue the understanding of law through history. He had read Maine and McClennan[17] and had benefited greatly. While Maine's *Ancient Law* had been around for some time, Maine's latest works were published in just

15. Holmes, note 9.

16. Introduction to O. Holmes, *The Common Law*, xvi (ed. M. Howe, 1963).

17. McClennan was a Scottish evolutionist, a contemporary of Maine. His principal work was *Primitive Marriage* (1865).

the period when Holmes was tinkering with expository jurisprudence. It would appear that *Village Communities in East and West* (1871) and *The Early History of Institutions* (1875) had a great influence on the Bostonian's thinking.

Both Maine and McClennan had analyzed primarily the Roman law and traced its historical development as a way of explaining the resulting concepts and principles. Holmes had immersed himself in learning the Roman law, but he had also learned the common law to a degree that superseded his British predecessors. He shared with them, however, a tendency to analyze legal concepts from the viewpoint of both systems. The concept of possession in the law of property, for instance, was discussed as though Roman and common-law concepts were essentially the same, or at most cousins. If the English and Roman concepts were different, some logical explanation related to history was summoned and usually provided. This curious mixture of phenomena from vastly different cultures, times, and political systems passed for comparative jurisprudence.

It is true that many Roman law concepts had entered the common law, but the two legal traditions were entirely different, and even where a Roman concept turned up in the common law, it often had a meaning quite different from the original. This way of analyzing legal ideas, made popular principally by Maine, opened the way for more thoroughgoing and objective comparative studies in the following years, but, as undertaken by Holmes and some of the English scholars at the time, it was scholarship resting on a shaky base. It is all the more curious that Holmes would engage in this sort of comparison and analysis, since he recognized that comparisons of this kind could be very misleading even when one was familiar with the terminology and concepts of both systems.[18]

Holmes displayed his historical erudition in several articles in the late 1870s,[19] and the culmination of this work, incorporating the substance of several of these articles, resulted in his landmark book, *The Common Law*, published in 1881. This book purports to be a history of the development of the common law, or some major aspects of it. But in fact it involves the selective use of historical sources to establish certain philosophical themes. The book also advances a primary thesis that the common law moved from a position in ancient times in which the intent or

18. See Holmes, Misunderstandings of the Civil Law, 6 Am. L. Rev. 37 (1871), reprinted in 44 Harv. L. Rev. 759 (1931).

19. They were Primitive Notions in Modern Law, 10 Am. L. Rev. 422 (1876); Primitive Notions in Modern Law, pt. 2, 11 Am. L. Rev. 641 (1877); Possession, 12 Am. L. Rev. 688 (1878); Trespass and Negligence, 1 Am. L. Rev. [n.s.] 1 (1880).

mental state of a person was paramount in determining legal liability to its modern position in which mental state has little to do with liability, although legal jargon still gives lip service to the old idea in many areas where it is no longer of real significance. He found that the law had moved from a subjective and internal perspective to an objective and external one.[20] It follows, according to Holmes, that Bentham and Austin were wrong in placing so much emphasis on the law's role in controlling conduct through the incentives of pleasure and pain. He recognized that much of the law, perhaps the bulk of it, did not rest on any attempt to regulate human behavior by rewards and penalties, but was aimed at results independent of the state of mind of the persons affected. "It may be thought that titles should be protected against even innocent conversion."

The parallel between Maine's *Ancient Law* and Holmes' *The Common Law* is so striking that it leads to the conclusion that Holmes was consciously trying to emulate the great Englishman. Perhaps the most famous theme of Maine's work was that the law in progressive societies (Roman-Continental and English common law) had moved over time from status to contract, that is, toward recognition of individual freedom. Maine's sources were, however, overwhelmingly Roman. Holmes' "internal to external" thesis purportedly proved a similar "evolution" in the English common law. Although he did not reject the value of "analytic" work in the law, as time went on Holmes tended to equate the "scientific" study of law with the evolutionary paradigm.[21]

The movement of Holmes' thinking from the expository to the evolutionary paradigm is even more clearly illustrated by his book review of the second edition of Langdell's casebook, where he said:

It is hard to know where to begin in dealing with this extraordinary production,—equally extraordinary in its merits and its limitations. No man competent to judge can read a page of it without at once recognizing the hand of a great master. Every line is compact of ingenious and original thought. Decisions are reconciled which those who gave them meant to be opposed, and drawn together by subtle lines which never were dreamed of before Mr. Langdell wrote. It may be said without exaggeration that there cannot be found in the legal literature of this country, such a *tour de force* of patient and profound intellect working out original theory through a mass of detail, and

20. For a contrary interpretation see Adams, The Modern Conception of Animus, 19 Green Bag 12 (1907).

21. See Holmes, Law in Science and Science in Law, 12 Harv. L. Rev. 443 (1899).

evolving consistency out of what seemed a chaos of conflicting atoms. But in this word "consistency" we touch what some of us at least must deem the weak point in Mr. Langdell's habit of mind. Mr. Langdell's ideal in the law, the end of all his striving, is the *elegantia juris*, or *logical* integrity of the system as a system. He is, perhaps, the greatest living legal theologian. . . .[22]

Holmes was not enthusiastic about legal theology:

> If Mr. Langdell could be suspected of ever having troubled himself about Hegel, we might call him a Hegelian in disguise, so entirely is he interested in the formal connection of things, or logic, as distinguished from the feelings which make the content of logic, and which have actually shaped the substance of the law. . . . No one will ever have a truly philosophic mastery over the law who does not habitually consider the forces outside of it which have made it what it is. More than that, he must remember that as it embodies the story of a nation's development through many centuries, the law finds its philosophy not in self-consistency, which it must always fail in so long as it continues to grow, but in history and the nature of human needs.[23]

Holmes' view of the science of law is obviously much broader than that of Langdell, although he perhaps does not give enough weight to the historical aspect, mostly implied, in Langdell's "habit of mind."

Through his authorship of *The Common Law*, we know that Holmes had become enamored of the evolutionary paradigm. Here again he offered keen insights but no follow-up, let alone systematic treatment. On the first page of that weighty book he says:

> The law embodies the story of a nation's development through many centuries, and it cannot be dealt with as if it contained only the axioms and corollaries of a book of mathematics. In order to know what it is, we must know what it has been, and what it tends to become. We must alternately consult history and existing theories of legislation. But the most difficult labor will be to understand the combination of the two into new products at every stage. The substance of the law at any given time pretty nearly corresponds, so far as it goes, with what is then understood to be convenient; but its form

22. Holmes, Review of Langdell, A Selection of Cases on the Law of Contract, 2d ed., 14 Am. L. Rev. 233 (1880). Holmes' remarks appear to be directed to Langdell's extended "summary" of the law of contracts that appeared at the end of the casebook.
23. Ibid.

and machinery, and the degree to which it is able to work out desired results, depend very much upon its past.[24]

Again, more questions are raised by these observations. What is the relationship between historical "growth" of the law and deliberate legislation? Does history limit what the law can be? If so, how? How does the distinction between substance and form correspond to public policy (or legislation) and history? How does the law "work out desired results"? We are given an inkling of the answer to these last two questions in the following passage:

A very common phenomenon, and one very familiar to the student of history, is this. The customs, beliefs, or needs of primitive time establish a rule or formula. In the course of centuries the custom, belief, or necessity disappears, but the rule remains. The reason which gave rise to the rule has been forgotten, and ingenious minds set themselves to inquire how it is to be accounted for. Some ground of policy is thought of, which seems to explain it and to reconcile it with the present state of things; and then the rule adapts itself to the new reasons which have been found for it, and enters on a new career. The old form receives a new content, and in time even the form modifies itself to fit the meaning which it has received.[25]

This passage describes a phenomenon very similar to the notion of cultural "survivals" elaborated by J. F. McClennan and E.B. Tylor.[26] How does such an old rule survive? Why don't all such rules survive? What are the causative mechanisms of these cultural developments? Holmes again leaves the development of these themes to later scholars. He is content to report the historical changes in the law itself; indeed, one of the serious problems with Holmes' historical work is that it consists principally of conceptual history. He says, in a much quoted line, "The felt necessities of the time, the prevalent moral and political theories, intuitions of public policy, avowed or unconscious, even the prejudices which judges share with their fellow-men, have had a good deal more to do than the syllogism

24. O. Holmes, *The Common Law*, 5 (M. Howe ed., 1963). Holmes inserted a note in the margin of his copy of the book at this point: "Imagination of men limited—can only think in terms of the language they have been taught. Conservative instinct."

25. Ibid., 8.

26. For McClennan see note 17. E. B. Tylor was an English evolutionist who initiated the field of anthropology in England. His most influential works were *Anahuac* (1861) and *Primitive Culture* (2 vols. 1871). For a discussion of survivals as that concept was used by Tylor and McClennan, see J. Burrow, *Evolution and Society*, 240 (1966).

in determining the rules by which men should be governed."[27] But if we examine his own texts, we find no investigation or description of these phenomena. Apart from occasional vague references to "public policy" or "general principles," we find no exploration of the felt necessities of the time; we are not directed to any prevalent political theory, and we are not made privy to any judge's prejudices; only the cases, the legislation, and the legal concepts are traced. The causative factors, according to the quoted statement, are ignored. Of course, to really identify these factors and show how they influenced the course of the law would involve a considerable sociological and anthropological study of history. Holmes was essentially a conceptual historian, opening up leads and suggesting relevant inquiry but providing no definitive answers. In his defense, however, it should be said that he did not differ in this respect from other noted legal historians of his time.[28]

There is one more important feature of Holmes' thinking. Whether in his early expository mode or in his sociological mode or in his historical mode, Holmes was emphatically concerned with the process of judicial decision-making. His eye was always on the courts. The process of legislation and the substantive policies embodied in the law did not interest him. In this he was half a disciple of Bentham. The world was divided for Holmes as Bentham had divided it. Considerations of justice, of utility to society, and of right and wrong did not concern him. They were left for the clergy or the speculative philosophers or the students of political economy or someone else. Holmes was a critic but not a reformer. It has been suggested that this was because of his skeptical attitude and his acceptance of the main tenets of social Darwinism.[29] Whatever the reason, his early leadership placed a tilt on American jurisprudence from which it has not altogether recovered, that is, the limitation of legal theory to a theory of judicial decision-making.

Amalgamated Jurisprudence: A Place for Every Idea

A considerably lesser light than Holmes was George H. Smith (1834–1915), something of a jurisprudential anomaly who had few if any followers and is today, perhaps undeservedly, completely unknown. Smith, a practicing lawyer in Los Angeles, attempted to create a jurispru-

27. O. Holmes, *The Common Law*, 6.
28. For example, Pollock and Maitland.
29. M. Howe, Introduction to O. Holmes, *The Common Law*, xxiv–xxv.

dence embracing elements of natural law, Austinian analysis, and historicism. While his attempt at combination seems to have failed, judged both from his time and from our own, it is interesting and instructive because Smith did try to integrate ideas from each of the great paradigms, and he recognized the significance of theory in the development of the law and in its unconscious application by practicing lawyers. Striving for ends he could not reach, he may have set some standards in aspiration. In discussing the "several theories of jurisprudence," Smith himself lumps the evolutionary and moral paradigms together.[30]

The failure of Smith to gain any followers appears to be because of his failure to accomplish the immense task that he undertook, although admittedly sometimes his terminology is confusing and his reasoning inconsistent. In one way Smith was the opposite of his contemporary William G. Hammond, who had much to say but wrote little; Smith wrote prolifically but had little to say beyond the limited but intriguing view he set out in his first book, *Elements of Right and of the Law*,[31] published in 1886. In this book he developed his main ideas, which were elaborated upon in subsequent books and articles (see bibliography).

Unlike Austin, Terry, and later Hohfeld and Kocourek (see chapter 4), who tried to analyze the ambiguous term "right" into its different meanings and thereby clarify legal discourse, Smith tried to subsume everything jurisprudential under the concept of right, hence the title of his main work. In Smith's view the science of right is a branch of the science of morality and in fact is coextensive with what is generally called the theory or science of justice. Smith distinguishes between positive morality, which is the body of rules and principles that people actually observe in practice, and scientific morality, which is the articulation and abstraction of those rules and principles into a consistent and uniform scheme. Smith maintains that positive morality is substantially the same in all societies, although there will be aberrations and differences because of accidents of geography, history, economy, and so forth. It is the job of scientific

---

30. See G. Smith, *Elements of Right and of the Law*, 249ff. (2d ed. 1887). The expository paradigm Smith labels "legal" or "legalistic."

31. G. Smith, *Elements of Right and of the Law* (1886, 2d ed. 1887). According to the preface to the second edition of this work, almost all copies of the first edition were destroyed in a fire at the publisher's warehouse. All citations to the work that have been found are to the second edition, and I have followed suit. When the second edition finally appeared, one reviewer, while sympathetic to Smith's aims, said, "We do not detect in Mr. Smith's contribution to jurisprudence anything strikingly original and what there is of original is not striking." Book Review, 35 Alb. L. J. 198 (1887).

morality to reform positive morality and rid it of its accidental and aberrational features. Both kinds of morality revolve around the essential notion of right: "We will therefore not attempt to define the term 'right,' otherwise than by saying we use it in its ordinary acceptation, as denoting a universal and apparently necessary conception of the human mind— leaving it to the reader to adopt a more specific definition, according to the theory he may adopt as to the abstract nature of right. . . ."[32]

Within this framework of thinking we find that law (Smith uses the Latin term *jus* with its built-in ambiguity) is that subset of rights that are actionable: rights that are recognized and enforced by courts of law. The science of jurisprudence, then, is a subdivision of the science of morality that deals only with positive law. The function of the science of jurisprudence is therefore to articulate, abstract, and reform the positive law into a logical and comprehensible system. Much of his book is devoted to this activity, and he follows the lead of Austin and Holland with some variations. He seems not to have read Terry.[33]

A notable feature of Smith's jurisprudence is his rejection of Austin's definition of law as a command. Following Maine, Smith maintains that law preexists any organized state and continues to regulate social relations after political authorities have been established. Following John Locke,[34] Smith believes that this law carries full moral force in an objective or absolute sense. The morality of the society is expressed in terms of rights, and these rights are equivalent to natural rights, subject, in Smith's view, to reform or purification by the operation of moral science. It follows that Austin had it wrong. Law flows not from a sovereign but from the people and their necessary relationships. Commands of the sovereign, called administrative legislation by Smith, can supplement the law but cannot contradict it.[35] Smith equates the natural-rights theories of the American revolutionaries and the founders of the constitution with these principles.[36]

32. G. Smith, note 31, 46.

33. For a discussion of Terry, see also chapters 3 and 4. Smith was, however, well read. He cites all of the leading legal philosophers from Plato to Holland frequently throughout his work.

34. J. Locke, *Two Treatises of Civil Government*, Book 2 (1690), reprinted in C. Morris, *The Great Legal Philosophers*, 134 (1959).

35. "But if a law is in excess of the rightful power, or right, of the legislature . . . it has no more force or validity in determining rights than the act of a private individual." G. Smith, note 31, 65.

36. Ibid., 23–24.

It is interesting to note that statutes have the same status as private legal instruments in Smith's view. The creation of rights comes about by the occurrence of acts and events. The execution of a will, the signing of a contract, and the conveyance of property by deed are examples of private acts that can create rights. Legislation is the typical example of the creation of rights by public act. However, these acts alone, in Smith's view, cannot create rights; they must be related to precedent rights (what would more commonly be called powers) already held by the actors. Smith says, somewhat obscurely:

> It . . . devolves upon the jurist, with reference to either, to ascertain the will of the party expressed in the instrument, whether that be of the state or a private individual; and thus far right includes the art of hermeneutics, or interpretation; but after the instrument is construed, its effect upon rights is still to be determined; and this must, at least ultimately, be determined by some principle of natural reason. . . .[37]

Smith finds a similar relationship between custom and right. A custom may lead to the recognition of a right if it is consistent with "independent principles of right." He elaborates:

> Neither laws nor customs, therefore, any more than other events, of themselves originate rights, but they do so only by virtue of principles of natural right, and therefore enter into the determination of rights merely as elements in the problem. In this way, and in this way only, can we reconcile the co-existence, in the law, of eternal and immutable justice with laws which are purely arbitrary, and customs which are . . . accidental.[38]

Unfortunately, Smith's attempts to reconcile the divergent notions of immutable justice, legislation, custom, and popular morality are not convincing. The main confusion comes from using the term "right" to mean anything and everything.[39] Further writing by Smith in the legal periodicals covers the same ground with the same results.[40]

---

37. Ibid., 66–67.
38. Ibid., 72–73.
39. See the comment of John Chipman Gray in *The Nature and Sources of the Law*, 16 (1909).
40. See, for example, Smith, Of the Nature of Jurisprudence and of the Law, 38 Am. L. Rev. 68 (1904).

The Evolving Conceptions and
Principles of the Common Law

Another significant scholar whose work was guided for the most part by the evolutionary paradigm was William G. Hammond (1829–94). Hammond was better educated than most of his contemporaries at the bar. He graduated from Amherst, where he was an outstanding scholar of the classics, apprenticed in a Brooklyn, New York, law office, and attended the University of Heidelberg in 1856 and 1857, where he studied German and Roman law and legal history. After practicing in New York for a short time, he went west and became a legal educator at the State University of Iowa and later at Washington University in St. Louis.

Hammond wrote many articles relating to comparative law and legal education, none of which purported to deal directly with jurisprudence; but it is possible to piece together much of his philosophical view of the law from fragments of these works. He prepared an extended introduction (later published separately) to an English translation of Justinian's *Institutes* in 1876.[41] This perhaps remains the best explanation in English of the classificatory system used by the ancient Romans, modified by the modern Continentals, and adapted by Hale and Blackstone to the English law. Hammond also edited a third edition of Francis Lieber's *Legal and Political Hermeneutics* in 1880[42] and in 1890 edited his own unique version of Blackstone's *Commentaries*.[43] Dr. Hammond, as he came to be called (he received an honorary doctorate from Grinnell College, Iowa), chaired the American Bar Association's committee on legal education in the early nineties just before his death.

While Hammond's view of law is distinctly historical—and he often cited Maine and Savigny in his scholarship—he sees value in the analytical method, or as he calls it, legal science. To obtain full and satisfactory knowledge of the law, both history and logical analysis must be used; in fact, each method serves as a check upon the other, and "we can prove the conclusions of each by the results of the other, as we do a sum in arithmetic."[44]

41. Sandar's *Institutes of Justinian* (1st American ed. 1876).

42. F. Lieber, *Legal and Political Hermeneutics* (3rd ed. 1880).

43. W. Hammond, *Hammond's Blackstone* (4 vols. 1890).

44. 15 Reports, Proc. A.B.A. 317, 352 (1892); this report is reprinted as Hammond, The Proper Course of Study for Law Schools, 26 Am. L. Rev. 705 (1892). This work is principally relied upon in the following discussion.

While admitting the usefulness of analyzing such concepts as right, duty, and person and the necessity of using technical terminology, Hammond nevertheless completely rejects Austin's definition of law as a command of the sovereign. He believes that students are misled when told that law is essentially a system of rules of action prescribed by a superior, and that law is divided into divine, natural, positive, written, and unwritten. Hammond maintains that such notions do not fit the facts of life and that students who have been indoctrinated into the law in this manner must unlearn the false doctrine.

The true, or "modern," doctrine is that the subject matter of the law consists of those relations between persons which are the necessary result of their dwelling together in a state and maintaining social and business intercourse. The law formulates these relations as reciprocal rights and duties, and the rules of law express these relationships as people know them. In cases of doubt resort must be had to a court for an authoritative determination, and enforcement by a court is proof of the existence of a legal right or duty. The courts, however, do not decide this point at their own caprice but in accordance with fixed standards of judgment. They find, not make, it a legal right or duty.

In this view the common law consists of principles. Lawyers learn through experience that specific rules in the books and in the opinions of the courts change their form but imply more general conceptions. All legal reasoning proceeds from these conceptions held in the trained professional mind. Except through legislation, these conceptions (necessarily expressed through legal terminology) belong to the community and cannot be changed by common consent or individual fiat.

> From these conceptions [may be deduced] a great variety of special rules; as that a contract must be mutual, or that it must be founded on a consideration, etc.; but no one of these rules can have any authority beyond what it derives from the fundamental conception. . . . Hence if we study our own thoughts upon legal questions carefully we shall see that what we take for principle is a deduction from these accepted terms or from their relation to each other and place in the system.[45]

It follows from this view that the common law is essentially a logical structure abstracted from empirical social relationships. This is not a universal law of nature, good for all times and places, but a law derived from the contingent social relationships of a particular society at a par-

45. Ibid., 351–52.

ticular time. Hammond rejects any notion of "innate ideas" and cautions against taking ideas arrived at by induction from social facts as being somehow necessary or fundamental, even though we may have difficulty imagining social relationships without them (an apparent critique of Austin).

Lawyers are called on to reason and reflect upon the principles of the common law as they apply them to new cases every day. But this law, being a logical structure abstracted from empirical social relationships, cannot be directly observed or verified as physical laws can. Hammond gives a perceptive description of the method that must be used to know the law or the "truths" of legal science:

> Truths must be formed by reflection alone and can only be tested or examined by the same process. All [the lawyer's] reasoning in these sciences depends on major premises of his own formation, which are themselves constantly undergoing reformation or insensible modification. Almost the only test of the accuracy of his generalizations that does not depend on other imperfect processes of the same kind is that of consistency between them.[46]

This is the extent to which Hammond articulates his theory of law. His view obviously draws heavily upon the thinking of Savigny, to whom he gives due credit; however, it displays much originality in that Savigny's notions are applied by Hammond to the Anglo-American common law found in the case reports, not the old Roman sources with which Savigny worked.

We should note Hammond's insightful observations on legal skepticism. In discussing the merits of Langdell's newly introduced case method of legal instruction, Hammond finds as an unavoidable limitation of the method that it is confined to the "doubtful part of the law." He agrees that the cases are the original sources for the growth and development of the law, but he points out that the law is developing at any given time only in certain areas. Other areas were fully developed long ago, their doctrines

46. Hammond goes on to say: "If two or more rules are conflicting, two or more general terms for the same class of things (or for classes of which one is a subdivision of the other), do not harmonize, there must be an error in the formation of one if not both. As no human error can introduce an authoritative inconsistency into the unwritten or common law (as legislation may), all its rules and terms should be consistent and harmonious; a conflict between them in their application to the same state of facts is proof that one or the other of the conflicting rules is wrongly stated or does not embody the true law." Ibid., 354. Compare this view with Hayek's "immanent criticism" discussed in chapter 10.

are well settled, and their concepts have become a part of our normal legal vocabulary. Much of the law is quite certain; no litigation ever arises over it. By constantly exposing the law student to difficult cases, the case method misleads the student into thinking that all law is equally indeterminate.[47] It produces law graduates "admirably calculated to argue any side of a controversy . . . but quite unable to advise a client when he is safe from litigation." Hammond asserts that "the student should not be so trained as to think he is to be a mere hired gladiator, fighting indifferently for one side or the other that pays his fee."

A learned scholar, William G. Hammond did not consider himself a legal philosopher and never wrote a comprehensive jurisprudential piece; but his works were cited by other scholars, and he did contribute to the advancement of the evolutionary paradigm in America.[48]

The American Austin and the
First Jurisprudence Treatise

The fifth scholar of this period who deserves careful consideration is Henry T. Terry (1847–1936), relatively unknown today but respected by some of the early twentieth-century scholars. The first American to write a serious treatise on jurisprudence, he was the American counterpart of Holland at Oxford, Clark at Cambridge, Hearn in Australia, and Salmond in New Zealand. His main work, *Some Leading Principles of Anglo-American Law*, was completed in 1883 and published in 1884.[49] Like the British authors, Terry accepted the expository paradigm, and he wrestled with basically the same problems as they, that is, exposition of the basic legal concepts—rights, duties, persons, acts, facts, and so on—clarification of terminology, and concern with the systematic organization of the legal system. His work compares favorably with that

47. Compare the similar thesis of H. L. A. Hart discussed in chapter 11.

48. A biographer has assessed his intellectual strengths and weaknesses in the following way: "Perhaps his mind was in its operations essentially analytical rather than creative, critical rather than constructive. There are detached fragments written with the deepest insight and in a style of remarkable clearness and force, a style perfectly classical in its adaptation of well-chosen language to the expression of profound thought; but the connecting links are missing." Emlin M'Clain in W. Lewis, ed., *Eight Great American Lawyers*, 232 (1909).

49. The full title is *Some Leading Principles of Anglo American Law, Expounded with a View to its Arrangement and Codification* (1884), hereinafter referred to as *Leading Principles*.

of his better-known contemporaries. Indeed, one of the greatest of the logicians of the law, Albert Kocourek, said of Terry's work more than a half century later: "It may be remarked that no analysis is to be found in the literature of jurisprudence which shows a more interesting and penetrating dialectic and which at the same time is more difficult of apprehension than Mr. Terry's discussion of 'correspondent' and 'protected' rights."[50]

Terry received a Bachelor of Arts degree from Yale in 1869 and immediately clerked in law offices in Hartford, Connecticut, being admitted to the bar in 1872. He had the opportunity to assume a professorship of Anglo-American law at the Imperial University in Tokyo, Japan, in 1877. He taught at the school until 1884, when he returned to New York to practice law. He resumed his professorship in 1894, finally retiring in 1912. He was awarded emeritus status and several other honors by the Japanese government in recognition of his long years of teaching. Terry wrote *First Principles of Law* in 1878, which was published in Tokyo as a text for his students, followed by *Leading Principles of Anglo-American Law*, written in Tokyo but published in Philadelphia in 1884, and finally *The Common Law*, published in Tokyo in 1898.

Terry's position as the scholar of a foreign legal system gave him a unique viewpoint from which to assess the Anglo-American law. This was the early Meiji period in Japan, when the Japanese were desperately seeking to "modernize" by bringing western institutions into the country. They imported all sorts of ideas and technologies from dairy farming to naval armaments, trying to "catch up," as they viewed it, with the modern western nations. One of the institutions thought to be important to modernize was the legal system.[51] The Japanese had been taken advantage of by western powers in various treaties and trade agreements, and they blamed their lack of a modern legal system for this failing. Hence, from roughly 1870 to 1900 they sent their students to western countries to study law, and they brought in scholars, including Terry, from those countries to teach Japanese students the foreign systems. The three principal forms of law studied were French, German, and Anglo-American. Thus, these three systems were in fact competing to become the model for the Japanese legal system.[52]

50. A. Kocourek, *Jural Relations*, 190 (2d ed. 1928).
51. See H. Tanaka, ed., *The Japanese Legal System*, chap. 3 (1976).
52. This is a fascinating history in itself. The German system proved to be the major victor. For the why and how, see Tanaka, note 51.

Terry could see that the Anglo-American law, while perhaps having some apparent advantages, was woefully deficient in organization and form. In contrast the French and, somewhat later, the German systems were highly organized and refined; they presented masterful codes of law governing the principal subject areas. The entire French and German systems of law could be encompassed in two or three volumes, while the common law required an extensive library of case reports and assumed a functioning court system that regularly reported appellate opinions. Not only was the common law diffused and difficult to find, but its only practical principle of organization was the alphabetical listing of minute topics found in the digests. Undoubtedly Terry could see that the chances of the Japanese adopting the common law were slim indeed.

In the preface to *Leading Principles* Terry reveals what he perceives to be the jurisprudential needs of the time:

> It is plain that the condition of our law, as to its form, is fast becoming unbearable. Whatever may be said in praise of its substance . . . it must be acknowledged to be shapeless, chaotic, bewildering, without any sufficiently intelligible arrangement or an orderly and clear exhibition of its principles, a mountainous stack of precedents. . . . The only remedy for this that I can see is a complete and systematic arrangement of the whole body of the law. . . .
>
> Not only is our law largely devoid of arrangement; it is also largely devoid of precise definitions, clear cut principles and legal conceptions. . . .[53]

As might be expected, Terry relies for inspiration and authority primarily on Austin, Amos, Holland, Holmes (*The Common Law*), Langdell,[54] and many English and American cases. He also occasionally cites Maine's *Early History of Institutions* and, surprisingly, a French edition of Savigny's *System des heutigen Römischen Rechts*.

The organization of Terry's magnum opus seems somewhat haphazard, especially for a writer so concerned about the systemization of the law. He begins with general observations on law, some of which are quite insightful. He devotes a chapter to persons and a chapter to things in a modest gesture toward the civilians and Blackstone. He proceeds to analyze what he regards as the fundamental concepts used in the Anglo-American

53. *Leading Principles*, i.

54. This appears to be the Summary from the second edition of Langdell's casebook on contracts, which was published separately in 1880 and again in 1883.

system: facts, acts and omissions, duties and rights, dispositive facts, and state of mind (negligence, intention, malice, and fraud). These chapters are followed by others on possession, property, rights in rem and their corresponding duties, rights in personam and their corresponding duties, and wrongs. In his final chapter he offers recommendations on the arrangement and codification of the law. He generally follows Austin and Holland; however, he often disagrees with them and makes persuasive arguments for his own position.

While scholars still debate whether Austin intended his definition of law and his categorization of it into rights, duties, and so forth, as universal, applicable to all legal systems at any time and place,[55] Terry immediately rejects this idea in his treatise. He first notes that both law and the meaning of the term "law" differ from culture to culture; thus, the western idea of law is peculiar to western culture, which leads to the idea that the fundamental concepts in different systems may also be different:

> As the conceptions of law change, the derived ideas of legal duty and right, as well as to some extent most of the elementary notions with which the law deals, such as those of persons, things, acts, contracts, property, etc., undergo parallel transformations. Technical meanings emerge different from the vulgar ones. Moreover, all these changes are in the course of a process of gradual development. There is no chasm between our own law and the rude and undifferentiated usages of a horde of savages. The one shades off into the other through innumerable small gradations; nor has the process of development gone on at all times and places in the same order.[56]

He concludes that no one definition of law will serve to cover all societies or even the same society in different historical times.

After this brief discourse, perhaps surprisingly, Terry concludes that Austin's definition of law is "in the main correct" so long as it is applied to the Anglo-American legal system. He is concerned, as Austin was, to maintain a sharp distinction between law and "policy." However, unlike Austin, Terry recognizes that there is an important relationship between law and extralegal principles. He says that the law usually expresses the general notions of right and expediency that prevail in a community and that efforts to reform law are attempts to bring about closer agreement between the underlying extralegal principles (or community morality) and the rules of positive law.

55. See Morrison, Some Myth about Positivism, 68 Yale L. J. 212 (1958).
56. *Leading Principles*, 3–4.

Terry points out that the distinction between the positive law and these extralegal principles is not likely to be confused when we are dealing with statutory law, and indeed the working of present statutory provisions into a general codification or systemization of the law will present fewer problems than would the working of case law, or what he calls "unwritten" law, into such a code. He says: "But in the department of judge-made law an immense amount of confusion has prevailed and still does prevail. The courts, not professing to legislate, have always been compelled to hide their innovations under the theory that they were only interpreting the existing law. A good deal of new law is actually made in this way."[57] Terry then imaginatively explains how the extralegal principles, which seem to be very much like customary morality, come to play a part in the positive legal system. He says that in the process of adjudication the courts often treat extralegal principles of justice or policy as part of the law and then deduce new concrete rules of law based upon them.[58] Terry then proceeds to give a number of illustrations of such extralegal principles to which the courts regularly appeal. They include various legal maxims, the general notion of fraud, and rules of construction.

Probably the most important contribution that *Leading Principles* makes to jurisprudence is in the analysis of rights and duties. Here Terry presents work that is in some respects more sophisticated than that of his contemporaries trying to do the same thing—Holland, Clark, Markby, Lightwood, and Hearn.[59] In particular Terry appears to have analyzed rights and duties into subcategories that carried greater explanatory power than those offered before.

Terry is not so explicit as Austin or Holland about the philosophical premises upon which he proceeds. He seems to accept the general notion that certain ideas or concepts are fundamental to the understanding of law.[60] He also claims the existence of certain principles of conduct that "have come, no matter how, to be generally accepted, and the municipal

57. Ibid., 7.

58. Ibid. Terry further points out: "The necessity of deducing each new rule from some recognized principle helped to keep their [the courts'] legislation within safe bounds, where it could not endanger the supremacy of the legislature or the balance of the constitution." See a similar argument made by Ronald Dworkin in chapter 11.

59. In the preface of the fourth edition of his work, appearing three years after Terry's *Leading Principles*, Holland rather backhandedly acknowledged Terry's "able treatise" as one that had adopted much of his (Holland's) terminology.

60. "The elementary legal ideas, therefore, are those expressed by the words person, thing, fact, act, omission, duty and right." *Leading Principles*, 17.

law is a more or less thorough-going and successful attempt to apply these to the regulation of conduct. . . ." In speaking of the arrangement or systemization of the law Terry says, suggesting both Kantian and empirical notions, "It must conform to the order in which the mind naturally works. . . . It must follow the principles of classification of other sciences."

Accepting the notion of fundamental concepts, Terry proceeds to analyze the notion of rights. He conceives of four kinds of rights with three corresponding duties. Following Holmes' lead, Terry defines duty before defining right; a duty is the condition of a person who is commanded or forbidden to do an act. A right is subsequently defined as the condition of having a duty owed to oneself.[61] A jural relation is defined as one in which duties and rights are correspondent. For example, A loans money to B. B is under a duty to repay the money to A. Following Holland, Terry calls B the person of inherence of the duty and A the person of incidence of the duty. But the duty is only one aspect of the relationship. The same facts also give rise to a right on the part of A to repayment of the money by B. A is the person of inherence of the right and B is the person of incidence of the right (the reverse of the duty).[62] The "content" of both the right and the duty is the same, namely, the act or omission that is owed, in this case repayment of the money. (This content Holland calls the "object," and Austin usually calls it "subject" and sometimes confusingly "object.") A breach of the duty also constitutes a violation of the right and gives rise to a cause of action. This kind of right-duty relationship in which the right and duty directly correspond, and in which we know who owes what and to whom it is owed, is a fundamental concept.

But Terry then argues that property rights generally are not adequately described by this concept of a correspondent right. In the case of A loaning money to B the same identical "investitive facts," that is, those facts which give rise to rights and duties, create both the right of repayment in A and the duty of repayment in B. The loaning of the money gives rise to the correspondent right and duty. Failure to repay gives rise to a cause of action. However, in many situations the investitive facts that give rise to the duty are different from the investitive facts that give rise to the right, and the breach of duty does not necessarily give rise to any cause of action.

Terry gives us this example. A municipality constructs and maintains

61. Ibid., 87. In spite of this beginning, Terry later makes the point that the definition of legal duties presupposes that of rights. *Leading Principles*, 94.

62. The "inherence—incidence" terminology used by both Holland and Terry originated with Bentham.

streets (investitive facts). It thereby imposes upon itself a duty to keep the streets in good repair so that they are not dangerous to life and limb of those who use them. The weather causes a large hole to form in a street. By allowing the hole to continue to exist the city breaches its duty to maintain in good repair. But whose corresponding right has been violated? Is it A's right to security of his property because he might drive his horse down the street, and the horse may injure itself by falling into the hole? Or is it B's right to bodily security, B being someone who might visit the city in the future and possibly fall into the hole? The correspondence between right and duty are incomplete, and the identification of the persons whose rights may be violated is problematic. Of course, if X walks down the street and falls into the hole, we can say that his right to personal security (or freedom from bodily injury) was violated. But there must be an additional set of investitive facts (falling into the hole) before we have a correspondence between right and duty and before a cause of action can arise.

Another example is given in which the right is claimed generally, because of certain investitive facts, but again the corresponding duty depends on another particular set of investitive facts. Suppose A owns sheep and keeps them on her farm. B, a neighbor, owns a vicious dog that has a propensity to kill sheep. In these circumstances we can say that the investitive facts, A owning sheep and B owning the vicious dog, give rise to a duty upon B to keep his dog from killing the sheep and to a right on the part of A to have her sheep free from attack by B's dog. The breach of this duty (which would also be a violation of A's right) would give A a cause of action against B (and establish liability, if proven). But what if B has no dog or has not yet obtained a vicious dog? He owes no duty to keep his dog in check until he obtains such a dog. Yet there is a sense in which we can legitimately say that A still has a right regardless of whether B or someone else has a corresponding duty. Terry would say that all property rights, and some others as well, are of this nature. They are what he calls "protected rights."[63]

In this view a protected right has as its content, not the act or omission of someone owing a corresponding duty, but a continuing condition of

63. The definition of protected rights is not a model of clarity: "A protected right . . . is the condition of a person for whom the State protects a certain condition of facts by imposing corresponding duties upon others, the content of those duties consisting in acts or omissions of acts which if done would cause or impair or tend to cause or impair the protected condition of facts, and the duties being enforceable at the option of the person having the right." *Leading Principles*, 97.

fact. The holder of this right may be said to be open to or entitled to being owed a corresponding duty whenever facts come into existence that throw upon another person such a duty, resulting, thereby, in a true jural relation. In the absence of the coincidence of the two sets of investitive facts, we may say that some persons have rights and others have duties to which they correspond, but there is no way to determine what duties correspond to what rights.

To return to the example of the defective street, we may say that the ordinary user of the street has a right to have the street kept in good repair. The city has a corresponding duty to keep the street in good repair. When the city fails to repair our hypothetical hole, it has breached its duty. However, no liability follows from this breach alone (there is no jural relation). Only when the user falls into the hole is his protected right of security violated, and liability follows.

This concept of protected rights, according to Terry, allows us to see the true nature of property rights, especially those usually designated as rights *in rem*. They differ, or more accurately their content and their corresponding duties differ, from what civilians call obligations or what Terry calls correspondent rights and duties. What we ordinarily call "title" or "ownership" is thus a kind of right, but nevertheless different from simpler notions.

Terry draws an interesting corollary to the analysis of protected rights. He says that the conditions of fact that make up the content of protected rights may be regarded as the end or object of the law that creates such rights. Among these conditions would be the unimpaired use of one's property, the freedom from pecuniary loss, an untarnished reputation, good bodily condition, and so on. These "conditions," which it is the law's purpose to provide, are necessary because they enable women and men in civil society to seek their own ends and happiness.[64] He says:

> In the case of most protected rights the situation of fact in which the law secures a person is more or less definitely conceived as a means of enabling him to do certain acts or gain certain ulterior ends. The possession and good physical condition of a thing, for example, which make up the content of the protected right of property, are of importance merely as enabling the owner to use and enjoy the thing.[65]

64. There is a striking similarity between Terry's limited notion of the function of law and Locke's idea of the relation between law and freedom. See J. Locke, *Two Treatises of Civil Government*, Book 2, in C. Morris, *The Great Legal Philosophers*, 141 (1959).
  65. *Leading Principles*, 100.

To complete Terry's analysis of rights and duties we should note his recognition of two additional types of rights (bringing the total to four) that are necessary to understand fully this basic conception; the first of these are "permissive rights." A permissive right is the condition of not being under a duty. The principal practical category of such rights is the license. For example, the owner of a patent may license X to manufacture and sell the subject of the patent. X is then no longer under a duty to refrain from manufacturing and selling the item; he has a permissive right to do so. The other category, "facultative rights," are legal capabilities to dispose of rights. Instead of having for their content acts or omissions, as do correspondent rights and permissive rights, or conditions of fact, as do protected rights, they have as their content other rights. There are no duties corresponding to these rights. Facultative rights are divided into two subcategories by Terry: powers and charges. Powers are illustrated by the classic power of appointment to the ownership of land. The holder of the power has no interest or right in the land, nor does she have a permissive use of the land. No duties are owed to her with respect to the land. Yet she has a right to designate ownership. Charges differ from powers in that it is necessary to invoke the aid of courts to enforce them. Typical examples would be the rights of a mortgagee under a mortgage or the rights of various lienholders who are required to resort to judicial proceedings to vindicate their rights (foreclose).

Terry's analysis of rights and duties is summarized in the following table:

JURAL RELATIONS

Type of Right	Content	Complement or Opposite
Correspondent Right of A	Act	Correspondent Duty of B
Permissive Right of A	Act	Correspondent Duty of B
Protected Right of A	Condition of Facts	Correspondent Duties of Others
Facultative Right of A	Other Rights	None

Consistent with the overall tenets of the expository paradigm, these careful and painstaking analyses of the concepts of duty and right, presented here only fragmentarily, were not engaged in by Terry for their own sake. Rather, they were considered preliminary to the full and accurate understanding of the positive law of the system. They, and other carefully analyzed concepts like "facts," "acts," "intent," and the like, were to be rigorously applied to case law and the interpretation of statutes with the ultimate goal of obtaining clarity, consistency, and certainty. In addition, Terry thought it especially important that this kind of analysis of basic concepts be undertaken before the even greater goal of codification could be achieved. Analysis must precede systemization; discovery or definition of fundamental concepts must precede analysis.

A fair consideration of Terry's jurisprudence should include a brief account of his thoughts on the classification of the law. This will be considered in some detail in the next chapter, since, apart from Holmes' brief excursion into this area recounted on pages 37–41, Terry's work also forms the starting point for American developments in this direction.

Thus, Henry T. Terry, from his unique standpoint halfway around the world, perceived the Anglo-American law as greatly in need of systemization and logical analysis. He contributed his own labors toward satisfying this need, and in doing so, he became the first American author of a significant text on jurisprudence.

3

THE DRIVE FOR

CLASSIFICATION

1870–1924

The question of classification of the law has also been called one of arrangement, of systemization, of form of expression, of codification, and of organization, each term having somewhat different connotations. While scholars were split on the question of whether codification by legislative enactment should be carried out, either expeditiously or at all, there was unanimity of opinion that some kind of scheme of classification would definitely improve the American legal system, or lack of system. This perceived need for system was especially congenial to those who embraced the expository paradigm. Indeed, it followed from the general inquiry which that paradigm sought to answer, namely, what is the law?

Considerable intellectual energy was spent in dealing with the problem of classification, and the success or failure of these efforts was tied to the degree to which certain basic jurisprudential ideas were accepted or rejected. Therefore, the history of efforts to classify the law is intertwined with the exposition of jurisprudential notions, primarily from the Austinian viewpoint. In this chapter we will examine the interplay between practical efforts at this type of law reform and the philosophical ideas that lay behind them.

Codification

There were parallel movements for codification on the continent of Europe, in England, and in the United States. In France the legal unification of the country, catalyzed by the great revolution of 1789, was accomplished through the enactment of the *Code Civil* (Napoleonic Code) in 1804. This code served as a model for other countries on the

Continent and in Latin America, where similar liberal revolutions in the nineteenth century took place. Austria enacted its own influential code in 1811. Germany was not unified until 1870, although efforts were made early in the century toward codification in some of the independent German states. After the imperial government consolidated its position, the codification movement proceeded apace in that country, resulting in the enactment of the German Civil Code in 1896, to take effect in 1900. Switzerland followed with a notable code in 1907, and, as noted in the preceding chapter, Japan had also codified in the 1890s, mainly along German lines. In England codification was much debated and was supported by many legal authorities, but it did not come close to becoming reality. There was, however, the special case of India, for which the common law was codified by the British in certain subject areas.[1] This practice was later extended to the African colonies and to Australia. Some American reformers wanted codification as early as the 1830s, and their efforts reflected an anti-British, anti-lawyer attitude with overtones of Jacksonian democracy.[2] This movement picked up impetus in 1848 with the work of David Dudley Field (1805–1894) and the New York Law Revision Commission. Codes of the Field type were enacted in some of the western states, notably California, and the issue was fought in New York and other states until the turn of the century.[3]

Many lawyers saw codification as a threat to their economic welfare, much as some early physicians saw vaccination against disease as a threat to their professional well-being.[4] These lawyers proved to be an effective lobby. However, others saw a need for some kind of organizing influence on the common law. After the Civil War the number of case reports coming from the appellate courts of the ever-increasing number of states began to appear as an obstacle to an accurate knowledge of the law. Treatises on various topics had proliferated but were of uneven quality. Most were little more than digests leading the practitioner to the case authorities; hence, they quickly became outdated. State laws on a single subject began to diverge. More and more transactions having legal import took place across state lines with potential differences in legal effect. Efforts were made to endorse codification at the national level through the

1. See M. Jain, *Outlines of Indian Legal History*, 600–696 (2d ed. 1966).

2. See J. Honnold, *The Life of the Law*, 100–143 (1964); Reimann, The Historical School against Codification, 37 Am. J. Comp. L. 95 (1989).

3. Ibid. For the scheme of classification used in the proposed New York codes, sometimes called the Field codes, see appendix D.

4. See Crystal, Codification and the Restatement Movement, 54 Wash. L. Rev. 239, 255–58 (1979).

American Bar Association, but they were only partly successful.[5] The bar was uncertain about the worth of codification, even apart from economic considerations.

The Perceived Need for Organization

Interestingly, as the codification movement itself lost steam in the last two decades of the nineteenth century, efforts to accomplish the objectives of the movement in other ways moved ahead. One of these objectives was uniformity of law among the states. The National Conference of Commissioners on Uniform State Laws was created in 1892 at the urging of the American Bar Association.[6] It adopted the first of many "uniform" laws, the Negotiable Instruments Law, in 1895. Through the years many of the statutes recommended by this organization were adopted by state legislatures, and the work of the commissioners continues to the present.

Two additional objectives of the codification movement, and of the expository paradigm more generally, were uniformity of legal terminology and clarity of expression in the law, or, in its more ambitious form, discovery and application of the inherent concepts innate to all legal systems. These ends, it was thought, could be achieved through careful analysis of basic legal ideas, which would lead to precise conceptualization embracing fine distinctions, which in turn would lead to less confusion. Such careful refining and redefinition of legal terms and concepts could be incorporated in a code, as was done to some extent in the German Civil Code,[7] but could also be accomplished independently by legal scholars. Such scholarly work would be used by the courts and the profession once its superiority over the prevailing sloppy thinking and careless use of language was realized and appreciated. The elaboration of the expository paradigm through the analysis of basic legal concepts is the subject matter of chapter 4.

Finally, two more objectives of the codifiers (and the Austinians generally) were what might be called organizational integrity and economy of rules. Ever since Bentham's time the complaint had been voiced over and over that the common law is a "ragbag," "chaotic," "a mountainous stack of precedents," "a confusing mass of legal lore"; that is, it displayed an

5. Ibid., 260–63.
6. See L. Friedman, *A History of American Law*, 408, 540 (2d ed. 1985).
7. See J. Merryman, *The Civil Law Tradition*, 74 (1969).

absence of any system of ordering. Within discreet subject areas of the law, like contract, bailment, easements, and injunctions, there may have been a fair degree of coherence and internal consistency in legal discourse (the expression of the law), but there were few principles that established the relationship between different categories. This meant that lawyers and judges must intuitively determine what law is applicable to a given case, and these intuitions can sometimes be wrong. The adversary system characteristic of the common law perhaps militates against mistakes of this kind, since opposing lawyers are likely to seek out any source of law that will help their own side; but this safeguard is not foolproof, nor is every legal determination made in an adversary setting.

There was also the feeling that a conceptual grasp of the whole was essential to an adequate grasp of the parts. One could learn about animals by studying them alphabetically (albatross, ape, aphid, and so on), but a system of organization based on general characteristics of the subjects to be classified (that is, into kingdoms, phyla, classes, and so forth) would not only expedite learning but would improve its quality because of the possibility of logical comparison and contrast. The argument that a student can more readily understand a body of knowledge that is organized upon easily understood principles and in which the various parts fall naturally into place is plausible and persuasive. But perhaps more realistically the abhorrence of a lack of organizational structure was because of a professorial prejudice in favor of the rational, the scientific, and the logical. For the classifiers, not all of whom were academics, organizational integrity was a pressing need.

The other objective of the classifiers, economy of rules, goes hand in hand with organizational integrity. In the absence of adequate organization many legal rules and concepts appear and reappear in different subject areas of the law, thus making the law appear to be a much larger and more complicated body than it really is. An example is the notion that infants lack the capacity to enter into legal relations. This is likely to be discussed under any general treatment of the law of contracts, under the requirements to pass title to property by deed, under the law of wills, and still again under the law of "persons" or the law of "legal capacity." What is worse, particular expositions of the law in each of these areas may use differing concepts or terminology resulting in potentially conflicting authorities and confusion. Observance of the principle of economy of rules would avoid this conflict and confusion and would help reduce the massive body of law to more manageable proportions. The classifiers considered this to be a high priority.

The Work of the American Bar Association

We have seen that Oliver Wendell Holmes, Jr., tinkered with the problem of classification early in his writing career,[8] and there had been considerable debate about the value of codification in connection with the proposed Field codes in New York.[9] Even the champion of the opponents of codification in New York, James C. Carter (1827–1905), agreed that some kind of scientific classification of the law based on principle would be of "priceless value" to the legal profession.[10] But it was none other than Henry T. Terry who ignited the spark that ultimately led to concrete results, mainly unintended, in classification in the United States (see chapter 2). In 1888 Terry wrote a long and detailed letter to the American Bar Association requesting that it take up the cause of classification along the lines he had outlined in his book. This matter was referred to the Committee on the Arrangement of the Law, and Terry's letter was published in the 1889 proceedings of the Association.[11]

Terry's reasons for advocating classification of the law were based on his vision of the law as a body of principles and concepts, independent of but reflected in the reported cases, which could be analyzed, refined, and logically related. He said in his letter:

> The only way that the law can be kept manageable and knowable is by its development along the lines of principle, by its having a logical frame-work upon which every special rule can be adjusted in its proper place. . . .
>
> Logic is simply the expression of the way in which the human mind naturally tends to arrange its thoughts the more it is trained and enlightened; and a logical arrangement of a positive science like law corresponds to that "natural" order in the physical sciences after which they are all striving. . . .
>
> A logical and natural arrangement must be based on and embody the results of an exhaustive analysis of legal conceptions and exact definitions of the elements disclosed by it. . . .[12]

8. See, for example, Holmes, Codes and the Arrangement of the Law, 5 Am. L. Rev. 1 (1870), and the discussion in chapter 2.

9. See Reimann, note 2.

10. J. Carter, *The Provinces of the Written and the Unwritten Law*, 45 (1889). For more discussion of Carter see chapter 5.

11. 12 Reports, Proc. of A.B.A. 327 (1889).

12. Ibid., 330, 332 (1889).

It is important to note that Terry had made the same recommendations in his ground-breaking treatise of 1884. His motivation is that of the lawyer, not the philosopher. He says:

> What is wanted is to get rid of a certain amount of antiquated material, mostly feudal, and the shells of obsolete theories that still stick in the law, to develop and further apply some sound and valuable principles already admitted into the law but not yet carried out and applied as fully and logically as they advantageously might be, and to so arrange the whole as to make it as easy as possible for persons who have occasion to do so to find out what the law is upon any given point. These are the only ends which it is of great importance to seek. Whatever arrangement best promotes these ends is the best, whether it is "philosophical" or not. To prefer any other to it is to play the doctrinaire or pedant. On the other hand the advantages of an arrangement of the whole law wisely adapted to such ends could hardly be overestimated. . . .[13]

But Terry recognizes the need for a thorough and logical system of organization. He rejects any short and simplified code or any code organized around superficial distinctions or current categories of convenience:

> Nor can any artificial or arbitrary system that amounts to merely an elaborate scheme of mnemonics answer the purpose. The arrangement must be logical. It must conform to the order in which the mind naturally works in trying to hold in its grasp and arrange a complicated mass of details. . . .

> Attempts at codification therefore are to be deprecated until such time as a plan of arrangement can be laid out based not upon mere traditional or empirical divisions and groupings expressed in loose popular language, but upon a thorough and comprehensive analysis of all legal ideas on which a truly philosophical synthesis can be raised and an exact and scientific nomenclature be elaborated for its expression. It would be desirable that a great deal of this work should have already been done by private hands and have become generally

13. *Leading Principles*, 607. Terry adds: "In making an arrangement of the whole body of the law the first and most important principle to be borne in mind is that the end in view is a purely practical one. It is not symmetry, *elegantia* or logical order for its own sake, or for the sake of the intellectual or aesthetic gratification to be derived from the contemplation of a code having such qualities, that would make it wise to enter upon the vast labor of codification."

familiar to the legal profession before the immediate task of codification was begun, since this would insure more intelligent criticism and
suggestion from outside to the codifiers as the work went on.[14]

Terry concludes that a purely logical arrangement of the body of the law
would be impossible, but that the attempt should be made to make it as
logical as possible, and, where impossible, convenience and expedience
will have to be given their due.

An outline of Terry's suggested arrangement for the law is printed in
appendix E. It follows Oxford's Holland to a significant extent. The great
divisions in this scheme are between public and private law and, within
the second division, between the law of normal persons and the law of
abnormal persons. The public-private law distinction is one that Blackstone chose to ignore and one that seems to be borrowed from the
civilians. Criminal law and procedure are included in public law, as are
constitutional law, administrative law, and related subjects.

Terry's rather odd division of private law into the law of normal persons
and the law of abnormal persons deserves some comment.[15] The origin of
this classification can be found in the *Institutes of Justinian*.[16] This was
essentially an instructional treatise compiled as a supplement to Justinian's famous code. It was divided into three parts—the law (*jus*, sometimes translated "rights") of persons, the law (jus again, sometimes rights)
of things, and the law of actions. This was really a restatement of the law
in three different ways. The first category focused on the different kinds of
persons recognized in Roman law (citizens, foreigners, plebeians, slaves,
servants, fathers, sons, daughters, wives, orphans, and so on) and how
their rights and duties differed. The second category, the law of things,
focused on the meaning of these rights and duties as they related to things
or property (property being construed very broadly to cover incorporeal
things as well as physical things). The third category, actions, dealt with
the procedure and remedies that could be invoked to enforce the same
rights and duties.

Blackstone used these same three categories when he organized the
English common law in his *Commentaries*, with two important exceptions. He included under the law of persons the legal powers, duties, and

14. Ibid., 608, 610–11.

15. The term "abnormal persons" was borrowed from Holland.

16. This matter is very ably discussed by another pioneer American legal scholar,
William G. Hammond. See Hammond's Introduction to Sandar's *Institutes of Justinian*
(American ed., 1876).

rights of public officials and governmental organs (the king, the Parliament, and so on), thus bringing constitutional and administrative law into this category. The latter two subjects were not dealt with at all in Justinian's *Institutes*.[17] Blackstone's second innovation was to rename the category of actions (procedures and remedies) as wrongs and to divide wrongs into private and public, meaning, thereby, civil and criminal.

Following the lead of Holland, Terry thought that the law relating to government, as opposed to the law that governs the relationships between private persons, should be treated as a separate subject: hence, the two major subdivisions of the law (which had been firmly established in civilian systems for a long time).[18] Terry recognized that the law of persons and the law of things were two sides of the same coin and could be dealt with more conveniently under one heading. This was especially true because the distinctions between different kinds of persons under English and American law were relatively small and less significant than under Roman law. Terry, therefore, did away with the category of the law of things, retained the nomenclature of the law of persons, but divided it into the normal-abnormal subcategories. The result was that the category of the law of normal persons is practically all of the private law (remedies and procedure being unceremoniously tacked on at the end). The law of abnormal persons presents the special law peculiar to those juristic persons singled out for special treatment, principally children, incompetents, women during coverture, and corporations.

It thus appears that while Terry favored a new and logical analysis, he could not escape the conventional organizational categories of which he was so suspicious, and the stamp of ancient Roman thought is found imprinted on his work. To this extent he failed to "conform to the order in which the mind naturally works."[19] Nevertheless, he introduced some significant minor changes in organization, which presumably moved the debate over the classification of the law toward a more rational plateau.

Terry offered a few practical suggestions on the arrangement or codification of the law that proved to be prophetic in light of twentieth-century developments. First, he had this to say about the form of a code:

> What is the best form of a code is of course a matter about which opinions will differ and no fixed principles of decision can be referred

17. Justinian's code also dealt only with private law, not public law.

18. Holland drew heavily on German sources and was probably convinced by them that the public-private dichotomy was fundamental, since it was regarded as such by all civilians.

19. See the quotations on pp. 58 and 67.

to. To my judgment the plan followed in the Indian codes—or partial codes—and in Sir J. F. Stephen's Digest of the Law of Evidence, strongly commends itself. A principle is stated; the explanations, qualifications and exceptions follow; and the whole is illustrated, when it seems necessary, by well chosen examples. The introduction of illustrations into statutes certainly at first sight strikes an American or English lawyer as strange; but there would be many cases in a code where they would be exceedingly useful.[20]

Regarding the organization and procedure to be followed in the preparation of a code, Terry suggests:

Some body of men representing the best legal learning of the country—I will say for convenience the recently organized American Bar Association, which ought to be such a body—should have the general supervision of the work. They should appoint a commission of from ten to twenty persons, chosen with care from the best lawyers of the country, to actually make the code. . . .

The commission should prepare a scheme for a code and submit it to the bodies by whom they were appointed for discussion and approval. From time to time, both while preparing this scheme and while at work on the details of the code itself, they might draw up schemes, outlines or statements of how they proposed to deal with some particular subject or special point and publish them in the legal periodicals or have them printed and send copies to leading lawyers to invite suggestions and criticism.[21]

This reorganization of the law would entail the radical creation of new categories and terms:

It is plain, too, that such an analysis and arrangement cannot be made without to a great extent remodelling our legal terminology. It cannot be expressed in loose and popular language, and our present technical terms are not sufficient. Some must be dropped, others be retained with more or less changed meanings, and many new ones introduced.

20. *Leading Principles*, 644.
21. Ibid., 644–45. Terry adds: "It would be a plain and gross waste of resources for each State to undertake to do separately what could just as well be done once for all; and moreover no one State could furnish so strong a committee of codification as could be selected out of the whole Union. . . . It must of course be kept wholly out of politics. . . . The expenses should be borne by the National government, which itself has need of a code for the District of Columbia, the territories and other places outside of State limits where it exercises jurisdiction."

> Also, the groupings will be very different from what we are ac-
> customed to. The distinction between law and equity, for example . . .
> rests mainly on historical accidents and not on any philosophical
> basis.[22]

Terry was sure that the somewhat drastic changes that were entailed in
such a logical rearrangement of the law would be worthwhile in the long
run.

The chair of the American Bar Association committee placed in charge
of Terry's proposal, Senator Johnson T. Platt of Connecticut, died within
the year. He was replaced by Emlin McClain, later to become chief justice
of the Iowa Supreme Court, and McClain's committee presented an extensive report at the annual meeting in 1891.[23] It recommended that the
Association support continuing efforts toward classification; more specifically, it suggested that two classifications be made. The first was a general
"theoretical" organization of the law into its major components, thought
by the committee to be primarily intended for students. A chart appended
to the report contained specifics (see appendix F). This was a simplified
version of Holland's scheme of organization rather than the variation
suggested by Terry in his treatise.

The second classification, which the committee regarded as the more
"practical," was to be an elaboration of a series of specific topics, related
to the general scheme but also largely self-contained. The committee
disagreed with Terry on introducing new concepts and terminology into
the classification. They found it "highly inexpedient to attempt to introduce any original scheme, however ingenious or satisfactory it might be
from a theoretical standpoint, or to employ in the arrangement newly
coined terms which have not already received some recognition." The
report did not make any positive proposals with respect to the second
classification. The committee took into account previous publications
that had proposed general schemes of classification, and a list of those
publications was included as an appendix to the report. The authors
referred to were Blackstone, Austin, Holmes, Digby, Hammond, Holland,
Smith, and Terry.[24]

22. 12 Reports, Proc. of A.B.A. 333, 335 (1889).
23. 14 Reports, Proc. of A.B.A. 379 (1891).
24. W. Blackstone, *Commentaries on the Law of England* (4 vols., 1765–69); J.
Austin, Lectures on Jurisprudence (1861); Holmes' early articles (see chapter 2); K.
Digby, *An Introduction to the History of the Law of Real Property* (1875); W.
Hammond, Introduction to Sandar's *Institutes of Justinian* (American ed. 1876); T.

The movement for classification received a boost from the prestigious Storrs lectures given at the Yale Law School in 1891–92 by John F. Dillon; they were published in 1894 under the title *The Laws and Jurisprudence of England and America*. Dillon carried considerable weight with the American bar. He was the author of a multivolume treatise on municipal corporations, a former justice of the Supreme Court of Iowa, a judge of the federal eighth circuit Court of Appeals, a lecturer at Columbia and Yale, and subsequently president of the American Bar Association. While his book was mainly historical, in the preface Dillon says:

> The pressing want of our substantive law is an authoritative, scientific, and comprehensive arrangement of its vast and scattered materials—a work which is yet in its formative stages. What has thus far been projected has made but little real advance, and has not always proceeded on the right plan or principles. My judgment is that, for this purpose, our law must be treated as substantially unique and distinctive, and arranged according to its real character,—arranged, so to speak, from within and not from without.[25]

By this Dillon means that schemes of organization based on Roman or German models should be rejected: "A Roman basilica cannot be transformed into a Gothic cathedral." In favoring a "conservative" type of codification, Dillon pointed to the problem of the proliferation of reported cases, often conflicting, and the fragmentary alteration of the common law by irregular state legislation.

While further efforts at codification by state legislatures collapsed before the turn of the century, progress on the ABA's attempts to classify was slow as committee membership changed and lack of time prevented these practicing lawyers from meeting or doing much constructive work on the project. This eventually proved to be a fatal defect in the accomplishment of the goals of the classification movement within the organizational framework of the ABA.

Renewed activity and interest in classification surfaced again in 1902 when James DeWitt Andrews (1856–1928) of Chicago (later, of New York) became chair of the ABA committee. Andrews was a practitioner with a scholarly bent. He had edited the works of founding father James

---

Holland, *Elements of Jurisprudence* (1880); G. Smith, *The Elements of Right and the Law* (2d ed. 1887); G. Smith, The True Method of Legal Education, 24 Am. L. Rev. 211 (1890); H. Terry, *Leading Principles of Anglo-American Law* (1884).

25. J. Dillon, *The Laws and Jurisprudence of England and America*, x (1894).

Wilson, had edited a new edition of an English author's work on pleading, and had put Cooley's annotation of Blackstone into a fourth edition. More important, he had written his own 1200-page treatise on the rather broad topic of "American Law."[26]

While Andrews' treatise contains an extensive discussion of the importance of classification and the necessity for a scientific approach to the exposition of the law, its organizational scheme is a disappointment because it turns out to be a variation of Blackstone's (see appendix G). Andrews' extended analysis of rights, duties, and so on places him squarely in the expository paradigm, although he relies on the authority of James Wilson and William G. Hammond as much as on Bentham, Austin, and Holland. He seems not to have been aware of Terry's treatise.

Andrews recognized that his own treatise, comprehensive as it was, did not supply the solution to the quest for classification of American law. His committee prepared a fifty-page report, published in the 1902 proceedings of the ABA, which urged collective action toward the goal of classification and offered some observations and suggestions toward that end.[27] Andrews' position on classification was much more in tune with the earlier view of Terry. He saw a clear need for scientific analysis and rearrangement of the law. Many German and English authorities are quoted in the report as well as American luminaries like Joseph Story and James C. Carter. The report borrows the notion from James Wilson that the common law consists of general principles and specific rules. An anatomical metaphor is suggested in which principles are likened to the unchanging skeleton and rules are likened to the muscles that are subject to growth and atrophy. The report continues: "In ordinary codification the principles remain untouched—they are presumed to exist and underlie the code, and to be known, while in legal classification the statement of the leading principals [sic], applicable to every department of law of necessity constitutes the chief end and aim."[28]

The report acknowledges that some new thinking must be done before a generally acceptable scheme of classification can be produced. It reviews the attempts by Blackstone, Austin, Amos, Holland, and others to establish principles of classification, and it points out their mistakes. Finally, as might be expected, a chart is offered suggesting one possible arrangement

26. J. Andrews, *American Law: A Treatise on the Jurisprudence, Constitution and Laws of the United States* (1900).

27. 25 Reports, Proc. A.B.A. 21, 425 (1902).

28. Ibid., 450–51.

of the law; and in this chart appear, in a prominent place, the old Roman categories of persons, things, and actions.[29]

Further respectability was lent to the movement for classification by the publication in 1909 of Harvard professor John Chipman Gray's *The Nature and Sources of the Law*. While introducing a number of jurisprudential innovations in this work (see chapter 6), Gray was at heart an analyst, and as such he had strong convictions about classification: "The task of an analytic student of the Law is the task of classification, and, included in this, of definition. It has been truly said that he who could perfectly classify the Law would have a perfect knowledge of the Law...."[30]

The Corpus Juris Project

Meanwhile the ABA committee had continued to exist with Andrews as its chair until 1908, but nothing further was accomplished. However, in 1909 an effort was made to institute a classification project outside the structure of the organized bar. Leading the way were the irrepressible James DeWitt Andrews, Lucien Hugh Alexander of the Philadelphia bar, and George W. Kirchwey, professor and soon to be dean of the Columbia law school and president of the Association of American Law Schools. The proposal, called the *Corpus Juris* project, started as a memorandum to one of the justices of the United States Supreme Court. It was generally circulated and was finally published in the *Green Bag* for 1910.[31] The project called for "tacit codification"[32] or "expository codification"[33] (as opposed to "legislative" codification) of the whole of the common law. After reviewing all of the usual authorities in favor of classification, the memorandum asks:

> Do not these citations of authority demonstrate the proposition that
> a great institutional digest, an expository digest, dealing with our law
> and the minutiae of its various ramifications, a complete logically

29. Ibid., 474–75. With a few minor variations the chart offered by the committee is identical to the organizational scheme proposed by James DeWitt Andrews in his treatise (reproduced as appendix G in this book).

30. J. Gray, *The Nature and Sources of the Law*, 6 (1909).

31. Alexander, Memorandum *in re Corpus Juris*, 22 Green Bag 59 (1910).

32. A term borrowed by John F. Dillon from Henry Maine. Ibid., 64.

33. Term attributed to John H. Wigmore. Ibid.

coordinated statement of the American *Corpus Juris*, is a vital necessity and that we must have it in order to prevent that ultimate chaos
so rapidly approaching, to which reference has been made?[34]

While the memorandum contains nothing philosophically new, it does
propose a method of organization and financing that would presumably
overcome the difficulty experienced by the ABA. The project would establish a board of editors that would maintain ultimate editorial direction
and control, the membership to be drawn from outstanding members of
the bar. An associate board of editors, composed of law school professors,
would be established to do the actual drafting. In addition, an advisory
council would be created to assist the board of editors, and a board of
criticism, consisting of one hundred to two hundred of the ablest lawyers
of bench and bar would round out the organizational structure. Funding
of the project would be through the creation of the Foundation of Jurisprudence, which would receive and disburse grants from private individuals and charitable organizations. The Carnegie Institution was targeted
as a possible donor.

The project was greeted with some enthusiasm by the lay press in 1910.
A later issue of the *Green Bag*[35] reports that a generally favorable attitude
toward the project is reflected in newspapers and magazines around the
country, with story headlines like "Wanted, An American Justinian,"
"Simplify the Law," and "Justinian, Napoleon—Who Next?" Articles in
legal periodicals by Andrews and Henry T. Terry also appeared.[36] Apparently as a result of these efforts, fifty-five "distinguished members of the
Bar" assembled in 1914 to organize the American Academy of Jurisprudence.[37]

34. Ibid., 69.

35. Comment, Survey of Editorial Comment on the Corpus Juris Proposal, 22 Green
Bag 457 (1910).

36. Andrews, The Next Great Step in Jurisprudence, 19 Yale L. J. 485 (1910);
Andrews, The Classification of the Law, 22 Green Bag 556 (1910); Terry, The Arrangement of the Law, 22 Green Bag 499 (1910). See also the articles appearing the following
year in the Green Bag: Gareis, Systematic Classification of the Law, 23 Green Bag 180
(1911); Spencer, Professor Gareis' Introduction to the Science of Law, 23 Green Bag
191 (1911). Andrews and Terry continued to advocate classification throughout the
decade. Andrews, Jurisprudence: Development and Practical Vocation, 25 Yale L. J.
306 (1915); Terry, The Arrangement of the Law, 17 Colum. L. Rev. 291, 365 (1917);
Andrews, Classification and Restatement of the Law, 14 Ill. L. Rev. 465, 622 (1920);
Terry, Arrangement of the Law, 15 Ill. L. Rev. 61 (1920).

37. 45 Reports, Proc. A.B.A. 82 (1920).

The AALS, ABA, and POIL

No funding was forthcoming, and the *Corpus Juris* project stalled. This led the president of the American Bar Association, Elihu Root, in 1916 to urge further effort and cooperation toward the goal of classification. "A few men are already taking the lead in classification. Some very able and public-spirited lawyers have been for some years urging the organization of a definite specific movement for the *restatement* of the law; for a new *corpus juris civilis*. They are quite right. It ought to be done."[38] At Root's behest another committee of the ABA was organized in 1917, to be called the Special Committee on the Classification and Restatement of the Law, ultimately to be chaired by James DeWitt Andrews. This group proceeded to act as a liaison with the American Academy of Jurisprudence and later with the American Law Institute.[39]

The Association of American Law Schools, an offshoot of the ABA created in 1900, also became interested in the project, and that group formed a Committee on the Establishment of a Juristic Center with aims allied to those of the ABA committee.[40] However, the AALS seemed more concerned to establish a physical facility where legal research and law-reform efforts could be conducted. With AALS encouragement, organizational meetings were held in 1922 of an entity called the Committee on the Establishment of a Permanent Organization for the Improvement of the Law (POIL), chaired by Elihu Root.[41] The POIL group's work resulted in the formation of the American Law Institute (ALI) in 1923 with funding of one million dollars from the Carnegie Corporation.[42] Elihu Root refused to accept the presidency of the Institute because of age and so was made

38. Italics added. Quoted in Report of the Special Committee on Classification and Restatement of the Law, 6 A.B.A.J. 420, 426 (1920).

39. See reports of this committee at 42 Reports, Proc. A.B.A. 194 (1917); 43 Reports, Proc. A.B.A. 90 (1918); 44 Reports, Proc. A.B.A. 42, 259 (1919); 45 Reports, Proc. A.B.A. 82 (1920); 46 Reports, Proc. A.B.A. 77, 481 (1921); 47 Reports, Proc. A.B.A. 82, 391 (1922); 48 Reports, Proc. A.B.A. 108, 364 (1923).

40. See Corbin, The American Law Institute, 15 Iowa L. Rev. 19 (1929).

41. See 1 Proc. of A.L.I., pt. 1, 52 (1923).

42. See 1 Proc. of the A.L.I., pt. 3, 29 (1923). It would appear that some of the same people who were involved with the American Academy of Jurisprudence (for example, George Wickersham) were also involved with the ALI. However, the Academy and James DeWitt Andrews apparently favored a plan of funding the project from the commercial sale of the product. This was officially disapproved by the ABA, and the Academy did not become the entity to carry out the project. See 47 Reports, Proc. of A.B.A. 82 (1922).

honorary president. George W. Wickersham was elected president. William Draper Lewis, dean of the University of Pennsylvania law school, was made executive director. The Institute saw its primary mission as remedying the problems of uncertainty and complexity in American law.

It is interesting to note that the initial "membership" of the American Law Institute consisted of more than three hundred and forty lawyers, judges, and professors from throughout the country, including the deans of all of the AALS member schools. The council, a smaller body of twenty-one, roughly comparable to the board of directors of a corporation, was made up of three judges, four academics and fourteen lawyers; of the twenty-one, nine were from New York City. The executive committee of the council, charged with running the more specific operations of the Institute, consisted of eight members from New York City, one from Richmond, Virginia, and one from Chicago; the only academic among them was Harlan F. Stone of Columbia University. The five officers of the organization were all from New York City except for Lewis, who became a permanent employee as executive director.[43]

This rather tight-knit group appointed the reporters (drafters) of each of the initial restatement projects. The reporter was supposed to be "the person who is, and who is recognized by the profession to be, best qualified for the work. . . ." Williston of Harvard, Beale of Harvard, Bohlen of Pennsylvania, and Mechem of Chicago were appointed reporters for the restatements of contracts, conflict of laws, torts, and agency, respectively. In addition the council was supposed to appoint a committee of three on classification and terminology; Dean Roscoe Pound (1870–1964) of Harvard would chair this committee. Later in the year the executive committee had second thoughts and decided to let Dean Pound handle classification by himself! He submitted his report late in 1923, and it was printed in the 1924 proceedings of the Institute.[44]

The Sudden Death of Classification

Dean Pound's report is a remarkable document. It is erudite, scholarly, historical, philosophical, and completely accurate; and it killed the movement for classification.

43. See 1 Proc. of A.L.I., pt. 3, 2 (1923).

44. 2 Proc. of A.L.I. 381 (1924). For an expanded exposition of Pound's thoughts on classification, apparently derived in part from his report, see Pound, Classification of the Law, 37 Harv. L. Rev. 933 (1924).

Pound's philosophy will be discussed in greater depth in chapter 6; suffice it to say here that he was a long-time enemy of the expository paradigm. He was the original American advocate of sociological juris-prudence, a mild skeptic of positivism, and a pragmatist. He perceived in the efforts to classify, as Holmes had forty years earlier, the handwriting of German metaphysics. He rejected the idea of the serious classifiers like Austin, Holland, Terry, and Andrews that the law must be radically rearranged around fundamental logical or natural concepts. His report said:

> At the outset we must renounce extravagant expectations as to what may be accomplished through classification. I doubt whether any classification is possible which will do anything more than classify. The most successful statements of law in legal history, the Digest of Justinian and the French Civil Code, are notoriously weakest on the side of classification. One might say that they have succeeded in spite of faulty classification.[45]

Pound traces the history of attempts to classify the law from the ancient Romans down to his own time. He includes an outline of the schemes of Pufendorf, Savigny, Puchta, Holland, Ahrens, the French Code, Wind-scheid, Planiol, the German Code, Hale, Blackstone, the ABA committee of 1902 (Andrews), and Terry. Of Terry's classification Pound says, "Terry has given us the most complete and most carefully worked out analytical arrangement from the standpoint of Anglo-American law." He also points out that the imprint of the ancient Roman classification (persons, things, actions) was stamped upon most of the suggested arrangements without any serious justification. Yes, Pound does leave us with a half-heartedly suggested outline based "on subjects usually taught in law schools." And yes, in spite of everything, one can see, faintly hidden in some revised terminology, the survival of at least part of the old Roman classification (see appendix H).

Although it was thought originally that general classification would proceed and be modified in step with the creation of the individual restate-ments,[46] the American Law Institute never took further action on Pound's report or made any other effort at general classification. A few writers in the 1920s suggested that the ALI should pay close attention to uniform ter-minology and classification, but little came of it with respect to classifica-

45. Ibid.
46. See 1 Proc. A.L.I., pt. 1, 45–46 (1923).

tion.[47] The last serious author to propose a new scheme of general categories was Albert Kocourek in 1934 (see appendix I).[48] By that time the
movement was dead and buried. The principal classifications proposed by
Americans over the years are printed in the appendixes to this book.

Exhumation and Autopsy

What happened to the movement for classification? In the
nineteenth century intelligent lawyers, especially those familiar with Roman law, saw a great need to systematize the common law. The Roman
law had been handed down to medieval and modern times as an organized
body of principles with its own technical vocabulary. It came in the form
of an official codification (Justinian's *Codex*) with an official textbook of
instruction (the *Institutes*). By comparison the common law, good enough
in substance, was an unorganized hodge-podge of rules, precedents, doctrines, and sources. To make the study of the common law something
more than merely low-level learning about approved maxims, technical
pleading, and alphabetical digests, in short, to make it a respectable
academic discipline, it was thought that rigorous "scientific" treatment
was necessary. This meant first and foremost some systematic organization. Blackstone's attempt was recognized by critics as inadequate, if
noble, and as time went by, obsolete.

In looking at the history of the drive for classification in America
recounted in this chapter we can see that scholars and lawyers throughout
the half century in question saw the problem in different lights. Terry
proposed radical reclassification in terms of logical and natural categories.
Field and his sympathizers wanted the stamp of authority on their statement of the common law. Others wanted uniformity among the states. As
early as the report of the ABA committee of 1891 we can recognize a
skepticism of the need for any radical rethinking, but an acknowledgment
of the desirability for clear and consistent expression of the "principles" of
the common law. While the 1902 report of the ABA committee reflected
the views of James D. Andrews, which were relatively radical, the 1910
push for the *Corpus Juris* project was ambiguous. It could be read as a
move for radical reclassification of the law or as a pitch for the clear and
consistent reexpression of the law. It is not at all clear what the members

47. See Goble, Terms for Restating the Law, 10 A.B.A.J. 58 (1924); Terry, Duties,
Rights, and Wrongs, 10 A.B.A.J. 123 (1924); Stone, Some Aspects of the Problem of
Law Simplification, 23 Colum. L. Rev. 319 (1923).
48. Kocourek, Classification of the Law, 11 N.Y.U.L.Q. 319 (1934).

of the Academy of Jurisprudence or the AALS backers of the Juristic Center had in mind. Elihu Root, committed as he was to "classification" of the law, seems to have introduced the term "restatement" in his famous speech of 1916. It is clear that when the dust had settled, and the leaders of the American Law Institute were firmly in control with their million-dollar Carnegie grant, that they had foremost in mind not reclassification of the law, but reexpression in the interests of clarity, consistency, and removal of the confusion supposedly inherent in the traditional case authorities.

Thus, classification meant different things to different people. For the codifiers, it meant getting the stamp of authority on otherwise vaguely expressed and confused doctrines of case law. For the radical reclassifiers it meant rethinking basic legal concepts and reclassification of the legal system according to logical or natural, as opposed to traditional, legal categories. For other interested parties, perhaps the great majority of the bar, it meant an attempt to state the common law in clear and consistent terms, divorced from the contingencies of particular cases.

The codifiers lost for a host of reasons, but mainly because the conservative attitude of the legal profession created a resistance to the unknown consequences of change and demanded adherence to the old ways. The radical reclassifiers lost for the same reason. Those seeking uniformity got half a loaf through the establishment and work of the Uniform Commissioners. Those seeking only clear and consistent expression won their battle. Their objective was the least controversial and the least intrusive in its potential effect on the vested interests of the bar. The American Law Institute's great venture would not have to be underwritten by the lawyers; it promised not to change the law, nor even to recommend legislative enactment of the restatements, and it further promised to proceed cautiously, always submitting drafts to the legal world. It held to these promises; it took ten years for the first restatements to gain ALI approval.

There is also a more intellectual explanation for the failure of the classification movement. The sociological movement in law began around the turn of the century, gradually gathering adherents, and the Austinian view became less and less fashionable (see chapter 6). At the very time when the ALI was beginning its great work of classification, a different view of why law was uncertain and complex was beginning to assert itself. The old idea of the scientific study of law as a matter of analysis and classification was being replaced by a newer idea of science. Ironically, it was the American founder of the new view who was placed in charge of formulating the plan for "classification." The lamb was given into the charge of the lion.

THE QUEST FOR
THE HOLY GRAIL
OF UNIVERSALS
1884–1935

Proper classification was deemed to be of paramount importance in understanding the law for Austin and his followers, but the classification they had in mind was not simply a matter of convenience or tradition. They wanted to classify the law according to its own fundamental
concepts and principles.[1] They seem to have had in mind such classifications as those in biology (invertebrates, vertebrates; fish, reptiles, birds,
mammals, etc.) where the categories were based upon the objective characteristics of the subject matter, or perhaps the more abstract concepts of
physics (gravitational attraction, inertia, etc.) which were conceived by
the physicists and imposed upon the phenomena as explanations.

Two different approaches to explaining basic concepts were suggested
in the nineteenth century.[2] The first approach is a priori, or what amounts
to almost the same thing, through definition. In this perspective, usually
associated with Kant or Continental rationalism, it is possible to think
about a particular subject only in certain ways. The idea of cause and
effect is a good example. We have great difficulty in thinking of anything
happening without a cause, although of course we may not know what the
cause is. It can be argued, as Austin did, that law, at least in "mature"
societies, cannot be conceived in the human mind without entailing certain other concepts. These concepts collectively are the basic building
blocks of the science of law.

1. Similar work was being done in Germany. See the numerous citations to German
authorities in T. Holland, *Elements of Jurisprudence* (8th ed. 1896).
2. These two approaches have been combined in more modern theory. See J. Losee, *A
Historical Introduction to the Philosophy of Science*, 173ff. (2d ed. 1980).

The second approach, associated historically with British empiricism, is to abstract the fundamental concepts from observation of the phenomena, a sort of induction. For example, by observing the relative variations of the temperature and pressure of a gas in an enclosed container, one can abstract a formula that will describe the relationship for all cases, including future ones. In law, one can observe the common characteristics of many legal systems and thereby derive general principles or concepts universally applicable.

Which method Austin thought he was following is a matter of debate.[3] However, it is clear that he regarded certain legal notions as fundamental and therefore the proper subject matter for analysis by the legal scientist. At one point Austin says, suggesting an empirical approach:

Although every system of law has its specific and characteristic differences, there are principles, notions, and distinctions common to various systems. . . . Accordingly, the various principles common to maturer systems (or the various analogies obtaining between them) are the subject of an extensive science: which science (as contra-distinguished to national or particular jurisprudence on one side, and, on another to the science of legislation) has been named General (or comparative) Jurisprudence, or the philosophy (or general principles) of positive law.[4]

On the other hand, when discussing these common notions specifically, Austin suggests an a priori, or Kantian, derivation:

Of the principles, notions, and distinctions which are the subjects of general jurisprudence, some may be esteemed necessary. For we cannot imagine coherently a system of law (or a system of law as evolved in a refined community), without conceiving them as constituent parts of it. Of these necessary principles, notions, and distinctions, I will suggest briefly a few examples: 1. The notions of Duty, Right, Liberty, Injury, Punishment, Redress; with their various relations to one another, and to Law, Sovereignty, and Independent Political Society. . . .[5]

3. See Morison, Some Myth about Positivism, 68 Yale L. J. 212 (1958); J. Stone, *The Province and Function of Law*, 58–70 (1950).

4. 3 Austin, 349–50.

5. Ibid., 351. Austin offers five additional categories of *necessary* principles, notions, and distinctions. He also discusses additional concepts, not necessary in the sense that we cannot think of a legal system without them, but which nevertheless "upon grounds

A substantial part of Austin's work lies in defining and analyzing the basic concepts of legal science. Starting from fundamental notions like *persons, things, acts* (and *forbearances*), and *events* or *incidents*, Austin constructs the concept of *duty* and *right*. Acts and forbearances are the objects of duties. Where there are rights correlative to duties, the same acts and forbearances are the objects of the rights. Rights are of two kinds: rights in or to things or persons and rights against other persons. With the former, the thing (or person) in which one has a right is called the subject of the right. Rights in things are further subdivided into rights *in rem* and rights *in personam*. Rights in rem (or real rights) are accompanied by corresponding duties on all persons generally; rights in personam (or personal rights) are accompanied by corresponding duties on determinate persons. The duties corresponding to personal rights are traditionally called obligations, and they can arise in three ways: by contract, by delict (tort), or by quasi-contract (restitution). Real rights are what we loosely know as property rights. Austin further elaborates his scheme of analysis in great detail.[6]

The British Expansion of Austinian Analysis

Austin's most influential follower in England was Thomas E. Holland, professor of law at Oxford, and it is he, along with Austin himself, who had the most impact on Americans. Holland amplifies Austin's idea of general jurisprudence; to him jurisprudence is to be carefully distinguished from the positive law itself—it is a science. "We have next to inquire what kind of science it is; and we shall find that it is formal, or analytical, as opposed to a material one; that is to say, that it deals with the various relations which are regulated by legal rules than with the rules themselves which regulate those relations."[7]

Holland compares jurisprudence with grammar; indeed, he calls it the grammar of the law. The grammarian develops concepts like the "possessive," "singular and plural," "verb and object," and "nominative and accusative," which express relationships existing in language, not just one language but conceivably many. So jurisprudence develops and analyzes

---

of utility" are found in all legal systems and therefore are also the subject of general jurisprudence. Ibid., 352–53.

6. Much of Austin's analysis is taken from the civilians and from Bentham. See 2 Austin, 1–41 and accompanying notes.

7. T. Holland, *Elements of Jurisprudence*, 5 (1880), hereinafter cited as Holland.

the concepts inherent in all legal systems.[8] This is not to be confused with comparative law, which examines the laws of various systems for similarities and differences and which must take into account the contingencies of historical and geographical accident. "Jurisprudence is therefore not the material science of those portions of the law which various nations have in common, but the formal science of those relations of mankind which are generally recognized as having legal consequences."[9]

Holland offers a scheme of classification to demonstrate where jurisprudence fits into related intellectual activity. The study of human action is divided into Ethic and Nomology.[10] Under Ethic are all of the sciences dealing with states of the will or internal morality. Under Nomology are the sciences dealing with the conformity of outward human acts to rules. Nomology is in turn divided into (1) the science of rules enforced by indeterminate authority, including social customs or morality, etiquette, codes of honor, and so on (and here Holland criticizes various notions of natural law that have in his view caused considerable confusion), and (2) the science of rules enforced by determinate authority, namely, jurisprudence.

Of the relations that form the subject matter of jurisprudence, none is more important than the concept of right. A legal right is "a capacity residing in one man of controlling, with the assent and assistance of the State, the actions of others." Putting aside psychological questions raised by this definition, Holland proceeds to analyze a right into its four component parts: the person entitled, the object, the act (or forbearance), and the person obliged. As an example, a testator dies, leaving his daughter a silver teapot. The daughter is the person entitled, the object is the teapot,

8. Henry Maine seemed to think that the kind of concepts Holland had in mind were analogous to the "laws" of economics (for example, law of supply and demand) that were being touted by political economists. See H. Maine, *The Early History of Institutions*, 346–47 (7th ed. 1897).

9. Holland, 7. Although this sounds Kantian, Holland further elaborates: "Jurisprudence is not a science of legal relations *a priori*, as they might have been, or should have been, but is abstracted *a posteriori* from such relations as have been clothed with a legal character in actual systems, that is to say from law which has actually been imposed, or positive law. It follows that Jurisprudence is a progressive science. Its generalizations must keep pace with the movement of systems of actual law. Its broader distinctions, corresponding to deep seated human characteristics, will no doubt be permanent, but, as time goes on, new distinctions must be constantly developed, with a view toward the coordination of the ever increasing variety of legal phenomena." Ibid., 8.

10. Holland, 22. This distinction is taken from German philosophy, particularly that of Kant. See J. Gray, *The Nature and Sources of the Law*, 92–93 (1909).

the act is delivering the teapot to her, and the executor is the person obliged. Holland points out that not all rights have objects. He also introduces some further terminology: the person entitled is called the person of inherence of the right, and the person obliged is the person of incidence. Holland further analyzes each of the four component parts of a right into their respective component parts.

Holland offers the following graphic representation to illustrate his analysis of right and duty:

| The Person Entitled | The Object | The Act or Forbearance | The Person Obliged |

While admitting that rights can be classified in various ways, Holland states that four categories are of prime importance. The first of them is the distinction between public and private rights and a corresponding distinction between the two bodies of law. Public rights are those in which the state is either the person of incidence or the person of inherence; private rights are those in which both persons are private. In this, Holland follows the nineteenth-century civilians and departs from Austin, who followed Blackstone in categorizing public law as a part of the law of "persons."

The second major division of rights is based upon the status of the persons holding rights or owing duties. A "normal" person is an adult male human being enjoying full rights. An "abnormal" person is a human being with some legal disability or incapacity (child, incompetent, adult woman under coverture, etc.) or an artificial person like a corporation, partnership, the state, and so forth.

The third major category of rights is based on whether or not the person of incidence is limited or unlimited. This is, of course, the old in rem–in personam distinction.

Finally, Holland classifies rights on the basis of whether the act required by the right is due for its own sake or upon default of another act. Thus, the owner of Blackacre has a right not to have it trespassed upon. When a trespass occurs, a new right to damages arises. This type of right is also called a secondary, remedial, or sanctioning right.

Many other concepts and distinctions are defined and analyzed by Holland: "rights at rest and in motion," "investitive and divestitive facts," "divisible and indivisible rights," and so on. These ideas are illustrated with examples drawn from both Roman and common law, but most of the new conceptual terminology seems to be drawn from nineteenth-century civilians, as indicated by the footnotes.

An even more sophisticated analysis of fundamental legal concepts was provided at the turn of the century by John W. Salmond. Salmond earned his master's and law degrees at University College, London, and became a professor of law at the University of Adelaide. He wrote a collection of essays on jurisprudence in 1891, followed by a small volume entitled *First Principles of Jurisprudence* in 1893. The latter work was greatly expanded and published in 1902 as Salmond's magnum opus under the title *Jurisprudence or the Theory of Law*. This book eventually came to supersede Holland's treatise as the premier text on jurisprudence in the British countries, running through twelve editions, the last in 1966.[11]

Perhaps partly in response to criticisms of Holland by Buckland, discussed on pages 91–93, Salmond carefully defined the scope of jurisprudence so that the subject does not exist independently of the law but simply as the theoretical, abstract, or general aspect of the law. It is the "science of the first principles of the civil law."[12] A chart explains the place of legal theory as he conceives it:

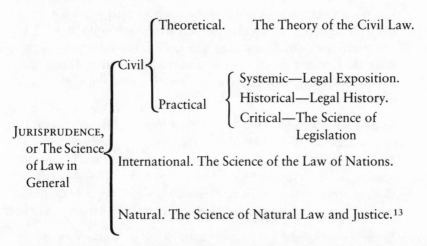

JURISPRUDENCE, or The Science of Law in General

Civil —
- Theoretical. The Theory of the Civil Law.
- Practical
  - Systemic—Legal Exposition.
  - Historical—Legal History.
  - Critical—The Science of Legislation

International. The Science of the Law of Nations.

Natural. The Science of Natural Law and Justice.[13]

11. Salmond drew upon Holland's work as well as Austin's. He gives no citations to the work of Terry in the original edition of his treatise, leading to the conclusion that he was not familiar with the American's work. In fact, the only American referred to by Salmond is Holmes (*The Common Law*).

12. J. Salmond, *Jurisprudence, or the Theory of Law*, 4–5 (1902), hereinafter referred to as Salmond.

13. In good positivist style Salmond recognizes that over the centuries a substantial body of literature dealing with natural law was created; but, he says, "Experience has shown . . . that this abstract theory of justice in itself, this attempt to work out *in abstracto* the principles of natural right, is a sufficiently unprofitable form of literature." See, however, Salmond, 222.

In this scheme Salmond's work falls under "Theoretical."[14] This concept of the scope of jurisprudence is broader than Austin's, Holland's, and others because it includes the theoretical side of all three branches of the science of civil law. In spite of this apparent expansion, however, upon closer examination we find that Salmond deals seriously only with the usual topics associated with the expository paradigm, that is, classification, definition of key terms, and analysis of fundamental concepts.

Like his predecessors in the Austinian tradition, Salmond declines to give very satisfactory reasons why some legal ideas or concepts are to be regarded as "fundamental." He does explicitly reject the empirical or inductive justification. "It is not . . . the science of those principles which all or most systems of law have in common." He holds that universal reception is neither sufficient nor necessary for a principle or concept to become a part of theoretical jurisprudence.

In another passage, stating what jurisprudence is not, he gives a clue to his vision of legal science:

> It is not an elementary outline of the concrete legal system. It deals not with the outlines of the law, but with its ultimate conceptions. It is concerned not with the simplest and easiest, but with some of the most abstruse and difficult portions of the legal system. Theoretical jurisprudence is not elementary law, any more than metaphysics is elementary science.[15]

Salmond departed from the Austinian structure in his definition of law, which he regarded as "the body of principles recognized and applied by the state in the administration of justice." He thus put the administration of justice as logically prior to the concept of law, a view shared and expanded upon by the American, John Chipman Gray. Salmond recognized that judges make decisions whether there is law on the issues or not.

> Even when a system of law exists, the extent of it may vary indefinitely. The degree in which the free discretion of the judge in doing

14. Salmond, 8. The author tells us that the matters included under the subject of theoretical jurisprudence are: analysis of the conception of civil law itself; analysis of the various subordinate and constituent ideas of which the complex idea of the law is made up; an account of the sources of law including the theory of legislation, precedent, and customary law; examination of the general principles of legal development; inquiry into the scientific arrangement of the law; analysis of the conception of legal rights together with the division of rights into various classes; investigation of the theory of legal liability, both criminal and civil; others deserving attention because of their fundamental character. Ibid., 6.

15. Salmond, 7.

right is excluded by predetermined rules of law, is capable of indefinite increase or diminution. The total exclusion of judicial discretion by legal principle is impossible in any system.[16]

While clearly recognizing that the principles and rules of law do not of themselves always determine judicial decisions, Salmond did not inquire what other sources or guides might influence or limit such decisions.

Salmond's work constitutes a real advance beyond the analysis undertaken originally by Austin. It redefines concepts and issues in a way that answers many of the critics' objections to the earlier works of Amos, Markby, Holland, and others as well as that of Austin, and it reflects some creative genius in doing so. We must content ourselves here, however, with consideration of Salmond's treatment of rights and duties.

Salmond maintains that all rights have correlative duties and vice versa.[17] Every right has the following elements: (1) the person in whom the right is vested, or the owner or *subject* of the right, (2) the person against whom the right avails, or the *subject* of the duty, (3) an act or omission required by the right or the *content*, (4) the thing to which the act or omission relates, or the *object* of the right, and (5) the facts or events that give rise to the right, or the *title*. This analysis is confined to the concept of right in its strict sense. Salmond recognizes, however, that the term "right" is used in a broad sense to include four distinct legally recognized interests: "In this generic sense a legal right may be defined as any advantage or benefit which is in any manner conferred upon a person by a rule of law. Of rights in this sense there are at least four distinct kinds, namely, *Rights* (in the strict and proper sense), *Liberties*, *Powers*, and *Immunities*."[18]

Rights in the strict sense, according to Salmond, may be considered the benefits that one derives from duties imposed on others. In contrast, legal liberties are the benefits that one derives from the absence of legal duties imposed on oneself.[19]

16. Salmond, 17.

17. "There can be no right without a corresponding duty, or duty without a corresponding right, any more than there can be a husband without a wife, or a father without a child." Ibid., 223.

18. Salmond, 231.

19. "Rights of the former class are concerned with those things which other persons *ought* to do for me; rights of the second class [liberties] are concerned with those things which I *may* do for myself. The former pertain to the sphere of obligation or compulsion; the latter to that of liberty or free will. Both are legally recognized interests. . . ." Ibid., 232. Examples of liberties given by Salmond include the "right" to express one's

Powers, in Salmond's view, are a third species of right (in the broad sense) in which the law enables one to effect some legal relationship.[20] Immunities are those benefits derived from the absence of legal control by others, or a legally protected freedom from the alteration of a legal relationship by someone else.[21] "Just as a right in the strict sense is the benefit derived from the absence of *liberty* in other persons, so an immunity is the benefit derived from the absence of *power* in other persons."[22]

Only rights in the strict sense have correlative duties. However, Salmond says that there are legal burdens analogous to duties that are correlative of the other types of "rights":

These legal burdens are of four kinds corresponding to the four varieties of legal rights already considered. Two of these classes, however, are not distinguished from each other in legal nomenclature, and are included under the same title, the classes being thus reduced to three in number. These are *Duties, Disabilities,* and *Liabilities.*[23]

Salmond then points out a further relationship between these various benefits and burdens, although he gives no special name to this relationship: "A duty is the absence of liberty. A disability is the absence of power. A liability is the absence either of a right or an immunity, and is the correlative either of a liberty or a power vested in someone else."[24]

A graphic representation of these ideas is provided by Salmond as follows:[25]

---

opinion on public affairs, the "right" to defend oneself against violence, and the "right" to use one's property as one sees fit.

20. Examples given by Salmond are the power to make a will, the power of sale vested in a mortgagee, the landlord's "right" of reentry, a power of appointment, the powers of legal officials, and the power to alienate property. He says, "A power is usually combined with a liberty to exercise it; that is to say, the exercise of it is not merely effectual but rightful. This however, is not necessarily the case. It may be effectual and yet wrongful; as when, in breach of my agreement, I revoke a license given by me to enter upon my land. Such revocation is perfectly effectual, but it is a wrongful act, for which I am liable to the licensee in damages. I had a right (in the sense of power) to revoke the license, but I had no right (in the sense of liberty) to do so." Ibid., 234–35.

21. Examples are the "right" a debtor acquires when the statute of limitations has run upon the debt, the "right" of the tenant to stay in possession when the landlord loses his right of reentry, and the right of a seller when the purchaser waives his right to rescind for fraud. Salmond, 235–36.

22. Salmond, 235.

23. Salmond, 236.

24. Salmond.

25. Salmond, 238.

RIGHTS in the generic sense—any benefit conferred by law

1. RIGHTS (stricto sensu) ....correlative to ....DUTIES
2. LIBERTIES ....correlative to ....LIABILITIES
3. POWERS ....correlative to ....LIABILITIES
4. IMMUNITIES ....correlative to .......DISABILITIES

1. RIGHTS (stricto sensu)—what others *must* do for me
2. LIBERTIES—what I *may* do for myself
3. POWERS—what I *can* do as against others
4. IMMUNITIES—what others *cannot* do as against me

Salmond does not try to make a case that lawyers and judges should follow this terminology, but the implication is that scholars and students should recognize these distinctions.[26]

Some Critical Questions

Austin set the wheels in motion, and his British disciples eagerly elaborated upon the expository theme. They were engaged in legal science. However, the gospel according to Austin was not universally accepted. Another English jurist, Professor W. W. Buckland of Cambridge University, raised a voice of dissent in a penetrating article published in 1890.[27]

By this time Austinian jurisprudence had become a standard course for law students at British universities. Buckland was sympathetic with students who failed to understand its significance.

Englishmen seem to have assumed as a fact a philosophy of law, but they have not been at the pains to indicate its nature. The student, observing a system of rules based on certain universal principles, turns over the leaves of his manual to find the demonstration of these universal truths. He fails to find it, but he finds instead the free assumption of those very principles which he had thought it the business of the writers to demonstrate.[28]

26. Roscoe Pound later suggested that Salmond borrowed the four- (or eight-) part schema from the German scholar Bierling. However, although Salmond does refer to Bierling in his book, he seems to refer primarily in this context to Windscheid. See Pound, Fifty Years of Jurisprudence, 50 Harv. L. Rev. 557, 571ff. (1937).

27. Buckland, Difficulties of Abstract Jurisprudence, 6 L.Q. Rev. 436 (1890).

28. Ibid., 437. Buckland expresses the purpose of this ten-page article as follows:

The principles to which Buckland alluded were those "necessary" concepts and distinctions announced originally by Austin. As refined by Holland, the two propositions or assumptions that Buckland attacks are stated as follows: "(i) There is a discoverable unity in law, i.e. it is possible to find, by comparison of systems of law, a skeleton of principles on which legal rules may be grouped; (ii) it is the object of the science of jurisprudence to develop these principles."[29] Buckland notes Holland's famous analogy between the science of grammar and the science of law, but concludes, "All this is, after all, nothing but a remote analogy." He points out that older theories of German transcendentalism have been rejected in England, and there are no eternal truths beneath the surface of positive legal systems. "Jurisprudence has no independent existence. Its formulae are meaningless except in relation to concrete legal rules. It is a part of the law. That the same jurisprudence is a part of all law is the point to be proven, not assumed."[30]

Buckland proceeds to argue that it has yet to be proven that any so-called universal legal principles or concepts actually exist. He discusses some of Austin's "necessary" concepts and demonstrates that they are not only unnecessary, but in some cases they involve considerable confusion. He also attacks Holland's and Markby's conception of a *res* as a right, concluding, "Is there not here a real confusion, and is it not . . . the result of an attempt to incorporate into a system aiming at universality incompatible rules drawn from various systems?"

While Buckland is not averse to teaching students some basic terminology and some concepts useful in various fields of law within the English system, he maintains that what the analysts are doing cannot be anything more than that. He suggests that any true science of law will follow the historical path marked by Henry Maine and Justice Holmes. Then,

> The result will be a science of great interest. But treatises on it will not at all resemble the current treatises on jurisprudence. Professor Holland's "unity underlying the phenomena with which jurisprudence has to deal" may still exist, but in another sense. It will no longer be

_____

"The object of the present paper has not been to deny the possibility of some universal philosophy of law, but to suggest that the English view of that philosophy is as unmanageable and stands on as doubtful foundation as the German, and to protest against the confusing conception of jurisprudence as having for its aim the exposition of universal principles which are only 'not unreasonably assumed.' " Ibid., 444–45.

29. Ibid.

30. Ibid., 438.

unity of principle obscured by difference in terminology, but differentiation of principle under the influence of social causes as to which general laws can be established.[31]

It is a monument to the hard conceptual shell created by the expository paradigm that its exponents seemed unmoved by this devastating critique delivered by Buckland. Holland's work continued to be published in ever new and updated versions. Competing with it as the standard treatise on jurisprudence was the 1902 treatise of Salmond and its subsequent editions.

Early American Efforts At Analysis

The first American to take up the expository paradigm was Oliver Wendell Holmes, Jr., as we have noted in chapter 2, but he soon dropped this endeavor to pursue other ideas. The second was Henry T. Terry, alternately professor of law in the University of Tokyo and practitioner in New York City (see chapters 2 and 3).[32] Also to be noted again is the jurisprudence of George H. Smith, discussed in chapter 2, which contained considerable analytic work. A third American to state and analyze fundamental legal concepts in some depth was Christopher Columbus Langdell. Langdell had been teaching a course in equity at the Harvard Law School for several years, and, as a result of this experience, he found it necessary to offer an explanation of certain fundamental concepts.

His first effort in this direction was published in the *Harvard Law Review* in 1887.[33] An expanded and somewhat modified scheme was published in 1900.[34] Langdell does not give the philosophical derivation of these fundamentals. He only tells us that he will discuss "those rights which it is the duty of courts of justice to protect and enforce. . . ."[35]

31. Ibid., 444.

32. Terry's treatise of 1884 is the most comprehensive and incisive work of analytical jurisprudence ever undertaken by an American, with the possible exception of Kocourek's *Jural Relations*. A. Kocourek, *Jural Relations* (2d ed. 1928).

33. Langdell, A Brief Survey of Equity Jurisdiction, 1 Harv. L. Rev. 55 (1887).

34. Langdell, Classification of Rights and Wrongs, 13 Harv. L. Rev. 537, 659 (1900). This essay was included in a collection of Langdell's articles published as a book in 1906, republished in 1908. C. Langdell, *A Brief Survey of Equity Jurisdiction* (1906).

35. Ibid., 538. In another passage, discussing how we obtain "knowledge" of a

Although Langdell cites Holland in his 1900 article, either he did not understand Holland's analysis of right and duty or he deliberately chose not to follow it. In any case, Langdell's work is clearly a step backward from the direction that both Holland and Terry had taken. Langdell does not appear to have read Terry's treatise.

Langdell divides rights into absolute and relative.[36] Absolute rights are further divided into personal and property rights. Personal rights are those inherent in any human being; they cannot be acquired or alienated. Although he gives no examples of such rights, presumably he means such things as the right to be free from bodily injury and assault, the right to life, the right to good reputation, the right to engage in lawful activities, and the like.[37] Curiously, in some passages Langdell discusses these rights as though they were the same natural rights associated with the moral paradigm.[38]

Property rights, in contrast to personal rights, must be acquired, must have pecuniary value, and can generally be alienated. They are further subdivided into corporeal and incorporeal rights. Under the heading of incorporeal rights Langdell includes rights created by obligations, powers, licenses and monopolies (including patents and copyrights), which he characterizes as "negative rights." He makes the puzzling assertion that absolute rights of both the personal type and the property type have no duties that correspond to them.

Relative rights are divided into those creating obligations and those creating duties. An obligation is created by act of the parties; it may be contractual, quasi-contractual (restitutionary), or tortious (some kinds of torts, at least). The right-obligation relationship is further subdivided into personal and real obligations. Examples of real obligations are servitudes (easements) and liens. A personal obligation can be illustrated by a simple contract to borrow money. A lends B $100, and B gives A his note for that

---

particular kind of right, Langdell rather obscurely says: "Courts of justice never have occasion to take cognizance of [personal rights] except when complaints are made of their infringement. . . . It follows, therefore, that all the knowledge that we have of personal rights relates to one question, what acts will constitute an infringement of them." Ibid.

36. This corresponds roughly to rights in rem and in personam as used by other authors. Langdell believes the use of these traditional terms should be restricted to procedure, and their use in classifying rights is inaccurate. See ibid., 546–47.

37. Langdell does not seem to have a category for political rights, that is, the right to vote or hold public office. These are not property rights, but they must be acquired (through majority, citizenship, residence) and can be lost.

38. See ibid., 538, 546, 659.

amount. A has a relative right against B to payment on the due date; B has an obligation to pay. Langdell points out that A also has an absolute property right against all the world to ownership of the note.

In contrast to an obligation, a duty is created by a command of the state rather than by an act of the parties; it applies to persons in certain situations. The persons upon whom duties fall will change from time to time; therefore, the "parties cannot properly be predicated." Langdell says, "A person can avoid incurring liability to a duty only by avoiding the situation to which such liability is incident. . . ." Langdell realizes that when a person breaches a duty (command of the state), he commits a tort, which is also an invasion of the victim's absolute rights, but Langdell is unwilling to find a correspondence between the duty and the right. It appears that here he may have taken the wrong fork in the road, twice. First, Langdell's distinction between inherent absolute personal rights and the duty-creating commands of the state that prohibit interference with those rights seems unnecessary and baseless. Second, Langdell seems unwilling to find a right correspondent with a duty unless the person owing the duty is identifiable. This does not involve a logical fallacy, but such an analysis seems to obscure more than it explains.

Langdell's analytic scheme can be represented graphically as follows:

                    Absolute Rights
Personal _____ No Corresponding Duty
Property _____ No Corresponding Duty
      Corporeal
      Incorporeal
            Created by obligation (as against the world)
            Powers
            Licenses
            Monopolies

                    Relative Rights
Right _____ Obligation (of the obligor)
                    Contract
                    Quasi-contract (restitution)
                    Tort (some)
Right _____ Duty

Apparently unaware of the advances made by Salmond, a Washington, D.C., lawyer by the name of Hannis Taylor (1851–1922), holding degrees from Edinburgh and Dublin, wrote a treatise entitled *The Science of*

Jurisprudence in 1908.[39] This work purports to be a combination of both historical and analytical scholarship. In fact, the two parts of the book could easily have stood alone as representative samples of the evolutionary and expository paradigms, respectively. The treatise is dedicated to Thomas E. Holland and Lord James Bryce, the principal British analyst and historicist, respectively, of the time.

In Taylor's view there are two approaches toward understanding law. The first, and the more fundamental, is the historical approach; the second is jurisprudence, or the analytic science of positive law. These approaches are not incompatible, but in fact complement each other in such a way that both are necessary for a complete grasp of the subject. A subdivision of historical inquiry is comparative law, the examination of different legal systems in their historical contexts, with cross-comparisons. This type of study furnishes the data from which jurisprudence abstracts its own concepts. Taylor argues that since the neo-Roman and English legal systems now encompass nine-tenths of the globe and are the most mature and sophisticated, the comparatist can be content with the study of only those two systems.

In the analytical part of the treatise Taylor presents the usual positivist discussion of legal concepts. In his view the "cardinal conceptions" inherent in all legal systems are state, law, rights, and duties. His specific analysis of these terms proceeds no farther, however, than that of Holland.

Taylor finds Holland's analogy between grammar and jurisprudence "the best possible" explanation of legal science. There is no Kantian side to Taylor, however; he maintains that the concepts used by analysts are generalizations of fact taken from the data supplied by comparative lawyers. He perceived, as Holland had, that since these data are always expanding, jurisprudence will also change as time passes; that is, it is a dynamic science. Taylor does express the hope, revealing some "taint" of idealism, that in the distant future the combined efforts of the historians, comparatists, and analysts will yield a "uniform conception of legal right" throughout the world.

In 1909, the year following the publication of Hannis Taylor's magnum opus, the first treatise on jurisprudence expressing original American themes was produced. This was Harvard professor John Chipman Gray's *The Nature and Sources of the Law.* Gray (1839–1915) regarded himself

39. H. Taylor, *The Science of Jurisprudence* (1908). For a short article that summarizes the conclusions (and assumptions) of the treatise, see Taylor, The Science of Jurisprudence, 22 Harv. L. Rev. 241 (1909). Taylor was an eminent diplomat and ambassador to Spain. He wrote books on international law, American constitutional history, and British constitutional history.

as an analyst, but his great contribution to jurisprudence does not lie in the domain of the expository paradigm; rather, it is in the modification of that paradigm so that sociological jurisprudence could obtain a foothold (see chapter 6). While he speaks admiringly of Savigny's ideas and the value of legal history generally, and he admits the persuasiveness of Holland's metaphor of jurisprudence and grammar,[40] Gray essentially accepts the Austinian analysis as a helpful clarification of terminology, but with a mild skepticism toward its theoretical pretensions. He took as his aim:

> To call your attention to the analysis and relations of some fundamental legal ideas, rather than to tell their history or prophesy their future development. Not that I am insensible to the value of historical studies, nor blind to the fact that legal conceptions are constantly changing, yet, to borrow a figure from the shop, it is well at times to take account of stock. . . .[41]

Why does Gray find some legal ideas "fundamental"? He never tells us but he does tell us what does not make them fundamental. Rejecting a priori approaches out of hand, he further explains why general jurisprudence based on necessary concepts as defined by Austin cannot be derived by empirical induction. If such a science involves the study of all rules common to all legal systems, it is impossible because of the enormity of the undertaking; and even if such a task could be undertaken, "the list of rules of Law received, *semper, ubique et ab omnibus*, from Kamchatka to Patagonia is likely to be a short one." If the list is limited to "necessary" principles, this science, too, becomes impossible, because it rests on a theory of metaphysical absolutes no longer tenable. While some of the same principles of law can be found in systems based on the Roman and the English, there is nothing necessary about them, and calling them so "has the evil result of suggesting the universal . . . when the fact merely is that they have been accepted as true or convenient by certain jurists in Rome and by certain judges in England."[42]

Taking a pragmatic or perhaps nonphilosophic approach, Gray thus refuses to explain why certain concepts are fundamental in understanding law. These concepts include, of course, rights and duties, which he analyzes in some detail. While generally following the lead of the English

40. J. Gray, *The Nature and Sources of the Law*, 131 (1909).

41. Ibid., Gray provides an interesting analysis using a plate of shrimp salad as the subject of rights and duties. This example is picked up and reanalyzed by other scholars. See the discussion of Hohfeld, pp. 101–107.

42. Ibid., 133. Gray follows and approves Buckland's argument made in 1890. See Buckland, note 27.

analysts, Gray's discussion proceeds farther down a certain track by introducing the concept of interests taken from Jhering.[43] In this way the legal term "right" is connected to sociological data. Gray's discussion of sovereignty also is particularly enlightening. In chapter 6 Gray's work in relation to the Poundian paradigm will be explored.

The Fundamental Categories Of Legal Knowledge

Other scholars in America took up the cause of analytic jurisprudence in the second decade of the century.[44] In particular two notable contributors at Northwestern University were very prolific, John H. Wigmore (1863–1943) and Albert Kocourek (1875–1952).[45] Wigmore, dean of the law school and a noted authority on the law of evidence and torts, had begun his thinking in the expository paradigm as early as 1894, when he was seeking a rational organization for the law of torts. In two related articles in the *Harvard Law Review* Wigmore suggested a way in which the multisubject field of "torts" could be considered one field of "tort."[46]

Following a lead suggested by Holmes, Wigmore bases his analysis on the idea of duty. After explaining that all legal relations (he likes the term "nexus") consist of a right at one end and a duty at the other, he distinguishes between duties (1) imposed on the obligor without reference to

43. Ibid., 18ff. For more on Jhering see chapter 6.

44. In addition, the works of two foreign scholars working in the expository paradigm were published in the United States in English during this period. K. Gareis, *The Science of Law* (trans. Kocourek, 1911), reviewed in Spencer, Professor Gareis' Introduction to the Science of Law, 23 Green Bag 191 (1911); N. Korkunov, *General Theory of Law* (trans. Hastings, 1909).

45. These two scholars edited a three-volume work known as the Evolution of Law Series. A. Kocourek and J. Wigmore, *Sources of Ancient and Primitive Law* (1915); A. Kocourek and J. Wigmore, *Primitive and Ancient Legal Institutions* (1915); A. Kocourek and J. Wigmore, *Formative Influences of Legal Development* (1918). The latter was reviewed critically by Edwin B. Gager in 28 Yale L. J. 617 (1919). Kocourek and Wigmore also collaborated in editing *The Rational Basis of Legal Institutions* (1923), reviewed by Underhill Moore in 23 Colum. L. Rev. 609 (1923). Kocourek translated volume 1 of the Modern Legal Philosophy Series, K. Gareis, *The Science of Law* (1911).

46. "Certainly the subject is in need of some accepted analysis. . . . If we are ever to have, as Sir Frederick Pollock puts it, not books about specific Torts, but books about Tort in general, some further examination of fundamental ideas is desirable." Wigmore, The Tripartite Division of Torts, 8 Harv. L. Rev. 200 (1894). The second article is in the same volume: Wigmore, A General Analysis of Tort Relations, 8 Harv. L. Rev. 377 (1895). A historical introduction to these articles can be found in Wigmore, Responsibility for Tortious Acts: Its History, 7 Harv. L. Rev. 315 (1894).

her wish or assent, or (2) in consequence of her wish or intent to assume it. The first type Wigmore calls recusable, the second irrecusable. Recusable duties are basically those incurred through contract. Among irrecusable duties are those imposed upon certain classes of persons (for example, duty of parent to support child) and those imposed upon persons generally, or universal irrecusable duties. This is the subject area of torts. But within this category torts are not to be broken down into the usual types (slander, trespass, negligence, battery, nuisance, and so on). Rather, three "generic component elements" common to all torts are to serve as the organizing principles. These are the damage (or harm) element, the responsibility (or causation) element, and the excuse (or justification) element. Wigmore goes on to explain how different parts of these elements combine to define or determine actionable torts.[47]

Wigmore seems not to have done anything further with his experiment in analysis until the publication of his two-volume casebook on torts in 1911–12.[48] This interesting work presents cases and text for student use organized into the three categories mentioned. In addition, a summary of principles is included as an appendix, containing further development of Wigmore's jurisprudential ideas. The same analysis of duties presented in the earlier articles is again presented, with some refinements and extensions.[49] In addition, Wigmore has developed a classification of all of the ways in which law can be scientifically studied. He takes Holland's distinction between the sciences of ethic and nomology and develops an

47. Ibid. On the nature of these classifications, Wigmore says: "The fundamental idea is, not to follow fancy nor to force a symmetrical grouping, but, neglecting accidents of appearance and surface differences, to examine reasons and causes, to ascertain the intrinsic meaning of principles and the considerations actually treated as controlling decisions, and thus at once to indicate the true lines of argument and discussion on which the development of principles must proceed."

48. J. Wigmore, Select Cases on the Law of Torts (2 vols. 1911–12).

49. Wigmore defines social, ethical, and legal relations. He analyzes the latter as follows: "A legal relation may be termed a Nexus. The converse fact, i.e. that the State force will not interfere to compel or protect the parties, is a non-Nexus. Theoretically, to define the nexus is to state the law sufficiently; practically, the organs of the law are constantly stating also a non-Nexus, i.e. that the State force will not interfere. . . . A Nexus has two elements: the Persons and the Interest. The Persons to a Nexus are two. From the side of the person by whom State force is demandable, the nexus is termed a Right. From the side of the person against whom it is demandable, the nexus is termed a Burden, Duty, Obligation, or Liability. The former person is termed Obligee, the latter Obligor." He then explains the relationships between interests, rights, and wrongs; this he connects with the concepts of "cause of action" and "form of action." He also makes the distinction between "primary" and "auxiliary" rights (Austin's and Holland's "secondary" rights). Ibid., 834–35.

entire regime of categories that purports to be exhaustive of the ways in which one can think about law.

This scheme was elaborated upon in a 1914 article in the *Harvard Law Review* in which Wigmore advocated the adoption of a universal technical vocabulary for legal scholarship.[50] He modestly proposed "to offer tentatively a terminology for legal science." He stated his thesis in these words: "The Science of Law—meaning all systematic knowledge about law—should be divided, not according to the kinds of law, nor the subject of law, but according to *the ways in which we conceive of law as an operative fact in its relations to the world.*"[51]

Wigmore proposes the use of new terms "to avoid the inherited curse of ambiguity." He suggests as the name of the science of law generally "nomology." In the finest Benthamite tradition, he offers as the branches of this science:[52]

1. *Nomo-scopy*:   broken down into
    Nomo-statics, the ascertainment of the actual law of a given moment.
    Nomo-genetics, the history of the law.
    Nomo-physics, the relation between law and other facts or sciences.
2. *Nomo-sophy*:   broken down into
    Nomo-critics, the logical analysis of the law.
    Nomo-thetics, the evaluation of law according to a standard of ethics.
    Nomo-politics, the evaluation of law from the standpoint of economics or social science.
3. *Nomo-didactics*: legal education.
4. *Nomo-practics*: the giving effect to law by organs of the state, broken down into.
    Nomo-dikastics, application of law by courts.
    Nomo-poietics, legislation.
    Nomo-drastics, administration or execution of the law by the executive.

Wigmore's suggestions were apparently not taken seriously by the scholarly community except for his colleague and sometime collaborator,

50. Wigmore, The Terminology of Legal Science, 28 Harv. L. Rev. 1 (1914).
51. Ibid., 2.
52. Ibid., 3 ff.

Albert Kocourek, who expanded and improved upon the terms in the 1920s.[53] While Wigmore did not attempt to distinguish between different kinds of rights and duties, he related nomology to legal education in another article published in the *Harvard Law Review* in 1917,[54] and in this piece he implies that he considered the various branches of legal science set out above as in some sense dictated by a priori, or what we have called Kantian, absolute categories. He says:

> Law, as a subject of thought and activity, has several distinct categories or modes of being, and cannot be thought about except in one or another of these processes. . . . All of the above ways of thinking about Law are inherent and unavoidable, and are used in a lawyer's practical activity. Some are used always more than others, and some are used at certain periods of a nation's history more than others. But all are used, and all are necessary and inevitable.[55]

At this abstract level of the "modes of being" of legal science Wigmore came very close to capturing the holy grail of universals.

While Wigmore clearly had a vision of law within the expository paradigm, he also could shift gears and view it from the standpoint of the evolutionary paradigm; his work in this vein will be explored in the next chapter. This dualistic thrust is perhaps the distinguishing feature of Wigmore's jurisprudence.

The Wondrous Schema

Wesley Newcomb Hohfeld's (1879–1918) modestly titled article, "Some Fundamental Legal Conceptions as Applied in Judicial Reasoning," was published in the *Yale Law Journal* in November of 1913, with the second part following in 1917.[56] This came closely on the heels of

53. In particular Kocourek's book, *An Introduction to the Science of Law* (1930), reflects the eclectic outlook of Wigmore. Kocourek's other major work, *Jural Relations* (1927), is in some ways the culmination of the Hohfeldian debate.

54. Wigmore, *Nova Methodus Discendae Docendaeque Jurisprudentiae*, 30 Harv. L. Rev. 812 (1917). The Latin title is borrowed from a jurisprudential work of Leibnitz.

55. Ibid., 820–22.

56. Hohfeld, Some Fundamental Legal Conceptions as Applied in Judicial Reasoning, 23 Yale L. J. 16 (1913). The companion article, or part two, discusses the distinctions between legal and equitable rights and rights in rem and in personam. Hohfeld, Some Fundamental Legal Conceptions as Applied in Judicial Reasoning, 26 Yale L.J.

the publication of the several analytic works that have already been mentioned.[57]

Hohfeld begins his now famous essay by suggesting that he is going to clarify some confusions that have arisen in the law of trusts and related areas of equity. His aim is practical; he seeks to help the practitioner. But rather quickly he finds it necessary to provide an analysis of "fundamental" or "basic" legal conceptions. These conceptions make up legal or "jural" relations, which must be distinguished "from the physical and mental facts that call such relations into being." Factual relations must be kept distinct from the "purely legal."

Hohfeld effectively makes the points that the legal vocabulary is far from precise and that the use of the word "right" to mean several things is among the worst abuses in lawyers' language. This is the one proposition upon which his critics and his supporters will emphatically agree, although it is far from original with Hohfeld. He accordingly undertakes to explain the various meanings of "right" in the broad sense and of its correlatives and opposites. With justification he takes Holland to task for certain confusions in his analysis. He is even harder on Gray, taking the latter's colorful example of the right to eat shrimp salad and showing that Gray has confused right, in the limited sense, with privilege (or liberty).

One might think that a scholar concerned with the precise use of language would give a definition or series of definitions of the terms that he intends to use in an exact way. Instead, Hohfeld says, "The strictly fundamental legal relations are, after all, *sui generis*; and thus it is that attempts at formal definition are always unsatisfactory, if not altogether useless." The reader is therefore left to determine the meaning of Hohfeld's terms from his discussion, primarily a discussion of cases in which the various terms are used.

As was the case with Terry and Langdell, Hohfeld gives us no adequate explanation of why certain concepts are regarded as fundamental. His ostensible practical orientation would suggest that he has no Kantian

---

710 (1917). Hohfeld created his scheme of correlatives and opposites, the heart of his analysis, before June 1913. It appears with very brief explanation as an appendix to an article entitled Relations between Law and Equity, 11 Mich. L. Rev. 537 (1913).

57. They were the following: Langdell's equity jurisdiction articles published as a book in 1906 (2d ed. 1908), Hannis Taylor's treatise in 1908, Gray's work in 1909, the eleventh edition of Holland in 1910, the third edition of Salmond in 1910 (4th edition 1913), and Wigmore's torts casebook in 1912. According to his footnotes, Hohfeld relied on the second edition of Salmond (1907) and the tenth edition of Holland (1906).

absolutes in mind, and his use of cases to illustrate and demarcate the meaning of his fundamental concepts would lead us to believe that they are empirically derived. This would account for the sources of the concept, but not for the reason these particular concepts are basic. In fact Hohfeld's use of cases is quite misleading. He carefully picks and chooses as illustrations the cases that use the concepts in the way he wishes to have them used. Other cases are dismissed as instances of using language loosely or as examples of sloppy thinking. Hohfeld goes so far as to cite many "wrongly" reasoned cases in support of his position that greater precision and clarity are needed. Since the terms he is talking about (right, duty, and so forth) are used differently and loosely in hundreds if not thousands of cases, his preferred usage cannot be established by any kind of nose count.

Indeed, we are driven back to reconsider whether Hohfeld's concepts are metaphysical entities after all. Not only are they not derived empirically from the cases, but he advances one concept (no-right) that he admits to creating himself[58] and another in which the common meaning of the term (liability) is disregarded and a wholly new meaning is attributed.[59] Nor is it merely a game of words that we are playing, for as Hohfeld revealingly says, after decrying the ambiguity of legal terminology: "The above mentioned inadequacy and ambiguity of terms unfortunately reflect, all too often, corresponding paucity and confusion as regards *actual* legal conceptions [emphasis added]."[60] Hohfeld also uses an interesting mathematical analogy to describe his fundamental concepts: the "lowest common denominator" of the law.[61]

Hohfeld's motivation in creating his scheme of fundamental legal conceptions is clearly in pursuance of the conventional aims of the expository paradigm. His derivation of these particular concepts is just as clearly an adoption or extension of the analysis of Salmond. Salmond identified

58. He says no-right is needed, "there being no single term available to express the latter conception." Hohfeld, note 56, 33.

59. Hohfeld rather apologetically points out that a "liability" as he uses the term may be desirable or welcome; it is not necessarily onerous. Ibid., 55.

60. Ibid., 29.

61. "If a homely metaphor be permitted, these eight conceptions,—rights and duties, privileges and no-rights, powers and liabilities, immunities and disabilities,—seem to be what may be called 'the lowest common denominators of the law.' Ten fractions (1/3, 2/5, etc.) may, *superficially*, seem so different from one another as to defy comparison. If, however, they are expressed in terms of their lowest common denominators (5/15, 6/15, etc.), comparison becomes easy, and fundamental similarity may be discovered." Ibid., 58.

right, liberty, power, and immunity as distinct meanings of the broader term "right," and he suggested as correlatives duty, liability, liability (again), and disability. This scheme was modified by Hohfeld so that liberty was called privilege and its correlative was denominated no-right.[62] In addition, in Hohfeld's scheme "opposites" as well as correlatives were identified. Salmond had, of course, recognized the relationship of "opposites" in his treatise, but he did not give the relationship a name. Hohfeld's system is graphically represented as follows:[63]

Jural Correlatives

right	*privilege*	*power*	*immunity*
duty	no-right	liability	disability

Jural Opposites

right	*privilege*	*power*	*immunity*
no-right	duty	disability	liability

By way of further explanation, the correlative relationship means that the existence of one of the correlatives implies the existence of the other in another person. Thus, a right in A implies the presence of a duty in B (whether B is identified or not, or vice versa), a privilege in A implies a no-right in B, and so on. The relationship of opposites means the existence of one of the opposite terms in oneself implies its absence in another. Thus, a right in A implies a no-right (the absence of a right) in B, a privilege in A implies a duty (the absence of a privilege) in B, and so on. It follows from this, if one cares, that the opposite of the correlative of a concept is the absence of that concept in another. Thus, a privilege in A is the absence of a right in B, an immunity in A is the absence of a power in B, and so on, or a duty in A is the absence of no-right in B, a liability in A is the absence of a disability in B, and so forth.

This scheme was essentially invented by Salmond, although Hohfeld did a more elaborate and instructive job of explaining it, and of course he made some minor modifications.[64] Did Hohfeld give proper scholarly attribution? Unfortunately, it is difficult to conclude that he did. He cites

62. Hohfeld suggests that the term "claim" might be used to stand for the limited meaning of "right" in his scheme. He also ventures "subjection" as a good equivalent of liability and admits that "liberty" could be substituted for "privilege."

63. Hohfeld, note 56, 30.

64. Hohfeld invented the term "no-right" to replace the ambiguous use of "liability," he changed Salmond's "liberty" to "privilege," and he gave a name to the "opposite" relationship.

Salmond's treatise twice in his 1913 article, the first time for the proposition that a trustee is in fact an owner of the trust property and not merely an agent.[65] The second citation is more relevant. In his text Hohfeld quotes an opinion by Justice Cave from an English report in which Cave uses the term "liberty." In a footnote to this Hohfeld thanks Salmond for the reference to the case, and, in passing, points out that Salmond "overlooks the importance of *privilege* in the present connection."[66] There is no reference to Salmond's analysis of rights, liberties, powers, and immunities, or their correlatives. A smokescreen? Hohfeld purports to find his fundamental concepts in the case law, but what a coincidence that they turn out to be almost exactly the same as Salmond's!

Roscoe Pound has suggested that Hohfeld's mathematic-like schema in which all of the components are locked in logical entailment can be attributed to Hohfeld's training in Hegel's philosophy.[67] Hohfeld gives no reference to Hegel and gives an inadequate if not deceptive reference to Salmond, from whom so much was borrowed. Nevertheless, he marginally advanced the analysis begun by Austin, his presentation suggested great practical value, and the schema he championed was elegant. Perhaps more important, Hohfeld's accomplishment breathed new life into the tired idea that legal scholarship could indeed be a science. It appears that Hohfeld had glimpsed the grail, albeit in the hand of Salmond.

The scholarly reaction to the publication of Hohfeld's articles was one of excitement and activity.[68] Both critics and supporters jumped into the fray with abandon, and the periodical literature was filled with commentary for a decade or more. It is difficult to account for the interest that Hohfeld's schema provoked. Both Holland and Salmond were well read in

65. Hohfeld, note 56, 17, fn. 7.

66. The entire footnote reads as follows: "For the reference to Mr. Justice Cave's opinion, the present writer is indebted to Salmond's work on Jurisprudence. Citing this case and one other, *Starey v. Graham* (1899), 1 Q.B. 406, 411, the learned author adopts and uses exclusively the term 'liberty' to indicate the opposite of 'duty,' and apparently overlooks the importance of *privilege* in the present connection. Curiously enough, moreover, in his separate *Treatise on Torts*, his discussion of the law of defamation gives no explicit intimation that *privilege* in relation to that subject represents merely *liberty*, or 'no-duty.'" Ibid.

67. Pound, Fifty Years of Jurisprudence, 50 Harv. L. Rev. 557, 572 (1937).

68. Except for Pound's early critique, the scholarly give-and-take really begins in 1919, although Hohfeld's first article (or part one) appeared in 1913. This suggests that Hohfeld's death in 1918 may have had a bearing on the prominence of his work after this date. World War I may also have had some effect on the attention devoted to his schema.

America, if we can rely on periodical footnotes. Terry's treatise was presumably available and had been cited in works by Wigmore and Pound. Taylor, Langdell, and others had treated the same subjects. Yet, none of these authors had provoked the kind of response that followed Hohfeld's work.[69] Hohfeld died in 1918 at the age of thirty-eight. Others took up his cause, notably Arthur Corbin (1874–1966) at Yale and George Goble (1887–1963) at the University of Illinois.

One of the first critics of Hohfeldian logic was Roscoe Pound. In an article appearing in a nonlegal journal in 1916 he gently but persuasively picked away at the wondrous scheme.[70] Pound pointed out that some of Hohfeld's "fundamental concepts" were not really concepts at all but the negation of a concept. Thus, no-right, the obvious target, means nothing more than the absence of a right; it is not a term used in legal discourse and has no more significance than "no-cure" has in medicine. The supposed opposite to power, Hohfeld's disability, and the correlative to power, liability, "are quite without independent jural significance, and each name is available and in use for other and important legal conceptions."

Pound also points out that Hohfeld fails to account for duties the breach of which does not necessarily entail any further legal consequences, or what Henry T. Terry described as "protected rights."[71] It appears that Hohfeld was unfamiliar with Terry's work since no reference to it is made in any of Hohfeld's writings. Pound takes the position, consistent with Austin and Terry, that some rights (or some senses of the term "right") and duties do not have correlatives at all, something Hohfeld would clearly deny as a matter of logic. Duties imposed by the criminal law, says Pound, have no correlative rights in any other person unless we are willing to talk about the right of the state. "But that 'right' is really dragged in by the heels to save the proposition that every duty must have a correlative right."[72] It is interesting to speculate where Hohfeld would find the correlative duty to the right to vote.[73] It seems possible, perhaps likely, that

69. One work attempting to explain Holland at this time was Drake, Jurisprudence: A Formal Science, 13 Mich. L. Rev. 34 (1914).

70. Pound, Legal Rights, 26 Inter. J. Ethics 92 (1916).

71. Ibid., 94–95. For an explanation of protected rights see the discussion of Terry's work in chapter 2.

72. Ibid., 94. Pound also maintains that there is no real correlative nor opposite to Hohfeld's "power." Ibid., 97–98.

73. If the right to vote means right (claim) in Hohfeld's limited sense, then a correlative duty would fall on someone or possibly all others. What would this duty be? Perhaps the duty not to interfere with my voting. But this would be like saying my right

the necessary connections that Hohfeld saw between his conceptions and their correlatives and opposites were inherent in the concepts themselves (we would say definitional if Hohfeld had given us any definitions), and, hence, counterfactual examples[74] either would have to be ignored or would become serious jurisprudential conundrums.

The Great Debate

In 1919 scholarly recognition of the significance of Hohfeld's work appeared in an article by Walter Wheeler Cook (1873–1943), one of Hohfeld's colleagues at Yale. Cook lamented the passing of the young Hohfeld and asserted that his work was as yet unappreciated by the legal academic community.[75]

In the same year another of Hohfeld's colleagues at Yale presented the legal world with a demand to adhere to "an exact terminology and a definiteness and accuracy of mental concept."[76] Arthur L. Corbin, a disciple who was sure Hohfeld had seen the holy grail, called upon scholars, practitioners, and judges to adhere to the components of the eight-part schema faithfully in their writing as well as to the additional terms that Hohfeld had used in his two seminal articles.[77] Possibly not sure of the authority his own name would carry with the legal profession, Corbin points out in the first footnote that his article was "prepared with the critical assistance of other members of the Yale Law Faculty." Corbin did finally give definitions for all Hohfeldian terms and gave his own explanation of how they should be used. Conceivably inspired by Wigmore's terminological offer to the legal world, Corbin announced his own definition of three additional terms: "fact," "act," and "event."[78]

---

to payment of a debt gives rise to a duty on the part of the debtor not to interfere with my collection of the debt, whereas we know that the corresponding duty is to pay the debt. Perhaps the right to vote is really a privilege. Then the correlative no-right would be the no-right to vote in another or others; but of course others may well have the right to vote.

74. Examples like the duty not to drive over fifty-five miles per hour or the right to run for public office.

75. Cook, Hohfeld's Contribution to the Science of Law, 28 Yale L. J. 721 (1919).

76. Corbin, Legal Analysis and Terminology, 29 Yale L. J. 163 (1919).

77. They included operative facts, evidential facts, legal (jural) relations, primary right, secondary right, multital right (in rem), paucital right (in personam), unital right (in personam), instant right, future right, conditional right, and joint right.

78. Corbin, note 76, 163–64.

According to Corbin, physical existence, physical relations, legal relations, and mental processes are all facts. Facts include acts and events. An
act is the willed physical movement of a human being or animal. An event
is any change of facts, including an act. From these definitions Corbin
moves on to the ideas of operative facts and evidentiary facts, categories
advanced earlier by Hohfeld (and, incidentally, by Salmond and Holland).
Amazingly, it does not appear that Corbin was aware of the more sophisticated analysis of these and similar terms by Holland, Terry, and Salmond.
Like Hohfeld, Corbin is not explicit about his criteria for "fundamental"
concepts, but he asserts that more complex legal ideas like contract and
trust can be analyzed into these "simpler and invariable elements," opening the way in theory for a strictly logical treatment of the law as a
whole.[79] In a subsequent work, Corbin explored this question further.[80]

At this point Albert Kocourek enters the discourse and presents a
broader perspective from which to view the question of fundamental legal
concepts. Kocourek was familiar with much of the German work being
done in the expository paradigm as well as that of Holland, Terry, and
Salmond. In an article published in 1920 he discusses the meaning of the
concept "jural relations" and surveys the various classifications of several
nineteenth-century German scholars.[81] He asserts that Austin, Holland,
Salmond, and Terry have borrowed heavily from the Germans in this field.
In another article by Kocourek in the same year he presents his own table
of jural relations, similar to but more complicated than Hohfeld's.[82]

It seems inevitable that Kocourek would take direct aim at Hohfeld's
schema by advancing some serious objections, and he did, indeed, get
around to this in the same productive year.[83] He found some merit in
Hohfeld's work, but not much. What proved to be Hohfeld's innovative
contributions were also the weak points of the system. For instance,
Hohfeld was the first to articulate the relationship of opposites in the jural
concepts. However, Kocourek finds that this relationship has no utility.
Moreover, he finds that the relationship Hohfeld conceived of as unitary
really consists of several logical relationships. "Opposite" in the Hohfeld-

79. Ibid., 165. Another author venturing down the "right-duty" road with no
knowledge of the work of other scholars, including Hohfeld, was Roland R. Foulke.
See Foulke, Definition and the Nature of Law, 19 Colum. L. Rev. 351 (1919).

80. Corbin, Jural Relations and their Classification, 30 Yale L. J. 226 (1921).

81. Kocourek, Various Definitions of Jural Relations, 20 Colum. L. Rev. 394 (1920).

82. Kocourek, The Plurality of Advantages and Disadvantages in Jural Relations, 19
Mich. L. Rev. 47 (1920).

83. Kocourek, Hohfeld's System of Fundamental Legal Concepts, 15 Ill. L. Rev. 24
(1920).

ian lexicon can mean negative, contradictory, or contrary, all carrying different meanings in the field of logic. In fact the meaning of "correlative" is never explained by Hohfeld, and Kocourek implies that it, too, may be used in different senses.

Kocourek also thinks that the terms "immunity/disability" and "privilege/no-right" are the invention or glorification of negatives, terms that the law does not conceptualize in any practical sense.[84] He gives his own "reconstruction" of the Hohfeldian tables:[85]

Table Of Contradictions

Right	Power	Liberty [Privilege]	Immunity
No-right	Disability	No-Liberty	No-Immunity

Table Of Correlatives

Right	Power	Liberty [Privilege]	Immunity
Duty	Liability	None	None

In addition, Kocourek takes Hohfeld to task for his unfamiliarity with the extensive German work done in this field, for borrowing heavily from Salmond, for failing to define his own terms, for ignoring the more fundamental legal conception of a jural relation as the starting point for analysis, and for the absence of any explanation of how these supposed "fundamental conceptions" were derived.[86]

Kocourek's critique touched off a jurisprudential debate in the legal periodicals that has perhaps never been equaled. The 1921 *Yale Law Journal* published articles by Kocourek and Arthur L. Corbin. Kocourek reasserted his criticism of Hohfeld's system and sought to demonstrate more clearly that jural negatives are not true legal relations at all and should not form a part of the classificatory scheme.[87] Corbin restated the Hohfeldian scheme and praised its merits but did not come to issue with most of Kocourek's criticisms.[88] Corbin did, however, introduce a new element into the discussion.

The logical or philosophical nature of "fundamental concepts" apparently bothered Corbin, and he made an attempt to ground them on an

84. "If A, the owner of a cigar, smokes it in his study, he exercises a liberty, or in the language of the Hohfeld system, a 'privilege.' No one has a claim against A that he shall not smoke the cigar. What is the possible juristic significance of the act?" Ibid., 36.

85. Ibid., 39.

86. Ibid., 38–39. Kocourek, perhaps overgenerously, does not criticize Hohfeld for failure to attribute ideas to Salmond.

87. Kocourek, Tabulae Minores Jurisprudentiae, 30 Yale L. J. 215 (1921). He also offered a new table of relationships.

88. Corbin, note 80.

empirical base. He borrowed the Holmesian notion that law is a prediction of what courts will do, thus incorporating an element of sociological jurisprudence (the Poundian paradigm). Gray had started in this direction by relating rights to interests. Corbin completed the job by showing that concepts such as "right" and "duty" were shorthand symbols for describing a situation in terms of how the parties would be treated by the action of a court or other governmental agency. He says:

> In dealing with *law*, therefore, we are considering the conduct of societal agents and the rules expressing that uniformity with which they are expected to act. These rules are rules of law; but the rules that enable us to predict merely the action of natural forces or of individuals who are not social agents are not rules of law. There is no supernatural or mystical distinction between physical relations and legal relations. Rules of physics and rules of law are alike in that they enable us to predict physical consequences and to regulate our actions accordingly.[89]

In this view, to state that someone has a right means that if he brings a lawsuit in court and proves his case, the court will give judgment for him and the sheriff will execute the judgment. Thus, the fundamental concepts are those words, used as symbols, that derive their ultimate meaning from what a court will do. They are fundamental in that they cannot be reduced to any simpler terms.[90] This predictive approach to explaining the significance of fundamental concepts raises many questions, which will be pursued in the discussion of the Poundian paradigm in chapter 6.

Kocourek's position was attacked in the following year by Professor George W. Goble, who made a persuasive argument that negative jural relations were an important part of the Hohfeldian analysis.[91] Goble pointed to several legal discussions in which the schema had been used successfully. He also made an interesting attempt to quantify the system. Kocourek replied in another article in which he maintained again that Hohfeld's negatives confuse several different things.[92] Kocourek had also been busy analyzing some related concepts.[93]

89. Ibid., 227.
90. "They are fundamental because they are *constant* elements, into which all of our variable combinations can be analyzed, common denominators to which the superficially dissimilar, like law and equity, property and contract, can be reduced." Ibid., 229.
91. Goble, Affirmative and Negative Legal Relations, 4 Ill. L. Q. 36 (1922).
92. Kocourek, Non-Legal-Content Relations, 4 Ill. L. Q. 233 (1922).
93. Kocourek attempted to unravel the difficult logical knot that Henry T. Terry had

A symposium in the *Illinois Law Quarterly* for 1922–23 brought the combatants together again. Charles E. Clark joins in on the side of his Yale colleague, Arthur Corbin, reasserting the Hohfeldian position. George W. Goble follows with a denial that legal relations must involve constraint, as Kocourek maintains. He states that a definition of law does not require any restraint on conduct, curiously citing Holmes' famous statement that the law consists of "prophecies of what the courts will do."[94] Arthur Corbin then lends his weight to the debate, essentially repeating Goble's arguments.[95] Kocourek is given the opportunity to restate his position, which he does,[96] and a concluding article by Professor Frederick Green attempts to bring a broader perspective to the debate and to highlight the points on which the parties agree and disagree.[97]

The debate shifted to the *American Bar Association Journal* with an article by Kocourek in which he explains to the practicing bar the need for systematic exposition of legal relations.[98] He offers his own newly modified tables and definitions. Goble counterattacks in a subsequent issue, giving a critique of Kocourek's tables but agreeing to change the meaning of "right" in the narrow sense to "claim." He suggests replacing Kocourek's "privilege" with "obligation," giving it the meaning that Hohfeld gave "privilege."[99] This proves to be the end of the direct debate in which issues are joined, but further argumentation over the relative merits of the Hohfeldian and Kocourek schemes continued in the literature.[100]

---

created in his discussion of "protected rights." Whether Kocourek was successful or not, the reader will have to judge. Kocourek, Rights in Rem, 68 U. Pa. L. Rev. 322 (1920). He also wrote two articles in which he introduced a variety of new terms and ideas, mostly his own, but some of which seemed to owe something to John H. Wigmore, Kocourek's long-time colleague. Such terms included *nomic* and *anomic* jural relations, the former including *mesonomic* and *zeugmanomic* relations; *regenerable, rescindable,* and *contingent* relations; and *elliptical, abscindable,* and *dormant* relations. Kocourek, The Classification of Jural Relations, 1 Boston U. L. Rev. 208 (1921); Kocourek, Nomic and Anomic Relations, 7 Cornell L. Q. 11 (1921).

94. Goble, Negative Legal Relations Re-examined, 5 Ill. L. Q. 36 (1922). Goble was probably following the lead of Corbin, stated in Corbin, note 80.

95. Corbin, What is a Legal Relation?, 5 Ill. L. Q. 50 (1922).

96. Kocourek, Non-Legal Content Relations Recombated, 5 Ill. L. Q. 150 (1923).

97. Green, The Relativity of Legal Relations, 5 Ill. L. Q. 187 (1923).

98. Kocourek, The Alphabet of Legal Relations, 9 A.B.A.J. 237 (1923).

99. Gobel, Terms for Restating the Law, 10 A.B.A.J. 58 (1924).

100. Kocourek, Juristic Knots and Nots; a Reconsideration of Juristic Terminology, 19 Ill. L. Rev. 285 (1923); Husik, Hohfeld's Jurisprudence, 72 U. Pa. L. Rev. 263 (1924); Kocourek, Sanctions and Remedies, 72 U. Pa. L. Rev. 335 (1925); Kocourek, Acts, 73 U. Pa. L. Rev. 335 (1925); Kocourek, Attribution of Physical Qualities to Legal Relations, 19 Ill. L. Rev. 435, 542 (1925); Randall, Hohfeld on Jurisprudence, 41 L. Q.

Kocourek himself published a book entitled *Jural Relations* in 1927,[101] in which he set forth his revised position on the matters debated in this chapter as well as on many others relating to legal analysis. In this work he used and expanded the bizarre Wigmorean terminology. As one meanders through the Kocourekian landscape, one encounters homomorphic and heteromorphic conflicts, not to be confused with plurinary integral conflicts. In one chapter alone can be found abscindable, intercalary, accrescent, and degenerated relations. In another chapter one comes across conjunctive, congruent, homomeral, homologous, dypolic, homadic, homotaxic, and even homogeneous relations. In spite of an enthusiastic endorsement of this work in the introduction by Wigmore,[102] the legal profession seems not to have taken it seriously. Kocourek did not take up the "predictive" account of fundamental concepts offered earlier by Corbin, but he seems to have remained a Kantian with respect to this question.[103]

Three additional commentaries must be scrutinized before abandoning the survey of the quest for universals. Two are articles that can be considered sympathetic to Hohfeldian aims, but critical of particulars. Isaac Husik, writing in the 1924 *Pennsylvania Law Review*, believed that Hoh-

---

Rev. 86 (1925); Dowdall, The Present State of Analytical Jurisprudence, 42 L. Q. Rev. 451 (1926); Willis, Some Fundamental Legal Concepts, 1 Ind. L. J. 18 (1926); Kocourek, Subjective and Objective Elements in Law, 21 Ill. L. Rev. 489 (1927); Goble, The Sanction of a Duty, 37 Yale L. J. 426 (1928); Heilman, The Bases of Construction of Systems of Legal Analysis, 26 Ill. L. Rev. 841 (1932). The last article contains a penetrating review of different authors' positions on various issues.

101. A. Kocourek, *Jural Relations* (1927, 2d ed. 1928). A former student and disciple of Kocourek's later edited and published a text for students grounded in analytic jurisprudence: O. Snyder, *Preface to Jurisprudence: Text and Cases* (1954).

102. Wigmore said, "It has long been my belief that the applied science of Law is capable of equal achievements with those of Medicine and of Engineering. Its concepts are as definite, and their logical operation is as sure. What has been lacking is, first, a complete realistic analysis of those concepts, and secondly, an apt and consistent terminology that will permit accurate discussion of the concepts. In this book, it is believed, we have the first presentation of such a system. May the profession show the courage to use it!" Ibid., xxiii.

103. "We have been unaware of the existence of jural relations just as the savage is unaware of gravitational force. . . . It is not an exaggeration to say that many of our legal explanations are as naive as the savage's explanation of gravity. . . . Let it be emphasized again that jural relationship is a fundamental idea. No legal phenomenon can exist without dealing with one or more jural relations." A. Kocourek, *Jural Relations*, iii–v (2d ed. 1928). Kocourek maintains that legal phenomena involve three elements, one of which is a body of rules. "First, there is a body of legal rules existing only in the abstract—potentially—awaiting application in concrete cases." Ibid., 1. Is this the kingdom of the holy grail?

feld's concepts were not scientifically fundamental.[104] For example, he argued that the concept of privilege can be defined or explained in terms of the more fundamental concepts of right and duty.[105] In this view a privilege in A to do X means that A has no duty toward B to do X; A has no right against B that B should refrain from interfering with A doing X; and A has no duty toward B not to do X. Thus, privilege is a function of several rights and duties or, more accurately, their negatives. Moreover, such a combination of negatives is, according to Husik, not a legal relationship at all, but a factual one.[106]

Writing a few years later in the *Illinois Law Review*, Raymond J. Heilman undertakes a careful analysis of both the Kocourek and Hohfeld schemes.[107] Of particular interest is his conclusion that the concept of power should be regarded as pervasive of the others. He seems to visualize power as having at its core a psychological and economic significance that also is necessarily included in the other terms. This use of the term "power" is adopted from the work of John R. Commons, a noted economist.[108] Heilman is not clear as to whether he means that power is the generic term of which "right," "privilege," and so forth are the species or whether he means that the others are somehow constructs made of the basic notion "power."

It fell to George W. Goble to formulate the latter conclusion and, in a

104. Husik, Hohfeld's Jurisprudence, 72 U. Pa. L. Rev. 263 (1924). "What we are after in jurisprudence, which is the science of law, is the *necessary* and *sufficient* basic concepts." Ibid., 267.

105. Husik uses Hohfeld's example of eating shrimp salad (originally John Chipman Gray's illustration) to be the principal exposition of the meaning of Hohfeld's privilege.

106. "If we can show that the relation is purely factual and extra-legal, its introduction among legal relations, and especially among fundamental relations, is not merely useless, but positively harmful, because it leads to a misconception. From the point of view of analytical jurisprudence no relation is legal, which the state does not regulate and protect. Privilege, as Hohfeld conceives it, is a relation between persons which the state does not regulate, nor protect. . . . You might as well say that my desire to be a rich man is a legal relation, because the state does not forbid me to have the desire." Ibid., 267–68.

107. Heilman, Bases of Construction of Systems of Legal Analysis, 26 Ill. L. Rev. 841 (1932). Heilman is sympathetic to Hohfeld, especially as presented by Corbin. He is much less sympathetic to Kocourek.

108. Commons became infatuated with the Hohfeldian schema and applied it to analyze economic as well as legal phenomena. He changed some of the terminology and made some distinctions that Hohfeld had not considered. See J. Commons, *Legal Foundations of Capitalism* (1924); J. Commons, *Anglo-American Law and Economics* (1926).

sense, to devise or discover the ultimate universal.[109] Goble argues that the power-liability relationship is the basic one, and the other Hohfeldian pairs can be defined in terms of it.[110] The argument is not so difficult as might be thought; Pound, Kocourek, and others had suggested most of it. Half of the Hohfeldian terms mean simply the absence of their counterparts in another person (opposites); hence, it is easy to define them in terms of the counterpart (for example, privilege=absence of duty). The other half of the Hohfeldian terms mean the presence of their counterparts in another (correlatives); hence, if one uses the absence of their opposites in place of these terms, the entire system reduces to two relationships, characterized by their presence/absence in oneself or another.[111]

Goble arranges the final synthesis by arguing that the right-duty relationship is simply a shorthand way of recognizing a chain of power-liability relationships. Thus, the right of A not to have B trespass on his land can be explained as the power of A to initiate legal proceedings for trespass and to pursue those proceedings to judgment and execution wherein B's power over his own property is altered. All legal relations thus

109. Goble, A Redefinition of Basic Legal Terms, 35 Colum. L. Rev. 535 (1935). Although the connection between Heilman's article, written in 1932, and Goble's seems obvious, Goble does not cite Heilman, nor indeed any jurisprudential discussion except Hohfeld's.

110. "Briefly such definitions might run as follows:

　1. Power—Capacity of a person to change the legal status of another person.

　2. Liability—Subjectivity of a person to the power of another.

　3. Disability—Absence of power in a person to change the legal status of another.

　4. Immunity—Absence of subjectivity of a person to the power of another.

　5. Right—The power of a person to initiate that sequential combination of powers and acts involved in obtaining a judgment against another person.

　6. Duty—Subjectivity of a person to that sequential combination of powers and acts involved in another's obtaining a judgment.

　7. No-right—The power in a person to initiate that sequential combination of powers and acts involved in giving a judgement to another person.

　8. Privilege—Absence of subjectivity of a person to that sequential combination of powers and acts involved in another's obtaining a judgment." Ibid., 540.

111. The Hohfeldian table, so revised, although not so presented by Goble, would then be as follows:

Table of Correlatives

Right . . . . Subjectivity to Right [Duty]

Absence of Subjectivity . . . . Absence of Right [No-Right]
to Another's Right [Privilege]

Power . . . . Subjectivity to Power [Liability]

Absence of Subjectivity . . . . Absence of Power [Disability]
to Another's Power [Immunity]

become a giant chain or blanket of chains stretching in various directions in which one end of a chain link is a power and the other a liability.[112]

The ultimate Hohfeldian table, not presented by Goble but implied in his argument, would be:

Table Of Correlatives

Power . . . . Subjectivity to Power [Liability]

Absence of Subjectivity . . . . Absence of Power [Disability] to Power [Immunity]

Power to Initiate Events . . . . Subjectivity to Power to Leading to Judgment [Right]   Initiate Events Leading to Judgment [Duty]

Absence of Subjectivity to . . . . Absence of Power to Initiate Power to Initiate Events Leading   Events Leading to Judgment to Judgment [Privilege]   [No-Right]

While a chain-link fence doesn't resemble a grail very closely, it seems certain that Goble thought he had created a veritable bedrock conception from which all matters legal could be derived. It is doubtful whether or not he took Corbin's suggestion of basing these "conceptions" logically in the form of prediction of empirical events. He did explain that such legal concepts could have a "real" existence as "pictures in the mind" whether they related to actual cases, hypothetical cases, or others.[113] In this respect his notion of "fundamental legal concepts," and especially what he regarded as the one fundamental concept (the power-liability relation), closely resembles Kocourek's idea of rules of law existing in the abstract.[114]

---

112. "Law is not so much a seamless web . . . as it is a blanket of chains each link of which is exactly like every other link." Goble, note 113, 536. Goble is forced to distinguish various kinds of rights and to explain the old secondary (remedial) versus primary right dichotomy in order to save this wonderful consolidation of terms into one. The short of it is that he does not really progress much farther than Austin. In addition, Goble's argument loses some of its shine when he is forced to define and explain several different types of duties, thus introducing complexity back into what attempts to be a simplifying scheme. Ibid., 540–43.

113. Ibid., 546–47.

114. See Kocourek, note 103.

Fundamentally What?

At the very time when the Hohfeldian logicians were reaching the zenith of their discourse telling the world how it must think about law, the entire expository paradigm was falling rapidly into obscurity, being replaced by "realism" and social science (see chapters 7 and 8). While rights analysis still has a certain appeal to legal academics and some scholarly literature continues to be generated, it has clearly been out of the mainstream since the mid-thirties.[115] Austin's general theory has been resurrected in England by H.L.A. Hart and his followers, a valiant band of analysts fighting a rear-guard battle; but rights analysis in the old style remains reasonably dead in the United States.

What, then, can be said for "fundamental concepts"? With the benefit of hindsight, we can say—not much. From its initiation by Austin the pursuit of universals was plagued by an ambiguity that it never resolved. Are these concepts empirical generalizations or are they inherent mental structures or inherent social structures? If they are none of these, as it turns out, then the alternative is that they are simply convenient word usages, technical terminology no different from that of the plumber or the cook, and, hence, having nothing to do with science.[116] As nothing more than a part of a technical vocabulary, fundamental concepts would have to prove their worth in the trade. Have lawyers and judges adopted them and used them rigorously? The judgment of time says no. The law has managed to limp along without terminological rigor, and indeed the "problems" of law are generally no longer thought to have their origin in defective words or concepts. The holy grail was, after all, a myth.

115. See, however, the anachronistic work of Hans Kelsen discussed in chapter 11.

116. This failure to establish "legal science" once again raised the question, so anxiously pondered in the late nineteenth century, as to whether law was a legitimate academic discipline. A major difference was, however, that the law school had become a well-established American institution by the second decade of the twentieth century.

5

THE EVOLUTIONISTS

1880 – 1923

The idea of evolution had a tremendous impact on intellectual life in the second half of the nineteenth century. It permeated discussions of religion, history, linguistics, philosophy, and law, and it became an integral part of the theoretical framework of the newly emerging social sciences—sociology, anthropology, and political science. Pioneer American social scientists like William Graham Sumner, Lester F. Ward, and Edward A. Ross incorporated evolutionary ideas in their scientific methodology.[1] These scholars in turn had an influence on many legal scholars in the waning years of the nineteenth and early years of the twentieth centuries.[2]

Almost everyone in the field of jurisprudence accepted the idea of evolution and gave lip service to the notion that it should be incorporated in the understanding of law. However, most of the adherents of the expository paradigm were unable to integrate the new idea into the older way of thinking. Many of them endorsed the notion that the historical or evolutionary study of law was a fine thing but was a science or branch of legal science different from Austinian analysis. An accepted and conve-

---

1. Sumner was a disciple of Spencer and a forceful social Darwinist. His earliest book, *What Social Classes Owe to Each Other* (1883), declares that being rich is not bad, that one must look out for himself, and that "poverty is the best policy," among other themes. His best known-work is *Folkways* (1906). Ward was a reform Darwinist who believed that social evolution could be aided by social planning and reform measures. His best-known work is *Dynamic Sociology* (1883). Ross was also a reform Darwinist, who believed in state intervention in "private" affairs to produce better social outcomes. He was a colleague of Roscoe Pound at the University of Nebraska for a few years and had an impact on Pound's jurisprudential thinking. Ross' best-known work is *Social Control* (1901).

2. For a good discussion of these social scientists and law see Hovenkamp, Evolutionary Models in Jurisprudence, 64 Tex. L. Rev. 645 (1985); see also Elliott, The Evolutionary Tradition in Jurisprudence, 85 Colum. L. Rev. 38 (1985).

nient way of avoiding the potential conflicts inherent in the different paradigms was to consider legal evolution as the science of past law, legal analysis as the science of present law, and legislation as the science of future law (as the law should be).[3]

This period also saw the flowering of conceptual legal history, the greatest monument of which was probably Pollock and Maitland's *The History of English Law before the Time of Edward I* (2 vols., 1895). It was generally assumed that the business of the historian was to trace the development, or evolution, of legal ideas. Followers of Maine and Spencer saw a progress in the development of these ideas. Some of them also saw a struggle in which the best survived. The boundary between legal history and historical jurisprudence was obscure. Several works by Americans in this period purported to give evolutionary or historical explanations of the law, but they were in fact simply legal history.[4]

More astute thinkers perceived, however, that an evolutionary perspective was in potential conflict with the basic tenets of the expository paradigm. Some, like Salmond and Gray, modified their views in order to make an accommodation. Others openly rejected important features of the dominant Austinian view of the legal world. The most important of them would include Oliver Wendell Holmes, Jr. (in his historical mode), William G. Hammond, James C. Carter, Brooks Adams, and John H. Wigmore.

3. A typical endorsement of the two complementary "methods" is illustrated in an article written by a Canadian: LeFroy, Jurisprudence: Derivation and Definition, 27 L. Q. Rev. 180 (1911).

4. The following books are typical. Guy Carleton Lee, *Historical Jurisprudence: An Introduction to the Systematic Study of the Development of Law* (1900), relates the history of law in Babylonia, Egypt, Phoenicia, Israel, India, Greece, and Rome, ending with a history of English law to the thirteenth century. A less scholarly work is H. Scott, *The Evolution of Law* (1908). Broader in scope of subject matter and covering a greater period of time than Lee's book, this volume manages to trace legal history from Hammurabi to Thomas Jefferson in only 153 pages including some gratuitous advice on political systems. The third work is H. Taylor, *The Science of Jurisprudence* (1908), discussed briefly in chapter 4. Part one of the work, labeled "Historical," does provide what amounts to a short summary of the philosophy of Savigny and Maine, but the bulk of it is history, mostly Roman and English, in some 400 pages. While Taylor's scholarship is respectable, he finds no inconsistencies between the evolutionary and expository paradigms. Having compartmentalized them, he regards them as complementary.

Survival of the Fittest Legal Concepts

The work of Langdell, Hammond, and Holmes reflecting acceptance of the evolutionary paradigm has been discussed in chapter 1, but further work by Holmes must be noted. The eminent judge gave an address to the New York State Bar Association at the beginning of 1899; this was later published as a short article in the *Harvard Law Review*.[5] "Law in Science and Science in Law" offers further insight into Holmes' evolutionary view of law which began with publication of *The Common Law*. His theme is the value of the scientific study of law. In expounding this, Holmes gives his view of what is meant by scientific study. It turns out to be a form of the evolutionary paradigm.

He says, "In our less theological and more scientific day, we explain an object by tracing the order and process of its growth and development from a starting point assumed as given." The objects he has in mind are legal concepts and doctrines. He gives numerous examples of how such concepts gradually evolved and worked their way through various stages in the growth of the common law. Some continue to survive long after their practical usefulness has disappeared. Others are eroded by more attractive or useful ideas. In his view there is a "struggle for life among competing ideas, and . . . the ultimate victory and survival of the strongest."

Holmes' most complete illustration of this thesis is in development of the law of contract. Through his extensive historical knowledge he is able to show that the modern concept of contract could have originated in several ways: from courts having to deal with an interrupted sale, from the practice of holding a hostage pending performance (which itself became the institution of the surety), from the solemnity of the early oath and the Church's insistence on good faith, from the blood covenant, or from some other early legal ideas. Whichever of these was the true ancestor, the modern concept of contract still had to work its way through the forms of action known as debt, covenant, and finally assumpsit before it took its present configuration as a complex doctrine of substantive law. "I mention these only to bring still closer home the struggle for existence between competing ideas and forms. . . ."

In Holmes' view the role of the judge is to apply traditional rules, concepts, and doctrines in deciding cases. "I do not expect or think it desirable that the judges should undertake to renovate the law. That is not

5. Holmes, Law in Science and Science in Law, 12 Harv. L. Rev. 443 (1899).

their province." On the other hand, "Whenever a doubtful case arises, with certain analogies on one side and other analogies on the other . . . what really is before us is a conflict between two social desires, each of which seeks to extend its dominion over the case, and which cannot both have their way. The social question is which desire is strongest at the point of conflict."[6] In such cases the judges must "exercise the sovereign prerogative of choice." And furthermore: "But inasmuch as the real justification for a rule of law, if there be one, is that it helps to bring about a social end which we desire, it is no less necessary that those who make and develop the law should have those ends articulately in their minds."[7] Thus, conscious deliberation and moral choice are characteristics of judicial decision, drawing upon "social desires" as a source of justification; yet legal concepts evolve in a struggle for survival of the fittest. By implication we can perhaps conclude that for Holmes conscious decisions to achieve social ends "help" the process of evolution along. Once again the elegant product of Holmes' pen raises more questions than it answers.

Customary Morality as Law

Less well known today than Holmes but certainly a figure with great influence among the organized bar was James Coolidge Carter (1827–1905).[8] Carter became the foremost American advocate for the evolutionary paradigm, although his work seems to have been missed by some scholars. With the exception of one book, all of his writing took the form of speeches or reports in pamphlets to bar associations, although some were reprinted in legal periodicals. Since Carter was the political leader of the opposition to the codification movement in New York, some of his work tended to be partisan and polemical, which may have discredited it in the eyes of some scholars.[9]

Beginning in 1883, Carter wrote a twenty-one-page letter to Theodore

6. Ibid., 460–61.

7. Ibid., 460.

8. Carter was an organizer of the Association of the Bar of the City of New York, a reform group whose work in part led to the downfall of the Tweed ring. He was a president of the National Municipal League, a frequent advocate in the Supreme Court of the United States, and an active participant in the American Bar Association, serving as president in 1895. He was one of the most successful trial lawyers in New York at the turn of the century. W. Draper, ed., *Eight Great American Lawyers*, 3–41 (1909).

9. A popularized version of Carter's views and a polemic against codification in New York was R. Clarke, *The Science of Law and Lawmaking* (1898).

W. Dwight, chair of the Association of the Bar of the City of New York's committee organized to oppose the Field Codes.[10] This was the first of a series of writings in which Carter began to advance arguments based on a historical or even an anthropological view of the law. In 1884 he wrote a 117-page report for the Association in which he further articulated his views.[11] His main argument in opposition to codification was that there were two kinds of law, written and unwritten (by which he meant legislation and case law), and that an attempt to change the unwritten law to the written form would result in injustice and confusion. This theme was further developed in an address (of sixty-three pages) to the Virginia State Bar Association in 1889.[12] Finally, in 1900 Carter addressed the American Bar Association, introducing further ramifications of his philosophy.[13]

Carter retired from practice in 1898 but kept active in politics and public affairs. He decided to prepare a series of lectures to be delivered at his alma mater, Harvard, in 1905. Though he substantially completed them, he died before they could be delivered. The lectures became a book entitled *Law: Its Origins, Growth and Functions*, published posthumously in 1907, although it was not fully completed; it lacked a table of contents, chapter titles, and proper citations.[14] Nor was it especially readable. Most of the ideas treated in the book had been articulated in his earlier work, although he was able to elaborate on certain themes more thoroughly.

The starting point in Carter's theory is that law is custom.[15] This is,

10. Carter, A Communication to the Special Committee (Assoc. Bar C.N.Y. 1883). The debate over codification in New York, carried on principally between Carter and David Dudley Field, was in many ways a repeat performance of the same debate in Germany in the first quarter of the nineteenth century between Savigny and Thibaut. See Reimann, The Historical School against Codification, 37 Am. J. Comp. L. 95 (1989).

11. Carter, The Proposed Codification of our Common Law (Proc. Assn. Bar C.N.Y. 1884).

12. Carter, The Provinces of the Written and Unwritten Law (Va. State Bar Assn. 1889).

13. Carter, The Ideal and the Actual in the Law, 13 Reports Ann. Meeting, A.B.A. 217 (1890). This was reprinted in 24 Am. L. Rev. 752 (1890).

14. Hereinafter referred to as *Origins*.

15. "But while all Law is Custom, all Custom is not necessarily Law. Law differs from custom as a part differs from the whole. There is a large range of human conduct of which the law takes no notice, though it is under the control of custom quite as much as that part which the law assumes to regulate. A great part of this conduct falls under the control of moral rules which are enforced mainly by public opinion and form the subject of the science of morality. . . . Other parts of it are such as are controlled by the

perhaps, an unfortunate choice of terms because both the connotations and the limiting denotation of the word "custom" may suggest something other than what Carter means. However, his meaning becomes clear as we follow his discussion. His explanation begins, much like Maine's, with a consideration of primitive society, in which folkways (normative behavior generally), undifferentiated into morality, law, grammar, etiquette, and so on, guide human behavior and also furnish the standards by which behavior is evaluated. Breaches of any of these norms are likely to be visited with some kind of sanction, whether it be ridicule, ostracism, or even physical reprisal. These customs are learned from early childhood through example, trial and error, and sometimes purposeful training.[16] The adult community is fully aware of what is right and wrong in most contexts, although questions may arise. While law, as a specialized set of norms whose enforcement is charged to a certain group of people, is not known, the customs of the group are well known, and the need for conformity to them may be described as a sense of justice.[17]

For Carter there is no necessity to invoke a "higher" law, although a particular people may think of their own customary norms as God-given or as the natural law;[18] nor is there any need for a priori assumptions, nor even a need for the mystical *Volksgeist*. The law is simply that custom which has grown up through the constant interactions of persons in society; it is neither invented nor handed down by a king, conqueror, or supernatural entity. It is generally unquestioned, is followed, and results in patterns of behavior that help the society function. Carter says that the result of this all-pervasive custom is social "control." This term, too, is perhaps a bad choice. Control suggests restraint directed toward some purpose or serving someone's desires. What he evidently means is that custom results in self-restraint. It is self-created, or the product of a society interacting with itself and its environment. No one person or group dictates these moral norms, nor can this be done; custom is irrepealable. It may grow, change, or wither, but it cannot be legislated.

It is important to note here that Carter's model is a completely natural

---

usages of fashion or etiquette, and there is still another most important part . . . within the sphere of religious thought and action." *Origins*, 120.

16. "Custom . . . is not the accidental, trivial, and meaningless thing which we sometimes think it to be. It is the imperishable record of the wisdom of the illimitable past reaching back to the infancy of the race, revised, corrected, enlarged, open to all alike, and read and understood by all." *Origins*, 127.

17. Carter, The Ideal and the Actual in the Law, 24 Am. L. Rev. 752, 758–59 (1890).

18. He notes that "polygamy may be wrong in New York, but it is right among the Turks." Ibid., 768.

one. Law, practically synonymous with justice, is derived from ordinary social intercourse. Like other aspects of society, it changes over time, growing in some directions and receding in others. It is the product of natural forces, whatever they are, as much as any other social phenomena; and knowledge of the law is ultimately derived empirically. From this viewpoint justice is determined by natural processes and has an objective existence independent of any individual's wishes or judgment. An analogy from classic economics would be the market price of goods, which is determined not by the wishes of any person or group but by market forces. The analogy that Carter actually gives is physical: "Justice refuses to be either *made* or *molded*. It *exists* as absolutely as the law of gravity. . . ."

Carter points out that, although customary morality is generally known and followed, deviation may occur. Usually deviant behavior is acknowledged to be deviant or wrong by the actor, as in the case of the common thief. However, occasions arise in which the deviant behavior is sought to be justified in terms of some customary principle that appears to be opposed to the principle deviated from. Norms collide or compete for recognition. A legitimate dispute may ensue. Even in a primitive society such disputes get resolved, and in the process the "law" will be articulated and applied to the case. But cases requiring authoritative resolution of the law will be exceptional. For the most part the law is self-executing, that is, people will conform their behavior to it because they believe it to be fair and just. Thus, the significance of law is much greater than its role in adjudication. How does modern society and its law differ from the primitive? According to Carter, not as much as we, under mistaken Austinian influence, might think. It may be true that in modern civilization law is differentiated from other customary morality and that government is created in which specialized experts are designated to determine and apply the law in disputed cases. The law also becomes more complicated because society is more complicated. The ways in which people can interact are greatly increased by advancing technology and growing population. We also have legislation: what purports to be a method of creating law. Legislation seems to be the paradigm of modern law, and its common use gives credence to the Austinian idea of law as the official commands of the sovereign. Carter acknowledges these features of modern civilization but sees them in a different light. He still maintains that, at bottom, law is custom.

It is at this point that the distinction between written and unwritten law becomes important. Written law is legislation, and historically it appears much later than unwritten law. Unwritten law is that law applied by courts in the absence of relevant statutes and also applied in the interpretation of statutes. But more than that, it is an application of the normative structure (body of customs) of society to the context of a particular dispute. What has traditionally been called common law in England and the United States—and equity would be included here as well—is equated by Carter to the unwritten law.

In this view the common law is not an authoritative body of rules established by precedent. The principle of precedent, or *stare decisis,* is a customary norm that is a part of our system along with the rest of the unwritten law. In Carter's view stare decisis should not be slavishly adhered to, and courts are sometimes justified in overruling prior precedent. On the other hand, it furnishes a short and expedient way of deciding cases, and it is based on the widely shared moral notion that like cases should be treated alike; hence, clearly applicable precedents should not be lightly disregarded.

For Carter, to see the common law solely as a body of authoritative rules or doctrine is to get the cart before the horse. The court's function is to do justice. This means applying and enforcing societal expectations and accepted norms. The judge must *discover* what these norms are. In doing this he is assisted and guided by the previous work of countless tribunals in which legal reasoning has related societal norms to a particular set of similar facts.[19] While it is true that some rules and doctrines become so firmly established and acknowledged that no one disputes them and they take on a life of their own, nevertheless, they were in the first instance fashioned in argument from basic societal norms, and in time they risk rejection if and when they lose their connection to the culture. Such lawyer's law provides a convenient mode of reasoning and often dispenses with the need for a court to resort to argument from basic norms, but legal rules and doctrine are always provisional and always subject to discard when something better and more in tune with the customary morality of the society comes along.

What, then, is the function of the judge in this view of law, and especially how is the judge to decide novel or difficult cases? The message Carter gives here is that the law applicable to any case was in existence when the facts of the case arose. It is the duty of the judge to discover it. One of the consequences of the continuous existence of the law is that a judge is bound to apply it and apply it consistently.[20] He is never free to decide simply as he wishes or as whim might dictate. He cannot legislate.

19. Carter says, "A precedent is but *authenticated* custom." *Origins,* 65.

20. The consistency required in judicial decision-making is not the logical consistency of articulated rules, but the consistency of the decision with customary morality. *Origins,* 80.

In an ordinary case where the facts present no novel situation, a decision might be easy. The relevance of the common morality may be obvious, or the relevance of lawyer's law in the form of well-established precedent or doctrine (which are predigested transitions from common morality to legal conclusions) might be obvious. The adjudicatory powers of the judge or jury need not be stretched. Doing justice requires simple application of the customary mores of the community to the case at hand.

A novel case is not different in principle. What is different is that the process of search and discovery is more difficult. It will not be immediately clear which principles of custom and which legal precedents should be applied. It may be that two courses of argument, leading to opposite decisions, will be equally persuasive. In such a case it might be said that the court has leeway, meaning that a choice either way would be reasonable. But the judge is *bound* to apply the law as he understands it. The fact that two or more arguments seem equally plausible does not simplify the judge's task or "free" his decision in any way. It just makes it more difficult.

Carter tells us that this view of judicial decision-making explains why the perceived problem of due process that arises in novel cases is really not a problem at all. For those who believe that judges "make" law in novel cases, a question of due process or ex post facto application necessarily arises. From that viewpoint in the novel case the court must apply new rules or doctrine to a case that arose before the new law was announced. This is inherently unfair to the losing party. But in Carter's theory the law is always known to the parties because it is the customary morality of the society, and legitimate judicial decisions must be based upon that custom. Of course, situations arise in which the application of customary morality may not be clear, or in which competing moral principles seem to dictate different courses of conduct. But the persons whose conduct is in question *know* that they risk violation of the law (customary morality) in such situations; for Carter everyone is not "presumed to know the law," everyone does know the law, and where the law is unclear or ambiguous, that is also known. Thus, no due-process questions can arise from lack of knowledge of the law.[21]

21. Carter hints at but does not develop a related point. This is the pseudo-problem of the separation of powers that appears to arise when judges "make" law. In our political theory only the legislature can make law, because the legislature is directly accountable through the political process to the people who are subject to the law. If courts can make law in novel cases, they exercise legislative power without political accountability. In Carter's theory judges cannot make law; they can only discover it. Hence, judges, acting within their proper judicial capacity, are not and should not be politically accountable. In making their decisions they are *bound* to apply the law.

For the regulation of relationships between private persons Carter thinks that the unwritten law is far superior to legislation. He cites four advantages of unwritten over written law. The first is the truth of its principles. Presumably Carter means by this that the law administered by the courts in common-law cases corresponds more closely (ideally there would be a perfect correspondence) with the actual customary morality practiced in society. Second, the unwritten law permits of self-development, that is, it can gradually change to meet new situations and it can bend to conform to changing customary morality. Third, it is more stable than the product of the legislature; it is not changeable with every political wind that blows. Finally, the unwritten law tends to unity. In contrast to the great variation in statutory enactment, even where statutes in different states have the same purpose, common-law adjudication encourages constant reconsideration of the law in light of new circumstances and emergent values, with consequent constant reformulation. So long as customary morality remains constant (or changes in the same directions) among different states or countries, the law will continue to work itself out uniformly.

But what of legislation? Of course, we have substantially more legislation today than in Carter's day, although by the turn of the century the creation of great amounts of law in this manner was well underway. Carter does not dispute the application of the term "law" to legislation. But legislation is secondary to customary law, not only in historical development but in cultural priority as well. It is necessarily supplemental, corrective, and limited. It presupposes a cultural matrix into which it must fit. The criminal law is one area that Carter maintains is appropriately legislative. It defines specific crimes and specifies the punishments; in doing so it reinforces customary law. But if a legislature were so unwise as to enact a criminal statute that prohibited an activity that customary morality regarded as something one should be free to engage in, then that statute would be widely disregarded, prosecutors would be reluctant to prosecute, and courts would construe it narrowly or, as occasionally happens, interpret it completely away.

Thus, legislation has a function, but it is at the periphery of the law.[22] It can amend the unwritten law, and it can provide the rules for the enterprise of government, but it cannot directly challenge the established morality of society that springs from habit and custom. Law in the broad

22. At another point Carter says that legislation is a "mere fringe upon the body of the common law." *Origins*, 204.

sense is determined by cultural development, not by legislative bodies. Law is a natural phenomenon.

In Carter's view there is, nevertheless, a legitimate, even necessary, place for legislation. Its principal worth is in the area of public law—the organization of government and the allocation and limitation of public powers. Carter seems to envision these areas of the law as analogous to a community enterprise, an undertaking in which voluntary choice between ways of doing things is an important aspect and one in which customary morality plays a negligible role.[23] In addition, certain other areas of the law may demand legislative treatment. These would include situations in which formalities are desirable (for example, requisites for making a will), the whole of court procedure, and criminal law—all being fields of law in which certainty and stability assume great importance and the actual substance of the rules is comparatively unimportant or uncontroversial. Carter also acknowledges that corrective legislation is sometimes, although rarely, necessary where legal doctrine is in dispute or where the common law must be changed more rapidly than the judicial process will permit.

Carter advances the notion, consistent with the rest of his philosophy, that legislatures are limited in what they can legislate, not only by the familiar written constitutional provisions but by the unwritten law itself. He gives an interesting analogy to the coining of money. Silver and gold have long been accepted as money; government can place its mark upon coins, authenticating them and certifying the quantity of their content. This imprint will be respected and accepted if it is affixed to the genuine product, but it will be treated with contempt if placed upon a debased product.[24] He says further:

> Legislation should never attempt to do for society that which society can do, and is constantly doing for itself. As custom is the true origin of law, the legislature cannot, *ex vi termini*, absolutely create it. This is the unconscious work of society. But the passage of a law commanding things which have no foundation in existing custom would be only an endeavor to create custom and would necessarily be futile.[25]

23. One wonders why the prominent example of the unwritten constitution of England did not give Carter pause before he conceded so much to the province of legislation.

24. Note that gold and silver were legal tender in Carter's day, and bills were usually gold or silver certificates.

25. Carter, note 17, 775.

The consequences of ill-considered legislation, that is, legislation running contrary to the unwritten law, are described by Carter:

> When any part of the private law is attempted to be covered by statutory enactments, the keenest intelligence is inadequate to clearly foresee the future conditions. Injustice and inconvenience at once begin to disclose themselves, and opposition to the statute arises. If the injustice is gross, the moral sense is shocked. The injured party exclaims against the wrong. Doubts are started as to the meaning of the statute. The plain sense of the words is insisted upon by the one side; the improbability that such injustice could have been intended, by the other. The difficulty is usually resolved by the employment of the subtle arts of interpretation, and the obvious meaning of the language is *expounded* away in favor of the interests of justice.[26]

Carter gives numerous illustrations from the history of federal and state law to prove his point. He further explains that the apparent success of the French and German civil codes is because these codifications unified what were previously separate bodies of law in those countries. He also adds that these codes need considerable judicial alteration to make them workable.

It is clear in Carter's theory that courts are bound to apply customary morality which neither they nor anyone else has deliberately created; and legislatures, while free to make law in certain areas, are themselves limited by this pervasive unwritten law. With law so determined by blind evolutionary forces, we are led to ask whether it is possible consciously to improve and reform the law and whether reason plays any part in law's development. In spite of the determinism that looms so large in his view, Carter says yes, progress can be deliberately made:

> Under the great process of Evolution, man began to advance—to go no farther back—from his savage condition to higher physical, moral, and intellectual levels; and this was not by virtue of his own conscious effort, but because of the nature of his original constitution and the environment in which he was placed. The progress thus begun has been carried forward by designed effort. . . .[27]

Carter tells us that improvements in the lot of humanity can come about through wise judging:

26. Carter, note 12, 39.
27. *Origins*, 321.

Customs, in many respects, are not settled and are in conflict. A judicial decision determines them so far as it extends. If it be a correct one—that is, if the true custom is chosen (and by true I mean the one most consistent with the largest usage), it is accepted, and conduct is regulated accordingly, and the conflicting practices are discredited and pass away. This is the reaction of the judicial power upon custom, one of the great instrumentalities of social progress.[28]

Legislation, too, can be the instrument of progress: "Within its province [legislation] is capable of a work of great and increasing beneficence. It is . . . the *conscious* activity of society to improve its condition by improving its laws."[29]

Thus, Carter falls into the category of reform Darwinist rather than social Darwinist.[30] That is, he did not believe that the path of legal evolution was determined from the beginning of time and would take its course regardless of human efforts at reform. Rather, he believed in the inevitable march of nonrational change toward "progress," while maintaining that progress can be helped by conscious human effort. But while conceding the possibility of social reform, the pessimistic Carter counsels us not to expect too much:

But if the judicial tribunals correctly declare and enforce custom, all remaining social evils are evils in the customs, and any improvement must be sought for in a reformation of custom itself, and custom being conduct it can be reformed or improved only by a reformation or improvement of conduct. Conduct, however, being caused by thought, can be changed and improved only by a change or improvement in their thoughts. . . . All substantial social reform must begin with individuals and by a change and improvement in their thoughts. The legislature cannot originate it, however it may aid it, and the sole

28. Ibid., 66.

29. Carter continues: "In the order of succession of this activity follows the work of the judge. Custom first operates unconsciously to produce law. In a further stage of social advancement, society becomes an organized power and consciously exerts itself to aid and perfect the development of law. Finally it comes to do what the judiciary from its inability to break suddenly from the past and from its limited capacity to continue political instrumentalities for the enforcement of custom is unable to do, not to *make* law, but to make rules relating to law, as well as the complex machinery which the practical administration of law by the state requires." Ibid., 136.

30. These terms are discussed in a useful article by Herbert Hovenkamp: Evolutionary Models in Jurisprudence, 64 Tex. L. Rev. 645 (1985).

function of the judicial power is to preserve the peace of society and leave its members to work out their own happiness and that of their fellows by a free exercise of their own powers. Men cannot be made better by a legal command.[31]

While escaping from a complete determinism that would foreclose any human efforts toward achieving more perfect justice, Carter points to no standard of right or ethical theory that could guide legislators, except perhaps a vague appeal to the cultural values of society. In this respect his theory is incomplete. Judges, of course, are admonished to make their decisions as closely as possible in conformity with popular morality, and if they do, this will somehow assist the evolutionary process along the road of progress. The idea of progress itself seems to be accepted on faith. Further explanation is demanded here as well. Carter presumably leaves to the social scientists and historians the study of those forces that slowly change society's customary morality.

Although many of Carter's ideas can be found in the works of Savigny and Maine, discussed in chapter 1, he develops some of these ideas further, and he presents a fairly complete exposition of the evolutionary paradigm in his final work. Relatively frequently he cites or quotes without citation Savigny, Maine, Spencer, Edward Gibbon, and, by way of critique, Bentham and Austin.[32] It appears that he has drawn heavily upon these sources, but he has generally worked out his own arguments and patched together his own version of the evolutionary paradigm. While Carter's work may have directed the attention of some social scientists toward study of the law within their disciplines,[33] it was not especially noted or well received in the jurisprudential community; he perhaps deserves a better reception than he has gotten.[34]

31. *Origins*, 323.

32. Another author Carter is fond of citing is J. A. Dixon, a "Glasgow lawyer." Roscoe Pound attributes Carter's adoption of the evolutionary paradigm to the influence of a series of lectures at Harvard by Luther S. Cushing during Carter's law-school days. Cushing had studied under Savigny. R. Pound, *Interpretations of Legal History*, 35 (1923).

33. See Ellwood, The Social Science Foundations of Law, 22 Green Bag 576 (1910); Lindsey, The Development of a Scientific View of Law, 45 Am. L. Rev. 513 (1911).

34. Carter's work was summarized and criticized in a very able article by Canadian M. J. Aronson in 1953. This, however, apparently stirred no special interest in Carter. Aronson, The Juridical Evolutionism of James Coolidge Carter, 10 Univ. Toronto L. J. 1 (1953).

Economic Determinism and the Class Struggle

A somewhat different manifestation of the evolutionary paradigm was presented by other turn-of-the-century scholars. This variation of the historical perspective, no doubt in debt to Karl Marx, emphasized economic determinism. Clearly in the minds of these authors, and sometimes in their papers, was the great struggle of the labor movement in the first decades of the twentieth century. The premier advocate for this view was Brooks Adams.[35]

Brooks Adams (1848–1927) was a member of the illustrious Adams family of Boston; he graduated from Harvard and attended one year at the Harvard Law School. Although he practiced law and lectured at the Boston University school of law from 1904 to 1911, his real interest was history. He wrote a number of histories, some of which were translated into French, German, and Russian.[36]

Adams advances two metaphors to help us understand the nature of law. First, he conceives of law as the resultant of conflicting forces just as the earth's orbit is the resultant of its own inertia and the sun's gravity.[37] The forces operating on the earth are physical, while the forces operating on the law are social. "Law is not the will of the strongest, for the will of the strongest is always deflected somewhat from its proper path by resistance. Sovereignty, therefore, is a compromise. American sovereignty, in especial, is the resultant of a series of compromises, which began long ago and which are still going on."[38]

Among social forces the economic are most significant. In each period of history a class of persons becomes economically dominant, and this class bends the law to best serve its own needs: "The dominant class, whether it be priests or usurers or soldiers or bankers, will shape the law to favor themselves, and that code will most nearly approach the ideal of justice of each particular age which favors most perfectly the dominant class."[39]

35. Adams' direct contributions to legal literature and jurisprudence are The Nature of Law: Methods and Aim of Legal Education, in M. Bigelow, ed., *Centralization and the Law*, 20 (1906); Law under Inequality: Monopoly, in M. Bigelow, ed., *Centralization and the Law*, 63 (1906); Adams, The Modern Conception of Animus, 19 Green Bag 12 (1907).

36. These included *The Law of Civilization and Decay* (1895), *America's Economic Supremacy* (1900), and *The New Empire* (1902).

37. Adams, The Nature of Law, note 35, 52.

38. Ibid.

39. Adams, Law under Inequality, note 35, 64. Aristotle first popularized this idea.

The other metaphor that Adams offers is law as an envelope of security for society.[40] He sees society as being surrounded and protected by an envelope that consists of rules of law. These rules are dictated primarily by the dominant class subject to modification through resistance from others. The law is flexible so that societal change can be accommodated and the law will conform slowly to the normal expansions and contractions of social change. If change occurs too rapidly or is too opposed to longstanding habit, the envelope is torn. This is political revolution.

As an illustration of his deterministic theme, Adams draws upon his extensive knowledge of English and American legal history to suggest that the law of contract emerged to benefit the mercantile class and more recently has become a tool of dominance in the hands of the industrial class. He says:

> The law is an example of Darwin's generalization of natural selection. Those fittest to survive in each particular environment prosper, those unfit suffer in proportion to their unfitness, and nowhere is the working of this process more evident than in the development of our civilization, which, in its passage from the middle ages, elaborated the conceptions of contract as its basis, and which now, under new forms of competition, is discarding them.[41]

There is nothing to indicate in Adams' legal writings that he saw a place for reform or improvement in the law. He reiterates the proposition that law is the product of blind social forces and advises the law student and lawyer to try to understand in what direction the economic forces of the present are moving the law.

While certainly an exponent of his own version of the evolutionary paradigm, Adams rejects what he calls the historical method. In doing so he is referring to the chronological study of the conceptual development of legal rules and concepts, abstracted from their social context. He says: "I fear that nothing can be more misleading than to read an historical series of decisions relating to corporations or carriers or contracts, for example, without a commentary on the social changes which have caused and are causing old legal notions to vary fundamentally from modern."[42] This may be an attack on the methods of Langdell, or conceivably it could be aimed at Holmes. Holmes, of course, recognized the influence of social change on the conceptual development of the law, but in writing his

40. Adams, The Nature of Law, note 35, 45–46.
41. Adams, Law under Inequality, note 35, 64. Adams thinks that society, having moved from status to contract, is moving (in his day) from contract to servitude.
42. Ibid.

history he stuck to the conceptual. It is certainly an interesting jurisprudential contrast to compare Holmes' discussion of the evolution of contract law in *Law in Science and Science in Law* with Adams' discussion of
the same development in *Law under Inequality: Monopoly*.

Adams also disagreed with William G. Hammond's idea of the nature of
the common law as a body of abstract principles. Adams thought that
thinking of law as a body of abstract standards, whether natural law,
divinely inspired ordinances, or evolved common-law principles, was a
fallacy and one that led to great mischief in legal thinking: "There are . . .
no abstract legal principles, any more than there is an abstract animal
apart from individual animals, or an abstract plant apart from individual
plants."[43] Adams viewed this notion of abstract legal principles as a
survival of scholasticism, and he traces its use and abuse from medieval to
modern times.

Adams was joined in his economic determinism by his colleague, Melville M. Bigelow (1846–1921), dean of the Boston University law school.
While not as doctrinaire or deterministic as Adams, Bigelow, nevertheless,
supported the main idea that law "is the resultant of conflicting social or
political forces."[44] He urged that legal education shed its old ways and
that law teaching be based on a model of social conflict.[45]

The viewpoint of economic determinism was further supported in a
book by socialist activist Gustavus Myers (1872–1942) published in
1912.[46] This was a thoroughly Marxist history of the United States
Supreme Court. It presents from the socialist perspective a very interesting
discussion of some famous court decisions. Unfortunately it is quite polemical and lacks persuasiveness for the unconverted.

Another book of this period seemed to imply through its methods and

43. Adams, The Nature of Law, note 35, 45.

44. Bigelow, Economic Forces and Municipal Law, 41 Am. L. Rev. 27, 28 (1907). He
further pointed out: "Law is continuous only in time. In point of substance it is broken
up into periods of the ascendency of certain social, economic forces. These periods,
acting upon judges and legislatures, are the main factors which make our law; accordingly the law of one period may be essentially different from what it was, or what it may
be, under another period. . . . In this view of the matter, the past does not govern the
present; the books do not contain, either in development or in germ, all the law. To
understand the law, past or present, the decisions of the courts and the acts of the
legislature must be read in the light of accompanying social history. This we call a
scientific school of legal thought." Ibid.

45. See also three essays by Bigelow, The Extension of Legal Education, Law under
Equality or Inequality Defined, and Scientific Method in Law, published in M. Bigelow,
ed., *Centralization and the Law*, 1, 135, and 165 respectively (1906).

46. G. Myers, *History of the Supreme Court of the United States* (1912).

assumptions a theory of economic determinism or some variation of Marxism, but it confined itself largely to the presentation of facts and eschewed philosophical speculation. This was Charles Beard's (1874–1948) celebrated *An Economic Interpretation of the Constitution of the United States*.[47] Beard's research showed that the framers of the constitution were representatives of and were themselves members of the relatively small class of business leaders, financiers, and speculators and that the constitution was designed to protect and promote their economic class interests. The book was instantly controversial, along with its author, a professor of history at Columbia University; it remained so for the next half century. It gave support and perhaps some respectability to the jurisprudential thesis that all law is dictated by the ruling class and is determined by economic factors evolving in society.

These Marxist notions did not go unchallenged. Professor Francis M. Burdick of the Columbia law school took issue with Brooks Adams in an article published in 1912.[48] Burdick analyzed the same cases that Adams had used and added some, coming to quite opposite conclusions. These cases dealt with the fellow servant doctrine, the constitutionality of certain prohibition laws, and the doctrine of contributory negligence. Burdick demonstrated that Adams' thesis—that strong economic interests prevailed over the weak—was not borne out by the evidence. In addition, since Adams had written his articles, the famous "trust-busting" cases had been decided against the monopolies. Burdick says, "The statement that litigants of 'vast power are protected accordingly,' while weak litigants 'fare in proportion to their weakness,' reads like a fairy tale in the light of . . . the Standard Oil and Tobacco Trust Cases." This exchange between a Marxist and a non-Marxist dealing directly with the relationship between economic determinants and specific areas of the law is perhaps unique in American legal literature before the 1970s.[49]

Two other authors who explained law in terms of class dominance in

47. C. Beard, *An Economic Interpretation of the Constitution of the United States* (1913). Beard was a historian and not a philosopher; he did not advance any theory in justification of his work but purported to follow the lead of Frederick Jackson Turner. In his introduction Beard cited Gustavus Myers, social scientist Arthur Bentley, historians Dodd, Ambler, and Seligman, and legal scholars Borchard (referring to German jurisprudence), Rudolf von Jhering, Roscoe Pound, and James C. Carter. An earlier book, similar to Beard's, which also caused controversy was J. Smith, *Spirit of American Government* (1907).

48. Burdick, Is Law the Expression of Class Selfishness?, 25 Harv. L. Rev. 349 (1912).

49. Roscoe Pound restated the arguments in *Interpretations of Legal History*, 95ff. (1923).

this period should also be mentioned. William M. Blatt (1876–1957) wrote two articles dealing with legal evolution and the forces that generate the law.[50] He says:

> Legal evolution is brought about by four causes:
> 1. Changes in the pressure of the lawmaking forces.
> 2. A clearer perception of economic needs.
> 3. The development of greater moral courage.
> 4. Improvements in legal machinery.
> All of these except the first are in line with the general evolution of the race and it may therefore be predicted that an unsettled law will eventually be settled in the direction of higher evolution unless deflected by the first influence.[51]

The lawmaking forces that Blatt refers to are ambition, hunger, climate, geography, education, and many others. These forces act upon the three great classes in society—master, middle, and subject groups—as well as upon special-interest or pressure groups. The classes and interest groups constantly apply pressure to the legal system for their own economic benefit. The law at any given time is the result of constant pressures balanced against each other. Although it is within the evolutionary paradigm, this view also has some affinity with the idea of law as a balancing of interests espoused by Roscoe Pound and originated by Rudolf von Jhering (see chapter 6).

Also writing in 1913, Simon N. Patten (1852–1922) gives an evolutionary-socialist view of how law is formed and at the same time critiques the Austinian position.[52] His article, devoid of citations, is creative and interesting but suffers from having a unique vocabulary all its own. Patten offers charts to clarify his view, but they make little sense. For him social justice consists in "the consensus of present social activity brought to a common consciousness by the similarity of local struggles for social betterment."

50. Blatt, Some Principles of Legal Evolution, 23 Yale L. J. 168 (1913); Blatt, The Law-Making Forces, 47 Am. L. Rev. 41 (1913). Blatt was a Boston practitioner of law and a moderately successful playwright as well.

51. Ibid., 168.

52. Patten, The New Jurisprudence, 62 Univ. Pa. L. Rev. 1 (1913). Patten was a professor of political economy in the Wharton School of Finance at the University of Pennsylvania. He wrote *The Theory of Social Forces* (1896), in which he outlined a social theory combining evolution, economics, and politics. He wrote a number of other works on economics.

The Planetary Theory

An entirely different view of matters was taken by John Henry Wigmore (1863–1943), another scholar enamored of the evolutionary paradigm, although much of his jurisprudential work was done within the confines of the expository paradigm (see chapter 4). An extremely prolific writer, Wigmore published in 1897 an article of ninety-eight pages entitled "The Pledge Idea: A Study in Comparative Legal Ideas."[53] In this work he described the emergence of the pledge (delivery of property for security of a loan) in about a dozen ancient and modern legal systems. He is careful not to make any philosophical claims, and indeed disclaims the proof of any broad generalizations, but the whole idea of the article implies that this institution will emerge in all societies when the conditions are right; the pledge is an adaptation to a certain social environment.

Wigmore kept his belief in legal evolution and the importance of legal history throughout his life. He edited two important series of books on legal history totaling thirteen volumes,[54] and he and his colleague, Albert Kocourek, edited an additional three-volume set entitled *The Evolution of Law Series*.[55] This was a remarkable work, for both its good and bad qualities.[56] Of special importance from a historical perspective, these volumes provided a resource in English where the works of both social scientists and European students of legal evolution were made easily available to American legal scholars. Wigmore also wrote an article for the *Virginia Law Review* in 1917 that explained his "planetary" theory of legal evolution as well as his more mature thoughts on the subject.[57]

From these publications it is possible to piece together Wigmore's thinking on the topic of legal evolution.[58] He optimistically suggests that

53. Wigmore, The Pledge Idea: A Study in Comparative Legal Ideas (pts. 1–3), 10 Harv. L. Rev. 321, 389 (1897), 11 Harv. L. Rev. 18 (1897).

54. J. Wigmore, ed., *Select Essays in Anglo-American Legal History* (3 vols. 1907–1909); J. Wigmore, ed., *The Continental Legal History Series* (10 vols. 1912–28). Wigmore was also the chair of the Association of American Law Schools' editorial committee for the *Modern Legal Philosophy Series* (10 vols. 1912–22).

55. A. Kocourek and J. Wigmore, *Evolution of Law Series* (3 vols. 1915–18).

56. See Hovenkamp, Evolutionary Models in Jurisprudence, 64 Tex. L. Rev. 645, 662 (1985).

57. Wigmore, Problems of the Law's Evolution, 4 Va. L. Rev. 247 (1917). This was the first of three related articles. The others, not dealing directly with legal evolution, were: Problems of the Law's Mechanism in America, 4 Va. L. Rev. 337 (1917); Problems of World-Legislation and America's Share Therein, 4 Va. L. Rev. 423 (1917).

58. In particular see the preface to volume 3 in the Evolution of Law Series, note 55.

the greatest value of studying legal evolution lies in the possibility of applying the "laws" of legal evolution, whatever they turn out to be, to the present and future so that the course of the law's change can be forecast. These laws of development, now only dimly understood, are the real natural law. He provides an analogy to the work of the paleontologist, who is able to reconstruct the entire dinosaur from a few bone fragments. The student of legal evolution will be able to reconstruct the many adaptations of law to their particular social and economic environments through the study of ancient and contemporary primitive societies.

Like many of his contemporaries, Wigmore thinks that present-day legal systems contain many "survivals" from previous history, and he subscribes to the notion that legislatures are inherently limited in what they can do. He says that various factors or influences that affect legal evolution must be isolated and studied in different cultures.[59] These "factors" seem to be a type of causation.

Wigmore is not entirely clear about what evolves. He states that the law consists of a substantial element and a formal element. The substantial element is made up of the habits, conduct, relationships, and institutions that people naturally form. Only some of them are legal. The formal element of the law is the "mode" in which such behavior is affected, and it contains three elements: uniform behavior, compulsion or coercion, and state power. He says: "The evolution of law, which we seek to discover, does not imply progress, either morally or otherwise, but merely movement in the *abstract elements* of the conduct shown in history, seeking always to proceed to the more and more abstract; but always including *the cause with the effect*."[60] The reader will have to determine just what this means; Wigmore does not clarify the matter.

However, Wigmore does suggest that general models of legal evolution advanced by others, primarily European scholars, are all much too simple to account for the process adequately.[61] Instead he proposes his own general model, the planetary theory. Reduced to its essentials, this theory analogizes any rule of law, legal doctrine, or concept to a particle of metal on the spoke of a wheel. The wheel is turning, but its axle is attached to other axes extending in different dimensions, which are themselves turn-

59. He identifies the following factors: geophysic, economic, biologic, religious, racial, political, psychologic, and social.

60. Wigmore, Problems of the Law's Evolution, 4 Va. L. Rev. 247, 256 (1917).

61. Ibid., 259ff. He specifically rejects the following models: the ascending straight line, the ascending jagged line, the undulating line, the angled line, Vico's circle (a cyclical theory), De Greef's spiral, and Goethe's expanding helix.

ing. The forces that turn these axes are the aforementioned factors or influences. Thus, the motion or evolutionary direction of the law is a composite or resultant of forces moving in different although not usually opposite directions. The point of this rather silly metaphor is that physical science can account for the apparently erratic or random movement of the metal in the wheel's spoke through the application of known physical laws and with the knowledge of the velocity and direction of the forces involved. So, in theory, the science of legal evolution can determine the course of the law by finding the laws of change and applying them to the known development of legal history.

This is a tall order. In fact, Wigmore slips into an uncharacteristic pessimism when he discusses the methods that must be devised to pursue such study successfully.[62] He illustrates his point with two examples of generalization about legal development from Henry Maine's work. Using the legal history of different peoples, Wigmore finds that the course of development suggested by Maine is far from universal; Maine's data and his hypotheses are too simple. "And so, just as we approach some explanatory factor, we find ourselves again baffled and doubtful."

In spite of his native optimism, Wigmore's thinking on legal evolution, culminating in the planetary theory, led to the conclusion that the evolutionary paradigm was at that point little more than speculation. Maintaining his belief in the general notion of cultural evolution, including legal evolution, Wigmore, nevertheless, argued (1) that it was much more complicated than most people had suspected, (2) that it was more than legal history, (3) that it did not entail "progress," and (4) that no scientific method had yet been devised that was likely to be effective in discovering the laws of change. We might add, although this was probably not apparent to Wigmore, that his work also suggested general confusion in what it meant to "evolve," in what evolved, and in what cause and effect meant in this context.

---

62. "Any rigidly scientific results must be based on at least the following elements: Taking a single idea or institution, its forms must be traced (1) in two or more successive epochs for the same communities; (2) then in two or more communities in successive epochs; (3) then the other legal institutions in the same communities and epochs must be mapped out, so that the connection if any may be disclosed; (4) then the main social forces in the same communities and epochs must also be mapped out, so as further to detect the possible causes of difference; (5) the whole must be conceived of as a simultaneous movement of forces. Perhaps such a rigid method is as yet impracticable, for lack of adequate data, but at least it is an ideal to be looked forward to." Ibid., 267–68.

These criticisms and others were voiced in a brief but incisive book review by Judge Edwin B. Gager of volume three of *The Evolution of Law Series*.[63] Gager was amazed that Kocourek and Wigmore really thought that the future course of the law could be predicted through the science of legal evolution.[64] He articulated and challenged all of the assumptions of the editors of the series, and he further noted, "The use of the term 'Evolution' as applied to the history and transformation of law is . . . vague or merely metaphorical or actually misleading." For Gager law was the deliberate product of the human mind; changes in it, whether by legislation or precedent, were also the result of conscious decisions. There is no internal mechanism by which the law moves or tends toward a certain development: "Perhaps it would be truer to say that law as law has no "tendency" whatever, any more than a quantity of bricks has a tendency to become a house. Strictly it never changes, but is changed from without; it does not develop, but it is developed."[65] Gager further pointed out the problem of reconciling explanations of phenomena using the idea of cause and effect with explanations that rely on the idea of human volition (the free-will-versus-determinism debate). Wigmore had explicitly declined to tackle this hoary philosophical conundrum.[66]

This broadside against the evolutionary paradigm brought an immediate reply from A. G. Keller (1874–1956), professor of the science of society at Yale University and author of *Societal Evolution*.[67] In a short article Keller restated the case for legal evolution,[68] relying upon a theory much more like James C. Carter's than Wigmore's. While Keller cites William Graham Sumner and Herbert Spencer as well as his own work, his article could well be a summary of Carter's philosophy; however, doing what Carter had never done, he draws careful attention to the analogy between Charles Darwin's theory and his own view:

63. Gager, Book Review of A. Kocourek and J. Wigmore, *Formative Influences of Legal Development, Evolution of Law Series*, vol. 3 (1918), in 28 Yale L. J. 617 (1919).

64. "Great stress is laid upon primitive and savage institutions, apparently with the notion that thus, from law in its infancy, a principle can be derived which will help to forecast what may take place in the realm of law in the immediate future. We wish it might be. The world would place upon its loftiest pinnacle of fame that person who, today, with the help of principles derived from the so-called evolution of law, would be able to forecast the events in the field of law within the next few years." Ibid., 619.

65. Ibid., 617–18.

66. A. Kocourek and J. Wigmore, note 55, xi.

67. A. Keller, *Societal Evolution* (1915). Keller was a disciple of William Graham Sumner.

68. Keller, Law in Evolution, 28 Yale L. J. 769 (1919).

The essence of evolution is adjustment to life-conditions. But adjustment to changing conditions implies change. Change is secured, in the organic range, by the element of variation. It is immaterial to the process whether or not the variation is pronounced enough to be called a mutation. The presence of variation in the mores, over space and through time, is a matter of observation. . . . We have . . . the fact of variation in custom. There is no analogy here; the phenomenon is present in the social realm entirely independently of its presence elsewhere.[69]

Keller further explains the relationship between evolution in the biological and the social fields:

If the fact of variation in the mores be granted, whereby some of them enjoy, under selection, a survival value over others, leading to their persistence, then the mores thus approved under test as superior in fitness become subject to the action of tradition. This is the factor in the social field that corresponds to heredity in the organic. . . . What is said of the mores in general applies *a fortiori* to law.[70]

Keller says that Gager's example of a pile of bricks exhibiting no tendency to become a house confuses the product of evolution with the process. A pile of bricks is like a horse's hoof or a camel's foot; each exhibits an adaptation to life conditions. "That is precisely what any legal enactment shows, or it becomes a dead-letter and nil. Each of these things is a *product* of the evolutionary process."

Judge Gager's same pile of bricks also prompted a response from a surprising source, Australian W. Jethro Brown, author of *The Austinian Theory of Law*[71] and a respected legal analyst. Brown also upholds the evolutionary paradigm against Gager's criticisms.[72] He says that the brick analogy is false because it fails to take into account the difference between the formal language of a statute (what he calls ostensible law) and its application by a court; he also insists that the meaning of legal texts, unchanged in form, nevertheless changes over time as they become viewed in a different light by different minds:

The actual rules which govern the life of the citizen, in so far as legal relations fall within the ambit of a particular statute, are determined

69. Ibid., 778.
70. Ibid., 779–81.
71. J. Brown, *The Austinian Theory of Law* (1906); see chapter 3.
72. Brown, Law and Evolution, 29 Yale L. J. 394 (1920).

both by the organic or *quasi*-organic interrelation of a totality of statutes and precedents, and by the mental attitude of judges who bring to the statute an equipment derived from the history of the race and the environment of a particular generation. We may say, if we like, that the statute remains fixed without any tendency to change or develop. As a matter of fact, however, the statute does not mean— cannot mean—to one generation just what it meant to a preceding generation.[73]

While admitting that the question of whether law "evolves" is partly a verbal one, Brown sides with the evolutionists. He believes that the historical development of law shows enough similarities to the evolution of plants and animals to permit the fair use of the term. He also suggests an answer to the apparent antinomy between cause and effect and human volition in the course of evolution. An analogy to the breeding of cattle and horses is offered. While the course of evolution has naturally brought the cow to a certain stage of development, careful breeding of the animal by human direction can produce bigger, healthier, and beefier varieties. Law, too, has evolved, but deliberate change by human direction can also improve it. Brown thinks that the mental processes of human beings can be one factor in the evolution of animals or of a social institution such as law. "All that we are justified in saying is that in the case of law conscious, if unformulated, purposes play a more important and a more apparent role than in biological evolution."

Other Voices

Other scholars of this period who did not endorse the evolutionary paradigm in their principal work nevertheless seemed to approve of some of its ideas. For example, noted analyst John Chipman Gray, in discussing the abstraction of the state and who actually exercises power, says that all governments are run by small groups of men, often behind the scenes, who act in their own interests.[74]

73. Ibid., 395–96.
74. He says: "In every aggregation of men there are some of the number who impress their wills upon the others, who are habitually obeyed by the others, and who are, in truth, the rulers of the society. The sources from which their authority flows are of the most diverse character. They may be, or may pretend to be divinely inspired. It may be their physical strength, their wisdom, their cunning, their virtues, their vices,—often-

Professor Francis H. Bohlen of the University of Pennsylvania, later to become the first reporter for the *Restatement of Torts*, also had a clear vision of how economic forces affected the law. In a 1911 article discussing the landmark case of *Rylands v. Fletcher*, Bohlen demonstrates the economic and ideological reasons why the case was decided as it was in England and why it was not followed in many American jurisdictions.[75] While Bohlen does not ignore the doctrinal aspects of the case, it is significant that he finds the argument running from historical change of economic circumstances the most fundamental explanation.[76]

Arthur L. Corbin, better known for his later championing of the Hohfeldian schema, also endorsed legal evolution early in his career.[77] Writing in a nonlegal periodical, Corbin advanced the Carterian notion that judges should apply community morality in deciding cases. After noting that the rules and doctrines of the law allow the judge more leeway than most people think, he says: "A judge's declared rules must compete for their lives with the rules declared by other judges and by all other persons. In the judicial world, as in the animal and vegetable world, the ultimate law is the law of the survival of the fittest."[78]

Another evolutionist worthy of mention was Nathan Isaacs (1886–1941), a professor at the University of Cincinnati. Isaacs wrote an article in 1917 advancing the thesis that law moves in cycles.[79] He thinks Henry Maine grasped only part of the truth when he envisioned law moving through the stages of fiction, equity, and legislation. Isaacs sees a circular movement from codification to fiction to equity to legislation to codifica-

---

est, perhaps, their assiduity and persistance,—that have given them their power. . . . Such rulers may have official position, but often they are without it. A king-maker or president-maker, the favorite of a monarch, the boss of State politics, may pride himself on his private station. Nor does the machinery of government make any great difference. The real rulers of a country are probably not much more numerous in a democracy than in a monarchy." *The Nature and Sources of the Law*, 65 (1909). For more on Gray see chapters 4 and 6.

75. Bohlen, The Rule in *Rylands v. Fletcher*, 59 Univ. Pa. L. Rev. 298, 373, 423 (1911).

76. Bohlen's analysis is critiqued by Roscoe Pound in *Interpretations of Legal History*, 105ff. (1923).

77. Corbin, The Law and the Judges, 3 Yale Rev. 234 (1914).

78. Ibid., 238. As noted in the text, this article appears in a nonlegal periodical and contains no citations. How scholarly did Corbin regard it to be? It may have been a speculative lark in view of Corbin's later analytical tendencies (see chapter 4).

79. Isaacs, "The Law" and the Law of Change, 65 U. Pa. L. Rev. 665, 748 (1917). Isaacs, a product of the University of Cincinnati and its law school, taught law at Cincinnati, Pittsburgh, Columbia, Yale, and Harvard in his short career.

tion again. This cycle starts with codification, the organization of unrelated parts of the law, to glossation or word study including the use of
fictions, to commentation or the study of principles and the use of equity,
to the drafting of specific legislation, then back to codification. These
stages can overlap so that at any given time lawyers can be working in
more than one stage of activity. Isaacs thinks that the history of both the
Roman law and the common law illustrates a cyclical development, but he
bases his proof on the history of Jewish law, which he traces in considerable detail. Indeed, this history is the bulk of his two-part article and may
also be his most valuable contribution to the literature.[80]

This survey of evolutionist jurisprudence must end with consideration
of the work of Roscoe Pound, a thinker certainly not known as a historicist. Like many legal scholars at the turn of the century, Pound was a
reformer, a progressive, a pragmatist, a mild skeptic of older ways of
thinking, and a believer in a general and vague idea of social evolution.
But he was also much more. He was able to advance jurisprudence on
several fronts almost single-handedly, and he attempted to construct his
own philosophy of sociological jurisprudence (see chapter 6).

Pound rejected what he called the historical school of jurisprudence,
including the evolutionary ideas of Savigny, Carter, and Holmes.[81] His
principal criticism was that the historical view was based on a metaphysical assumption that history revealed an unfolding idea of progress, often
in the form of increased personal liberty, an assumption attributable
originally to Hegel and Kant. This inevitable unfolding led to an extreme
conservatism, a "what will be, will be" attitude, which was anti-reform.
This was diametrically opposed to Pound's idea of social engineering
through law, and the a priori methodological assumptions were equally
unacceptable to Pound. He also rejected what he termed the ethnological-
biological and economic-biological views of legal development, including
those of Brooks Adams. Here, again, the proponents of this view in
Pound's mind assume a race struggle or a class struggle behind empirical
reality but one that operates on the law in a deterministic fashion. There is
no room for deliberate engineering of legal solutions to problems, no
possibility of reform. Pound also thinks that the facts of legal history do
not support the case for either of these views.

80. Another author who advanced a cyclical theory of sorts was A.F. Albertsworth of
Western Reserve University. See Albertsworth, The Changing Conception of Law, 8 A.
B. A. J. 673 (1922); Albertsworth, Is There a Legal Cycle?, 11 Calif. L. Rev. 381 (1923).

81. See R. Pound, *Interpretations of Legal History*, 34–37, 85–86 (1923). The
following discussion is based primarily upon this source.

How, then, does Pound contribute to the evolutionary paradigm? First, he generally subscribes to Maine's idea that legal development moves through certain stages.[82] Particularly important for Pound is the idea that law in modern societies contains both customary or traditional elements and authoritative or legislative elements. Failure to take into account the traditional elements (which incorporate a vast amount of customary morality) results in a theory of law that is untrue to the facts and makes impossible a workable theory of judicial decision-making. Pound sees this, of course, as the sin of the Austinian analysts.

Pound's second contribution is his suggestion for resolving the determinism—free will dilemma as it relates to the evolutionary paradigm.[83] He offers a powerful metaphor. The law or legal system of a society is like a large building constructed over a long period of time. Many contemporary hospitals and university libraries serve as good examples. The building starts as a small structure carefully and deliberately designed for a particular purpose. As time passes the building no longer adequately serves the needs of those who use it; an addition is constructed. Later, another addition is added. A fire occurs and part of the building is gutted. It is reconstucted. With each construction different materials and different building techniques are used, because they are currently the least costly and most effective. In the course of this process the use of the building changes, perhaps imperceptibly, but substantially. When we look at the ultimate product after all of these changes, we find a building that no one has designed, often one that no one in her right mind would design. Yet, at each stage of change, the changes are deliberately made with specific purposes in mind. So it is with the law. The system we have inherited as a part of our culture was designed by no one; it is irrational in many ways. Yet, it is a product of rational choices.

The "evolution" of the large, old building is, of course, only a metaphor. But it is an instructive one that steers a path between pure determinism and rationalistic utopianism. As such, it is typical of Pound.

Extinction of the Evolutionists

The evolutionary paradigm began to wane in the early twenties. In any of its forms it was never particularly useful for the practicing

82. R. Pound, *Law and Morals*, 29–33 (1924).

83. Pound, note 81, 40. Pound refers back to Blackstone's characterization of the common law as a great medieval castle.

lawyer or judge or legislator. It may have been helpful in arguing against legal reforms, or in justifying racial segregation, or in furthering expansive notions of substantive due process that destroyed social legislation, but it was shaky. Besides, the new Poundian paradigm incorporated some aspects of the evolutionary paradigm, and it made much more sense for the times. As Wigmore had demonstrated, research that might prove at all fruitful in bolstering the theory would have to be undertaken by historians or social scientists, not legal scholars. That work did proceed; but for lawyers the theory was held on faith or else acknowledged as extremely speculative. In fact, there was not one theory but a whole family of theories.

That the evolutionists did not agree among themselves can be shown from the various statements of the evolutionary paradigm already summarized. First, it is clear that the authors have different ideas about what "evolves" or changes. For William G. Hammond it is the abstract principles of the common law, incapable of being authoritatively articulated and known only through their application in individual cases, a truly metaphysical view. For Holmes it is legal concepts like seisin, possession, bailment, entail, and consideration. These concepts have a "life" that carries them through the generations. For Carter it is the grassroots morality or customs of a social group, generally unarticulated but found and applied by judges in the legal process. For Adams it is the official rules of law, whether legislated or established by precedent, and the specific policies of the "sovereign," who is the mouthpiece for the ruling class. Wigmore is unclear on the point, but he seems to waiver between the Holmesian conceptual notion and the Carterian customary morality.

Second, what does it mean to evolve? Some authors seem to equate simple historical change with evolution. Hammond gives no explanation. Holmes suggests a survival of the fittest among ideas, an apparent analogy to biological natural selection. The selection, however, seems to be done by judges who weigh competing alternatives. Carter gives perhaps the most persuasive but disappointing answer. All kinds of things affect changes in customary morality (law): economic need, religious belief, political events, climate, geography, and so forth. No method is suggested for systematizing or analyzing these influences. Adams is more explicit about how the mechanism works. Economic activity is the engine of change. As economies change, certain elites become the dominant classes. Each type of economy will have its own ruling class: the soldier-landlord in feudal society, the merchant prince or banker in commercial society, the robber baron in industrial society. Each dominant class molds the law to its own best advantage. Discover the type of economy, and the form and nature of the law inevitably follow. Wigmore's position on this point is more sophisticated. He identifies certain "factors" that influence legal evolution, but he also seeks the laws of change. The laws of change, as yet unknown, operate on these factors to produce an evolutionary process.

Several of the evolutionary authors make use of the concept of survivals, that is, current legal rules or doctrines that seem anachronistic. Widely accepted was the idea that these anachronisms had evolved in an earlier age, that they had adapted to the social environment, and that time had then passed them by. Like a few strange animals and plants that today seem to belong to a more ancient epoch, they are destined to disappear. While this is possible if one subscribes to an evolutionary theory, it may on the other hand be a way of rationalizing data that do not fit the theory. Survivals may be the great hedge against the evidence. Whenever legal history shows us a doctrine or institution that should not exist at that time in that society according to some evolutionary or historical theory, it can be labeled a survival, thereby saving the theory.

In retrospect it is possible to see that the evolutionists did not agree on what evolved or how it evolved. The process of legal evolution was also difficult to document empirically, although the use of the concept of survivals perhaps helped keep otherwise messy data in line. Wigmore seemed to realize these things, and Pound certainly did. Others very likely found the various versions of the evolutionary paradigm not to their taste for the same reasons.

Apart from the merits of any theory of legal evolution, the more general notion of social Darwinism and the allied idea of white supremacy became unacceptable to many in America after World War I. German militarism was blamed on false ideas of Teutonic superiority. People justified racial discrimination on evolutionary grounds, and their opponents tended to oppose not only the discrimination but the concept of evolution as well. Faith in the general notion of progress in western culture, an important part of evolutionary theory for some, was substantially undermined by World War I itself. In this milieu legal evolution was bound to suffer, and it did. As the Poundian paradigm ascended, the evolutionary paradigm went into eclipse.

THE FORMATION OF
THE POUNDIAN PARADIGM
1872–1923

In response to the shortcomings of the older philosophies, a different point of view began to emerge around the turn of the century, and several intellectual currents of thought came together just before the beginning of World War I. The person most instrumental in welding this new view of the legal world into a whole and of developing it further was Roscoe Pound: hence, the Poundian paradigm.[1] Pound was the earliest of the Americans to expound a relatively complete new theory. This theory has been called sociological jurisprudence, legal realism, free law, functional jurisprudence, the jurisprudence of interests, and instrumental pragmatism.[2]

1. By "Poundian paradigm" is meant a comprehensive philosophy of law. Pound's particular version of it came first and is representative. Other authors shared some of his theory, but not all of it. All of it was acknowledged and supported by others but not by any one scholar, and many of the later exponents of the paradigm were unaware of their intellectual debt to the pioneering Pound. Thus, if differences are emphasized, as in White, From Sociological Jurisprudence to Realism, 58 Va. L. Rev. 999 (1972), more than one theory emerges. If similarities are emphasized, as in R. Summers, *Instrumentalism and American Legal Theory* (1982), a single jurisprudence is found. In my view the differences between the traditional moral, expository, and evolutionary paradigms and the Poundian are much greater than any variations within the Poundian paradigm, and so it is treated here as a single theory. It is clear that the seminal thinking, in terms of putting the various strands together, was Pound's.

2. Unlike the more traditional paradigms advanced in American jurisprudence, the Poundian paradigm, especially in its version as legal realism, has received considerable attention from historians of legal scholarship. See especially, L. Kalman, *Legal Realism at Yale, 1927–1960* (1986); R. Summers, *Instrumentalism and American Legal Theory* (1982); A. Hunt, *The Sociological Movement in Jurisprudence* (1978); G. White, *Patterns of American Legal Thought* (1978); W. Twining, *Karl Llewellyn and the Realist Movement* (1973); E. Purcell, *The Crisis of Democratic Theory* (1973); W.

Four currents of thought that led to the formation of the Poundian paradigm can be identified in the period immediately before World War I. They include a marked American tendency to view law indirectly through the activity of courts, that is, not as an independent body of rules or principles but as a "source" given life and effect when courts draw upon it to justify decisions. This kind of thinking suggests that rules and principles derive their authority, perhaps even their "existence," from the fact that courts rely on them, not the other way around. A second current of thought was pragmatism, both a formal philosophical position and a diffuse attitude held by many American intellectuals. A third was the notion of explaining social phenomena in terms of the conflict of group interests. The Marxist idea of class struggle was just one manifestation of this larger concept. Finally, a skeptical movement in German jurisprudence, called both "free law" and "sociological jurisprudence," worked its way across the Atlantic. We will describe the contributions of various thinkers to each current of thought; then we will discuss how Roscoe Pound put them all together into a more or less coherent whole.

Looking at Law from the Other End

We must begin again by noting the suggestions of Oliver Wendell Holmes, Jr., related to this new perspective. Holmes had great insight; but, as in other areas, he did not develop his ideas.[3] He suggested as early as 1872 that many factors could motivate a judge to decide a case in a certain way; some of them might be prior precedents or statutes, but others might be the custom and practice of the trade or the judge's economic views or his sense of justice or even his prejudices. The notion that social practices and norms as well as personal idiosyncrasies, in addition to the formal law, or even in opposition to the formal law, play a

---

Rumble, *American Legal Realism* (1968); Schlegel, American Legal Realism and Empirical Social Science: From the Yale Experience, 28 Buffalo L. Rev. 459 (1979).

3. The insight appears originally in an 1872 article in which Holmes stated: "It is clear in many cases custom and mercantile usage have had as much compulsory power as law could have, in spite of prohibitory statutes; and as to their being only motives for decision until adopted, what more is the decision that adopts them as to any future decision? What more indeed is a statute. . . ? Any motive for [a judge's] action, be it constitution, statute, custom, or precedent, which can be relied upon as likely in the generality of cases to prevail, is worthy of consideration as one of the sources of law. . . ." Holmes, The Law Magazine and Review, 6 Am. L. Rev. 593 (1872), reprinted in 44 Harv. L. Rev. 788, 789–90 (1931). See also the discussion of Holmes in chapter 2.

role in judicial decision-making challenges the autonomous legal world of the Austinians and threatens to undercut the entire expository paradigm. At the same time, the idea that judges deliberately make policy also undermines the concept of "legal evolution."

In 1891 Ezra Thayer, in what was no doubt one of the finest student essays ever written, addressed the topic of legislation by courts.[4] He compares the analytical jurisprudence of Austin with the historical jurisprudence of Hammond and Carter and finds each of them to contain only part of the truth. According to Thayer, failure to understand and take into account how courts reason and how they create law leads Bentham and Austin to regard legislation as the only proper form of law and enforcement the key to its identification. On the other hand, the historicists, seeing the important role that custom and morality play in judicial decisions, fail to distinguish between such norms and the law that is actually enforced. Thayer gives a brief definition of law that seeks to combine what is best in both views: "Law . . . is a body of rules . . . which are enforced by the sovereign power in a state and those only. The source and support of these rules, in a civilized and self-governing community, must be justice; that is to say, the opinion of the community as to what is right and expedient."[5] The point at which justice and enforcement come together, of course, is in the operation of courts.

In 1892 Professor John Chipman Gray attacked the Austinian and Carterian views of law and carried the reasoning farther than Thayer.[6] He persuasively demonstrates that Austin's definition of law as the command of the sovereign is entirely inadequate. Law, in Gray's mind, includes much that is not the command of the sovereign, and conversely many commands of the sovereign are not law. He says that rules of infantry tactics and postal regulations directed to postal officers are commands of the sovereign but not law. Likewise, customs of the trade and judges' views on public policy are given the effect of law but are not commands of the sovereign.

While rejecting the notion of sovereign command, Gray, nevertheless,

4. Thayer, Judicial Legislation: Its Legitimate Function in the Development of the Common Law, 5 Harv. L. Rev. 172 (1891). This article was the prize-winning essay of the class of 1891 selected by the Harvard Law School Association, according to the note at the end of the article. Ezra Thayer subsequently became dean of the Harvard Law School.

5. Ibid., 178.

6. Gray, Some Definitions and Questions in Jurisprudence, 6 Harv. L. Rev. 21 (1892).

does not accept custom as the primary basis for judicial decision. First, he points out that much of the law is technical and could not possibly be the subject of customary morality. For example, a contract is considered completed in New York when it is deposited in the mail; in Massachusetts it is not completed until received in the mail. Gray asks rhetorically if this reflects a deep difference in the customs of the peoples of the two states. A second argument against law as custom is equally effective. The reason that custom appears to be applied by the courts is because the judge's own morality will usually coincide with custom; therefore, when she applies her own notions of right and wrong (including notions about what is the best public policy), she is applying a rule identical with "custom." However, in those cases where the judge's convictions differ with popular custom or morality, the judge will apply her own view.[7]

In addition, custom will give rise to expectations on the part of persons engaged in legal transactions. Where no statute, precedent, or conflicting moral principle is applicable, the judge will give effect to the reasonable expectations of the parties, not simply because such expectations are the result of custom but because it is a moral principle accepted by all judges that reasonable expectations should not be disappointed.

While Gray admits the authority of legislation and precedent, he finds that these sources of law can be approached and understood most effectively through the courts. He says, "Jurisprudence is the science which deals with the principles on which courts ought to decide cases." He defends the deontological (ought) element of this definition against positivist criticism by arguing that how courts ought to decide cases is very much a practical concern of the lawyer and judge. An example is given of conflicting circuit-court-of-appeals decisions rendered by two courts on the same point of law. What the law is in this situation is equivalent to what the law ought to be. Similarly, in any situation in which the law is not clear or obvious, the legal inquiry shifts to what the law ought to be.

In 1897 Holmes gave further support to the idea of viewing law through

7. Ibid., 31. "Where the custom is one way and the judge's judgment of what is moral is another way, the judge follows the latter, and disregards the former. He would not so disregard a precedent, still less a Statute. Judges are constantly following Statutes and precedents which they consider pernicious; but has it ever been heard that a judge declared a custom to be without precedent in the courts and pernicious, and yet followed it? On the contrary, judges constantly refuse to follow customs which they deem unreasonable, *a fortiori* customs which they deem immoral; that is, they set their judgment of whether a practice is reasonable and moral higher than the mere fact of the practice as a source of law."

the courts in an address given to the graduating students at the Boston University law school.[8] Perhaps his most quoted line comes from this address: "The prophecies of what the courts will do in fact, and nothing more pretentious, are what I mean by the law." In this short address, directed, it should be kept in mind, to young graduates about to enter the practice of law, Holmes gives his now famous example of the bad man.[9] He counsels the practitioner to look at the law from the standpoint of a bad man who has no respect for morality and who will try to enhance his own interests at the expense of others if he can get away with it. Only when he sees that the force of the state may be brought to bear on him by requiring him to pay money or by putting him in jail, does he become concerned about his behavior. This, and only this, is the law bearing down upon him. The lawyer must always distinguish between the dictates of morality and the force of the law. Her professional activities are concerned only with the latter. Thus, lawyers are in the business of predicting what courts may do to their clients. Whatever aids in that prediction is a source of law, and law itself is the correct prediction, a statute or precedent to the contrary notwithstanding.[10] The bad-man metaphor not only emphasizes the separation of law and morality but also places the lawyer's focus squarely on the courts.

A sense of the creative role of the judge and the failure of the current legal theories to account for it prompted Jabez Fox (1850–1923), a Massachusetts judge himself, Harvard law graduate, and sometime lecturer in the Boston University law school, to some inspired criticism at the turn of the century. Reviewing J. B. Thayer's "Treatise on Evidence" in the *Harvard Law Review*,[11] Fox points up the difference in the evolutionary and Holmesian views of extralegal sources. Rejecting both the expository and evolutionary paradigms, he says, "We shake off the notion that law is

8. Holmes, The Path of the Law, 10 Harv. L. Rev. 457 (1897).

9. The famous metaphor of the bad man was suggested by Rudolf von Jhering in 1883. R. Jhering, *Der Zweck im Recht* (2 vols. 1877–83), translated by Isaac Husik as *Law as a Means to an End*, 33 (1913).

10. It should be noted that even in this address itself Holmes recognizes that law can be looked at from other standpoints. Lines seldom quoted from the same piece are: "Theory is the most important part of the dogma of the law, as the architect is the most important man who takes part in the building of a house. The most important improvements of the last twenty-five years are improvements in theory. It is not to be feared as unpractical, for, to the competent, it simply means going to the bottom of the subject." Holmes, note 8, 477.

11. Fox, Law and Fact, 12 Harv. L. Rev. 545 (1899); see also Fox, Law and Logic, 14 Harv. L. Rev. 39 (1900). Fox cites Holmes' famous Path of the Law article, note 8.

the mandate of the sovereign only to substitute the mandate of society or the 'social standard of justice' or some other unseen power."[12] This unwarranted assumption of some external social standard, in Fox's view, leads to a fruitless search. "In assuming that it is the duty of the judge simply to declare and apply the law we are compelled to look for the outside source of supply. . . ."

Following Holmes and Gray, Fox does not go so far as to suggest that courts give deceptive reasons for their decisions nor that they are not bound by clearly applicable statutes or precedents. But he recognizes that they do make law and that this creative function necessarily leads to uncertainty:

> Beyond this [the need to follow indistinguishable precedent] the judge has a free hand to decide the case before him according to his view of the general good. It may be that his decision will be governed by the "social standard of justice," but the essential point is that no human being can tell how the social standard of justice will work on that judge's mind before a judgment is rendered. It is this element of uncertainty which gives to every new judgment the force of a new rule.[13]

Interestingly, the eminent British analyst John W. Salmond expressed a kindred view just a few years later (see chapter 4). In the introductory part of his 1902 treatise Salmond maintains that law, in the positivist sense of a body of authoritative autonomous rules, is secondary to the administration of justice, by which he means the functioning of courts. He recognizes that courts can perform their function of administering justice without law and, indeed, that this actually happens in some societies.[14] He offers a definition of law as an alternative to the traditional Austinian one: "The law consists of the rules recognized and acted upon in courts of justice." But Salmond does not pursue this line of inquiry; the rest of his text is concerned entirely with the analysis of the formal positive law. It is

---

12. Ibid., 546. Fox adds, "It is astonishing with what tenacity we cling to the notion that the administration of justice presupposes the existence of a body of law imposed upon the judges by some external force."

13. Fox, Law and Logic, 14 Harv. L. Rev. 39, 43 (1900).

14. He adds: "The primary purpose of the judicature is not to enforce law, but to maintain justice, and this latter purpose is in its nature separable from the former and independent of it. Even when justice is administered according to law, the proportion between the sphere of legal principle and that of judicial discretion is different in different systems, and varies from time to time." J. Salmond, *Jurisprudence, or the Theory of Law*, 23 (1902).

perhaps noteworthy that the only American cited in the original edition of Salmond's major work is Holmes.

Gray gave greater currency to the idea of understanding law by looking at it through the courts in his widely acclaimed jurisprudential treatise of 1909, *The Nature and Sources of the Law*, an essentially analytic work.[15] Recognizing that a court-oriented view is analogous to studying medicine from "the clinical or therapeutic side," he, nevertheless, contends that his approach avoids the common confusion between law and sources of law fostered by the prevailing legal paradigms. Although he repeats the arguments made in his earlier article, sometimes verbatim, he extends the earlier position to incorporate substantially the definition of law suggested by Salmond, namely, "The Law . . . is composed of the rules which the courts . . . lay down for the determination of legal rights and duties." He does not, however, cite Salmond's work or indicate that he was familiar with it. Gray identifies common sources of the law, in order of their binding authority on judges, as statutes, judicial precedents, opinions of experts (by which he means scholarly legal opinion), custom, morality, and equity (the judge's own morality). He makes a strong statement for judicial creativity and argues that courts constantly make law ex post facto. His refutation of the Austinian and Carterian doctrine on many points is persuasive.

The gaslight Harvardians can be credited, then, with originating the idea that law can be most fruitfully understood by looking at it through the operation of the courts—a major part of the Poundian paradigm. Skeptical of the mechanical operation of legal rules and doctrines, they saw merit in speaking of law as a prediction of what courts will do. In taking this approach they found that various social, moral, economic, and other factors, certainly nonlegal from the positivist perspective, could and did affect judicial decision-making. Of course this last idea in a slightly different form was an inherent part of the earlier evolutionary paradigm. For example, James C. Carter's version of that paradigm, equating common law to customary morality as declared by the courts, clearly identified an "extralegal" source of law. However, the evolutionists generally regarded the influence of these sources as inevitable, determined by evolutionary forces, or at the very least not understood or capable of investigation by legal scholars. In contrast, the Harvard thinkers left open the questions of what and how extralegal matters impinge upon judicial

15. J. Gray, *The Nature and Sources of the Law* (1909). This was a publication of lectures given the preceding year at Columbia University.

decision, thereby inviting the study of such matters. They deserve credit for the idea of looking at law through the lens of the courts.

This view of legal phenomena was carried a significant step farther by a young law professor at Stanford University. The work of Joseph W. Bingham (1878–1973) is brilliant, but singular and narrow. It emphasizes certain aspects of the Poundian paradigm that are downplayed in Pound's own work. Bingham made his entire contribution to jurisprudence in a series of four articles published from 1912 through 1914.[16]

Bingham appears to have conceived the science of law as analogous to the physical sciences. In this view the field of study is the patterns of activity of government officials, perhaps primarily but certainly not limited to court activity. The law is reflected in the actions of these officials, not in law books, not in doctrine, not even in the reasoning and pronouncements of courts themselves. Bingham recognizes that this characterization runs contrary to the way the word "law" is used in normal parlance, but he does not wish to fight a verbal battle. What are normally called laws, that is, legal propositions, rules, and concepts, are verbal formulations of what potentially is the law. They are mere predictions, like formulas or "laws" in the physical sciences; they are not the basic subject matter of study but are instrumental in understanding and communicating about the subject matter. They may be true or accurate, or they may not. It does not matter whether a legal rule or concept is announced by a court or legislature or by a private attorney; its validity or truth depends on whether it accurately states what officials will do.

Bingham's writing contains some extreme language that drew hostile criticism at the time.[17] He says that principles and rules of law do not really exist, and he advances a crude empirical epistemology that denies any objective reality to ideas or concepts. However, his basic insight is simply an extension of the Holmesian idea that we use legal rules and terminology—define rights and duties—for the purpose of characterizing or predicting the activities of government officials. The verbal or conceptual side of law is dependent on and derivative of the actions of human

16. Bingham, What is the Law? (pts. 1 and 2), 11 Mich L. Rev. 1, 109 (1912); Bingham, Science and the Law, 25 Green Bag 162 (1913); Bingham, The Nature of Legal Rights and Duties, 12 Mich. L. Rev. 1 (1913); Bingham, Legal Philosophy and the Law, 9 Ill. L. Rev. 98 (1914). Some of Bingham's jurisprudential thinking had developed by 1909 and appears somewhat tangentially in Bingham, Some Suggestions Concerning "Legal Cause" at Common Law, 9 Colum. L. Rev. 16, 136 (1909).

17. See Kocourek, Review of Bingham, 8 Ill. L. Rev. 138 (1913); Spencer, Jurisprudence Not an Objective Science, 25 Green Bag 74 (1913).

beings or what would be the actions of human beings in certain circumstances.

Bingham's discussion of the effect of precedent is instructive. He says courts are not bound by precedent in the way that they are bound by legislation. What previous courts have said they are doing, what rules they have said they are applying, and their reasons are always open to challenge and reinterpretation. Thus, any notion of a strict doctrine of stare decisis is rejected by Bingham. He says that courts feel the right decision before they can intellectually justify it, and their justifications are often erroneous. Predicting actual decisions like "judgment for plaintiff" is the ultimate business of the lawyer, not the manipulation of doctrine for its own sake.

In the course of his writings Bingham gives no hint of indebtedness to Holmes, Gray, or even Pound, who was marching in the same general direction. One is also tempted to think that he was influenced by the behaviorism of Bentley, discussed on pages 160–62, and he may have heard Bentley lecture at the University of Chicago in his student days. Bingham never wrote anything jurisprudential after 1914, although he taught law for many years thereafter.[18]

Pragmatism

The American political experience, especially in the ever-moving democratic West, shows that early in the nineteenth century people came to regard law as instrumental; it was felt that laws could and should be enacted to promote particular objectives.[19] Later in the same century American philosophers began to elaborate a philosophical theory of pragmatism that matched this homespun insight. The leaders of this movement were Charles S. Peirce (1839–1914), William James (1842–1910), and John Dewey (1859–1952).[20] None of these scholars were lawyers, but

18. He did summarize his original ideas much later in a contribution to Northwestern University, *My Philosophy of Law: Credos of Sixteen American Scholars*, 5 (1941).

19. This theme is developed in J. Hurst, *Law and the Conditions of Freedom in the Nineteenth Century United States* (1956).

20. The most important works are: W. James, *The Will to Believe and Other Essays in Popular Philosophy* (1897); W. James, *Pragmatism: A New Name for Old Ways of Thinking* (1907); W. James, *A Pluralistic Universe* (1909); J. Dewey, *Studies in Logical Theory* (1903); J. Dewey and J. Tufts, *Ethics* (1908); J. Dewey, *Reconstruction in*

Dewey had some interest in the law, and some of his writings could be regarded as peripherally jurisprudential. More important is the impact that their writings had on the major theorists of the law.[21]

From the point of view of general philosophy and the history of ideas perhaps the most important aspect of American pragmatism is its epistemology. To greatly oversimplify, but nevertheless to give a rough general picture, truth is a function of what works. In science a theory is true, or more accurately better than another, if its accounts of phenomena, past and predicted, proved to be correct, that is, if it could be relied on for human purposes. General knowledge of a nonscientific nature, including common sense and inherited traditional wisdom, also have to justify themselves in the currency of hard results. Pragmatism, then, has strong elements of empiricism and skepticism; but, unlike the empiricists of the eighteenth and early nineteenth centuries, the pragmatists do not accept the idea that there is a knowable objective reality "out there" discoverable through scientific means. Theoretical or abstract knowledge is not somehow a copy of physical reality. The reality or truth of any concept lies in its usefulness, that is, its capacity to aid human beings in understanding their world and thereby in achieving their ends. This instrumental view of truth and knowledge indirectly had an impact on jurisprudence.

More directly significant for jurisprudence is the pragmatists' view of morality. In morals no a priori, metaphysical, or religious principles are acceptable, but a moral precept might be regarded as true or right if its observance led to consequences that were more desirable than their alternatives. The results of conduct are the key to evaluation. What are the best overall alternatives, the most desirable general ends? In the view of the pragmatists, this question had led philosophers in the past into quagmires of speculation and abstract theory that discredited the whole enterprise of moral inquiry. Ultimate moral precepts are rejected by the pragmatists. The important moral questions are more specific. What is the best choice among competing alternatives in a given practical situation? Real moral life constantly presents these kinds of questions; one is seldom if ever required to justify ultimate values. Indeed, the values subject to choice,

---

Philosophy (1920); J. Dewey, *Human Nature and Conduct* (1922); Dewey, Logical Method and Law, 10 Corn. L. Q. 17 (1924). The earlier work of Peirce, upon whom James and Dewey drew, was principally in periodical literature, some popular and some technical. For a good historical discussion of pragmatism, see P. Wiener, *Evolution and the Founders of Pragmatism* (1949).

21. An authoritative book exploring the relationship between pragmatism and jurisprudence is R. Summers, *Instrumentalism and American Legal Theory* (1982).

once exposed and analyzed, are as likely as not uncontroversial, although the choice might be. A wrong or an injustice usually can be perceived and understood in terms of generally accepted values. The real moral problem is to engineer a solution, and solutions are likely to be temporary and relative to a specific context.[22]

The pragmatic philosophy took the form of "progressivism" in the political arena.[23] Both major political parties had their progressive and conservative wings. These positions were contrasted with radical socialist views espoused by many at the turn of the century. Conservatives were generally skeptical about political and legal change; progressives favored all kinds of specific causes. They considered the prevailing legal and political systems to be basically sound but believed in reform as a necessary concomitant to social progress. This attitude was tied in some cases to a corresponding belief in evolutionary progress, although the concept of evolution could serve the conservative camp equally well or better.

A pragmatic view of moral choice offered an alternative in jurisprudence to the moral theory of the older paradigms. The expository paradigm, from its beginnings with Bentham, divided the legal world into the science of legislation and the science of jurisprudence (see chapter 1). Only the former was concerned with questions of value, and Bentham's psychological utilitarianism with its *felicific calculus* had not proved workable in practical arenas. This branch of science was not pursued by Austin or any of the analytic lawyers who followed him. They left problems of moral choice in the hands of legislators, where they became a matter of politics. The theoreticians of this subject were utilitarian philosophers, theologians or popular preachers, political economists, and politicians themselves.

The evolutionary paradigm suggested a more passive and unimportant role for morality (see chapter 5). While embracing the idea that morality and law were intimately entwined, the evolutionists believed that both developed according to blind historical forces. Even among evolutionists who admitted that human efforts could aid in the march of progress, the direction of progress was itself dictated by evolution, and deliberate improvement in society was perceived as difficult.

The devotees of the moral paradigm, of course, placed precepts of morality at the center of their legal theory (see chapters 1 and 9). But their

22. The pragmatists' approach to morality suggests a kinship with utilitarianism; however, the pragmatists did not accept the simple pleasure-pain psychology of Bentham.

23. The classic historical work on progressivism is R. Hofstader, *The Age of Reform: From Bryan to F.D.R.* (1955).

theory was largely discredited in the late nineteenth century. A few advocates of this view tried to overcome the general opinion among legal theorists that natural law was a figment of philosophers' imaginations, or was a metaphysical abstraction of dubious credibility, or was an ingenious attempt to characterize as objective the personal prejudices and convictions of a deluded theorizer. Talk of a "higher law" might be useful in Fourth of July orations or occasional constitutional rhetoric, but it carried no weight with hard-headed lawyers.

Into this intellectual milieu, where morality had fallen through the cracks, stepped pragmatism. Pragmatism offered a way to justify changes in the law on moral grounds. It offered the chance to advocate a position on questions of public policy that was not based on religion or metaphysics or evolutionary forces, but on the basis of the consequences that the policy would engender. Such an approach had great appeal to reformers who saw the law becoming more and more obsolete in a time when the industrial revolution was rapidly reshaping society. From a theoretical standpoint it only remained to work the general idea of pragmatism into a framework of jurisprudential thinking.

The works of James and Dewey were known to legal thinkers as evidenced by citations in the scholarly literature. Perhaps more important, a popularized but significant pragmatic perspective gradually penetrated the thinking of the time and became a part of the personal credo of many leaders of American society from Theodore Roosevelt to Roscoe Pound; accordingly it eventually became a part of the Poundian paradigm.

Competing Group Interests

Another element in the Poundian paradigm, the notion of law as the result of the conflict of competing interests, owes its origin to the work of a German scholar, Rudolf von Jhering (1818–1892).[24] Jhering was a brilliant follower of the historical school in Germany. Then, in mid-

24. Jhering was a highly respected professor of law at several German universities, his last and longest affiliation being with Göttingen. He was a prolific writer, his best-known works being *Der Geist des römischen Rechts auf den verschiedenen Stufen seiner Entwicklung* (4 vols. 1852–65); *Der Kampf um's Recht* (1872), fifth edition translated as *The Struggle for Law* (trans. Lalor 1879); *Der Zweck im Recht* (2 vols. 1877–83), translated as *Law as a Means to an End* (trans. Husik 1913); *Scherz und Ernst in der Jurisprudenz* (1885); *Der Besitzwille: Zugleich eine Kritik der herrschenden juristischen Methode* (1899). For further biographical and bibliographical information on Jhering, see the introduction and appendixes in R. Jhering, *Law as a Means to an End* (trans. Husik 1913).

career he had doubts; he became a mild skeptic of dogma and advanced the thesis that the law changes and develops as a result of competing social interests. Decisions of courts and enactments of legislatures balance these interests. The balancing may be done intuitively or consciously, usually through the forms of traditional dogma but based on utilitarian considerations.

Of all the parts of Jhering's philosophy the concept of balancing interests was most influential in the development of the Poundian paradigm. The two works most easily available to Americans were *Der Kampf um's Recht* (1872) and *Der Zweck im Recht*.[25] Both went through numerous editions in German.[26]

Jhering argues against Savigny's view that law evolves silently and peaceably as customary morality generally working its way into the culture of a people; rather, he suggests that law is the result of the conflict (struggle) between different interests. Interests themselves are the result of the common egoistic motivation of individuals in society, that is, individuals and groups seek to accomplish their own purposes. For Jhering law does not originate in custom but in legislation (possibly including judicial legislation?); custom conforms itself to the law thus handed down from the crucible of conflict. In spite of a similarity to Marxism on this point, Jhering's thesis suggests that the process is a struggle not between economic classes but between individuals, and especially the myriad groups within society that individuals associate themselves with. Further, he maintains that when enlightened self-interest prevails, there is a "solidarity" of the interests of society and the individual.

Although considered more closely allied to the evolutionary paradigm discussed in chapter 5, the American economic determinists, or neo-Marxist legal theorists, led by Brooks Adams, supported and advanced the principle of the Poundian paradigm that Jhering had identified. They saw law as the result of conflicting interests. For Adams, who envisioned a struggle between economic classes, the public policy that becomes law is not purely the policy of the dominant class. There is always an element of compromise because of the resistance of those people adversely affected. Some of the other authors following this mode of thinking saw the conflict

25. See note 24.

26. Jhering's most extensive and original work was never translated into English but was read by some Americans. This was *Geist des Römischen Rechts auf den verschiedenen Stufen seiner Entwicklung* (4 vols. 1852–65). Also often cited in American jurisprudence was R. Jhering, *Scherz und Ernst in der Jurisprudenz* (1884). A humorous part of this work was translated into English and published in M. Cohen and F. Cohen, eds., *Readings in Jurisprudence and Legal Philosophy*, 678 (1951).

as between various vocational, religious, economic, and other interests, much as Jhering saw it. They also shared a skepticism of the efficacy of formal doctrine to determine judicial decisions.[27]

The most powerful statement of the competing-interests idea offered in the American literature came in 1907 in the form of Arthur F. Bentley's *The Process of Government*. Bentley (1870–1957) was much influenced by Jhering as well as by the German sociological jurist Georg Simmel and by the Austrian Ludwig Gumplowicz.[28] While not a lawyer, Bentley was fully informed about the legal process and about developments in jurisprudence. One chapter of the book is devoted to law and another to the pressure of interests on the judiciary. Bentley's mission was to establish a behavioral approach to the study of government, including law. He was far ahead of his time.

Bentley thought, much like Auguste Compte, that the great impediment to progress in social science was the persistence of ghosts in explanatory theory. The term "ghosts" includes metaphysical and religious concepts as well as "feelings," "faculties," and "capacities." It means the personification of qualities or characteristics. For example, horses are not mistreated today as they were in times past. This is explained by saying that people are becoming more humane.[29] This apparent explanation is no explanation at all. In law legal theory serves as a ghost to "explain" why one wins or loses a case in the courts. Social science must eliminate these ghosts and concentrate on what people (government officials, judges) actually do.

Once attention has been focused on social reality—on activity—it will become apparent that it is a process that the social scientist is attempting to explain. Government becomes comprehensible in terms of competing interest groups and the ways that they exercise influence on officials and

27. See especially an early article by William M. Blatt, The Effect of the Imitative Instinct on the Common Law, 37 Am. L. Rev. 892 (1903).

28. A. Bentley, *The Process of Government* (1907). Bentley devotes an entire subchapter to the work of Jhering. Ibid., 56-90. According to the introduction by Odegard to the 1967 printing of this work, Bentley studied in Germany and was greatly influenced by Simmel and Gumplowicz. Ibid., x. See also ibid., 465–80.

29. Bentley says, "The ordinary question concerns the creating of new psychic qualities, the increasing of the amount of some old ones, the suppressing of some other old ones. The real question we must face—is, why the living, acting men and women change their forms of action, cease to do now what they did formerly, use their 'qualities' in some places and not in others, in short live the particular lives they do live. . . . So long as such 'stuff' is used in explanation of the forms of our social actions on no better ground than that we assume changes in the 'stuff' from the mere fact of the changes in the modes of action, then it is no explanation." Ibid., 18.

on how officials mediate between different groups. Advocacy and technique in advancing a cause become important parts of the explanation of the process. The notion of group struggle is the key to understanding government. Bentley acknowledges the earlier starts in this direction of thinking made by Marx, Jhering, Gumplowicz, and Simmel, but in his view they all failed to rid themselves of ghosts.

Bentley is somewhat impatient with definitions, and his idea of what constitutes the process of government is not clearly spelled out. However, it is a comprehensive view and includes the judicial process. While the judicial process has its peculiar forms, traditions, and personnel, it is at base no different from other governmental activities like legislation and administration.

> When we talk about law we think not of the influencing or pressure as process, but of the status of the activities, the pressures being assumed to have worked themselves through to a conclusion or balance. Of course, the pressures never do as a matter of fact work themselves through to a final balance, and law, stated as a completed balance, is therefore highly abstract. Law is activity, just as government is. It is a group process, just as government is. It is a forming, a systematization, a struggle, an adaptation, of group interests, just as government is.[30]

The basic information that the social scientist must use in explaining the phenomenon of law "cannot be found in the lawbooks. . . . It cannot be found in the 'law' behind the lawbooks. . . ." Nor can it be found in the proceedings of constitutional conventions, legislative histories, or scholarly essays. It can be found in the activity of people. Language, of course, is one form of activity, but it must be placed in the overall context of conflicting interests. Traditional concentration on written sources leads to "an enormous overvaluation of the forms of activity which appear in words." For Bentley legal theory has a role to play in the legal process, but it does not necessarily determine the outcome of cases. Legal theories can be made at various levels of abstraction all the way from what is called legal philosophy down to a particular doctrine of product liability. Advocates devise and advance theories that serve their clients' interests:

> The courts make this theorizing a dignified portion of their work. But they do not decide cases purely in the highly rarefied atmosphere of such theorizing. They decide them by letting the clash of the underly-

30. Ibid., 272.

ing interests work itself out, and then making the theorizing follow suit (not crudely, remember, but as a representative process). Within fairly broad limits theories will be found available for either apparent alternative of activity.[31]

Thus, principles of law or doctrine are peripheral to the real legal process itself, but they may have some stabilizing effect on decision-making.

The theory therefore may be said to function as holding together the system of interests, and as furnishing a short-cut through which the interests that have balanced themselves once may escape being compelled to make their fight all over again and to work out the balance all over again at any and every moment in the process when their adjustment is threatened.[32]

Bentley's contribution was a giant stride toward formation of the Poundian paradigm. He elaborated the conflict-of-interests idea; he played down the importance of substantive law and written doctrine; like Bingham, he directed attention to the actual behavior of courts; he used the notion of function in describing particular activities; and he emphasized a process model rather than a static one. His concept of a total governmental process in which court decision is simply one phase would also prove fruitful.

Sociological Jurisprudence in Germany

Before we can say that the Poundian paradigm became fully articulated in the United States, we must take into account certain developments that were occurring in Germany at the turn of the century.[33] Most of the German scholars and drafters of the German Civil Code were adherents of the evolutionary or expository paradigms. They perceived the new code, a product of the collaboration of many legal workers, as the most advanced and refined statement of law to be found anywhere in the world.[34] For the evolutionists the code represented the restatement of traditional German law as it had evolved over many centuries, but now

31. Ibid., 294–95.
32. Ibid., 397.
33. For a more complete discussion of these developments, see Herget and Wallace, The German Free Law Movement as the Source of American Legal Realism, 73 Va. L. Rev. 399 (1987).
34. The code, in German the *Bürgerliches Gesetzbuch* (BGB), was enacted in 1896 after many years of trial drafts, to become effective January 1, 1900.

shorn of accidental historical quirks and aberrations. For the positivists the code brought authoritative statement, organization, and logical clarity to a law that was theretofore obscure. It was optimistically thought that answers to all questions of civil law could be found authoritatively expounded within the four corners of the code. The duty of the judge, regarded in Germany as a civil servant, was to study the code carefully, construe its provisions in the context of the case at hand, and deduce a conclusion leading to judgment. A resort to extraneous matters in aid of judgment was impermissible; there were no gaps in the code that could not be overcome through analysis and exegesis of the text.

Against this mechanical and formalistic view of the law arose a scholarly reaction that came to be known as the free-law movement.[35] At first led by the novel ideas of French professor François Geny, through his work entitled *Methode de Interpretation et Sources en Droit Prive Positif* (1899), a number of German thinkers led a spirited fight against the dogma about gaps (*die logische Geschlossenheit des Rechts*). Some went farther to challenge the idea of an autonomous legal system and to question the entire expository paradigm itself. The movement reached its high point around 1906 and then faded away when World War I began. In its later stages the scholars of the free-law movement tended to call their work "sociological jurisprudence."

The outpouring of articles, books, and pamphlets that constitute the free-law movement established a jurisprudential position that is almost equivalent to that manifestation of the Poundian paradigm later to be known in the United States as "legal realism." The free-law thinkers regard the function of the judge as creative. They call for better-educated judges trained in the social sciences who would reject mechanical arguments, balance the competing interests present in every lawsuit so as to maximize the public good, and use their knowledge of society to arrive at just decisions. Such creative judicial labor is called "free-law finding." Traditional methods of interpretation and reasoning, regarded as outmoded scholasticism, are to be distrusted. The free-law thinkers believe that certainty in the law is illusion: indeed, formal legal opinions in which conclusions are reached through highly conceptualized reasoning are regarded as false and illusory. Free-law advocates urge judges to direct their attention to the real sources of law, those sources outside the hollow formal system. They stress the importance of applying the methods and tools of empirical social science to law.

The literature of the free-law movement served as the main source of in-

35. Herget and Wallace, note 33, 407.

spiration for Roscoe Pound in his early years and as a rich lode to be mined by other Americans somewhat later. The free-law message would seriously change American thinking about the legal process and its problems.

Roscoe Pound's Consolidating Work

Roscoe Pound (1870–1964) was a remarkable man.[36] He was a success at everything he undertook, at least until around the age of sixty-five. He was briefly a first-rate botanist; he was good at the practice of law; he served as an appellate judge for a few years in Nebraska, his home state. He absorbed an immense amount of learning about the law in only one year at the Harvard Law School. He became one of the best-known legal reformers of the progressive era. He promoted an unprecedented harmonious relationship between the practicing bar and the law schools. He became the guru of American jurisprudence, writing a truly amazing number of articles and books. His ideas and insights were not original, but he had an unusual capacity for assimilating the thinking of diverse scholars. Above all, the man read everything.

Although Pound's native language was English, he began reading German at age six. He developed a voracious appetite for legal literature in both languages, especially on jurisprudence. His citations to sources are accurate, and his discussion of them indicates that he understood them. We are, therefore, safe in concluding that he actually read and digested the great bulk of the material that he cited. The German authors he principally relied upon included Dernburg, Ehrlich, Gumplowicz, Jhering, Kohler, Stammler, the jurisprudential encyclopedias of Fritz Berolzheimer, and a half-dozen free-law scholars;[37] Pound was especially impressed with the thinking of Jhering and Kohler. He was also familiar with the work of all of the British theorists, including Bentham, Austin, Amos, Holland, Clark, Salmond, Pollock, Dicey, and Maine, as well as the classic seventeenth- and eighteenth-century European philosophers. He occasionally cited French and Italian sources. Among his own compatriots he frequently cited lawyers Gray, Wigmore, Carter, and Holmes, and less frequently Terry, Brooks Adams, Kocourek, George H. Smith, and Hammond. He was especially fond of the sociological theories of Albion Small, Edward Ross, and

36. See D. Wigdor, *Roscoe Pound: Philosopher of Law* (1974); P. Sayre *The Life of Roscoe Pound* (1948).

37. Among the free-law thinkers, Pound's favorite was Hermann Kantorowicz. Pound often translated quotations at length from his works.

Lester Ward. He admired Bentley's work, and he drew upon the thought of William James. Pound was a colleague and associate of many of these individuals in his successive university tenures at Nebraska, Northwestern, Chicago, and Harvard. He also was personally familiar with others.[38]

Pound began articulating many of the ideas of the free-law movement early in his scholarly career. In fact his first jurisprudential article, published in 1904, described the emerging viewpoint of the free-law thinkers as "A New School of Jurists."[39] In the next seven years he published almost a dozen articles pursuing this theme, compounding it with the thought of the American sociologists and his pleas for reform.[40] In 1911 and 1912 Pound produced a three-part article in the *Harvard Law Review* that consolidated much of his previous work and presented in outline form what sociological jurisprudence was all about.[41]

In Pound's view sociological jurisprudence was a scholarly activity to be engaged in by theorists of the law like himself. This theoretical work would presumably guide judges, legislators, and legal scholars. However, at certain points in his writings Pound almost equates sociological jurisprudence with sociology itself. At other points, less frequently, he blurs the distinctions between political reform, social work, and sociology. In his program for sociological jurisprudence there are elements that would be compatible with all three kinds of activity.[42]

Pound suggests that the following positions and attitudes characterize sociological jurisprudence.[43] Study of the law should move away from the analysis of appellate court opinions and toward the effectiveness of trial-

38. See Wigdor, note 36.

39. Pound, A New School of Jurists, 4 U. Neb. Studies 249 (1904).

40. Pound, The Decadence of Equity, 5 Colum. L. Rev. 20 (1905); Pound, Do We Need a Philosophy of Law?, 5 Colum. L. Rev. 339 (1905); Pound, Spurious Interpretation, 7 Colum. L. Rev. 379 (1907); Pound, The Need for a Sociological Jurisprudence, 19 Green Bag 607 (1907); Pound, Enforcement of Law, 20 Green Bag 401 (1908); Pound, The German Movement for Reform in Legal Administration and Procedure, 1 Bull. Comp. L. Bureau A.B.A. 32 (1908); Pound, Mechanical Jurisprudence, 8 Colum. L. Rev. 605 (1908); Pound, Common Law and Legislation, 21 Harv. L. Rev. 383 (1908); Pound, Law in Books and Law in Action, 44 Am. L. Rev. 12 (1910). For a fuller discussion of these works, see Herget and Wallace, note 33.

41. Pound, The Scope and Purpose of Sociological Jurisprudence (pts. 1–3), 24 Harv. L. Rev. 591 (1911), 25 Harv. L. Rev. 140, 489 (1912).

42. See Geis, Sociology and Sociological Jurisprudence: Admixture of Lore and Law, 52 Ky. L. J. 267 (1964). Pound himself participated in only one empirical study, the "Cleveland Project." See Wigdor, *Roscoe Pound: Philosopher of Law*, 242–46 (1974).

43. See Pound, note 41.

court operations. The emphasis should be on the process of law in its social context; the study of abstract doctrine should be deemphasized. The main province of the scholar's inquiry should be the actual effects— the factual consequences—of legal doctrine, court decisions, and legislation. This means that legislation should be based on empirical studies of social consequences, not merely on comparative analysis of the statutes themselves or armchair speculation about statutory efficacy. Likewise, legal history should abandon the sterile chronicling of doctrinal change and relate legal changes to the social context. Courts and scholars alike should recognize that certainty in law is illusory and that legal precepts should be taken as flexible guides to decision-making so that justice can be achieved in individual cases. Purposes of the law, not sanctions, should be emphasized. Finally, law must be treated instrumentally; it is always a means to an end. The pragmatic philosophy must be adapted to the legal enterprise.[44]

These elements were all in place in Pound's theory by 1912. In footnotes to several articles he reveals that the law-review materials advancing sociological jurisprudence are to be incorporated in a forthcoming book that will set forth a complete statement of the new theory. Although Pound published numerous books in subsequent years, the long-awaited treatise on sociological jurisprudence never materialized. Very likely Pound recognized that his early theory was incomplete. It originally contained no critical element, no basis for determining good from bad law. Pound went to work on this problem sporadically in the period from 1912 through 1923 and gradually worked out a theory of "interests" and "jural postulates." In this endeavor Pound again drew from the thinking of other scholars. Because Pound never integrated all of his insights systematically, he appeared to have no grand theory, thus prompting numerous writers in the twenties and thirties to offer their own versions of Pound's "sociological jurisprudence."[45] This lack of a systematic statement also made it more difficult for critics to attack his views.

Pound was not concerned with defining the word "law" or in straightening out terminological puzzles. For him law consisted of those precepts,

44. In an early essay Pound said, "The sociological movement in jurisprudence is a movement for pragmatism as a philosophy of law." Pound, Mechanical Jurisprudence, 8 Colum. L. Rev. 605, 609 (1908). However, in 1911 he modified his view to say, "A pragmatist philosophy of law is yet to come. When it is promulgated it may expect many adherents from the sociological jurists." Pound, note 41, 516.

45. Pound's own theory is improved upon and elaborated by his disciple, Julius Stone, in J. Stone, *The Province and Function of Law* (1950).

techniques, and ideals used in the process of decision-making by courts and legislatures; but it was the entire process itself that jurisprudence was required to take into account, and this involved much more than the formal law. Law was to be made on the basis of the consequences it would bring about. Formal legal doctrine and often legislation were sufficiently vague and general that they did not dictate the judicial decision in individual cases, at least in novel cases, and attempts to rely solely on formal sources could lead to unjust results. Courts must not mislead themselves or others by manipulating legal concepts to arrive at conclusions actually dictated by other reasons. In order to decide well, courts must know as much of the consequences of their decisions as possible. This is a task for the sociological investigator, which the legal scholar must therefore become. Empirical data is essential. Funds must be channeled into empirical legal research through the universities and institutes established for that purpose. The old-fashioned judge's method of relying on abstract doctrine or principles arrived at deductively from absolute moral principles must be rejected. Legislators, likewise, must look to consequences in the enactment of laws.[46]

What is lacking in this view is some means to evaluate the consequences of the adoption of legal precepts and rules. Once a court has put aside its previous bad habits and looked squarely at the probable alternative effects of its decision, on what basis does it choose the "right" alternative? As a confirmed reformer, Pound believed that objective moral standards existed, but he could not accept the dogmatic and metaphysical approach of the natural-law school. Instead, he drew upon the theory of three eminent scholars, Jhering, Kohler, and James, to formulate his own theory. While the critical side of Pound's theory is not spelled out in any single work, it can be pieced together from several sources.[47]

---

46. As applied to legislation this view is not markedly different from Bentham's (without the apparatus of the felicific calculus). In fact, Jhering, upon whom Pound relied for his theory of social interests, was sometimes called the German Bentham. However, in the arena of judicial lawmaking, Bentham did not have a sophisticated conception; indeed, his view of this is diametrically opposed to Pound's. See the discussion in chapter 1.

47. See, R. Pound, *Outlines of Lectures on Jurisprudence* (2d ed. 1914); R. Pound, *Introduction to American Law* (1919); R. Pound, *The Spirit of the Common Law* (1921); Pound, Legislation as a Social Function, 18 Am. J. Sociol. 755 (1913); Pound, Justice According to Law (pts. 1–3), 13 Colum. L. Rev. 696 (1913), 14 Colum. L. Rev. 1, 103 (1914); Pound, The End of Law as Developed in Legal Rules and Doctrines, 27 Harv. L. Rev. 195 (1914); Pound, The End of Law as Developed in Juristic Thought

Pound was tempted to find the ethical basis for the evaluation of law in the same place Bentham had found it—in the psyche of the human animal.[48] Instead of a crude psychology of pleasure and pain, however, Pound was attracted to the notion of "instinct" as it was being propounded by contemporary psychologists. If instincts common to all human animals could be identified and categorized, then the satisfaction of those instincts would be the goal of social life in general and of the legal system in particular. A teleology could be established in which the ultimate test of good or bad would lie in the harmonization of human instincts. But Pound concluded that psychologists had not come to any firm agreement on the nature of instincts, and therefore such a concept would make a shaky foundation for any theory of morals.

Instead Pound turned to the more familiar juristic notion of interests, but interests empirically established. To Pound the processes of both adjudication and legislation are viewed as an activity of government officials in which various claims are made by groups or individuals upon the decision-making body. To have a chance of being accepted, these claims must be more than mere personal demands; they are asserted to be morally right, accepted by society, and generally applicable to some particular class or group of persons. Following the lead of Jhering, Pound calls these claims "interests" and classifies them into individual interests, social interests, and public interests; however, any interest can be cast in terms of a social interest,[49] and it is this category that becomes significant in Pound's solution to the problem of evaluating the law.

After surveying substantially all of the interests that have been and are being urged upon courts and legislatures in a given society, as well as those that seem to be incorporated into legal institutions themselves, one can generalize the specific interests into a smaller inventory of social interests

---

(pts. 1–2), 27 Harv. L. Rev. 605 (1914), 30 Harv. L. Rev. 201 (1917); Pound, Juristic Science and Law, 31 Harv. L. Rev. 1047 (1918); Pound, A Theory of Social Interests, 15 Proc. Am. Sociol. Soc. 16 (1921); Pound, The Theory of Judicial Decision (pts. 1–3), 36 Harv. L. Rev. 640, 802, 940 (1923). See also, R. Pound, *An Introduction to the Philosophy of Law* (1922); R. Pound, *Interpretations of Legal History* (1923); Pound, *Law and Morals* (1926).

48. Pound, A Theory of Social Interests, 15 Proc. Am. Soc. Sociol. 16, 30–32 (1921). The psychological and sociological writings cited by Pound on this matter are: W. McDougall, *Introduction to Social Psychology* (11th ed. 1916); E. Hayes, *Introduction to the Study of Sociology* (1918); S. Colvin and W. Bagley, *Human Behavior* (1913); E. Ross, *Principles of Sociology* (1920); H. Marshall, *Instinct and Reason* (1898).

49. See J. Stone, note 45, 490–91.

stated in more general terms. Admitting some arbitrariness in this process, Pound lists seven prime social interests for his own society: (1) general security, (2) security of social institutions like family, church, and state, (3) general morals, (4) conservation of resources, (5) general progress, that is, cultural development, individual economic and personal self-realization, (6) aesthetic improvement, and (7) individual life and liberty.

These social interests, or some similar categorization, derived empirically from the actual interests asserted (and often but not always realized or "secured") in a given society imply or "presuppose" even more general normative propositions that Pound, following Kohler, calls "jural postulates."[50] It is not entirely clear whether these postulates are derived through generalization from social interests or through generalization from the rules and principles of the legal system. If the latter, of course they would simply generalize the public policy of the status quo. Pound asserts, however, that both the social interests and the jural postulates may change over time as a civilization changes, and indeed these postulates are supposed to be the general moral principles that a civilization cultivates in order to advance itself. This Hegelian notion of self-development comes through the work of Kohler but seems not to be essential to Pound's scheme. In fact, there seems to be some duplication of function between the social interests and the jural postulates.[51]

Whether social interests or jural postulates are used as the measuring stick, the consequences of legislative and judicial decisions can be measured against them. The question can be asked: what social interests would be advanced by invoking or enacting rule of law X, and what would be impeded? However, even with the availability of these standards, a decision is not necessarily determined, because in most cases a particular legal decision will advance some social interests and impede others. The ultimate test is taken from the pragmatism of William James. "The law is an attempt to reconcile, to harmonize, to compromise these overlapping or conflicting interests . . . so as to give effect to the greatest number of interests or to the interests that weigh most in our civilization, with the least sacrifice of other interests."[52]

In the Poundian paradigm there are no absolute moral standards, but there are objective standards to guide decisions that relate to the specific

50. A formulation of these jural postulates can be found in R. Pound, *Outlines of Lectures on Jurisprudence* (2d ed. 1914); they are revised in R. Pound, *Outlines of Lectures on Jurisprudence*, 168–84 (5th ed. 1943).

51. See Stone, A Critique of Pound's Theory of Justice, 20 Iowa L. Rev. 531 (1935).

52. Pound, note 48, 44.

society and legal system in question. These standards are to be derived empirically by surveying and cataloging the various interests asserted and recognized in that society. This activity of inventorying and abstracting also becomes a task of the legal-sociological scholar. But it is not a task that can be accomplished once and for all. "New wants and new forms of old wants speedily make the best products of social engineering no less than of mechanical engineering insufficient and obsolete, and our instincts of curiosity and construction lead us to new devices by which to satisfy a greater number of wants."[53]

Although he continued to revise and assert his theories throughout the rest of his long life, Pound's significant contributions to jurisprudence were essentially completed by 1923. In that year he published a three-part article in which he brought several of the various strands of his theory to bear on the process of judicial decision-making.[54] Just a few years later his views surprisingly seemed to come into conflict with views of scholars who had come later to adopt the Poundian paradigm. Although this debate proved to be intellectually a superficial tempest in a teapot, it did precipitate other critiques of the Poundian paradigm and its extension, legal realism, that were of greater significance.

---

53. Ibid., 45.
54. Pound, The Theory of Judicial Decision (pts. 1–3), 36 Harv. L. Rev. 640, 802, 940 (1923).

THE NEW PARADIGM
ACCEPTED, EXTENDED,
CRITICIZED
1912–41

Although the second and third decades of the twentieth century were in many respects the high point of the expository paradigm, the legal literature nevertheless had room for more than one point of view. Others besides Pound began to articulate the new paradigm. In 1910 the Association of American Law Schools authorized the publication of a series of books containing translations of foreign legal philosophy.[1] This resulted in the publication of Jhering's *Law as a Means to an End* in 1913, *Kohler's Philosophy of Law* in 1914, and *The Science of Legal Method* in 1917. The latter contained a number of the better works of the free-law movement, including seminal pieces by Geny, Wurzel, and Ehrlich. Some of the free-law ideas were also discussed by Albert Kocourek in a 1914 article.[2]

As others began to explore the contours of the new way of thinking,[3] a second edition of John Chipman Gray's *The Nature and Sources of the*

1. This project, called the Modern Legal Philosophy Series, was guided by Pound and Wigmore. See the bibliography.

2. Kocourek, The Formal Relation between Law and Discretion, 9 Ill. L. Rev. 225 (1914).

3. See, e.g., Cohen, The Process of Judicial Legislation, 48 Am. L. Rev. 176 (1914); Brandeis, Living Law, 10 Ill. L. Rev. 461 (1916); Ehrlich, Montesquieu and Sociological Jurisprudence, 29 Harv. L. Rev. 582 (1916); Drake, The Sociological Interpretation of Law, 12 Mich. L. Rev. 599 (1918); Schroeder, The Psychologic Study of Judicial Opinions, 6 Calif. L. Rev. 89 (1918); M. Smith, Jurisprudence (1919); Vinogradoff, The Crisis of Modern Jurisprudence, 29 Yale L. J. 312 (1920); Oliphant, Current Discussions of Legal Methodology, 7 A.B.A.J. 241 (1921).

Law was published in 1919, and a second edition (in French) of free-law thinker François Geny's *Method of Interpretation and Sources of Law* came out in 1921. Perhaps most important in giving credence to the new view was the publication of Benjamin Cardozo's (1870–1938) Storrs lectures at Yale University in 1921.[4] Relying heavily on Pound and the free-law authors, Cardozo (acknowledged) that he and other judges did and should use the "sociological method."

Entitled *The Nature of the Judicial Process*, Cardozo's work offered an analysis of the methods that he and presumably other judges used in the resolution of cases. His approach was eclectic. He described first the method of philosophy, or logic: straightforward logical application of the obviously relevant rules of law to the facts of a case. This was presumptively the preferred method if it worked, reflecting the traditional approach of judges in the lawmaking process. However, Cardozo noted that the obvious method did not work in many cases, especially at the appellate level. The alternatives were the method of history, or tradition, and the method of sociology. The former involved an effort to find the rationale for a decision in its historical growth; the latter was a more deliberate legislative approach in which the judge tries to craft a decision that meets the needs of public policy as best she can ascertain it. To do this she must have a contextual understanding of the consequences of her decision and an understanding of the social wants and needs of the time; in short, she must take a sociological approach.

Cardozo's lectures showed that he accepted the major premises of the Poundian paradigm without, however, offering any original theoretical contributions. At the same time, because of his eclecticism, he was willing to see some truth in the expository and evolutionary paradigms, which were in opposition to the Poundian. His exposition was, therefore, philosophically unsatisfactory, but it had considerable influence because of his prestige as an eminent appellate judge (later a Supreme Court justice) and because it was one of the first sophisticated public discussions by a judge of judicial legislating.

Further elaboration of the Poundian paradigm followed in the legal periodicals. Charles Grove Haines (1879–1948) reiterated the teachings of the free-law thinkers in a provocative article.[5] He also introduced some statistics that suggested arbitrary decision-making by New York City

4. B. Cardozo, *The Nature of the Judicial Process* (1921).

5. Haines, General Observations on the Effects of Personal, Political, and Economic Influences in the Decisions of Judges, 17 Ill. L. Rev. 96 (1922).

magistrates in minor criminal cases and called for the gathering of more statistical information. Haines even proposed a classification of factors likely to influence judicial decisions.[6]

The year 1919 saw the popularization of Watson's influential work on behaviorism in psychology,[7] which eventually had its impact on legal scholarship. Professor G.H.T. Malan of Cape Town University, South Africa, was commissioned to explain to members of the American Bar Association how the science of law should be placed on a behavioristic basis.[8] Professor Underhill Moore (1879–1949) of Columbia University gave an incisive and caustic review of the Wigmore and Kocourek book, *The Rational Basis of Legal Institutions*, in the pages of the *Columbia Law Review*.[9] While debunking the book, Moore maintained that only a rigorous behaviorist approach to the study of law can be scientific. Moore continued his crusade for behaviorism in law in subsequent years (see chapter 10). Other articles reflecting the adoption of part or all of the Poundian paradigm began to multiply,[10] including an important speech in

6. Ibid., 116. His rather unimaginative scheme was as follows:
"A. Remote and Indirect—
    1. Education—
      (a) General.
      (b) Legal.
    2. Family and personal association; wealth and social position.
B. Direct—
    1. Legal and political experience.
    2. Political affiliations and opinions.
    3. Intellectual and temperamental traits."

7. J. Watson, *Psychology from the Standpoint of a Behaviorist* (1919). Watson's original work was J. Watson, *Behavior: An Introduction to Comparative Psychology* (1914).

8. Malan, The Behavioristic Basis of the Science of Law (2 pts.), 8 A.B.A.J. 737 (1922), and 9 A.B.A.J. 43 (1923).

9. Moore, The Rational Basis of Legal Institutions, 23 Colum. L. Rev. 609 (1923).

10. See Oliphant, Study of the Operation of the Rules of Law, 9 A.B.A.J. 497 (1923); Frank, An Institutional Analysis of the Law, 24 Colum. L. Rev. 480 (1924); Wormser, Sociology and the Law, 1 N.Y.U.Q.L. Rev. 8 (1924); Wu, The Juristic Philosophy of Roscoe Pound, 18 Ill. L. Rev. 285 (1924); Dewey, Logical Method and the Law, 10 Corn. L. Q. 17 (1924); Radin, The Theory of Judicial Decision: Or How Judges Think, 11 A.B.A.J. 357 (1925); Cook, Scientific Method and the Law, 13 A.B.A.J. 303 (1927); Harper, Forms of Law and Moral Content, 22 Ill. L. Rev. 259 (1927); Yntema, The Hornbook Method and the Conflict of Laws, 37 Yale L. J. 468 (1928); Green, The Duty Problem in Negligence Cases, 28 Colum. L. Rev. 1014 (1928); Hutcheson, The Judgment Intuitive: The Function of the "Hunch" in Judicial Decision, 14 Corn. L. Q. 274 (1929).

1927 by Herman Oliphant (1884–1939), president of the Association of American Law Schools.[11]

After Pound became dean at the Harvard Law School in 1916, it might have been expected that the Harvard law curriculum would be reformed to some extent to reflect the new line of thinking. This was not to be the case, however. Instead, the Columbia University law school led the way in applying the new paradigm to legal education.[12] A two-year curriculum study was undertaken by the Columbia faculty in 1926. The reforms suggested and debated were essentially of two kinds. First, the traditional curriculum with its courses based on common-law categories like estates in land, torts, contracts, and so on, seemed to be out of touch with the realities of modern law.[13] The industrial revolution had also revolutionized the practice of law, introducing new subject areas and changing the relevance of old ones. It was proposed that courses be restructured to cut across traditional lines so as to reflect the contemporary functions of law. Second, teaching and research in law was to be made more scientific, not in the old Austinian or Langdellian sense, but in the mode of contemporary social science. Students and faculty were to explore law in its social context with a view toward improving it.

The Columbia curriculum study was the first and only significant effort to reorient legal education in America since the time of Langdell. A two-hundred-page summary of the recommendations prepared by Professor Oliphant in 1928 was circulated throughout the law-school world. This summary was nothing less than the program of sociological jurisprudence applied to legal education, and if the authorship had not been known, a reader would likely assume that Roscoe Pound had written it.

For various reasons, mostly unrelated to the merits of the curriculum recommendations, the sweeping reforms were not adopted by the Columbia faculty. This resulted in several professors leaving Columbia for greener pastures, including three who founded the Law Institute at Johns

11. Oliphant, A Return to Stare Decisis (2 pts.), 14 A.B.A.J. 71, 159 (1928). This printed speech, actually delivered in 1927, has sometimes been noted as the beginning of the "realist" movement. L. Kalman, *Legal Realism at Yale, 1927–1960* (1986); Herget and Wallace, The German Free Law Movement as the Source of American Legal Realism, 73 Va. L. Rev. 399, 431 (1987).

12. The best short account of this is W. Twining, *Karl Llewellyn and the Realist Movement*, 41–69 (1973).

13. These were essentially the course categories established at Harvard under Langdell's administration. It should be pointed out, however, that these courses were contemporary in Langdell's day and differed markedly from the categorization of subject matter presented a century earlier by Blackstone.

Hopkins University,[14] and two who went to Yale, where a movement toward "scientific" legal research was beginning.[15] However, many of the reforms did eventually work their way piecemeal into law-school programs at Columbia, Yale, and elsewhere.

Critique Of The New Wisdom

As the Poundian paradigm became increasingly respectable, a few doubts about it were raised in print. As early as 1916 Morris R. Cohen (1880–1947) scolded Pound, Bentley, Brooks Adams, and some of the free-law thinkers for their denigration of deductive logic, although Cohen was sympathetic to their exposure of the misuse of logic.[16] French lawyer Pierre Lepaulle argued incisively against Pound's theory in 1922.[17] He thought that Pound's theory of interests was subject to the same intractable difficulties as Bentham's utilitarianism, that is, the weight to be accorded various claims in the balancing process was problematic, and the impracticality of such a balancing process made it futile. Lepaulle further pointed out that Pound had assumed the doubtful proposition first advanced by William James that the assertion of a claim and nothing more legitimates it. He also stated that sociological jurisprudence was a misnomer in that sociology dealt with facts, was value-neutral, and could not define or produce social goals.

Three years later Fordham law professor Walter B. Kennedy (1885–1945) attacked pragmatism as a philosophy of law from the standpoint of natural law.[18] He argued that Pound's failure to admit the validity of natural rights and take them into account poisoned his whole scheme. Kennedy further maintained that Pound's balancing of interests by judges was practically impossible and that interests, as collective demands for satisfaction of wants, were poor guides to decision because they were not

14. They included Leon C. Marshall, Herman Oliphant, and Hessel Yntema. See the discussion in chapter 8.

15. The two were William O. Douglas and Underhill Moore. In 1927 Robert Maynard Hutchins had been appointed dean of the Yale Law School at age twenty-eight partly because he favored empirical research directed toward reform. See Schlegel, American Legal Realism and Empirical Social Science: From the Yale Experience, 28 Buff. L. Rev. 459, 468–77 (1979).

16. Cohen, The Place of Logic in the Law, 29 Harv. L. Rev. 622 (1916).

17. Lepaulle, The Function of Comparative Law with a Critique of Sociological Jurisprudence, 35 Harv. L. Rev. 838 (1922).

18. Kennedy, Pragmatism as a Philosophy of Law, 9 Marq. L. Rev. 63 (1925).

necessarily good. He offered the analogy to a child who wants to eat all the candy he can; in Kennedy's view Pound's theory would require that this unworthy demand be satisfied or at least "balanced" with others. These early criticisms, however close to the mark, were nevertheless few and far between, and Pound's general approach was gradually accepted by more and more scholars, and it remained mostly unchallenged by others through the 1920s.

Some intellectual jousting in the law journals in 1930 and 1931 seemed to demonstrate that the Poundian paradigm, if it had not become dominant, was indeed taken seriously by all those who dealt in the currency of legal theory. In fact, it was accepted by many younger scholars as the guide to new directions in legal research. Youthful exuberance led to some extreme statements of jurisprudential positions that were simply extensions of the Poundian paradigm by these younger academics, leading in turn to severe criticism of what came to be called "legal realism."

The Great Nondebate

What at the time appeared to be a great jurisprudential battle[19] began in 1930 with the publication of two books, Jerome Frank's (1889–1957) *Law and the Modern Mind*[20] and Karl Llewellyn's (1893–1962) *The Bramble Bush*,[21] and a law-review article by Llewellyn.[22] The Frank book was devoted to the thesis that law, in the sense of what courts will actually do, is inherently uncertain, and this must be hidden through techniques of illusion because of a Freudian desire for security that makes people crave certainty in their law. The Llewellyn book was a series of lectures that the author had given to entering law students at the Columbia law school in which he explained that courts have immense discretionary leeway in their decision-making and that much of the art of the lawyer

19. A cursory summary is given here since this has already been recounted in some detail. See W. Twining, *Karl Llewellyn and the Realist Movement*, 70–83 (1973); G. White, *Patterns of American Legal Thought*, 122–31 (1978); Hull, Some Realism about the Lewellyn-Pound Exchange over Realism, 1987 Wis. L. Rev. 921.

20. J. Frank, *Law and the Modern Mind* (1930). Frank was a New York practitioner and part-time lecturer in law at Yale. He later became a judge of the Second U. S. Court of Appeals in New York.

21. K. Llewellyn, *The Bramble Bush* (1930). Llewellyn had been a participant in the great curriculum debate at Columbia.

22. Llewellyn, A Realistic Jurisprudence—The Next Step, 30 Colum. L. Rev. 431 (1930).

is in knowing how to stretch or shrink precedents. It is this booklet that contains the famous statement by Llewellyn, "What these [government] officials do about disputes is, to my mind, the law itself."

The law-review article by Llewellyn, then thirty-four years of age, suggested that a group of young law teachers (of which he was one) was implementing a new method or approach toward the study and understanding of law. In a loose and rambling discourse, perhaps not well thought through, Llewellyn terms this new method "a realistic jurisprudence," although he denied several times that it constituted a "school of thought" or "philosophy of law." The features of the new method, it turns out, are almost exactly those spelled out in Pound's 1912 article on sociological jurisprudence, perhaps supplemented in details by the Bingham and Bentley works.[23] In fact Llewellyn admits that the ideas are not new,[24] but have only recently been put into practice by "realists." He says of Pound's past work, "It is full to bursting of magnificent insight," but he criticizes Pound for not applying his jurisprudential insights to everyday scholarship and for the "constant indeterminacy of the level of his discourse." Had this article stood alone, it might have been interpreted as an elaboration of Pound's earlier work in certain directions, in spite of its mild criticism of the Harvard dean.[25]

However, in the following year Pound saw fit to respond to it and apparently to the two books of 1930.[26] The response was not up to Pound's standards, and, indeed, it impresses the reader as something

23. Pound, The Scope and Purpose of Sociological Jurisprudence (pts. 1–3), 24 Harv. L. Rev. 591 (1911), 25 Harv. L. Rev. 140, 489 (1912). See the discussion in chapter 6.

24. "I am not concerned here with whether prior writers may have contributed to, or anticipated, some or all of these ideas. Pound saw them, he formulated them, he drove them home. But these brilliant buddings have in the main not come to fruition." Llewellyn, note 22, 435, fn. 3.

25. The unusual prose style of Llewellyn could conceivably have led readers to think that what he was saying was more revolutionary than it was. A sample: "I see no value to be gained from the interests-rights and rules-remedies set up except to bring out, to underscore, that law is not all, nor yet the major part of, society; and as a matter of method, to provide words which keep legal and non-legal aspects of the situation and the interactions distinct. And it would seem to go without demonstration that *the most significant* (I do *not* say the *only* significant) aspects of the relations of law and society lie in the field of behavior, and that words take on importance either because and insofar as they are behavior, or because and insofar as they demonstrably reflect or influence other behavior. This statement seems not worth making." Llewellyn, note 22, at 443. The use of italics for emphasis peppers the text throughout.

26. Pound, The Call for a Realist Jurisprudence, 44 Harv. L. Rev. 697 (1931).

carelessly dashed off between more important endeavors (fifteen pages, no footnotes). Pound rather generously gives encouragement to the "younger teachers of law." He says, "Here is an important movement in the science of law, and it behooves us to understand it and be thinking of it." But he also offers five rather mild criticisms, duly qualified,[27] of "current juridical realism." In retrospect they seem to be aimed primarily at Frank's rather extreme book and at some unnamed enthusiastic statistics-gatherers, but Pound does not say who his targets are. Pound then offers, somewhat officiously, his own seven-point program to expand the new jurisprudence, all of which had appeared in his earlier writings. Perhaps most regrettable on Pound's part was his failure to recognize that the "realist" work that Llewellyn endorsed and encouraged was simply the application of the Poundian paradigm to specific fields such as commercial law, contracts, procedure, evidence, and others. These applications were for the most part empirical studies of the consequences of legal rules, decisions, and concepts. The young scholars were doing exactly what Pound had said they must do back in 1912.

Pound's reply prompted a response from Llewellyn and Frank that perhaps generated more heat than light.[28] Taking their own selections and evaluations of realist scholars' writings, they show that Pound's criticisms were generally wide of the mark. Having proved their case in this way, they proceed to outline nine "common points of departure" that are characteristic of "real" realists.[29] Again, these proved to be the main components of the early Poundian program for sociological jurispru-

27. "It is unfair to take any one item, or even set of items, from one or more of its adherents and assume that it may be fastened upon the formative school as characteristic dogma." Ibid., 700.

28. Llewellyn, Some Realism about Realism—Responding to Dean Pound, 44 Harv. L. Rev. 1222 (1931). Llewellyn states in a footnote that the article is really a joint product of Jerome Frank and himself, but for reasons not explained Frank declined to put his name to it.

29. In abbreviated form these were: (1) The conception of law in flux . . . and of judicial creation of law. (2) The conception of law as a means to social ends and not as an end in itself. (3) The conception of society in flux . . . so that the probability is always given that any portion of law need reexamination. . . . (4) The temporary divorce of Is and Ought for purposes of study. (5) Distrust of traditional legal rules and concepts. . . . (6) . . . Distrust of the traditional theory that traditional prescriptive rule-formulations are the heavily operative factor in producing court decisions. (7) . . . Grouping cases and legal situations into narrower categories than has been the practice. (8) An insistence on evaluation of any part of the law in terms of its effects. . . . (9) Insistence on sustained and programmatic attack on the problems of law along any of these lines. Ibid., 1229ff.

dence.[30] The article then traces some of the work being done, much of it involving empirical studies, within the realist perspective. The lack of an ethical or normative dimension to this perspective is explained by saying that realism is not a philosophical school. At another point the authors seem to regard this as a positive feature.[31] Yet, the amazingly naive statement is also made that "there is very general agreement on the need for courts to face squarely the policy questions in their cases, and use the full freedom precedent affords in working toward the conclusions that seem indicated."

So what was debated in the great debate? The tone of the argument and the roles of the participants probably made it seem more confrontational than it was; the brash young Turks full of enthusiasm were pitted against the old master of bygone truths. But it seems clear, with the advantage of historical hindsight, that Pound and the realists displayed no significant jurisprudential differences in the course of the scholarly exchange.[32] At the time, however, it must have appeared that Pound was on one side of the jurisprudential fence and the realists on the other. This also meant that "realism" would be regarded by many contemporaries as a new jurisprudence.

There did remain one serious difference in overall theory, although it was obscured by the form that the pseudo-debate took. While Llewellyn was pragmatic in his outlook, he seemed to assume that empirically solid legal scholars could somehow distinguish bad from good results and that they had a firm grasp of what public policy required in any particular context. He failed to see the ethical problem, the problem of evaluation of law, as being inherent in the type of work he endorsed.[33] As we have seen,

30. The reader will recall that Pound developed his early program without the ethical side (Pound, note 23); Llewellyn had arrived at the same point in his own thinking and went further to approve explicitly a "divorce of the Is from the Ought."

31. "When the matter of *program in the normative aspect* is raised, the answer is: *there is none.*" Llewellyn, note 28, 1254.

32. Others have come to the same conclusion. See R. Summers, *Instrumentalism and American Legal Theory*, 23 (1982); W. Rumble, *American Legal Realism*, 13 (1968); A. Hunt, *The Sociological Movement in Law*, 38, 41 (1978); Hull, Reconstructing the Origins of Realistic Jurisprudence, 1989 Duke L. J. 1302; Herget and Wallace, note 33; Walter, The Legal Ecology of Roscoe Pound, 4 Miami L. Q. 178 (1950).

33. In fairness to Llewellyn it should be noted that he did develop an ethical dimension in his best work, *The Cheyenne Way*, in the guise of "law jobs." The law jobs are those functions that law must perform in order to hold society together. His articulation of the law jobs is strikingly reminiscent of Pound's general "social interests." See K. Llewellyn and E. Hoebel, *The Cheyenne Way*, 290–309 (1941); also, W. Twining, *Karl Llewellyn and the Realist Movement*, 153–69 (1973).

Pound had faced that problem as early as 1913 and had ultimately worked out his own theoretical solution.

The Real Debates

In the months and years following the great nondebate, a series of real debates took place over the worth of the Poundian paradigm, particularly in its realist version. The course of this scholarly exchange was obscured, however, by the fact that there were several points at issue, although many of the participants seemed to think there was only one. While the intellectual give and take was important for American jurisprudence, we will have to be content in this account with a brief description and an identification of the main proponents and the principal points they made.

One of the more interesting direct exchanges was one between Felix S. Cohen and Walter B. Kennedy over "functionalism" in jurisprudence, with Cohen, the realist, advocating a functional approach and Kennedy, the traditionalist, debunking it.[34] Equally enlightening was an attempt to follow a pure behavioral approach in a study of banking law by Underhill Moore and Gilbert Sussman,[35] which was devastatingly criticized by Lon L. Fuller.[36] Of course, Jerome Frank's *Law and the Modern Mind* led to a flurry of critiques and defenses.[37]

To recreate the atmosphere and some of the substance of these debates, it will be helpful to examine two of them in some detail. These particular controversies originated with the publication in 1935 of two books by

34. See Cohen, Transcendental Nonsense and the Functional Approach, 35 Colum. L. Rev. 809 (1935); Kennedy, Functional Nonsense and the Transcendental Approach, 5 Ford. L. Rev. 272 (1936); Cohen, Letter to the Editor, 5 Ford. L. Rev. 548 (1936); Kennedy, More Functional Nonsense: A Reply to Felix S. Cohen, 6 Ford. L. Rev. 75 (1937).

35. Moore and Sussman, Legal and Institutional Methods Applied to the Debiting of Direct Discounts, 40 Yale L. J. 381, 555, 752, 928, 1055, 1219 (1931); Moore, An Institutional Approach to the Law of Commercial Banking, 38 Yale L. J. 703 (1929). See the discussion of this in chapter 8.

36. Fuller, American Legal Realism, 82 U. Pa. L. Rev. 429 (1934).

37. Frank, *Law and the Modern Mind* (1930); Adler, Legal Certainty, 31 Colum. L. Rev. 91 (1931); Bohlen, Book Review, 79 U. Pa. L. Rev. 822 (1931); Morris, Book Review, 16 St. Louis L. Rev. 181 (1931); Shartel, Book Review, 29 Mich. L. Rev. 541 (1931); Frank, Mr. Justice Holmes and Non-Euclidean Legal Thinking, 17 Corn. L. Q. 568 (1932); Frank, Realism in Jurisprudence, 7 Am. L. Sch. Rev. 1057 (1934).

realists, followed by a series of critical reviews. The books are *Law and the Lawyers*[38] by Edward S. Robinson (1893–1937) and *The Symbols of Government*[39] by Thurman Arnold (1891–1969). These works represent the Poundian paradigm carried to its extreme in two directions.

Robinson's book attempts to deal with the traditional problems of legal theory at various levels from the point of view of psychology. More than that, it is an argument that traditional legal thinking must be completely discarded in favor of the psychological approach. Using the term "jurisprudence" to include all kinds of legal discourse, Robinson says, "This book attempts to show that jurisprudence is certain to become one of the family of social sciences—that all of its fundamental concepts will have to be brought into line with psychological knowledge." He adds, "The claim that all juristic problems are ultimately psychological will not be readily accepted in jurisprudence." His assessment of traditional legal discourse is not kind:

> Of all the social studies jurisprudence has collected perhaps the largest assortment of theories which, though obviously in disagreement with the facts, are said to be convenient. Falsifications of history, economics, and sociology, as well as of psychology, are the devices by means of which juristic thought simplifies a baffling world.[40]

Robinson stresses that the role legal concepts, doctrines, and theories are supposed to play in the world of law is illusory. Lawyers, legislators, and judges are motivated by irrational considerations more than rational ones; thus, legal discourse is used to cover up or rationalize what is at base irrational. In his view concepts like intention, negligence, and stare decisis will be studied by the new "naturalistic jurisprudence," but not from the old standpoint of rational explanations. Rather, they will be analyzed

38. E. Robinson, *Law and the Lawyers* (1935). Robinson was a prominent psychologist at the University of Chicago when he came to Yale in 1927. He conducted a joint seminar at the Yale Law School with Thurman Arnold. Robinson died in 1937 at age forty-four.

39. T. Arnold, *The Symbols of Government* (1935). Arnold was a many-faceted individual. One-time dean of the law school at West Virginia, he was successively a law professor at Yale, a New Deal bureaucrat, a federal appeals judge, and a founder of one of Washington's most prestigious law firms (Arnold and Porter). Arnold also wrote *The Folklore of Capitalism* (1937) and other books. See Freund, Book Review, 51 Harv. L. Rev. 1132 (1938); Hook, Book Review, 5 U. Chi. L. Rev. 341 (1938); Lerner, Book Review, 47 Yale L. J. 687 (1938); Mechem, Book Review, 23 Iowa L. Rev. 443 (1938).

40. Robinson, note 38, 73.

from the standpoint of behavioral psychology and psychiatry. The whole of legal doctrine will have to be psychoanalyzed, and those who want to engage in jurisprudential scholarship will have to be prepared. "The student of jurisprudence will be required to throw himself into psychology completely enough to become his own competent critic on the matter of psychological theory. There is no easy way."

Anticipating critics who will argue that Robinson leaves out the crucial roles of logic and morality in explaining law and judicial decision-making, he says:

> It will be well therefore to approach the judicial process with the simple, naturalistic notion of deliberation. Logic and ethics should be considered merely as types of values by which judges are sometimes swayed. The details of judicial deliberation and the additional types of evaluation that permeate it may profitably be settled factually rather than through slavish adherence to traditional categories and distinctions. . . . We may well repeat in this connection that the naturalistic, psychological view of deliberation does not minimize the practical importance of logical and ethical values. Rather it seeks to understand and place those values by looking at them from the outside.[41]

Thus, for Robinson the scientific or naturalistic method, and particularly psychology, becomes the basis upon which logic, philosophy, ethics, and other traditional modes of thinking can be studied. Presumably, from the point of view of participants in a social process like adjudication, the steps to be taken and the choices to be made are logical and perhaps based on ultimate moral principles. However, from the viewpoint of legal science in its new garb as naturalistic jurisprudence or radical empiricism, all of the factors that motivate and produce behavior are to be considered and accounted for, and most of them are not rational.

As to the possibility of a science of law or ethics outside of the naturalistic approach, Robinson says that it is "nothing but a pious wish." Further, those who refuse to submit all of their serious thinking to the confines of the naturalistic jurisprudence are creating a "domain for fairies and magic," and "there is really nothing to be done about a man when he decides upon such a course." To those to whom it seems paradoxical to study nonscientific (naturalistic) legal thinking from a scientific perspective, Robinson says:

41. Ibid., 187.

As soon as it is appreciated that a naturalistic jurisprudence will be, not only a body of knowledge about knowledge, but that it will be knowledge about a variety of bodies of knowledge, we shall no longer be troubled by the apparent paradox which arises when the naturalistic view of legal thinking shows that legal thinking is essentially non-naturalistic. We do not have to reform all of the judges and juries in order to give an intelligible account of how they think.[42]

Finally, Robinson maintains that the pursuit of knowledge about the legal process through the new naturalistic jurisprudence will bring about healthy changes in social institutions. Although such scientific study deals only with what is, facts and generalizations about facts, the knowledge gained will lead to enlightenment, which in turn will lead to improvement in society. "A naturalistic philosophy of law will help men to accept some valid facts about legal behavior and the legal institution to which they are inclined to close their eyes." And further, "The naturalistic student of the law who is concerned not only with how courts act and talk, but also with the changing trends in such talking and acting, will find himself supplying doctrines for the courts of the future."

Arnold's work takes an anthropological approach to the study of government, including law, and appears superficially quite different from Robinson's. However, as we begin to absorb Arnold's train of thought, it becomes apparent that the two realists see much the same world but from somewhat different standpoints. Arnold is concerned to demonstrate that the world of law and government is populated with ideals, fictions, and half-truths which, regardless of their unreality, play an important part in determining how people behave.

Arnold would have us explore our own society in much the same way that an anthropologist would study a remote jungle tribe. The anthropologist notes and describes the tribal people's understanding of how the rain-god makes rain, how the god of fertility may be appeased to assure offspring, why the shaman has curative powers, and how certain ceremonies assure good crops. In other words, she explains the structure of the tribe's thinking in terms of the symbols and ideas that they themselves use, all the while knowing that most of the structure of reality that they hold is quite unreal. In our own society we maintain similar shibboleths, signs, and symbols that help us manage our lives and our environment, yet they are equally unreal. Among the false symbols in our legal folklore are the notions that law consists of principles and rules, that courts logically

42. Ibid., 315.

apply these rules to decide cases, that the constitution is a body of principles laid down in 1789 (occasionally modified by amendment) that govern the operation of our government today, and that legal philosophy explains how morality, enacted law, and legal logic all fit together. Arnold says, "Law is primarily a great reservoir of emotionally important social symbols." He also gives an elaborate analogy between legal discourse and theology.

According to Arnold, the reason that the anthropologist knows that these symbols are unreal is that she sticks to the facts, avoiding preconceived categories, theories, and doctrines. Indeed, the theories and concepts of the people under study are themselves facts; therefore, our own ideal conceptions like the separation of powers, due process of law, and the duty of care toward others are simply facts from the point of view of the scientific observer. With their truth or falsity the observer is not primarily concerned. "The process of objectively examining the theories behind our own institutions, rather than of arguing their truth or falsity, gives us a shock. We can discuss savage taboos and understand them. Then we may use our information in guiding the savages. The same point of view toward our own institutions seems to undermine them."[43]

The necessity of seeing the factual world through idealistic conceptions leads to behavior that is not necessarily in the best interest of those saddled with the blinders. In the law these conceptual blinders often induce unwarranted conservatism. "Though the notion of a 'rule of law' may be the moral background of revolt, it ordinarily operates to induce acceptance of things as they are. It does this by creating a realm somewhere within the mystical haze beyond the courts, where all our dreams of justice in an unjust world come true."[44]

Behind this anthropological approach to social study lies a psychology that will further explain social phenomena. Why do we need symbols in doing what we do? Why do we accept symbols that often fly in the face of facts? Why do we rationalize behavior that is not rational? Arnold would refer us to a psychology like Robinson's for the answers to these kinds of questions. In this book he is content to point out the many ways in which we rationalize the irrational through the use of symbols and ideals. Among some of the symbols unmasked are the traditional account of judicial decision-making, the idea that the common law consists of principles and rules somehow having an independent existence, the artificial

43. Arnold, note 39, 95.
44. Ibid., 34.

legal propositions of the American Law Institute restatements, and the iron laws of classic economics as well as many constitutional doctrines.

The scientific observer is not concerned with whether a particular symbolic concept is true or false or whether it is morally good or bad. Indeed, to raise such questions is to misunderstand the objective fact-gathering activity of the social scientist. Whether behavior is morally right or logically consistent is irrelevant from the scientific point of view. What is important is that the scientist account for as many facts as he can, including the fact of the psychological use of certain symbols. If patterns of behavior emerge and if laws of behavior can be formulated, so much the better. But morality and logic become matters to be studied within a given social framework; they do not play a role in the scientific method itself. All moral and philosophical principles thus become relative, become a part of a particular society's vision of itself. "The result of uniting legal and social sciences is to take away many of the faiths on which our present social organization depends."

The critics of the Robinson and Arnold books, selected for their sophistication, are philosopher Morris R. Cohen[45] and law professor Phillip Mechem (1892–1969),[46] who consider the contentions of our two realists exaggerated and arrogant. After labeling the Robinson book "high and mighty censoriousness," Cohen points out, "We certainly cannot, by calling psychology a natural science, deny that a great deal of what is published under its name today is highly speculative and the object of a great difference of opinion." He adds, "It is well that legal scholars in this country should show a willingness to learn from all possible sources. But it is also necessary to be on guard against the easy assumption that any proposition becomes true when someone labels it natural science."[47]

Mechem regards the attacks on conventional legal thinking by Robinson and Arnold as attacks on a straw man whom he calls the "average

45. Cohen's critiques can be found in Cohen, Book Review of Robinson, *Law and the Lawyers*, 22 Cornell L. Q. 171 (1937), hereinafter referred to as Cohen I, and Cohen, Book Review of Arnold, *The Symbols of Government*, 31 Ill. L. Rev. 411 (1936), hereinafter referred to as Cohen II. For more on Cohen see chapter 8.

46. Mechem's critique can be found in Mechem, The Jurisprudence of Dispair, 21 Iowa L. Rev. 669 (1936), hereinafter referred to as Mechem. For other critiques of Arnold, not discussed herein, see Corwin, Book Review, 30 Am. Pol. Sci. Rev. 581 (1936); Laski, Book Review, 45 Yale L. J. 951 (1936); Stone, Book Review, 25 Geo. L. J. 224 (1936); Lerner, The Shadow World of Thurman Arnold, 47 Yale. L. J. 687 (1938); Levi, Natural Law, Precedent, and Thurman Arnold, 24 Va. L. Rev. 584 (1938); Sullivan, The Speculation of Thurman W. Arnold, 1 Polamerican L. J. 3 (1938).

47. Cohen I, 177–78.

unreasonable lawyer." This dimwit suffers under the delusion that the law is perfect reason and judges apply it mechanically.[48] Opposed to the straw man, of course, is "the omnipotent psychologist." Mechem thinks that the omnipotent psychologist in reality has made only one contribution to legal science, the application of psychiatric theory to criminals; the rest is huff and puff.[49]

Arnold's concern with false symbolism is also attacked. His favorite analogy between law and theology is found by Cohen to be lacking in objective merit:

> Rhetorically effective, but of dubious value scientifically is thus the parallel between jurisprudence and theology which, whether intended or not, will be generally taken as an argument against the truth of the former. But as such, it is simply an appeal to the anti-theologic prejudice. To a really detached or scientific observer, the question would remain open whether this parallel does not indicate rather some shrewd insight on the part of both theologians and jurists.[50]

Along with Arnold's skepticism of legal logic, Robinson's substitution of psychological for logical reasons is also attacked:

> Under the guise of showing the psychological origin and motives of certain doctrines, there is often a good deal of intimation that therefore these doctrines are false. Taken seriously, such an argument, based on a confusion between the truth of a proposition and the motives of the one who professes it, is of course an old fallacy.[51]

An important argument of the critics is that failure of the realists to understand scientific method results in confusion and error. "Facts will not evaluate themselves."[52] Theory, deprecated by the realists, is essential

48. "The straw man so viciously attacked in their writings may be christened 'The Average Unreasonable Lawyer.' He sees nothing and knows nothing. He thinks the Common Law is the perfection of reason. He believes that rules of law are certain and unvarying, that judges apply them with mechanical perfection. . . ." Mechem, 676.

49. "We may note [the psychologist's] disproportionate reliance on the psychiatric aspect of criminal law. This is his great resource, his constant theme. When he reaches into his bag to pull out an illustration of the usefulness of psychology to jurisprudence—somehow he always pulls out the same one. The suspicion grows that it may be the only one he has." Ibid., 680.

50. Cohen II, 418.

51. Ibid., 417.

52. Mechem, 678.

for scientific study. Arnold has a naive faith in the popular myth that science is a matter of observing facts. He fails to understand the role and importance of hypothesis and theory.[53] Furthermore, Robinson and Arnold confuse the application of science with science itself. The engineer draws on science in his construction of a bridge, but science cannot tell him where to build the bridge or whether it should be built at all. This involves deontic or normative considerations:

> For Professor Arnold himself is, because of the realistic misinterpretation of the method of natural science, quite confused as to the distinction between existential and normative considerations, between problems as to what exists and problems as to what is desirable or what ought to be, irrespective of whether it is or is not yet in existence.[54]

This point raises a broader issue, namely, do Robinson and Arnold adequately account for the normative aspects of law? Cohen says that those who believe they can deal with social life without making normative judgments fail to realize the ethical assumptions implicit in their undertakings.[55] Mechem agrees:

> It may be wondered how the New Realist expects a judge to decide cases, when there neither is nor can be any law. One answer is that, as a matter of observation they *do* decide them; why bother further. Some stress the judicial hunch, some the judicial digestion or indigestion, and some point out that it is far too complicated a matter to express any opinion about, until more statistics are available. Yet, insofar as any opinion is ventured on how they really should decide them, it is this: on the merits. But this is preposterous! In a world without value judgments there are no merits. And value judgments are impossible without rules.[56]

Mechem follows with an illustration: "There is plenty of 'scientific evidence' to the effect that we should kill fewer people if we drove more slowly; unfortunately this leaves quite open the question at what point we *ought* to harmonize the interest in speed with the interest in preserving life."

53. "If . . . we follow the progress of some actual scientific research, it becomes obvious that without some guiding principle, idea, or theory as hypothesis, we cannot even determine what facts to look for." Cohen II, 412.

54. Ibid., 414.

55. Cohen I, 176.

56. Mechem, 672–73.

Not only does the failure to recognize the normative aspects of law vitiate the methodology of the realists; it leads to a quite unacceptable conclusion. "The refusal to recognize the distinction between what is and what ought to be naturally leads to the assumption that what is, is right. . . ."[57]

Mechem concludes:

[Arnold's] view [is] that society and its most important institutions are a great joke. A parade of fools whose folly is all the more comical in that they take it so seriously. . . . [It] cannot fail to be a jurisprudence of despair. . . . Robinson's world is different—but only on the surface . . . satisfactory to those who want a chromium world. Some may prefer the older sort, full of creaks and imperfections in the form of aspirations and beliefs and faiths and distinctions between right and wrong and good and bad. . . .[58]

The Special Case of Felix S. Cohen

One realist who was willing to acquiesce in the need to account for a moral dimension in jurisprudence was Felix S. Cohen (1907–1953), son of Morris R. Cohen.[59] Almost alone, Felix Cohen supported the main thrust of legal realism—skepticism of formal legal rules and doctrine, a keen interest in the extralegal factors that determine what courts actually do, and a faith in the power of social science to explain law; yet he advanced a moral philosophy that he thought was compatible with his realism. This was set forth briefly in a law-review article published in 1931[60] and was followed by a more extensive exposition in book form in 1933.[61] This book is remarkable in that it is the only work in American history before World War II, except for natural-law writings, to present a full-blown ethical theory that explains the relationship of ethics to law.

Cohen maintains that every jurisprudential outlook has within it ethical presuppositions. In the case of natural law these presuppositions are open and explicit. In other paradigms they are hidden or unnoticed.

57. Cohen I, 177.
58. Mechem, 692.
59. Felix S. Cohen was educated in both philosophy and law. As a lawyer for the government, he was the nation's foremost expert in federal Indian law. See Symposium, To the Memory of Felix S. Cohen, 9 Rut. L Rev. 355 (1954).
60. Cohen, The Ethical Basis of Legal Criticism, 41 Yale L. J. 201 (1931).
61. F. Cohen, *Ethical Systems and Legal Ideals* (1933).

An ethics, like a metaphysics, is no more certain and no less dangerous because it is unconsciously held. . . . A historical school of law disclaims concern with ethics and repeatedly invokes a *Zeitgeist* or a *Volksgeist* to decide what the law ought to be. An analytical school of jurisprudence again dismisses questions of morality, and again decides what the law ought to be by reference to a so-called logical ideal, which is not an ideal of logic at all, but an aesthetic ideal of symmetrical analogical development. . . . And those who define law in terms of actually prevailing social demands or interests make frequent use of the undisclosed principle that these demands *ought* to be satisfied.[62]

Cohen argues that the evaluation of law must be done openly and candidly in the light of an ethical theory. Such theory can be developed rationally through a dialectical process. Indeed, philosophers have been working in the field of ethical science for many years, and their labors have not been fruitless. Cohen's idea of a rational ethical science seems to follow the methods of his philosopher father, Morris R. Cohen (see chapter 8). Using such methods, he reviews some of the major standards for legal criticism that have been used in the past, and he critiques each of them, including simple intuition, natural law, liberty, social interests, and others. He concludes that each of these approaches has its limitations and that only a teleological ethical system that aims at the good life is adequate to serve as a basis for legal criticism.

What theory of the good life is best? Cohen examines several possible ethical theories and concludes that hedonism, or utilitarianism without specific Benthamite connotations, is the best alternative. He recognizes that the arguments for this position are not entirely conclusive, but he maintains that those who refuse to acknowledge the merit of a hedonistic approach are obligated to come forth with better arguments for their own preferred system.

Settling upon an ethical system is, of course, only the beginning of the attempt to evaluate law. The ramifications of the system must be worked out, and then it must be applied to the positive law. Since the positive law changes with changing social conditions, and social conditions are constantly changing, the evaluation of law becomes an ongoing activity that can never terminate. The vision of positive law that Cohen has in mind is not the same as John Austin's, however; it is the same vision that was shared by Llewellyn, Frank, Oliphant, and other realists, a vision not too

62. Ibid., 4–5.

far removed from that of Roscoe Pound. Thus, Cohen presents a jurisprudential view analogous to that of Bentham. On the one hand we have
positive law, the law that is, and this must be carefully studied by scientific
method for an adequate understanding. On the other hand we have the
ethical theory of utilitarianism that enables us to evaluate the positive law
and recommend change. The great difference from Bentham's position is
that the positive law is conceived in realist terms, not in the formal terms
of the expository paradigm.

The Attack Of The Moralists

Another attack on legal realism in the 1930s and 1940s from a
different direction came from the natural-law believers, led for the most
part by legal scholars at Roman Catholic universities, especially Professor
Walter B. Kennedy of Fordham.[63] As might be expected, these critics saw
in the theoretical writings of the realists the failure to account for the
moral dimension of the law, or, in the case of extremists like Robinson and
Arnold, the failure to appreciate the necessity of accounting for the moral
dimension of the law. Identifying the realists with political theories of
"might makes right," they implied that legal realism led directly to au-
thoritarianism and supported the ever-more-menacing regimes of the
Nazis in Germany, fascism in Italy, and the governments of Stalin and
Franco in Russia and Spain. For Walter Kennedy legal realism was a
"goose step philosophy."[64]
While in some respects the extreme realists embracing a radical empiricism were easy targets for the natural lawyers to hit, Pound himself and

63. See Kennedy, Pragmatism as a Philosophy of Law, 9 Marq. L. Rev. 63 (1925);
Kennedy, Principles or Facts?, 4 Fordham L. Rev. 53 (1935); Kennedy, Legal Realism,
What Next?, 8 Fordham L. Rev. 45 (1939); Kennedy, A Review of Legal Realism, 9
Fordham L. Rev. 362 (1940); Kennedy, A Required Course in Jurisprudence, 9 Am. L.
School Rev. 593 (1940); Kennedy, Psychologism in the Law, 29 Geo. L. J. 139 (1940).
See also the articles cited in note 34.
64. Kennedy, My Philosophy of Law, in Northwestern Univ., *My Philosophy of Law:
Credos of Sixteen American Scholars*, 151 (1941). Edward Purcell in his perceptive
history of this period says, "[Legal realism's] philosophical assumptions had undermined the concept of a rationally knowable moral standard. Its apparent ethical
relativism seemed to mean that no Nazi barbarity could be justly branded as evil, while
its identification of law with the actions of government officials gave even the most
offensive Nazi edict the sanction of true law. Juxtaposing that logic to the actions of the
totalitarian states, the critics painted realism in the most ominous and shocking colors."
E. Purcell, *The Crisis of Democratic Theory*, 172 (1973).

others like John Dickinson (1894–1952)[65] and Lon Fuller (1902–1978)[66] were more difficult to criticize because they recognized the important ethical side of legal phenomena. Nevertheless, Pound's pragmatism and theory of social interests came under attack as well. An excellent critique of the ethical side of Pound's philosophy from the standpoint of the moral paradigm was offered by Karl Kreilkamp in the 1940 *Fordham Law Review*.[67] In addition to pointing out the difficulties in using the theory of interests, Kreilkamp showed that Pound lacked a coherent psychology necessary for establishing a universal human nature, this being essential to the development of moral theory in Kreilkamp's view.

The attack on the realists' apparent lack of morality in an international setting in which dictatorship challenged traditional American political values and world war loomed on the horizon prompted some writers to defend the "new" movement and others to retreat from their earlier positions.[68] Notable among those drawing back were Karl Llewellyn[69] and Jerome Frank.[70] A book by Edward Garlan published in 1941 also attempted to demonstrate, somewhat unconvincingly, that the realists did indeed have a theory of justice.[71] Apparently inspired by the same motivation, another book appeared in the same year containing the "credos" of sixteen legal theorists.[72]

---

65. See Dickinson, The Law Behind Law, 29 Colum. L. Rev. 113, 285 (1929); Dickinson, Legal Rules—Their Function in the Process of Decision, 79 U. Pa. L. Rev. 833 (1931); Dickinson, Legal Rules—Their Application and Elaboration, 79 U. Pa. L. Rev. 1052 (1931). These articles constitute a substantial defense of the original Poundian paradigm against most of the charges leveled at the extreme legal realists.

66. See Fuller, American Legal Realism, 82 Pa. L. Rev. 429 (1934). See also Kantorowicz, Some Rationalism about Realism, 43 Yale L. J. 1240 (1934).

67. Kreilkamp, Dean Pound and the End of Law, 9 Fordham L. Rev. 196 (1940).

68. See Purcell, note 64, 167–78.

69. Llewellyn, One Realist's View of Natural Law for Judges, 15 Notre Dame Lawyer 3 (1939); Llewellyn, On Reading and Using the Newer Jurisprudence, 40 Colum. L. Rev. 593 (1940); Llewellyn, On the Good, the True, and the Beautiful, in Law, 9 Univ. Chi. L. Rev. 247 (1942). In retrospect it is interesting to note that Llewellyn, in his initial nondebate with Pound, listed among scholars doing "realistic" work around the world one Justus Wilhelm Hedemann. Hedemann became a leading scholar at Hitler's Academy for German Law in the late 1930s.

70. Frank's reversal of position was later in coming than Llewellyn's, but it was more radical. See J. Frank, *Fate and Freedom: A Philosophy for Free Americans*, 98, 259, 295 (1945).

71. E. Garlan, *Legal Realism and Justice* (1941).

72. Northwestern Univ., *My Philosophy of Law: Credos of Sixteen American Scholars* (1941). The unlikely assemblage of scholars included Bingham, Morris Co-

A Summary Of The Critiques

While the impending war between the dictatorships and the democracies of the world tended to turn the debates into strident polemics, we can, with the advantage of historical distance, recognize the most important criticisms of legal realism that emerged in this period. They fall into two main categories. First, there was discussion of what the scientific study of law should mean. Critics charged the realists with a false scientism. This meant (1) that they had an uncritical faith in both the methods and the substantive knowledge of the fledgling social sciences; (2) that they failed to understand how logic, hypothesis, and theory were actually employed in using the scientific method, relying instead on a crude notion of pure empiricism; and (3) that they attempted to transfer the determinist cause-and-effect assumptions of physical science to the realm of human studies, thus denying the possibility of free will or choice as any part of an explanatory scheme.

Second came questions of right and wrong. Critics faulted the realists for failing to provide a normative dimension to their thinking. For some this meant that the realists took the detached, objective scientific observer's perspective on the legal process as the only possible perspective. Thus, the legal scientist can study the way in which judges decide cases but cannot speak to the question of how the judge should decide. In the less-sophisticated realist writings there was an assumption that the judge should obviously decide in accordance with public policy, an unwitting shorthand for a whole realm of moral questions. For others this criticism meant that the realists omitted the most important kinds of legal questions from consideration or else pretended that they were not real questions. This was not limited to the grand philosophic questions of justice in society but included more mundane puzzles like how a judge should decide a case when presented with conflicting arguments, or how we know what court has jurisdiction, or how the legislature should balance the need for security against the interest in free expression. Felix Cohen emerged as the only realist who acknowledged these criticisms and met them head on with his own ethical theory.

The criticisms could not so easily be applied to the theory of Roscoe Pound himself, but there is an element of validity to them even here. One difficulty with Pound's theory was, as Llewellyn so correctly observed,

---

hen, Cook, Dewey, Dickinson, Fuller, Green, Kennedy, Kocourek, Llewellyn, Moore, Patterson, Pound, Powell, Radin, and Wigmore.

that it was never integrated into a coherent whole and that some of it was pitched at one level of abstraction and some at another. Pound continued to defend and elaborate his theory for another twenty years or so, but without ever overcoming these problems. But the Poundian paradigm had by this time taken on a life of its own extended and modified by other thinkers.

THE SOCIAL SCIENCE

OF LAW

1928-70

The Poundian paradigm became the dominant legal theory in America in the third decade of the twentieth century. Many of the developments of the thirties, forties, and fifties were direct extensions of that theory but contained novel elements that distinguished them from the older, more general view. One main line of development was to make a social science of the law. This chapter will cover the most significant efforts to extend the Poundian paradigm in this direction: the behaviorism of Underhill Moore, the experimental jurisprudence of Frederick Beutel and Thomas Cowan, the social science of law advocated by Herman Oliphant, Walter Wheeler Cook, Hessel Yntema, and others, and the law, science, and policy (LSP) of Harold Lasswell and Myres McDougal. The antiscientistic critical views of Morris R. Cohen will also be taken into account.

At the turn of the century the social sciences were in their infancy, and it was not entirely clear to legal scholars what constituted science or what its method was. This changed with time; psychology, sociology, economics, and anthropology all became sophisticated disciplines, each with methods of its own. While philosophers debated about methods, the practice of social science marched on. Characteristically, this practice involved empirical observation. Some of the results, especially from anthropologists, inspired the law professors.

In law schools the more academically oriented professors worried, like Langdell in the previous century, about how scientific their own scholarship was. The adherents of the expository paradigm supported the development of the restatements and clung to the old science of logical analysis whose prophets were Austin and Hohfeld. But for those who accepted the Poundian paradigm, science had to signify the newer social science; yet, what did this mean? Was law as an academic discipline to become a part of the social sciences, carved up into psychology of law, sociology of law, and so forth? Or was there to be a separate social science of law? Or was law applied social science, using scientific studies as the basis for legislation and court decision just as medicine uses the products of physical and biological science to cure illness? All of these questions were answered in the affirmative by one group of thinkers or another. Driven by the craving for scientific respectability, the most ambitious of the new scholars wanted to build up an entirely new science of law, each having his own idea of what that science was supposed to be. These new ideas constituted, of course, a new kind of jurisprudence. As a rough starting point for these developments we will use 1928, the year the Institute of Law was established at Johns Hopkins University for the empirical study of law, followed by Yale's establishment of the Institute for Human Relations, devoted to promoting social science research, in the following year.[1]

Underhill Moore's Behaviorism

William Underhill Moore (1879–1949) practiced law in New York City and taught at the universities of Kansas, Wisconsin, and Chicago before returning to his alma mater, Columbia.[2] His specialty was commercial law; he produced his own casebook and wrote conventional articles on the subject. Although he had earned a master's degree in political science while attending law school, he was not trained or experienced in empirical social science. After returning to Columbia, however, he underwent a great intellectual transformation under the influence of John Dewey, Thorstein Veblen, and James H. Robinson.[3] He saw the light; and the light was Watsonian behaviorism.[4] This seems to have been more a leap of faith than the result of any in-depth study of a social science discipline or of the philosophy of science.

1. See W. Twining, *Karl Llewellyn and the Realist Movement*, 60–63 (1973).
2. An exhaustive and well-written work on Moore's intellectual life is Schlegel, American Legal Realism and Empirical Social Science: The Singular Case of Underhill Moore, 29 Buff. L. Rev. 195 (1980).
3. Ibid., 237.
4. Watsonian behaviorism took its name from the radically empirical approach of the American psychologist J. B. Watson. See J. Watson, *Psychology from the Standpoint of a Behaviorist* (1919). Moore's new intellectual suit of clothes was first revealed in a book review in 1923: Moore, The Rational Basis of Legal Institutions, 23 Colum. L. Rev. 609 (1923).

Moore was involved in the great Columbia curriculum study (see chapter 7); he was also on the losing side in the contest for the deanship (supporting Oliphant). Partly because the Columbia law school seemed to be under the control of a vocational-oriented administration and faculty and partly because Robert M. Hutchins, dean of the Yale Law School, made a tempting offer to Moore, he resigned and went to Yale in 1929. Part of the arrangement was that Moore, in addition to being a full professor on the law faculty, would become associated with the newly formed Institute of Human Relations and would have access to researchers and funding for empirical studies. The Institute, established with Rockefeller Foundation money, was created to foster social science research.

Moore undertook two major research projects during his tenure at Yale. The first was a series of empirical studies of banking practices, supposedly designed to determine whether court decisions followed certain customs of the banking business. The hypothesis was that court decisions are determined in large part by the practice or custom of the parties engaged in any particular activity. In the principal study Moore found appellate court decisions from different states that reached opposite conclusions on a specific point of banking law. A customer may sometimes have a checking account with a bank and also owe the bank on a note that has become due and remains unpaid. In this situation is the bank legally entitled to charge the amount due on the note to the customer's checking account? In Pennsylvania and Connecticut the courts said yes. In South Carolina the court said no. Moore's hypothesis was that the courts followed the banking practice in the state. He conducted an empirical study in those states to explore the banking practices. His meticulous findings and conclusions, complete with charts and mathematical notation, took up 246 pages in the *Yale Law Journal*.[5] Whether he proved anything or not is a matter of debate.[6]

The parking study, a ten-year project in New Haven, Connecticut, was intended to measure the relationship between traffic regulations and driving behavior. Moore borrowed a psychological theory from Yale col-

5. Moore and Hope, An Institutional Approach to the Law of Commercial Banking, 38 Yale L. J. 703 (1929); Moore and Sussman, Legal and Institutional Methods Applied to the Debiting of Direct Discounts, 40 Yale L. J. 381, 555, 752, 928, 1055, 1219 (1931); Moore, Sussman, and Brand, Legal and Institutional Methods Applied to Orders to Stop Payment of Checks, 42 Yale L. J. 1198 (1933); Moore, Sussman, and Corstvet, Drawing Against Uncollected Checks, 45 Yale L. J. 1, 260 (1935).

6. For a devastating critique of Moore's banking study see Fuller, American Legal Realism, 82 Pa. L. Rev. 429, 453 (1934).

league Clark Hull as the framework for his investigation. This was Hull's "learning theory" involving the notions of stimulus and response, or more accurately "drive, cue, response, and reward." Moore hypothesized that traffic signs provided a "cue" that stimulated a response that could thus be explained by learning theory. Correlation was to be made between parking behavior with and without regulation by signs. Apparently Moore was able to get the cooperation of the police chief and city officials, who changed the regulations in the course of the study so that Moore and his researchers could observe the results. An actual experiment was conducted, in fact, three of them: the main parking study observed the difference in parking behavior before and after regulation of the time of parking; the "tagging" studies observed the difference in parking behavior between persons who were given tickets for overparking and those who were not; the "rotary" studies involved observation of motorists at a multiple-street intersection before and after a sign and painted markings were introduced requiring traffic to circulate around the intersection instead of crossing directly to another street.

The findings and conclusions of this study were published in 136 pages of the *Yale Law Journal*, complete with charts, graphs, and an abundance of mathematical notation.[7] Interpretation of the data proved to be a serious problem, and the conclusions related to the main parking study are inconclusive. The tagging study presumably showed that those receiving parking tickets got their learning reinforced and adjusted their behavior. The rotary study was said to have proved the hypothesis that: "There will be a decrease in the frequency of drivings through and to the left of the oval, and the amount of this decrease in each lane-category will vary with the distance in space between that lane and the nearest lane which passes to the right of the oval and will vary in such a way that the greater the distance the less the decrease."[8]

Moore did not claim to be a legal philosopher, although he egoistically deprecated all previous efforts in jurisprudence. Nevertheless, in the course of working out his empirical method he was forced to justify and explain what he was trying to do. A particular jurisprudential view can, therefore, be pieced together from parts of his various articles,[9] although his theory changed over a period of twenty years.

7. Moore and Callahan, Law and Learning Theory: A Study in Legal Control, 53 Yale L. J. 1 (1943).

8. Ibid., 86.

9. The most significant statement of his jurisprudential theory can be found in Moore, The Rational Basis of Legal Institutions, 23 Colum. L. Rev. 609 (1923); Moore

After his conversion to social science, Moore seems to have started out with something close to an anthropological approach. He regards human institutions, including law, as habits of behavior on the part of the persons associated with the institutions. In some respects this is like the views of Bingham and Bentley in that what people do is the only social reality. What people think they are doing becomes rationalization and is not to be trusted to reflect reality, although their rationalizations are facts that the social scientist must observe and record along with other facts of behavior. Institutions have a rational aspect in that they are at least in part deliberately created as means to some end. However, they also have a life of their own, and they may serve other ends, or putting it differently, they may generate consequences that were unforeseen.

As a good realist, Moore considers the prediction of judicial decisions to be a major function of legal science, and he rejects the idea that legal rules determine the outcome of cases. In taking this position he seems to misinterpret the traditional view of how rules are supposed to determine the outcome of cases.[10] Instead of viewing the operation of rules as normative, that is, as statements of what the judge ought to do, he characterizes the traditional view as causative—rules are causes of the judge's behavior. For a strict behaviorist, normative statements have no reality; consequently Moore points out the obvious, that legal rules do not predict the decision in many cases; hence, they cannot be the "cause."

He suggests that there are in fact many determinants (causes) of a judicial decision. By "cause" Moore says that he means neither logical entailment nor statistical probability; rather, he conceives of it in terms of the likelihood that a will follow b.[11] The myriad of causal determinants will always vary from case to case so that, even if the individual determinants could be known, the new combination of them would make perfect prediction of decisions impossible. Nevertheless, according to Moore, certain determinants may be more influential than others; if these can be

and Hope, An Institutional Approach to the Law of Commercial Banking, 38 Yale L. J. 703 (1929); Moore and Sussman, The Lawyer's Law, 41 Yale L. J. 566 (1932); My Philosophy of Law, in Northwestern Univ., ed., My Philosophy of Law (1941); introductory part of Moore and Callahan, Law and Learning Theory: A Study in Legal Control, 53 Yale L. J. 1 (1943).

10. See Moore and Hope, An Institutional Approach to the Law of Commercial Banking, 38 Yale L. J. 703, 704 (1929).

11. Ibid., 706, fn.2. Moore does not explain why this concept of cause is not mere statistical probability. Moore also developed a convoluted social science jargon worthy of Bentham himself, and he used mathematics or symbolic notations at every opportunity.

isolated, they may lead to some degree of successful prediction. Institutional practices are hypothesized by Moore to be such a determinant, hence the hypothesis of the banking study that court decision will follow the practice of the bankers.[12]

Moore insisted on pure empirical methods to ascertain what institutional practices actually prevailed.[13] While there may have been some direct observation of the acts of bank officials in his study, much of the information was gathered through questionnaires and interviews. Thus, the information given by the bankers must have been, in part, the result of what they thought they were doing. In other words, to answer Moore's questions the bankers had to have some concept of "banking," "discounting," "depositing," and so forth, all of which are theoretically outside the realm of Moore's empirical reality. What Moore called behavior was not at all like mice running through a maze, but it incorporated purposeful rational choice in a complex and technical framework of concepts. In fact, the application of his hypothesis to the banking world in itself entails the adoption of these same banking concepts by the investigator. This means that Moore succeeded, if he did succeed, only in providing an empirical input into a highly conceptualized mental structure, a structure that itself incorporated many legal concepts.

In the banking study and the theory behind it Moore was concerned about the effect of institutional behavior on law. In the second phase of his work, the parking study, Moore became concerned about the effect of law on behavior. However, he departed from his original approach by taking up a psychological theory as the framework for the study. This time the law was the "stimulus," and the compliance or noncompliance the "response."[14] As with the banking study, a difficulty concerning the conceptualization of those doing the parking (their understanding of compliance, of enforcement) taints the purely empirical observations that Moore was

12. One of the shortcomings of Moore's extensive banking study, pointed out by many critics, was his failure to show how the courts knew what the banking practices were that were supposed to determine the outcome of their decisions. It took Moore himself several years to find out what those practices were.

13. Moore suggests that he adheres to the position associated with the "logical positivists" of the Vienna Circle to the effect that all statements must ultimately have an empirically verifiable referent in order to be meaningful; all statements failing to meet this requirement are merely emotive. See Moore, My Philosophy of Law, in Northwestern Univ., ed., My Philosophy of Law, 203–204 (1941). See also Schlegel, note 2, 285.

14. One authority on Moore has suggested that his theory changed to meet the professional biases of those who held the purse of grant money. See Schlegel, note 2, 284ff.

trying to make. Indeed, intuition or common sense that took into account what people were trying to do could provide a superior explanation for the behavior in the parking study. One of these studies was conducted in front of the post office; people parked for much shorter durations than at other locations, perhaps a surprise to Moore and a problem for him to explain! Such a thing as the purpose of parkers (to mail a letter or buy stamps) is an element that Moore's strictly behavioristic method would not permit taking into account.[15]

Moore's approach to the study of law deliberately and relentlessly attempts to exclude normative factors. He purports to study only what is; his purpose is the understanding of what is. Therefore, his type of inquiry does not purport to provide guidance other than information to the judge who must decide a case or to the reformer who wants to change the status quo. Moore's jurisprudence is accordingly, at best, incomplete. Moore certainly held strong political opinions,[16] but he never sought to relate them to his legal theory.

More important than the theory of Moore's radical behaviorism was the effect that his studies had on contemporary academics. The parking study was the butt of jokes among law professors for years.[17] Some thought that the amount of funds Moore expended in his research (enormous by law-school standards) produced a poverty of results. Others thought that the jargon and mathematical notation common to Moore's scholarship was pure affectation.[18] Karl Llewellyn, himself the arch-realist, in reviewing the early attempts by realists to do empirical research, said in 1956: "It was at Yale that the nadir of idiocy was achieved when Underhill Moore 'tested out' whether law has mystical operation by an elaborate observation, metering and statisticking of the noneffect on the parking practices of New Haveners of a change in the official traffic regulations which he had arranged to keep carefully from coming to the knowledge of any trafficker."[19] Most lawyers couldn't make heads or tails of Moore's studies; social scientists considered him an amateur, neither

15. Further, even though the behavior of parking is much simpler than banking, Moore as the investigator is forced to accept and operate within the community's general conceptual picture of what a law is, who can promulgate it, why it should be obeyed, what common morality thinks of disobedience, in short, the legal culture of New Haven, Connecticut. Again, a large nonempirical element is assumed by the study.

16. See Schlegel, note 2, 241.

17. See Clark, Underhill Moore, 59 Yale L. J. 189 (1950).

18. See Lucey, Book Review, 30 Geo. L. Rev. 800 (1942); Hanft, Book Review, 20 N.C.L. Rev. 123 (1941); Bullington, Book Review, 20 Tex. L. Rev. 644 (1942).

19. Llewellyn, On What Makes Legal Research Worthwhile, 8 J. Leg. Ed. 399, 401 (1956).

admitted to the guild of the Ph.D. nor privy to the trade secrets of empirical research. His work gave credence to the idea, widely held among lawyers in the forties and fifties and by some academics as well, that lawyers shouldn't meddle in social science and that social science has little of significance to contribute to the understanding of law.[20]

The Experimental Jurisprudence of Beutel and Cowan

Frederick K. Beutel (1897–1983), educated at Cornell and Harvard universities in the twenties, was very much a Poundian as he entered the teaching ranks of the profession.[21] His professional interests were divided between commercial law and jurisprudence, especially the extension of sociological jurisprudence into what he called "experimental jurisprudence." He wrote a definitive article in 1934 that made a plea for such an approach.[22] There were overtones in this article that suggested Beutel thought little of self-government and might support a more total-itarian regime so long as it proceeded "scientifically." Perhaps because of negative reaction to these implications of his proposal, or perhaps because he was very much involved in the development of commercial law, Beutel did not write anything more in the jurisprudential field until the early 1950s, although he did conduct several empirical studies that supported his theory.[23] In the meantime he became dean of the law school at the University of Nebraska in 1946, when he encouraged Thomas A. Cowan (1904–   ), a former colleague at Louisiana State University, to join him there. Cowan stayed at Nebraska only one year, but the two shared a faith in the promise of experimental jurisprudence.

20. Later appraisals of Moore's work have been more sympathetic. See generally Schlegel, note 2. See also, Verdun-Jones and Cousineau, The Voice Crying in the Wilderness: Underhill Moore as a Pioneer in the Establishment of an Interdisciplinary Jurisprudence, 1 Int. J. Law and Psychiatry 375 (1978).

21. Beutel received his B.S. and LL.M. degrees from Cornell and an S.J.D. from Harvard in 1928. He taught at Tulane from 1928 to 1935, was dean at Louisiana State from 1935 to 1937, professor at William and Mary 1940–45, dean at Nebraska 1945–49, and professor there until his retirement in 1963. He was also assistant general counsel for the Department of the Interior from 1943 to 1945. Beutel was the editor and revisor of a multivolume treatise on negotiable instruments originated by Brannan; he also wrote several articles opposing the adoption of the Uniform Commercial Code.

22. Beutel, Some Implications of Experimental Jurisprudence, 48 Harv. L. Rev. 169 (1934).

23. These all appear to have been undertaken in the late 1940s and early 1950s in Lincoln, Nebraska.

Beutel's most important writings for jurisprudence consisted of a series of law-review articles in the early fifties, which were turned into a book published in 1957.[24] Called *Some Potentialities of Experimental Jurisprudence as a New Branch of Social Science*, Beutel's book consisted of two parts. The first addressed the methodology of experimental jurisprudence. The second was a report on certain pilot studies involving, among other subjects, traffic regulation, sterilization of barber instruments, sale of tobacco to minors, and regulation of the size of bricks. This introductory subpart was followed by an extensive empirical study of bad-check law in Nebraska.

Beutel describes the method of experimental jurisprudence in terms of eight steps. Slightly edited, these steps are: (1) the nature of the social problem, the phenomena, should be studied empirically; (2) the legal regulation of the phenomena should be accurately stated; (3) the effects of the regulation should be observed and measured; (4) an hypothesis should be constructed that accounts for the results of the regulation; (5) the hypothesis should be generalized to cover similar cases (thus generalized, it is called a "jural law"); (6) if the results are inefficiently achieved, new methods of accomplishing the desired results should be suggested; (7) the suggested new regulation should be imposed and the whole process repeated; (8) continuing reform or experiment with new regulation may result in change of the objective or even modification of the social and political ethics related to such objective. The jural laws produced through this process of empirical testing will serve as guides to further lawmaking. They do not represent any kind of absolute truth but are pragmatic and subject to further modification through experience and testing.

This approach departs from that proposed in one form or another by Roscoe Pound in only two ways: the introduction of step seven and a failure to articulate the evaluative standards by which the experiments are to be measured. In fact Pound favored many reforms, not as experiments but as pragmatic steps in improving the law; but it was implicit in Pound's view that reforms that didn't work should also be reformed. More signifi-

---

24. Beutel's articles were Outline of the Nature and Methods of Experimental Jurisprudence, 51 Colum. L. Rev. 415 (1951); Traffic Control as Experimental Jurisprudence in Action, 31 Neb. L. Rev. 349 (1952); and The Lag Between Scientific Discovery and Legal Procedures, 33 Neb. L. Rev. 1 (1953). The book that resulted from these earlier works and the extensive empirical study of bad checks was *Some Potentialities of Experimental Jurisprudence as a New Branch of Social Science* (1957). See also Oikawa, Application of Beutel's Experimental Jurisprudence to Japanese Sociology of Law, 39 Neb. L. Rev. 629 (1960).

cant, Beutel seems not to have perceived the many normative choices that would have to be made in employing his "new" method. He discusses the idea of interests but makes little of it. He also devotes a chapter to demonstrate that "values" are of no consequence in experimental jurisprudence. In an interesting metaphor he suggests that the concept of "value" as used in the social sciences and jurisprudence is equivalent to the concept of "phlogiston" used by eighteenth-century chemists to account for certain aspects of burning.[25] Beutel seems to regard values held by individuals as mere personal preferences with no rational basis and values held by a sizable part of the community as a fact to be taken into account by the legal scientist.

In presenting his own empirical work, especially the bad-check study, Beutel is on firmer ground. He investigates the phenomena of passing bad checks, as opposed to analysis of the formal law dealing with the same subject, and he arrives at some conclusions that one who attended only to the formal law would perhaps never have known. His focus is the Nebraska statute that makes it a misdemeanor to issue a check without sufficient funds in the amount of $35 or less and a felony to issue such a check in larger amounts. His study found that gas stations, liquor stores, and restaurants received many more bad checks than other businesses. Over half of all bad checks were for $10 or less. The criminal statute, however, was spottily enforced; only 2 percent of all bad checks reached the attention of officials. Of these, most were not prosecuted; rather, the official (75 percent of prosecutors and 50 percent of sheriffs) informally brought pressure to collect the check for the merchant. In those prosecutions that were initiated many were dismissed after the merchant was reimbursed. In spite of all this, 25 percent of male inmates in state prisons and jails and 40 percent of female inmates were incarcerated for writing bad checks. The deterrent effect of the felony was no greater than that of the misdemeanor; most of the convicted were in fact habitual bad-check writers.

This, of course, is all in the best Poundian and realist tradition. However, it seems significant that in his studies Beutel, although using the usual statistics, interviews, and other sociological data, does not engage in any type of experiment! Nor does he seem to be familiar with Moore's parking

25. The early chemists noted that when a metal was consumed by fire the resulting residue was heavier than the original metal. They postulated a substance known as phlogiston having negative weight. The phlogiston inhered in the metal, but the fire set it free; thus, the ash weighed more and the smoke went up.

study, which did involve experiment. This is more than merely ironic, because it suggests a serious difficulty with Beutel's proposed advance on the Poundian paradigm, namely, that experiments with the law run counter to democratic theory and practice.

Not only is it difficult to induce elected public officials or their appointees to change a policy that they think their constituents favor, but it runs counter to the tradition of self-rule through representatives. Beutel recognizes that the voting public may not be capable of understanding the results of scientific study and therefore may be opposed to experiments that change what they regard as satisfactory law. His recommendation in general is to leave this "scientific decision-making" to experts and remove it from the usual political processes. Of course, this actually occurred to some extent during the New Deal with the creation of many administrative agencies having wide powers of discretion to make rules and even to "experiment." The extent to which this antidemocratic theme should be carried is not spelled out by Beutel.

Beutel's ideas were severely criticized by almost all reviewers of his book; two reviews in particular carefully elaborated the shortcomings of his theory.[26] His antidemocratic inclinations were attacked, as might be expected, and his idea of science was also found to be faulty. Experimental jurisprudence, at its best, was thought by critics to be nothing more than good legislative practice enlightened by scientific evidence wherever possible.

Thomas Cowan followed the master's footsteps for a short time, then moved on in his writings to other themes relating to the relationship between science and law.[27] In spite of the similarity of outlook and common experience on two law faculties together, Cowan does not cite Beutel's work in his own scholarship; he did, however, see fit to reprint Beutel's original article on experimental jurisprudence in a book of selected jurisprudential readings that he edited.[28]

26. Cavers, Science, Research and the Law: Beutel's "Experimental Jurisprudence," 10 J. Leg. Ed. 162 (1957); Robson, Book Review, 26 U. Chi. L. Rev. 492 (1959). For a reply to some of his critics, see Beutel, Elementary Semantics: Criticisms of Realism and Experimental Jurisprudence, 13 J. Leg. Ed. 67 (1960).

27. Cowan received B.S., LL.B., and Ph.D. degrees from the University of Pennsylvania and the degree of S.J.D. from Harvard. He taught on the law faculties at Louisiana State, Pennsylvania, Nebraska, Wayne State, and Rutgers.

28. T. Cowan, *The American Jurisprudence Reader*, 194 (1956). This book of readings contains a subchapter entitled "Legal Experimentalism" in which Beutel's early article is included along with those of Underhill Moore, a team of Cohen, Robson,

Cowan has great faith in experimental science, and he believes that law can be brought within the domain of the social sciences; indeed, he predicts that legal science, or the rational study of law, will be absorbed by the social sciences.[29] Until this comes about, however, he recommends that lawyers, judges, and legal scholars make better use of the findings of social science and that legal scholars encourage social scientists to do research in areas of the law by clarifying the law as it relates to specific aspects of social life. He also endorses Beutel's notion that the law itself should be used as a means of control for experimentation.[30]

Cowan perceives that experimentation in law will run into theoretical difficulties.[31] He regards the cause-and-effect explanations used in the physical sciences as inappropriate for the study of human action, but neither can he accept a moralistic or a priori approach to law. A new method is needed, one cutting across traditional philosophies of empiricism and rationalism. Inspired by Dewey's pragmatism, Cowan proposes a set of "postulates" for experimental legal science. These postulates are only slightly analogous to the legal postulates of society devised earlier by Pound. Pound's postulates were derived through empirical generalization from the assertion of interests by the people of the society, and they represented ideals to which law should be made to conform. Cowan's postulates, in contrast, are guides to the conduct of inquiry into the law; they are not derived empirically but are asserted as a working hypothesis. They constitute "part of a creed for scientific humanism in the law."[32]

Cowan's interest in experimental jurisprudence gave way to a broadened interest in other aspects of social science; indeed, he competed for the role as head cheerleader for "law and science" in the early sixties.[33] Beutel

---

and Bates, and Cowan himself. Cowan also credits Beutel as a founder of this movement. Ibid., 27.

29. Cowan, The Relation of Law to Experimental Social Science, 96 U. Pa. L. Rev. 484 (1948).

30. Ibid., 502.

31. Cowan, Postulates for Experimental Jurisprudence, 9 Rutgers L. Rev. 404 (1954).

32. The five postulates are: "I. The mechanical aspects of a legal system are meaningless without purpose; the purposes or ends of law are impotent without form, order, rule, mechanisms. II. There are no pure a priori elements in legal science; neither are there any basic unalterable facts. III. The science which law uses must be based on experience and experience must ultimately rest on experiment. IV. Every social experiment involves ultimately a question of legal control. V. Every question of legal control involves a moral choice." Ibid.

33. See Cowan, Group Interests, 44 Va. L. Rev. 331 (1958); Cowan, Studies in Legal

continued to defend his experimental jurisprudence in the sixties, but few listened.[34] The ideas of these two scholars were eclipsed or perhaps absorbed into the mainstream of social-science work in law.

The New Social Science of Law

Meanwhile another group of scholars had set out in the same general direction seeking to establish their own version of a social science of law. Among this group were those expatriates of the Columbia law faculty who had left to form the Institute of Law at Johns Hopkins University in 1928 (see chapter 7). Included were Herman Oliphant (1884–1939), who had a background as a philologist and teacher of literature, Hessel Yntema (1891–1966), who had a background in Roman and comparative law, and Leon Marshall, not a lawyer but an economist with empirical leanings who had been recruited to chair Columbia's fruitless curriculum study of 1928. They joined Walter Wheeler Cook (1873–1943), who had left the Yale law faculty to become director of the Institute in June of that same year. Cook had been trained as a mathematical physicist as well as a lawyer. None of these legal scientists had ever practiced law. The mission of the Institute at Johns Hopkins was to become the first institution devoted solely to research in law; the Institute had no students. The researchers were to employ only scientific methods in developing the social science of law.

The jurisprudential ideas of the Institute scholars were not particularly well formed; their views can be ascertained from several articles published in the late twenties and early thirties. Looking at Herman Oliphant first, we find that he did not have a scientific background, but he had been inspired by the writings of Roscoe Pound. His commitment to empirical studies was based more on faith than on a clear understanding of social science. With associate Abram Hewitt he wrote a twenty-five-page introduction to a translation of Jacques Reuff's *From the Physical to the Social Sciences*.[35] This work was published by the Institute and presumably was intended to demonstrate that the methods of the physical sciences could be applied to social phenomena. Although it was cited as authoritative for

Philosophy: Nietzsche, 14 Vand. L. Rev. 151 (1960); Cowan, Decision Theory in Law, Science and Technology, 17 Rutgers L. Rev. 499 (1963).

34. See F. Beutel, *Democracy and Scientific Method in Law* (1965).

35. J. Reuff, *From the Physical to the Social Sciences* (Green trans. 1929).

this proposition in many legal articles and books in the thirties, it was in fact a terribly naive and backward work. In the introduction Oliphant and Hewitt completely confuse the traditional expository and moral paradigms, calling them "transcendental" theories. They also confuse the application of law, or the use of law by lawyers and judges, with the objective study of law. They eschew metaphysics while unconsciously adopting a metaphysics of their own that involves the assumption that the same cause-and-effect relationships utilized in the physical sciences will be applicable in the social science of law. Worse still, they fail to distinguish between normative and descriptive propositions. The introduction, however, is better than the book itself, which does not go much further in explaining science than Auguste Compte did a century earlier. For example, the social sciences are said to include psychology, ethics, and political economy.[36]

Oliphant again addressed the problem of the theoretical basis of legal science in an article published in 1932.[37] There he attempts to refute two objections "advanced most frequently" to the scientific study of law: that it is impossible to quantify the social data of law and that values, being a part of legal phenomena, cannot be subjected to scientific inquiry as facts can. The first objection is easily handled by Oliphant, who points out that not all of the other sciences are quantified and that much of legal phenomena can in fact be quantified. Oliphant hedges a bit on the problem of values. He says, first, that the legal scientist is not concerned with values but only with identifying "the social consequences of particular legal measures and devices."[38] Evaluation can be left to others. However, Oliphant also offers another rather pragmatic and compromising answer. He says that it is unnecessary for the empirical investigator to become concerned with ultimate ends and goals. The immediate end is obvious enough to allow the scholar to carry on his work.[39]

Oliphant's colleague Walter Wheeler Cook wrote several short essays concerning the aims and method of legal science but contributed nothing really jurisprudential.[40] This is somewhat surprising, since Cook was

36. For a good critique of the book see Radin, Scientific Method and the Law, 19 Calif. L. Rev. 164 (1931).

37. Oliphant, Facts, Opinions and Value Judgments, 10 Tex. L. Rev. 127 (1932).

38. Ibid., 137.

39. Ibid., 138.

40. See Cook, Scientific Method and the Law, 13 A.B.A.J. 303 (1927); Cook, The Possibilities of Social Study as a Science, in Brookings Institution, ed., Essays in Research in the Social Sciences (1931); Cook, Legal Logic, 31 Colum. L. Rev. 108

regarded as the "brains" behind the scientific movement at Columbia, Yale, and ultimately the Institute.[41] He took a flexible view toward the methodological underpinnings of the social science of law. He was clearly not a radical behaviorist like Underhill Moore, but he had confidence in the worth of empirical research.

It turned out that Hessel Yntema, the third lawyer-scientist at the Institute, had the most to say about the definition of the social science of law. His debate in the literature with Morris R. Cohen brought out several important issues. Cohen published a collection of his essays in 1931 as a book entitled *Reason and Nature*.[42] Some of them dealt with the relationship between science and law. In the same year Cohen published an article that was critical of Justice Holmes' conception of the law.[43] Hessel Yntema also published an article on Holmes giving a much more sympathetic view.[44] A clash between these two heavyweights seems to have been inevitable.

Cohen's jurisprudential position and his role in the social science controversy is detailed on pages 217–19. However, it will be helpful to summarize the thrust of his attack on the legal realists and their social-scientist allies. Those who would make of law a strictly empirical science, Cohen accuses of nominalism.[45] He sees in their approach (having in mind primarily Frank and Bingham) a rejection of the reality of legal rules and concepts. Such rejection, according to Cohen, flies in the face of all that has been learned in the fields of natural science: that generalizations and concepts formulated as laws or theories are the subject matter of scientific knowledge, not the contingent facts to which those theories relate. While factual verification of theory is a necessary part of scientific inquiry, the observation of facts can be undertaken only when hypotheses

---

(1931); Cook, "Facts" and "Statements of Fact," 4 U. Chi. L. Rev. 233 (1937). This is the same Walter Wheeler Cook who, earlier in his legal career, was enamored of Hohfeldian analysis. See Cook, Hohfeld's Contribution to the Science of Law, 28 Yale L. J. 721 (1919), and the discussion in chapter 4.

41. See W. Twining, *Karl Llewellyn and the Realist Movement*, 40–42, 60 (1973).

42. M. Cohen, *Reason and Nature* (1931).

43. Cohen, Justice Holmes and the Nature of Law, 31 Colum. L. Rev. 352 (1931).

44. Yntema, Mr. Justice Holmes' View of Legal Science, 40 Yale L. J. 696 (1931). Yntema also elaborated upon the empirical approach to law in Yntema, The Purview of Research in the Administration of Justice, 16 Iowa L. Rev. 337 (1931).

45. Nominalism, in brief, is the metaphysical position that the only reality consists of individual external objects; universals like "horse" or "rule," as well as all concepts, are fictions of the mind. Nominalism is usually contrasted with essentialism, which holds that universals do exist.

are conceptually linked to experiment or other data-finding. The would-be legal social scientists, purporting to devote themselves to facts alone, ignore much of what is crucial for an intelligent inquiry into law. A second criticism of legal social science by Cohen, the failure to provide a critical or normative theory, will be addressed in the context of Hessel Yntema's arguments.

Yntema took on both Morris R. Cohen and Mortimer Adler in his article, "The Rational Basis of Legal Science."[46] He maintains that the study of law has traditionally been carried on in the United States in a style that is scholastic, literary, and speculative. This has led to sterility and to the diversion, delay, and impairment of scientific movements in law. Because of this history, empirical legal science was certain to be attacked by traditionalists: "It is inevitable that a nascent empirical legal science, now at the threshold of its endeavors, should be put to its formal justification, before it can be in fact proved. . . . It is inevitable that . . . [it] should be challenged anew in the name of the traditional abstract values of reason, truth and justice."[47]

Yntema takes Cohen to task for "invalidating" empirical legal science on the basis of a faulty metaphysics, namely, nominalism, before it ever has a chance to get off the ground. In particular he declines what he perceives as Cohen's invitation to join the philosophers in the "metaphysical quagmire." He says that science will march on regardless of whether the philosophers ever terminate their debate on the "correct" epistemology of science. Scientists need not become philosophers before they can engage in the scientific enterprise, nor need they wait for philosophers to resolve the methodological problems; in fact, most scientists are indifferent to questions of epistemology. He says:

The indifference of the scientist to the epistemological problem—as a scientist—is warranted by two striking considerations: first, that the theory of knowledge has been disputed ever since the days of Plato and Protagoras and is still disputed—which suggests either unreality in the problem or defect in the methods of solution; second, that while it is yet to be shown that a scientific demonstration is at all validated by the theory of knowledge of the scientist, any more than by his religion or the language in which the results are stated, scien-

46. Yntema, The Rational Basis of Legal Science, 31 Colum. L. Rev. 925 (1931). Yntema's attack on Adler was aimed at the latter's critique of Jerome Frank's *Law and the Modern Mind* in Adler, Legal Certainty, 31 Colum. L. Rev. 91 (1931).
47. Ibid., 935.

tific discoveries seem to have been often made irrespective of or in spite of metaphysical naivete.[48]

Yntema thus dismisses Cohen's methodological objections to the empirical science of law as impertinent and irrelevant.

Yntema then directs his attention to Cohen's thesis that an empirical science of law will be inadequate because it attempts to exclude the normative aspects of law. He suggests that the idea of a normative science or a science of ethics is ambiguous, indeterminate, and historically unsuccessful.[49] "It would seem that the theory of justice, after two thousand years, is in about as parlous a state as the theory of knowledge."[50] He analyzes and criticizes Cohen's concept of a normative theory of law, although he appears to misunderstand Cohen at certain points. He thinks that an evaluation of legal rules used by the courts in terms of other legal norms and of ethical principles would unnecessarily restrict legal science. "An inelegant analogy would be the restriction of a science of dietetics to the 'norms' of a cookbook since they are used by the *chef*."[51]

Cohen replied in the 1932 issue of the *Columbia Law Review.*[52] He suggests that Yntema misunderstands the nature of philosophy, viewing it as some sort of short-cut to scientific knowledge through the use of mirrors.[53] Cohen maintains, in contrast, that philosophy is not a phony substitute for science but concerns itself with the fundamental problems underlying all intellectual enterprise. Cohen chides Yntema for confusing metaphysics, the study of ultimate reality or what is, with epistemology, the study of how we know what we know. Scientists in every field make both epistemological and metaphysical assumptions when they engage in their work, sometimes consciously and sometimes not.

Students of law, like all other intellectual workers, are likely, sooner or later, to make assumptions which involve one or another answer

48. Ibid., 938–39.

49. Note here that Yntema is not talking about the empirical study of norms, which he favors, but about philosophical theories of ethics, which he dismisses.

50. Yntema note 46, 943.

51. Ibid., 952.

52. Cohen, Philosophy and Legal Science, 32 Colum. L. Rev. 1103 (1932).

53. "Philosophy to Professor Yntema, and to many others, appears to be a peculiar method of thought which sets itself up as a short-cut to knowledge and thus seduces travelers from the arduous road of science. Indeed there seem to be three short-cuts to legal knowledge offered by philosophy, and these are the paths of Mind, of Logic, and of Ought. It seems therefore incumbent upon the defenders of legal science to mark the quicksands which underlie these paths, so that men may continue to walk on the firm highways of verifiable knowledge." Ibid., 1103–1104.

to the basic problems of metaphysics. When one of these answers happens to be untenable it does not help the situation to urge that we are lawyers and not metaphysicians. The untenable assumption remains untenable no matter what the professional occupation of the one who makes it.[54]

Cohen proceeds to explain nominalism and its faults and reasserts that the empirical legal scientists are falling into this particular metaphysical hole.

Cohen then takes up Yntema's argument that scientists do not and should not involve themselves in epistemology. Cohen believes that Yntema has confused psychology with logic. Two distinct questions are presented: How do people in fact think?—a question for psychology; and, Is the evidence adequate for any particular asserted proposition?—a question for logic. "The argument that scientific propositions sometimes have epistemological presuppositions is not answered by the statement that 'most scientists are not epistemologists.' Not the 'theory of knowledge of the scientist' is in question, but the objective implications of his premises."[55]

Cohen then turns to Yntema's assertion that there can be no meaningful normative science of law. Cohen's exposition of what is meant by the term "norm" is especially lucid. He maintains that it is intellectually legitimate to study law from a normative point of view whether or not we call such study science. His main objection to a strictly empirical science of law is that it claims to be the only science of law. He says normative study can be pursued in three ways: historically, sociologically, and through normative jurisprudence. The first two methods are essentially descriptive. The third is critical or evaluative.

Cohen states that there is nothing transcendental, as Yntema implies, about any of these norms or the study of them. They are no more mysterious than the standards of literary craftsmanship, the requirements of economic efficiency, or the rules of good carpentry. Norms in each of these technical areas may be evaluated and rationally organized. Likewise, more general norms applicable throughout a broader spectrum of social activities and applicable as well to the legal system may be rationally assessed with a view toward promoting consistency and effectiveness in human action.

Cohen dismisses the contention that normative jurisprudence is not science but merely art or technique.[56] He says:

54. Ibid., 1105.
55. Ibid., 113 fn.21.
56. Cohen uses the term "science" here in a broad sense, including any kind of organized and systematic study that uses logic and reason.

If normative jurisprudence is an art, it is certainly not an art which deals directly with the organization of physical things. Rather does it seek to organize judgments into a rational or harmonious system. And in this sense all science may be viewed as a rational art. Physics may thus be regarded as the art of transforming all our judgments of natural existence into a coherent system which will not be in conflict with any physical observation. Similarly, ethics or the general theory of value is an attempt to organize all our judgements of approval or preference into a coherent system, so that every one of them will be determinate, rather than purely arbitrary, and in the long run best express our emotional and volitional nature.[57]

Cohen then relates the importance of ethical norms to the everyday business of law. He explains that elements of discretion are present in most cases of judicial decision, and indeed some cases are completely novel. "In asking whether an existing rule should be extended or restricted, the judge's opinion as to its justice is bound to be influential."[58] Here the lawyer must take into account the judge's ethical views and in addition how those ethical views can be fitted into a larger whole, so that argumentation can be directed to change the judge's views if necessary. Therefore, some appreciation of the interrelationship between ethical theory and law is necessary for a full understanding of how the legal process works.

Further statements of Cohen and Yntema on these issues appeared in the literature of the thirties, but no resolution of them was to come about, although Yntema softened his views somewhat.[59] Yntema and his colleagues at Johns Hopkins undertook a score or more empirical studies, concentrated mainly on gathering judicial statistics, and the results of these were eventually published.[60] Judging from the lack of reference to them in the literature of legal scholarship, they did not make much of an impression on lawyers. The Johns Hopkins Institute of Law closed its doors in 1933 for lack of funding, a victim of the Great Depression. Oliphant ultimately went into practice with the government. Yntema and Cook found their way to the law faculties of Michigan and Northwestern,

57. Cohen note 52, 1125.
58. Ibid., 1126.
59. See Yntema, The Implications of Legal Science, 10 N.Y.U.L.Q. Rev. 279 (1933); Yntema, Legal Science and Reform, 34 Colum. L. Rev. 207 (1934). See also the critique by Cohen of Thurman Arnold's *The Symbols of Government* in chapter 7.
60. For a list of the published studies of the Institute see W. Twining, *Karl Llewellyn and the Realist Movement*, 403–404 (1973).

respectively. In this same period the Institute of Human Relations at Yale also experienced cuts in funds. However, projects involving empirical research were carried on by Charles E. Clark and William O. Douglas of the Yale law faculty as well as the more notorious work of Underhill Moore. Needless to say, funds for this sort of academic activity were unavailable during World War II.

Various other scholars in the late twenties and thirties endorsed the idea of a separate social science of law. Cassius Keyser (1862–1947), a professor of mathematics at Columbia, explained rather naively the method and program that such a science would have to follow.[61] Herman Kantorowicz (1877–1940), formerly a prominent member of the free-law movement, outlined a comprehensive science of law that contained a social-science component, but his views reflected a tradition of German legal scholarship alien to Americans.[62] Reinold Noyes (1884–1954), a prominent economist, also presented his views on how the new science should go about its work.[63] Noyes' suggested approach was essentially behavioristic, although not as dogmatic as that of Underhill Moore. Noyes recognized that the value side of law could not be treated scientifically, but he thought that a descriptive science could be developed that would help make the law "more certain."

One of the most ardent advocates for a new and independent social science of law was Huntington Cairns (1904–   ).[64] Cairns had written a book called *Law and the Social Sciences* in 1935 that received mixed reviews. Its central theme was that the social sciences could provide valuable insights and information to legal scholars, something most Poundians had taken to heart by this time. In 1941 Cairns' more mature thought was presented in *The Theory of Legal Science*.[65] With the exception of the work of Morris R. Cohen, this was the most sophisticated

61. Keyser, On the Study of Legal Science, 38 Yale L. J. 413 (1929); Keyser, The Nature of the Doctrinal Function and its Role in Rational Thought, 41 Yale L. J. 713 (1932).

62. Kantorowicz and Patterson, Legal Science—A Summary of its Methodology, 28 Colum. L. Rev. 679 (1928).

63. Noyes, Law and the Scientific Method, 55 Pol. Sci. Q. 496 (1940).

64. Cairns was educated at the University of Maryland, practiced law in Baltimore, and served as assistant general counsel in the Treasury Department for several years. He also served as secretary, treasurer, and general counsel for the National Gallery of Art and was a lecturer at Johns Hopkins University from 1947 to 1959.

65. Cairns also contributed a significant historical work a few years later: *Legal Philosophy from Plato to Hegel* (1949). See also, *Law and Its Premises* (1962); *What Is Law?* (1970).

effort to date to explain the theoretical underpinnings of the social science of law. Cairns distinguishes the professional or vocational aspects of law as mere "technology." Such technology or vocational wisdom in most fields of human endeavor would amount to the application of science to specific tasks. However, in the case of law there is only the pseudoscience of analytic jurisprudence. Thus, the law taught in law schools is not even a full-fledged technology, since it has no real science to draw upon. Cairns advocates a radical change in the academic study of law to make it a true social science. He believes that in the long run the development of such a science will improve the practice of law because it can then become a legitimate technology.

Unlike the Institute scholars and Underhill Moore, Cairns recognizes that a serious jurisprudential question is presented by the assertion that the academic study of law should be a separate and independent social science. He devotes his first chapter to this proposition. Cairns sees all of the social sciences as studying human behavior, but each from its own point of view or with its own focus. He says that the social science of law can join the others with its peculiar focus being "disorder."[66] Relying on many anthropological studies, he establishes that every human society has order of various kinds and that such orders are of human creation; he then points out that disorder nevertheless occurs. How society deals with disorder is the focus of legal science, or, as he prefers to call it, jurisprudence.[67] Cairns says that the idea of disorder as a focus for investigation is borrowed from Lawrence K. Frank.[68]

Cairns discusses many of the questions of the philosophy of science, including causation and determinism, but he seems to offer no new thoughts on these subjects, and indeed vacillates between a completely deterministic social science and one in which rational choice is assumed. He relies on Morris R. Cohen for some of his discussion, and his recommended scientific method is that of "hypothesis and verification," which turns out to be the hypothetico-deductive model that had been worked

66. "Jurisprudence as here conceived may be defined provisionally as the study of human behavior as a function of disorder." H. Cairns, *The Theory of Legal Science*, 1 (1941).

67. Cairns is not entirely consistent in this matter, since in a later chapter he lapses by saying, "Law is but one of the many systems of order which operate in society." Ibid., 112.

68. See Frank, The Principle of Disorder and Incongruity in Economic Affairs, 47 Pol. Sci. Q. 515 (1932); see also Frank, An Institutional Analysis of the Law, 24 Colum. L. Rev. 480 (1924).

out for the physical sciences.[69] Cairns advocates a "pure" science of law as opposed to research directed toward some pragmatic end. He thinks Pound and others, including the researchers at the Johns Hopkins Institute, seriously erred in directing research toward legal reform. The mission of science, as Cairns conceives it, is to produce scientific knowledge, not to support political causes.

In the last chapter of *The Theory of Legal Science* Cairns comes to grips with the question of values. He makes explicit what the practice of the anthropologists had demonstrated: that values can be studied scientifically and empirically as fact, but the evaluation of values cannot. Recognizing that law is normative, he concludes, following the lead of Morris R. Cohen, that three lines of inquiry could be followed. First, a postulational science of law could be created. This is the kind of empirical science that Cairns advocates throughout the book. It would treat the values of any given culture as fact. Second, a postulational science of ethics could be created. This would serve as a basis for evaluation of the law. Third, a postulational science of law and ethics in combination could be created. This would presumably provide us with a fuller understanding of law than either of the other alternatives. However, it would be much more complicated and difficult. For this reason Cairns thinks that the first alternative should be pursued, at least until some progress has been made in that direction.[70]

While not contributing much in the way of new ideas, Cairns' book was a sophisticated summary of the philosophy of the social science of law as it stood in 1941.[71] The model of the physical sciences is accepted as the guide for social science. The problem of free human action and causal determinism is recognized but not resolved. Likewise, the problem of how to fit values into scientific inquiry is well stated but also left unresolved.

69. Although there is a citation to Max Weber's *The Protestant Ethic and the Spirit of Capitalism* (1930), Cairns does not seem to be acquainted with Weber's ideas relating to the social meaning of behavior or his idea of "ideal types." Cairns briefly discusses ideal types, but means by that term something quite different. Cairns, note 66, 108.

70. "Whether, in the construction of a science of law, the postulational scheme should include the normative or whether, for the time being, it should omit it, is a matter of opinion. Legitimate considerations, however, indicate that omission is the wiser course. We have more chance of success if our initial field of inquiry is not too ambitiously staked out." Cairns, note 66, 144–45.

71. For commentary on the book see Hall, Book Review, 28 Va. L. Rev. 851 (1942); Cohen, Book Review, 8 U. Chi. L. Rev. 807 (1942). For a somewhat later discussion of social science method by Cairns, see Cairns, Book Review [reviewing F. Kaufmann, *Methodology of the Social Sciences* (1944)], 13 U. Chi. L. Rev. 126 (1945).

The case is explicitly argued for a social science of law, in addition to the existing social sciences, and divorced from the technology of law practice; but the argument is not convincing.

After World War II no one came forth to champion the idea of a social science of law.[72] The reasons for advocating such an independent science, as opposed to sociological or anthropological work in the field of law, were articulated only by Cairns, and not very persuasively. For the earlier scientists a simple but unconscious argument seemed to underlie the whole enterprise: law is not a natural science or an art, but it is a recognized discipline in the academic community; therefore, it must be a social science. It implied that a choice must be made by the academic lawyer: be a scientist, or be a trade school teacher, a "Hessian trainer."[73]

In addition, from its beginnings in the twenties a social science of law did not inspire institutional support. The legal social scientists did not know it at the time, but the failure to adopt the great Columbia curriculum study with all its implications for social science research proved to be the rejection of an independent social science of law for the foreseeable future. Assembled at Columbia were the most promising and enthusiastic legal scientists ever in place at one institution. Yet they could not overcome the inertia of the institution's role as professional trainer of the bar. The institution of the law school had become so firmly fastened in American educational culture that it could be moved only incrementally, and not too far at that. Most of the bar, including many law-school teachers, ridiculed efforts of the would-be scientists. The other social scientists viewed the legal scientists with suspicion and jealousy, a threat to their rightful turf, as indicated clearly in the case of Underhill Moore. The jurisdictional lines had been drawn. There was no place for the law scientists.

Other circumstances combined to defeat the idea of a separate social science of law. The Depression and the war combined to eliminate funds for this type of research for the ten or fifteen years that were crucial to the development of this new discipline. At the same time the sociologists, the anthropologists, and the psychologists were beginning to make some headway into the study of legal phenomena under the premises of their own disciplines. By 1946 forward-looking legal scholars were beginning

72. Oliphant died in 1939, Cook in 1944, Moore in 1949. We may distinguish the experimental jurisprudence of Beutel and the LSP of Lasswell and McDougal as programs of a somewhat different nature.

73. See Bergin, The Law Teacher: A Man Divided Against Himself, 54 Va. L. Rev. 637 (1968).

to talk about the need for "interdisciplinary research" in the law.[74] In looking back on the situation in 1956, Karl Llewellyn observed with the benefit of hindsight that the early efforts toward legal social science failed for several reasons: lack of an interested public; correspondent lack of funding; lawyer-investigators untrained in social science; failure to learn and follow techniques already established in related disciplines; lack of organization and recording of projects; and failure to choose manageable projects likely to bear fruit.[75] Whether Llewellyn's assessment of the early efforts at a social science of law were correct or not, they undoubtedly represented the postwar thinking on the subject.

At the same time that the social scientists of law were trying to make headway, that competing symbol of "science" in the law, the great monument of the expository paradigm, the restatement, was marching forward to the acclaim of bench and bar. Not only had the American Law Institute been well funded, but the prestige of its projects in legal academia drew young scholars into its orbit.

All of these factors combined to kill the movement for an independent social science of law. Curiously, this occurred without anyone ever having directly refuted the idea.

The Place of Morris R. Cohen: Restoring the Balance

Morris R. Cohen (1880–1947) was not an enthusiast for a legal social science, nor was he an enemy; but he played a very important role in the development of jurisprudence in the context of the "new" science; hence, some attention must be given here to this role and to his views.[76] Cohen was trained not as a lawyer but as a philosopher. However, early in his career he took an interest in jurisprudence, writing significant articles as early as 1913.[77] He was influenced by Pound and by German theorist Rudolf Stammler, but most of the ideas he developed

---

74. See, for example, Symposium, Integrating Law and other Learned Professions, 32 Va. L. Rev. 695 (1946).

75. Llewellyn, On What Makes Legal Research Worth While, 8 A.B.A.J. 399 (1956).

76. The definitive work on Cohen is D. Hollinger, *Morris R. Cohen and the Scientific Ideal* (1975). This book also contains a bibliography of Cohen's works.

77. See, for example, Jurisprudence as a Philosophical Discipline, 10 J. Phil. Psy. and Sci. Methods 228 (1913); The Process of Judicial Legislation, 48 Am. L. Rev. 161 (1914); History vs. Value, 11 J. Phil. 710 (1914); Jus Naturale Redivivum, 25 Phil. Rev. 761 (1916); The Place of Logic in the Law, 29 Harv. L. Rev. 622 (1916).

came from his philosophical background in logic and the philosophy of science. He was neither an idealist nor a pragmatist, although he had studied at Harvard under the leading American exponents of those schools of philosophy, Royce and James. Cohen tended to view issues or problems in terms of polar opposites, taking the position that a subject can be distorted by being carried to extremes and counseling that the truth was likely to be found in the middle. His jurisprudence displayed this same moderation.

Cohen did not put his philosophy of law into one scholarly work; indeed, he did not touch upon all of the issues of jurisprudence in his writings, as Pound substantially did. Hence, Cohen's theory is fragmentary; but what he had to say was particularly important for the time because he came to jurisprudence from an intellectual world quite different from that of the lawyers. In his skepticism of positivism (of either the expository or empirical variety) he anticipated the more explicit arguments of Fuller (see chapter 9). He saw behind both approaches a tendency to equate what is with what ought to be, translated as "might makes right." Against what he viewed as a warped empirical scientism, most of his writings tended to be arguments for the recognition of the normative or ethical side of law and for the importance of logic and reason in understanding law. In a sense he was bucking the trends of the period at every turn.

However, in a broader perspective Cohen accepts the Poundian paradigm. He is not a defender of the strict analysts or of the theory underlying the *Restatements*; nor does he accept traditional natural law. He agrees that law is a social phenomenon, and that the activity of legal decision-makers is determined by many factors other than formal rules. Nevertheless, formal rules are an important part of law, and in his view a true understanding of law requires an account of how those rules bind judges and why they should. This means that he insists at the very least on a normative component to an overall science of law. In the twenties and thirties when such ideas about normative theory were under indiscriminate attack by the realists, Cohen found himself constantly defending this side of the Poundian paradigm.

Cohen did not, however, subscribe to Pound's theory of social interests. Instead he offered a "normative science of law" that arguably gave a greater role to reason and logic.[78] Cohen is ambiguous on whether his

78. Cohen's normative theory is best stated in Jus Naturale Redivivum, 25 Phil. Rev. 761 (1916), and Philosophy and Legal Science, 32 Colum. L. Rev. 1103 (1932).

approach can yield ultimate values. He seems to envision a system in which one starts with clearly accepted specific judgments about right and wrong as evidenced by both societal acceptance and personal intuition. Then, proceeding rationally, the normative scientist will fit these specific judgments into a logical scheme of organization. Logical consistency requires that priorities be established and means and ends be articulated. As the system becomes clearer, more abstract principles can be postulated. Cohen analogizes the postulation of such principles to the postulation of scientific hypotheses, to be taken as valid until proven wrong because they lead, again logically, to unacceptable moral judgments in specific circumstances. Whether or not this type of dialectical science can lead to ultimate principles, it will have the effect of clarifying the relationship between various ethical precepts. Needless to say, legal norms can be evaluated within such a normative system. It should be emphasized that Cohen also insists that such a system depends entirely upon an adequate understanding of society and hence upon the fruits of social science. Cohen was not an enemy of social science.

Except to the extent that it might have influenced Fuller, Cohen's normative theory did not seem to collect many immediate adherents; however, the theory was never answered or refuted in the jurisprudential literature.[79] It might have been thought that Felix S. Cohen, Morris Cohen's lawyer son, would follow his father's lead. However, Felix Cohen defended realism, combining it with a utilitarian ethics.[80] More important than the normative theory for this historical period, however, was Morris Cohen's superior grasp of the philosophy of science; this had a great impact on the debate about empirical approaches to law. Particularly in his exchanges with Yntema and his critique of Arnold, Cohen came out ahead. This should not be surprising since the game was philosophy of science, not science, and this was Cohen's ballpark. Cohen can be credited more than any other scholar with establishing the idea that a radically behaviorist social science of law, as the exclusive science of law, was on a shaky if not completely untenable foundation. Cohen's view of this matter was to prevail.

79. The reader is directed to two strikingly similar theories advanced much later by Rawls and Hayek. See J. Rawls, *A Theory of Justice*, 46–53 (1971) ("reflective equilibrium"); F. Hayek, *Law, Legislation and Liberty: The Mirage of Social Justice*, 24–27 (vol. 2, 1976) ("immanent criticism"). See also R. Dworkin, *Law's Empire*, 254–66 (1986) ("Hercules' " decision process).

80. See F. Cohen, *Ethical Systems and Legal Ideals* (1933).

The Law, Science, and Policy of
Lasswell and McDougal

Myres McDougal (1906–   ) studied at the universities of Mississippi, Yale, and Oxford. He taught briefly at the University of Illinois and returned to Yale in 1934.[81] He began as a realist, defending the movement against the critique of Lon Fuller.[82] When visiting at the University of Chicago he met Harold Lasswell (1902–1978), a political scientist.[83] The two became mutual admirers, and later, when the opportunity arose, Lasswell was invited to join the faculty at Yale as a professor of law and social science, which he did. This was part of Yale's "realist" policy of bringing in social scientists to complement the teaching of traditional law materials.[84] McDougal and Lasswell cooperated in research and writing efforts for a period of thirty years, and in the process they formulated a jurisprudential system usually called law, science, and policy, or LSP, after the name of the seminar that they jointly taught for many years.

McDougal regarded the realist movement as a healthy remedy for the intellectual backwardness of the entrenched expository paradigm; but he also saw that it was primarily negative, successful in exposing old myths and lame theory but offering little to take its place. While McDougal acknowledged the value of empirical study in the legal field, he knew that such scholarship alone could not replace the old ways of thinking. He recognized that law is normative, or, to use LSP's phrase, a matter of policy. Lasswell, who regarded himself as a "policy scientist," brought to bear on law all of the intellectual techniques and devices used by the political scientists of the day. McDougal and Lasswell came to see the need

81. McDougal taught property law initially, but the war and its aftermath turned his attention to international law; he became a world-renowned scholar in this field. McDougal served as president of the Association of American Law Schools and as president of the American Society of International Law.

82. McDougal, Fuller v. The American Legal Realists: An Intervention, 50 Yale L. J. 827 (1941).

83. Lasswell was educated at the University of Chicago and served on its political science faculty from 1926 to 1928, then joined the Yale law faculty. In addition to the application of policy science to law, he taught international law. Lasswell served as president of the American Political Science Association.

84. Reflecting the realist concern for the development of social science and law, in the 1930s the Yale Law School added to its faculty Walton Hamilton, an economist, Edward Robinson, a psychologist, and Harold Lasswell, a political scientist. In the 1940s Yale hired F.S.C. Northrop, a philosopher of science. For a discussion of Northrop see chapter 9.

for a new type of legal science incorporating the insights of realism and empirical legal study but capable of being used to formulate, promote, and critique policy. This science would have to escape from the conceptual strictures of traditional legal science, including old terminology and the traditional way of framing issues and problems.

The two scholars had worked out some of the framework of the new science by 1943, when they coauthored an extensive article proposing radical reforms in legal education.[85] This plea for educating law students to be policy-makers brought Lasswell and McDougal considerable attention in the law-school world, but they were unable to proceed further because of the war. Work was resumed in the late forties, and the exposition and application of LSP proliferated in articles and books published over the next quarter century.[86]

LSP has as its focus authoritative decision-making. This means that the policy scientist is concerned with how the process of decision-making is carried on by persons having political authority. The system applies to the processes of decision by legislatures, courts, administrative agencies, arbitrators, city councils, school boards, international organizations, homeowners' associations, and many other institutions. It is significant that how judges decide cases is only one aspect of the scheme.

LSP is, in fact, one grand scheme, a giant system of analysis.[87] Decision-

85. Lasswell and McDougal, Legal Education and Public Policy: Professional Training in the Public Interest, 52 Yale L. J. 203 (1943).

86. R. Arens and H. Lasswell, *In Defense of Public Order* (1960); H. Lasswell and A. Kaplan, *Power and Society: A Framework for Political Inquiry* (1950); H. Lasswell, *The Analysis of Political Behavior: An Empirical Approach* (1949); Lasswell, The Interrelations of World Organization and Society, 55 Yale L. J. 870 (1946); Lasswell, The Impact of Psychiatry on Jurisprudence, 21 Ohio St. L. J. 17 (1960); Lasswell, The Interplay of Economics, Political and Social Criteria in a Legal Policy, 14 Vand. L. Rev. 451 (1961); Lasswell, A Brief Discourse about Method in the Current Madness, 57 Proc. Am. Soc. Int. L. 72 (1963); Lasswell and McDougal, Jurisprudence in Policy Oriented Perspective, 19 U. Fla. L. Rev. 486 (1967); M. McDougal and Associates, *Studies in World Public Order* (1960); M. McDougal and F. Feliciano, *Law and Minimum World Public Order: The Legal Regulation of International Coercion* (1961); McDougal, The Law School of the Future: From Legal Realism to Policy Science in the World Community, 56 Yale L. J. 1345 (1947); McDougal, The Role of Law in World Politics, 20 Miss. L. J. 253 (1949); McDougal, Law and Power, 46 Am. J. Int. L. 102 (1952); McDougal, Law as a Process of Decision: A Policy Oriented Approach to Legal Study, 1 Nat. L. Forum 53 (1956); McDougal and Reisman, The Changing Structure of International Law: Unchanging Theory for Inquiry, 65 Colum. L. Rev. 810 (1965); McDougal, Jurisprudence for a Free Society, 1 Georg. L. Rev. 1 (1966).

87. For a short sympathetic explanation of LSP, but more detailed than the one given

making processes may be broken down in various ways for purposes of study. Categorization of the process by the community affected (international, national, local, institutional) is an obvious option. Study according to phase (phase analysis) is another method. The standard phases, or components of the process, used by Lasswell and McDougal are participants, perspectives, situations, base values, strategies, outcomes, effects, and conditions. Any decision-making process can also be broken down into authority functions, or "steps," appropriate to decision. The authority functions utilized in LSP are intelligence-gathering, promotion, prescription, invocation, application, termination, and appraisal. The concepts of authority (decision in conformity with community expectations) and control (effective sanction) are central to the whole scheme. The process of decision is viewed as combining authority and control to promote community values resulting in the sharing of those values among members of the community. Future consequences of decisions measured in terms of community values become important in shaping and evaluating those decisions. If a definition is needed, law is thus "the sum of the power decisions in a community."[88] The application of LSP also requires that the observational standpoint (as policy scientist, decision-maker, other participant) be taken into account in using the scheme of analysis.

Another important and controversial aspect of LSP is value analysis, or the analysis of specific values held by the participants that enter into the decisional process. A value, for Lasswell and McDougal, is a preferred or desired event, something valued. Obviously many things in life are valued, but it is possible to classify these values into more general categories. LSP has settled on eight such general values as being most convenient: power, or participation in the making of decisions; enlightenment, the discovery and dissemination of information and knowledge; wealth, control of economic goods; well-being, physical and mental health; skill, the development of talents; affection, the development of close personal relations; respect, recognition of merit by others; and rectitude, righteousness in social relationships. The values are presumably empirically derived, and their particular manifestation in a given society will vary with other aspects of the culture. These general values are obviously similar to Pound's social interests, although perhaps more individualistic, and they also resemble Fuller's shared human purposes (see chapter 9).

---

here, see Moore, Prolegomenon to the Jurisprudence of Myres McDougal and Harold Lasswell, 54 Va. L. Rev. 662 (1968).

88. McDougal, The Law School of the Future: From Legal Realism to Policy Science in the World Community, 56 Yale L. J. 1345, 1348 (1947).

In any discussion of values in the LSP schema it is important to keep in mind the observational standpoint. While all persons probably desire all of the eight general values used in the system, they may differ greatly in the importance they attach to particular values. Thus, an individual who will be subjected to or affected by a decision may have a particular set of values that differs from another person affected; both sets of values may differ from the decision-maker's. Community expectations may differ again. These are generally questions of fact from the standpoint of the scientific observer. It is, of course, possible to assess an individual's or group's values against those of the greater community or those of some authoritative decision-maker and thus make a value judgment. Such a value judgment will be relative to the respective participants. Thus, the ethical relativism of earlier realists reappears in a different setting.

The system of LSP is not limited to use by neutral or objective scientific observers, however. Any participant can also use it as an intellectual tool in playing her part in the decisional process. Thus, a legislator, a judge, an advocate, or an interested citizen can utilize the system of analysis to understand better what he or she is or should be doing. The system does presume that anyone using it, including participants, always acts rationally as a value maximizer, a proposition questioned by those inclined toward a psychological approach. When a judge, lawyer, or legislator applies the system, however, the participant's own values are not a question of fact. Each participant must articulate and clarify her own values, deriving them from whatever rational sources are appropriate. This process of value articulation and clarification is regarded as an important aspect of LSP. Further, the social scientist himself is seldom if ever neutral, usually directing his study toward some reform; hence, he also must insert his own values into the analysis. McDougal and Lasswell have openly stated the values that they conceive to be paramount, although they have given no further justification for these values. They seem to regard "human dignity" as an overarching end with three subordinate principles: shared knowledge, shared power, and shared respect.[89] These are thought to be "democratic values" sought and urged by McDougal and Lasswell in their analysis of various fields of law.[90] Some observers have consequently seen a natural-law aspect to LSP.[91]

89. Cf. the traditional natural-law principle, Do Good and Avoid Evil, discussed in chapter 9.

90. McDougal was primarily interested in international law, and almost all of the LSP analysis done by him and his students is in that field.

91. See, for example, E. Bodenheimer, *Jurisprudence: The Philosophy and Method of*

The different methods of analysis and the categories established for each in LSP are created in order to assure systematic consideration of all aspects of decision-making. They are glorified "checklists," or perhaps more accurately, "tasklists." The particular categories selected by Mc-Dougal and Lasswell are not God-given or a priori but are simply the ones found to be convenient in the course of using the system. Because the system of analysis is broader than the methods of traditional legal analysis and is multifaceted, it also helps avoid confusion and mistake by insuring that aspects of the process are considered in their proper place.

LSP combines features of "decision theory," "systems analysis," and other inventions of the social scientists. It is expected that social-science methods will be used, including empirical studies of all kinds. The methods of sociology, psychology, anthropology, political science, and economics can be brought to bear on questions of fact raised by application of the analysis.

Thus, LSP brings legal realism to a sort of completion. Where the realists discounted the operation of formal legal concepts and rules but provided no substitute for the function of such legal abstractions, LSP allocates a minor place to such traditional law (as "perspectives") while at the same time focusing on the broader process of authoritative decision-making, which systematically includes all of the other factors that go into the decisions. These factors, of course, include the values held by participants, something that the radical empiricists among the realists failed to account for.

The advantages of LSP over previous kinds of jurisprudence are claimed to be several. Use of a new terminology and set of concepts frees discussion from the constraints of traditional conceptual categories and the connotations of the traditional vocabulary. LSP joins fact, as scientifically determined, with values in a workable way that makes evaluation and guidance of decision-making possible. Although McDougal and Lasswell advance certain values that might be regarded as peculiar to American culture, the LSP system itself can be used to promote the values of any ideology; in this sense it is universal. Because of its elaborate methods of analysis, LSP will yield more precise and usable results for decision-makers in contrast to traditional vague exhortations to "balance interests," "exercise wise discretion," and the like. LSP also places legislative, judicial, and other processes of concern to lawyers in the wider context of

---

the Law, 151 (rev. ed. 1974), where the author includes the work of Lasswell and McDougal in a chapter on the revival of natural law.

social processes of which they are a part; the autonomy of the legal system can thus be seen to be illusory, and the lawyer can relate social phenomena once thought to be nonlegal to their proper place in legal processes. The checklist aspect of the LSP analysis forces the inquirer to examine things that might otherwise be ignored and to challenge otherwise unconscious assumptions. Finally, use of the system is said to provide greater clarity and insight into legal problem-solving than alternative approaches.

An argument can certainly be made that LSP is simply the Poundian paradigm brought to maturity. It takes into account the same basic insights, but it organizes and systematizes the study of legal institutions in a way that Pound and the realists were never able to do. Indeed, from this perspective LSP is the book of sociological jurisprudence that Pound never wrote. Two things stand out in the system of LSP that no one has criticized and that seem to be real advances on the traditional Poundian paradigm. These are, first, the wide focus on authoritative decision-making to include court decision, legislation, and other similar processes. Certainly ever since Holmes the focus in American jurisprudence had been almost exclusively on court decisions.[92] Second, by indicating the importance of the observational standpoint in jurisprudence, LSP has clarified or resolved what had become an intractable methodological problem.[93]

On the negative side LSP has been criticized along four lines. First, the terminology of the system is overpowering. It does not seem likely in the foreseeable future that the legal profession would be willing to change its words and concepts so drastically. Yet, the system is supposed to be capable of use by the participants in it, not just by academics in ivory towers. At the very least LSP will have to prove itself highly superior to alternative ways of thinking about the legal process before any terminological revolution will occur. Many would say that it has thus far failed to do so.

Second, it has been charged that LSP provides a fancy analytical scheme with new terms that does nothing more than lawyers, judges, and legislators do all the time. The lawyer's intuition, combined with his admittedly antiquated legal education, plus a little experience, allows him to get to

92. This advantage of LSP would certainly please and vindicate Arthur Bentley. See the discussion of Bentley in chapter 6.

93. For example, there was much argument over how law could be viewed as the prediction of what courts will do. In deciding a case, of course, a court is not predicting what it will do. Recognition of the different observational standpoints of participants in the process (judge, advocate, party, and so forth) as well as outside observers can remove much confusion in this debate.

the important issues involved in any legal problem as fast or faster than LSP. In this view the checklist aspect of LSP is also oversold. Instead of directing attention to shaky assumptions or unknown facts, the checklists direct attention to trivia that any legal analyst would intuitively reject as remote and unimportant. The principle of "economy" is brought in by McDougal and Lasswell as a way of saving the system from this criticism; but it amounts to an admission that the system is far too cumbersome for solving all but the most complex legal problems.

A third criticism relates to value analysis. The eight-category checklist, designed to provide value input to any process analysis, suffers from the same defects as Pound's categories of social interests. They are too general and thus too capable of manipulation to provide any real guidance. While the use of such a checklist presumably forces one to articulate and clarify the values involved, the LSP classification of values does not really take us much beyond talking about the "public policy" in favor of this or that.

A similar criticism can be made of Lasswell and McDougal's own paramount values, human dignity, shared power, shared respect, and shared knowledge. These are hardly less general than the precepts of natural law which Lasswell and McDougal relegate to the intellectual trash barrel. In addition, no epistemological, metaphysical, theological, or other justification for the insistence on these values is offered. Hence, the LSP system fails to provide what many think most important in a jurisprudence, an objective moral grounding for the legal system.

McDougal served as director of the graduate program at Yale for many years. A large number of students receiving advanced law degrees from Yale in the fifties and sixties went into law teaching at universities across the nation, and many of them spread the gospel of LSP. Thus, a following for this type of jurisprudence was built up. McDougal retired from Yale in 1977, although he has remained active; Lasswell died in 1978. But since the initial flurry of excitement in the jurisprudential world in the forties and fifties, LSP has been in decline. Michael Riesman has carried on the tradition at Yale, and others have tried elsewhere. However, the severe rethinking about legal process required by LSP, including adoption of its terminology, combined with some of the defects of the system, created too much of a burden to overcome. Most of the system's believers gave up trying to proselytize it by 1970.

The efforts to extend the Poundian paradigm to make an independent science of law can be said to have failed. However, the enterprise of social science directed toward understanding legal institutions undertaken by social scientists themselves increased substantially in the years following

World War II (see chapter 11).[94] New funding was obtained, new journals were established, and cooperative efforts between lawyers and social scientists became commonplace.[95] The presence of social scientists on law faculties, so radical at Yale in the thirties, became generally accepted, if not generally prevalent. What, then, happened to the jurisprudence of law and social science?

Legal scholars reverted to the more traditional Poundian view that social science in the field of law should be used to investigate the consequences of legal decision and the causes of legal problems; and it should be undertaken by qualified social scientists with the assistance of lawyers. This meant that the jurisprudential issues raised by the social science of law—questions of scientific method, of determinism and free choice, of values and facts, of "pure" science versus reform—were sent back to the philosophy of science from which they originated. They did not surface again in jurisprudential literature in the century here under consideration.

94. See L. Friedman and S. Macaulay, *Law and the Behavioral Sciences*, 1–35 (1969).

95. Some of the most successful pioneering efforts to study law through social science methods can be found in the following sources: K. Llewellyn and E. Hoebel, *The Cheyenne Way* (1941); Schwartz, Social Factors in the Development of Legal Control: A Case Study of Two Israeli Settlements, 63 Yale L. J. 471 (1954); P. Bohannan, *Justice and Judgment Among the Tiv* (1957); J. Cohen, R. Robson, and A. Bates, *Parental Authority: The Community and the Law* (1958); J. Carlin, *Lawyers on Their Own: A Study of Individual Practitioners in Chicago* (1962); Macaulay, Non-Contractual Relations in Business: A Preliminary Study, 28 Am. Soc. Rev. 55 (1963); A. Conard, *Automobile Accident Costs and Payments* (1964); W. LaFave, *Arrest: The Decision to Take a Suspect into Custody* (1965); H. Kalven and H. Zeisel, *The American Jury* (1966).

NATURAL LAWYERS AND

KINDRED SOULS

1 9 3 9 – 6 4

The moral paradigm is the oldest of them all, going back in one form or another to Plato and Aristotle. It received its most sophisticated treatment in the philosophy of St. Thomas Aquinas, which combined Christian theology with Aristotelian ethics and metaphysics in a theoretical schema not since equaled. This jurisprudence was a part of an elaborate philosophic system of the thirteenth century. Intellectual thought moved on, for better or worse, to address the new problems that presented themselves as time passed. Foremost among them from an epistemological standpoint was the problem of modern science, beginning with the scientific theories of Copernicus, Galileo, and Newton, theories that could not be fitted easily into Thomistic ways of thinking. Just as important on the ethical side was the need to rationalize the newly emergent political structures that were taking the place of feudalism. Proponents of rigid Thomistic philosophy, perhaps because of its intellectually overpowering, comprehensive, and systematic character, refused to find the new questions relevant and refused to relate to the newer social and intellectual developments. Thomism was originally replaced in the epistemological field by cruder but more responsive theories like those of Descartes and Bacon, and in the ethical and legal field by a secularized, "rational" natural law represented by Grotius, Locke, Pufendorf, Burlamaqui, and others.

The Reformation had a major impact on the theory of natural law. The universities in Protestant countries began to deviate from the Roman Catholic schools in their teaching of ethics and law, including the bridging doctrine of natural law. In Protestant countries the general idea of natural law was turned into a secular notion of natural rights. Catholic academics generally reacted by reasserting the old doctrine. In the eighteenth century the break was completed. Kant on the Continent, Hume and Adam Smith in Scotland, and Bentham in England formulated sophisticated new ideas about the relationship between morality and law, completely free from any religious basis. Eclipsed by the new philosophies, the Thomistic version of natural law was already an intellectual museum-piece before the United States became a country.

This is not to say, of course, that popular ideas of natural rights in secular garb did not play an important part in the governmental and legal theory of the founding fathers. The United States Constitution to the present day institutionalizes certain natural-law notions.[1] The rejection of Thomism did not mean that questions of morality were not important in the public discourse in both England and the United States in the eighteenth and nineteenth centuries. But the theoretical bases for such discourse, if there were any, tended to be found in ideas of Jeffersonian natural rights, Protestant theology, utilitarianism, American transcendentalism, social Darwinism, and socialistic utopianism, none of which held traditional natural law to be of any significance.

Scholastic natural law never quite died, however. It was preserved as formally taught doctrine in some European countries, especially France and Italy, and at Roman Catholic universities in the United States. A rough notion of natural law also had a certain popularity in Anglo-American society as the basis for the ultimate "principles" of the common law; but natural-law theory itself was part of a minority intellectual culture in America until the late 1930s.

The radical empiricism and ethical relativism of the legal realists combined with frightening dictatorial dominance in European politics to raise a loud cry for a "moral" theory of law, especially one that would justify democracy. Later the postwar "trial" of German leaders for "war crimes" proved to be both a vindication of natural law and a call for its further explanation or justification. Finally, the use of the awesome atomic bomb by the United States and its presence a few years later in the arsenal of the Soviets led many thinkers to demand a worldwide moral and legal order to avoid human self-destruction. Therefore, the preoccupation of many jurisprudential scholars in the 1940s and 1950s was to provide a theoretical framework for the moral basis of American democracy, the American

1. The dated but classic works on this theme are Haines, The Law of Nature in Federal and State Judicial Decisions, 25 Yale L. J. 617 (1916); Corwin, The Higher Law Background of American Constitutional Law, 42 Harv. L. Rev. 149, 365 (1929); C. Haines, *The Revival of Natural Law Concepts* (1930).

legal system, and ultimately a system of world order and security. This invited the exposition of schemes of natural law, both new and old.

It is because of these circumstances that the moral paradigm attains prominence in America beginning around 1940. Only then, as a reaction against relativism and scientism and as a response to an ideological world war, does it become a part of the mainstream of American jurisprudence. It is accordingly treated in this chapter even though in one form or another it appeared in works by earlier American writers.

It is important to note that not every theory having a moral or ethical component belongs to the moral paradigm.[2] Indeed, that would obliterate much of the distinction between the various perspectives. Bentham and the Austinians had their own way of relating morality to law through utilitarianism and the science of legislation. The evolutionists saw moral principles as the moving force in the development of law. Pound articulated a pragmatic ethical theory that was based upon the satisfaction of social interests empirically derived from the legal process itself. None of these theories qualifies as a version of natural law.

It may be helpful to state the essential elements of the moral paradigm and explain how it differs from the others. It can be summed up in four key ideas: first, all human beings have a basic biological, psychological, and (for some) spiritual "nature" that is constant through time and circumstances; second, this basic nature dictates that certain kinds of conduct be mandated or prohibited to preserve and promote the good human life; third, this mandatory conduct can be understood by ordinary adult human beings and can be organized into a system of rules or principles; fourth, these principles, the natural law, are the basis for all moral and legal rules; that is, they are the justification for and the ultimate test of the validity of all rules of positive law. There are many variations of natural-law thinking, and kindred theories sympathetic in aim and outlook have been offered that depart in some respects from these four key ideas.

Voices in the Wilderness

In the period between the Civil War and the Great Depression a number of books and articles appeared that advanced the idea of natural law, or natural rights.[3] Most of them seem unrelated to each other and

2. For explanation of the traditional paradigms see chapter 1.

3. See, for example, D. Heron, *Jurisprudence and Its Relation to the Social Sciences* (1877) [English]; L. Spooner, *Natural Law or the Science of Justice: A Treatise on*

generally went unrecognized by the larger community of jurisprudential scholars. Nor did they have any impact on contemporary jurisprudential thought; in fact, occasional gratuitous slaps were taken at the notion of natural law.[4] Nevertheless, some acknowledgment of this work is in order, and I will summarily review a few of the major statements.

The first post-Civil War attempt at a theoretical exposition of the moral paradigm was the work of George H. Smith in 1886.[5] Smith regarded the work of Bentham and Austin as "absurd and pernicious in its consequences as it is ridiculous in its origin—being, in fact, subversive of human rights and liberty, and of the very foundations of justice and morality."[6] Nevertheless, he could not escape the influence of the dominant expository paradigm, and his treatise closely resembles those of Austin and Holland. In Smith's view positive law is derivative of moral law, and jurisprudence is that branch of moral science that deals with positive law. Smith's attempt to combine the expository and moral paradigms is perhaps unique (see a fuller discussion of Smith's philosophy in chapter 2). A work by Edward L. Campbell very similar to Smith's was published in 1887, although it was more elementary.[7]

Professor Rene I. Holaind, S.J., lecturer on natural and canon law at Georgetown University, published a series of lectures in 1899.[8] Directed to law students, this book attempted to relate the significance of Thomistic natural law to law practice and particularly to the ethics of the profession. Father Holaind uses the occasion to attack utilitarianism and evolutionary theories of law.

Natural Law, Natural Justice, Natural Rights, Natural Liberty, and Natural Society; Showing that All Legislation Whatsoever is an Absurdity, a Usurpation and a Crime (1882); D. Ritchie, Natural Rights, A Criticism of Some Political and Ethical Conceptions (1895) [English]; J. Andrews, American Law: A Treatise on the Jurisprudence, Constitution and Laws of the United States (1900); G. Raymond, Ethics and Natural Law, A Reconstructive View of Moral Philosophy Applied to the Rational Art of Living (1920); W. Robson, Civilization and the Growth of the Law (1935) [English]; Joslyn, Philosophy of Law, 12 Green Bag 142 (1900); Gavet, Individualism and Realism, 29 Yale L. J. 523, 643 (1920); Vinogradoff, The Foundations of a Theory of Rights, 34 Yale L.J. 60 (1924); Hill, The Natural Law, 13 Geo. L. J. 367 (1925).

4. See, for example, Thayer, Natural Law, 21 L. Q. Rev. 60 (1905); Holmes, Natural Law, 32 Harv. L. Rev. 40 (1918). A rejoinder to Holmes can be found in Noonan, Natural Law, 3 Marq. L. Rev. 91 (1919).

5. G. Smith, Elements of Right and of the Law (2d ed. 1887).

6. Ibid., v.

7. E. Campbell, The Science of Law According to the American Theory of Government (1887). Campbell seems to envision an intuitive knowledge of natural law or natural rights.

8. R. Holaind, Natural Law and Legal Practice (1899).

A puzzling work by William S. Pattee, dean of the College of Law at the University of Minnesota, appeared in 1909.[9] Dean Pattee attempts to explain all of the various meanings of the word "law" and organize them into a coherent system. He assumes that various kinds of laws exist that correspond to the different uses of the word and that some kind of logical relationship exists between them. The possibility that the word is used metaphorically or by analogy without any other relationship between the various uses seems not to have occurred to him. Thus, physical laws, divine laws, moral laws, spiritual laws, laws of progress, laws of thought, and many others are classified and related in an overall taxonomy. Natural laws are one type. He states that natural law, or the principles of justice, benevolence, and veracity, is the basis for systems of positive human law, but the relationship is not well explained. Pattee seems to endorse the idea that the moral or natural law is known intuitively.

A course called "Pure Jurisprudence" was initiated at the Fordham University law school by Professor Terence J. Shealy and was later taken over by Francis P. LeBuffe in the early twenties. The teaching materials for this course were published in 1924 under the title *Outlines of Pure Jurisprudence*.[10] They proved to be a very rigorous, systematic, carefully developed exposition of Thomistic jurisprudence, together with practical application of the theory and references for further reading. Two subsequent expanded editions appeared with the altered title *Jurisprudence with Cases to Illustrate Principles*, the third edition (1938) being coauthored by James V. Hayes.[11] The third edition also contains discussions of contemporary American schools of jurisprudence and "totalitarian" theories of law as viewed from the Thomistic perspective. It thus proved useful as the first Thomistic jurisprudential teaching text in the twentieth-century resurgence of the moral paradigm.

The Revival of Thomism

While Walter B. Kennedy and others had been criticizing the Poundian point of view from the Thomistic perspective since 1925 (see chapter 7), the legal literature began to promote the positive statement of natural-law theory, beginning in 1939 with the publication of Karl Kreil-

9. W. Pattee, *The Essential Nature of Law, or The Ethical Basis of Jurisprudence* (1909).

10. F. LeBuffe, *Outlines of Pure Jurisprudence* (1924).

11. F. LeBuffe and J. Hayes, *Jurisprudence with Cases to Illustrate Principles* (3d rev. ed. 1938).

kamp's *The Metaphysical Foundations of Thomistic Jurisprudence*.[12] The author acknowledges that his work is not original—what restatement of an old philosophy would be? But he maintains that this exposition is appropriate for the times, and he is especially concerned with expounding the connection between natural law and positive law:

> If St. Thomas were now as well-known as the stature of his thought warrants, this study would not have been written. . . . Its one purpose is to present with as much clarity and unity as possible certain aspects of St. Thomas' philosophy of law. The central theme examined is the primacy of the natural law with respect to systems of man-made law. . . . Thomism presents a view of human nature and a general technique for deriving positive laws from the law of that nature.[13]

Relying on the writings of St. Thomas as well as on interpretations of those writings, primarily by European scholars, Kreilkamp presents a comprehensive explanation of the relationship between natural and human laws. In doing so he is forced to draw upon and use the concepts and terminology of medieval metaphysics, with its science of "ends" and "essences." In short, he explains his subject in a thirteenth-century language.

The Thomistic view can be summarized briefly, using Kreilkamp's exposition, in terms of the four key ideas mentioned previously.[14] The Thomists see similarities among all people, and these similarities are considered the "essence" of the human being, differences being considered accidental. The principal features of this essence are materiality, vitality, animal sensitivity, and a distinctive form of rationality. This rational capacity has two sides, speculative reason and practical reason. Speculative reason is capable of apprehending reality and understanding it. Practical reason is capable of apprehending ends, the most general of which is the human good. If a human would be true to his essence, therefore, he must seek his proper end, sometimes called happiness, and this becomes the cardinal principle of moral obligation.

Since all people have a determinate nature shared by all members of the

---

12. K. Kreilkamp, *The Metaphysical Foundations of Thomistic Jurisprudence* (1939). Kreilkamp's comparison of Thomistic and contemporary jurisprudential views on various points (pp. 9–25) is of particular interest. See also Brown, Natural Law and the Lawmaking Function in the United States, 15 N.D. Lawyer 9 (1939). Occasional writings may be found in this period which advocate a more rationalistic natural law akin to the seventeenth- and eighteenth-century theories. See, for example, L. Stapleton, *Justice and World Society* (1944).

13. Ibid., 5.

14. See also the discussion of the moral paradigm in chapter 1.

species, and part of this nature is practical reason, or the capacity to understand one's ends, it is possible to ascertain principles of conduct that will lead to the ultimate end of the human good through the exercise of reason. It is also possible to disregard the true apprehension of ends and act in ways that defeat the achievement of true ends. Instead of following right reason, we may be driven in the wrong direction by the animal inclinations in our nature; sin is well known. The derivation of natural-law principles proceeds by applying knowledge of the details of universal human nature (biological needs, mental capacity, and so forth) to the overarching end. The capacity to derive natural laws in this way, sometimes called the exercise of right reason, inheres in every normal adult human being because each has "built in" the capability of apprehending ends, that is, a practical reason, or the knowledge of good and evil.

The mind can organize those principles in terms of a hierarchy running from general to specific. The ultimate principle, usually stated as "Do good and avoid evil," is universally true and demands obedience, but of course it lacks concreteness. Second-level precepts combine contingent knowledge of human nature with the ultimate precept to define more specific activities necessary to achieve the ultimate goal. Third- and lower-level precepts utilize more specific knowledge, including knowledge of existing economic situations, traditional social institutions, and other cultural features. Therefore, the lower-level precepts are not universal because they must incorporate specific circumstances that do not universally prevail. To the extent that they reflect correct knowledge, however, they carry the same validity and obligatoriness as the more general natural law. Our understanding of natural law is, therefore, perfect at the most general level and becomes subject to error as we reduce it to more specifics. The more specific precepts are, however, subject to correction through rational argument and the addition of more experience or information.

What, then, is the relationship of these moral principles, the natural law, to positive law? Positive laws are rules of conduct that serve as means to ends. Their ultimate end is to promote the common good. The common good is not conceived, however, as something opposed to the individual good; rather, a harmony of ends, the achievement of happiness for self and others, is contemplated. Human laws deserve obedience because they are conducive to this ethical end. Indeed, because of certain features of universal human nature, it turns out that human laws are necessary to achieve the common good. However, human law and natural law are not coextensive. Much of human law has no substantive moral content, like the rule requiring driving on the righthand side of the road, but even laws of this morally indifferent type command obedience because they are necessary to further higher objectives that do have a moral content. Natural law pervades the system of human laws to the extent that those laws carry specific moral content, that is, are means to ethical ends. Obedience to human law is therefore obligatory in two ways: first, much human law contains direct ethical content, or is a specific application of the natural law itself; and, second, a system of human laws is necessary in itself to achieve both the common and individual goods; therefore, all laws of the system become obligatory.

It is necessary to qualify the last statement in an important way. Laws that contain no moral content in themselves are obligatory because they are part of the whole system that requires obedience. But this is not true of human laws contrary to the natural law such as, presumably, laws of slavery. Because such immoral laws derogate from the achievement of ethical ends, they lose their obligatoriness. Whether they should be called invalid laws, nonlaws, illegal laws, or defective laws is a question resolved in different ways by different thinkers, but it seems more a matter of semantics than one of substance.

Natural law is therefore different from human law in several ways: it is not enacted but occurs naturally; it consists of a teleologically organized set of principles with the ultimate human good at their apex; it can be understood not by reading authoritative statements of it or by exercising some intuitive sixth sense but by exercising right reason; and it applies, in its more abstract principles, universally to all human societies in all places at all times; but its more concrete principles are contingent upon the particular culture. On the other hand, natural law pervades human law; it gives human law its obligatoriness and validity. It serves also as the great guide to the legislator, and to the judge when the judge legislates, in choosing the principles of human law that will govern conduct in a particular society.

Kreilkamp's scholarship was followed by other works that sought to accomplish similar objectives. Proceedings of a symposium on natural law were published in the *Notre Dame Lawyer*.[15] Anton Chroust, a professor at the Notre Dame law school, published a number of articles detailing the Thomistic position.[16] Mortimer Adler of the University of Chicago rein-

15. Symposium, Natural Law, 15 N.D. Lawyer 1 (1940).
16. Chroust, The Jus Gentium in the Philosophy of Law of St. Thomas Aquinas, 17 N.D. Lawyer 22 (1941); Chroust and Collins, Basic Ideas in the Philosophy of Law of

forced the Thomists.[17] French scholar Jacques Maritain, visiting at the University of Notre Dame, authored an influential book in English showing how basic human rights were anchored in the natural law;[18] a few years later Maritain was able to show how natural law also led to democracy.[19] Heinrich Rommen, a German Catholic scholar who emigrated to the United States in 1938, also contributed to this literature (see bibliography).

A theme taken up by the Thomists in response to the totalitarian threat might be termed "Holmes-bashing."[20] Oliver Wendell Holmes, Jr., died in 1935, and his private correspondence with Sir Frederick Pollock was published in 1941. The letters revealed more of Holmes' thoughts and opinions than had been publicly known. They proved to be a gold mine of ammunition for some of the Thomists. They revealed that Holmes was, indeed, a skeptic and was highly critical of absolutist moral theories, religious or otherwise, and he really did believe in some form of survival of the fittest. The letters of the ever-quotable Holmes were used to show that he and "his kind," the realists, the behaviorists, the pragmatists, Pound, and the pseudosocial scientists, were responsible for creating an amoral intellectual climate that led directly to totalitarianism.[21] Hitler and all he stood for were the end product of Holmesian thinking. This kind of critique was carried on mostly in Roman Catholic-sponsored publications and lasted until the end of the war.

Another strategy of some Thomists was to demonstrate that Americans

---

St. Thomas Aquinas, 26 Marq. L. Rev. 11 (1941); Chroust and Osborn, Aristotle's Conception of Justice, 17 N.D. Lawyer 129 (1942); Chroust, Law and the Administrative Process: An Epistemological Approach to Jurisprudence, 58 Harv. L. Rev. 573 (1945). These articles were published in the wartime period. Chroust continued to expand upon his explanations of natural law for many years thereafter.

17. M. Adler, *Aquinas and the Gentiles* (1938); M. Adler, *Scholasticism and Politics* (1940); M. Adler, *A Dialectic of Morals* (1941).

18. J. Maritain, *The Rights of Man and Natural Law* (1944).

19. J. Maritain, *Man and the State* (1951).

20. This is discussed in some detail in E. Purcell, *The Crisis of Democratic Theory*, 167–71 (1973).

21. See Simms, A Dissent from Greatness, 28 Va. L. Rev. 467 (1940); Lucey, Jurisprudence and the Future Social Order, 16 Social Science 213 (1941); Ford, The Fundamentals of Holmes' Juristic Philosophy, 11 Ford. L. Rev. 255 (1942); Lucey, Natural Law and American Legal Realism, 30 Geo. L. J. 498 (1942); Gannon, What Are We Really Fighting For?, 11 Ford. L. Rev. 254 (1942); Gregg, The Pragmatism of Mr. Justice Holmes, 31 Geo. L. J. 294 (1943); Ford, The Totalitarian Justice Holmes, 159 Cath. World 115 (1944); Palmer, Hobbes, Holmes, and Hitler, 31 A.B.A.J. 569 (1945).

had always maintained a philosophy of natural law,[22] although the facts were obscured by historical circumstances and some confusing choices of terminology. The story was told that the founding fathers really appreciated natural law and sought to base the new American government on Thomistic principles. This modest rewriting of history was finally countered by the publication of two books by authors sympathetic to Thomism but more sympathetic to the historical truth.[23]

The enthusiasm for Thomistic jurisprudence did not diminish at the end of the war.[24] Influenced by the Nürnberg trials and the potential consequences of the capacity for massive destruction of atomic weaponry, scholars saw the need for a universal set of moral-legal principles to govern international relationships. After 1950, when the Soviets exploded their first atomic device, the need for standards and rules for international security was underlined to Americans, and renewed efforts were made to establish Thomism as the jurisprudential answer.

The Thomists organized themselves well to win the crusade for the revival of scholastic legal philosophy. As early as 1933 the American Catholic Philosophical Association established a committee on the philos-

22. See, for example, Sternberg, Natural Law in American Jurisprudence, 13 N.D. Lawyer 89 (1938); Crane, Natural Law in the United States, 15 N.D. Lawyer 195 (1940); Manion, The Founding Fathers and the Natural Law, 35 A.B.A.J. 461 (1949); E. Barrett, The Natural Law and the Lawyer's Search for a Philosophy of Law, 1 Cath. Law. 128 (1955).

23. See C. LeBoutillier, *American Democracy and Natural Law* (1950); E. Gerhart, *American Liberty and Natural Law* (1953). A Thomistic reviewer of Gerhart's book said, "Every Catholic lawyer trained in natural law knows enough not to take Mr. Gerhart seriously." Constable, Book Review, 1 Cath. Law. 143 (1955).

24. See, for example, Catholic Lawyers Guild, *The Natural Law and the Legal Profession* (1950); A. D'Entreves, *Natural Law: An Introduction to Legal Philosophy* (1951) [lectures given at the University of Chicago in 1948]; J. Maritain, *Man and the State* (1951); C. Wu, *Fountain of Justice* (1955); R. Begin, *Natural Law and Positive Law* (1959); S. Buchanan, *Rediscovering Natural Law* (1962); Center for Study of Dem. Inst., *Natural Law and Modern Society* (1963); D. O'Connor, *Aquinas and Natural Law* (1968); Marceau, A Descriptive Theory of Justice, 6 La. L. Rev. 350 (1945); McKinnon, Higher Law: Reaction Has Permeated Our Legal Thinking, 33 A.B.A.J. 106, 202 (1947); Rooney, Law without Justice? The Kelsen and Hall Theories Compared, 23 N.D. Lawyer 140 (1948); Palmer, Natural Law and Pragmatism, 23 N.D. Lawyer 313 (1948); Wilkin, Natural Law: Its Robust Revival Defies the Positivists, 35 A.B.A.J. 192 (1949); Kreilkamp, Dean Pound and the Immutable Natural Law, 18 Fordham L. Rev. 173 (1949); Palmer, Groping for a Creative Legal Philosophy: Natural Law in a Creative and Dynamic Age, 35 A.B.A.J. 3 (1949); Schmidt, An Approach to Natural Law, 19 Fordham L. Rev. 1 (1950).

ophy of law and government.[25] This group became increasingly active and vocal, publishing the results of its proceedings.[26] The law reviews of the Catholic universities also devoted many pages to the advancement of Thomistic jurisprudence. At St. John's law school the St. Thomas Moore Institute for Legal Research was established in part to publish *The Catholic Lawyer*, a periodical with the dissemination of jurisprudential doctrine to practicing lawyers as one of its aims.[27] In 1947 Notre Dame University established its Natural Law Institute, an annual convocation of scholars. Its objective was to lead "the struggle to revest the natural law philosophy as the keystone of American jurisprudence."[28] The Institute received enthusiastic support from Roman Catholic legal scholars during the next five years. At that point new ways of disseminating the Thomist message were explored, and it was decided to establish a journal devoted to the topic.[29] The first issue of the new *Natural Law Forum* appeared in 1956.

However, by the late 1950s it was clear that the Thomists were talking to themselves.[30] To accept the medieval doctrine of natural law one had to accept the other trappings. Thomistic natural law was unconvincing unless a scholar was willing to see the world through its accompanying and reinforcing metaphysics, epistemology and perhaps theology. It was anachronistic in the best and worst senses. No department of philosophy outside the Catholic universities concerned itself much with these medieval doctrines except as part of the history of the discipline. Apart from the merits of the philosophy, it was difficult to accept a doctrine purporting to lead to democracy and justice that had historically justified a feudal

25. E. Purcell, note 20.

26. See Rooney, Law and the New Logic, 16 Proc. Am. Cath. Phil. Assn. 217 (1940); Desvernine, Philosophy and Order in Law, 17 Proc. Am. Cath. Phil. Assn. 135 (1941); Rooney, The Movement for a Neo-Scholastic Philosophy of Law in America, 18 Proc. Am. Cath. Phil. Assn. 185 (1942); Manion, The American Metaphysics in Law, 18 Proc. Am. Cath. Phil. Assn. 132 (1942); Hildebrand, The Dethronement of Truth, 18 Proc. Am. Cath. Phil. Assn. 9 (1942). All of these are cited in E. Purcell, note 21, 299–300.

27. See Tinnelly, The Catholic Lawyer: An Idea and a Program, 1 Cath. Law. 3 (1955).

28. Scanlan, Natural Law and Notre Dame, 1 J. Leg. Ed. 438 (1949). The proceedings of the Natural Law Institute were published in five annual volumes.

29. See O'Meara, Foreword, 1 Nat. L. Forum 1 (1956).

30. It is interesting to note that the *Natural Law Forum* changed its name to the *American Journal of Jurisprudence* in 1969. See Noonan, Foreword, 14 Am. J. Juris. vi (1969).

system, slavery (in Aristotle's time), and an ultra-authoritative, antidemo-cratic church structure. Most American scholars were unable to digest this revisionist menu of thirteenth-century ideology.

The Intuitionism of Jerome Hall and Edmond Cahn

In 1938 Professor Jerome Hall (1901–   ), then at Louisiana State University,[31] published a collection of readings and editorial com-ments intended for law students on the subject of jurisprudence.[32] Until this time almost all textbooks on jurisprudence, with the exception of Father LeBuffe's work discussed previously, dealt exclusively with the expository paradigm.[33] Hall's book of almost twelve hundred pages pre-sented the writings of authors from Plato to Pound with every conceivable point of view and concern. The book was hailed as a breakthrough and as evidence that law must look outside itself for guidance and input through interdisciplinary studies, and that a moral justification for the existing legal system and government must be expounded. Hall, who saw an "emerging, distinctive, socio-legal discipline," felt his collection was a step in both of these directions.

Hall included in the text one of his own early articles discussing the relationship between criminology and the drafting of a penal code.[34] It is apparent that Hall subscribed to the Poundian paradigm at this time, and, indeed, he seems to have been one of its foremost exponents in the field of criminal law. Unlike the extreme realists, Hall acknowledges the norma-tive aspect of law and the need for the legislator to think in terms of "the accomplishment of certain ends by appropriate means." The legislator and the judge are problem-solvers. Hall describes their enterprise:

31. Educated at the University of Chicago and Harvard University, Hall served successively on the faculties of the law schools at the University of North Dakota, Louisiana State University, Indiana University, and the Hastings College of Law of the University of California. His major publications are *Theft, Law and Society* (1935); *General Principles of Criminal Law* (1947); *Living Law of Democratic Society* (1949); *Comparative Law and Social Theory* (1963); *Foundations of Jurisprudence* (1973).

32. J. Hall, *Readings in Jurisprudence* (1938).

33. See chapters 3 and 4 for discussion of some of these works. Pound had previously published his *Outlines of Lectures on Jurisprudence*; however this was not a text, but outlines with extensive bibliographical references.

34. Hall, Criminology and a Modern Penal Code, 27 J. Crim. L. and Criminol. 1 (1936).

The [judge or legislator] has some knowledge, but not enough. He has some sense of what the desirable end or ends should be, but his understanding in that regard is vague and uncertain. So, too, as regards effective means. Social problem solving is a process that consists of increasing his knowledge, and, at the same time, of discovering *particular* objectives and the *particular* means to their attainment.[35]

While Hall took a pragmatic approach to these moral problems, he was uncomfortable with general statements of moral principles. He certainly distrusted abstract natural-law theory, and he may have questioned Pound's system of interest balancing.

The formulation of broad generalizations as ends, though acquiesced in by most persons, provides not the slightest aid in solution of social problems . . . since such generalities can include almost any actual content imaginable, they include nothing of value in social problem solving. . . . The discovery of specific ends and means is, indeed, inconsistent with acceptance of broad generalizations as already representing desirable ends and means.[36]

As Hall continued to write in the field of criminal law, his concern for a jurisprudential antidote to cultural relativism and radical empiricism also grew. His vision matured when he was invited to give a series of lectures in 1947, later published under the title *Living Law of Democratic Society*.[37] In this work Hall expounds three important themes. The first was a partial concession to relativism: that legal theory is always conditioned by the culture of the theorist, and there are no absolute truths of jurisprudence; yet, through critical and intuitive methods, a kind of objective truth can be found or approximated and understood. The key to this method is to place oneself in the cultural milieu of the theorist under study and to appreciate the problems that the theorist was trying to solve as he saw them. Second, Hall suggests some ways of improving the definition of positive law, which is his way of describing the epistemological problem of identifying law, that is, the seeming dichotomy of the pure fact of the empiricists and the pure law of the analysts; in this he tries to utilize the

35. Hall, note 32, 1075. Note the similarity of this idea with Lon Fuller's "collaborative articulation of shared purposes."

36. Ibid.

37. J. Hall, *Living Law of Democratic Society* (1949). Like others during this period, Hall was partly motivated to establish the legitimacy of the American democratic legal system in the face of the totalitarian challenge. See pp. 53–54.

concept of "living law" popularized by Eugen Ehrlich. Third, Hall maintains that moral value is inherent in law and that rational, objective judgments can be made. It is this last contention that is of special interest to this study.

Hall tells us that our common moral experiences, those situations where one senses duty, fairness, guilt, and so on, are difficult to explain, and writers on ethics and morality seem to be in endless disagreement in their attempts to do so. Yet, Hall says that our common experience is not myth; it is as real as any other experience. Not only that, but our moral sense provides the basic underlying datum for moral judgments, although more than the moral sense may be needed to make a correct judgment. He says that he accepts

> theories which rely on intuition and coherence. These terms, especially the former, are very unpalatable to some scholars, especially operationalists. But we may hazard the opinion that at some point, and probably at many crucial ones, these persons make various ultimate assumptions which they designate "axioms," "postulates," or "hypotheses," but to which they attach some degree of validity, in brief, that intuition, whatever it is termed, is inescapable.[38]

Hall presents two arguments in justification of moral intuition. First, he asks us to reflect upon our most basic experiences in perceiving the reality of what exists and in perceiving the reality of what is right or wrong in the most concrete situations. He reiterates his point that these experiences are unanalyzable, but real. "Intuitive knowledge is the direct apprehension of a fact or idea, exhibited in a flash but, often, only after much preliminary study and reflection. The only way to 'prove' the authenticity of intuitive knowledge is to get people to experience the same kind of situation."[39]

His second argument, one sometimes made by eighteenth-century natural-law philosophers, is that the same basic moral values have been recognized and insisted upon in all cultures across the span of history. While this is a difficult argument to prove, Hall makes a plausible summary of it. Having shown that human moral values are fundamentally the same for all societies, even though morality has been justified in different ways in these societies, Hall infers that humanity shares a common intuitive moral sense.

Hall recognizes that moral problems are often quite difficult, and hav-

---

38. Ibid., 72–73.

39. Ibid., 74–75. Hall relies on the work of the contemporary English philosophers Ewing, Reid, and Lewis.

ing a moral sense is not enough to solve them. What is required as well is "coherence." By this he means rational analysis of normative problems, discussion, reflection, bringing to bear wider experience, utilization of unbiased and informed opinion, and discovery and use of the experience of diverse cultures. This dialectic and heuristic approach, fully utilizing the moral sense, "may be regarded as a modern version of a central thesis of the perennial natural law philosophies." Hall distinguishes his theory, however, from traditional natural law by rejecting the notion of a code of moral principles, the necessity of God, or the idea of a body of natural laws somehow distinct from and superior to positive law. Hall also adds a special factor to his intuitive version of natural law. He suggests that a legal system that incorporates self-rule, also called the consent of the governed or democracy, attains a moral authority that other systems lack. Not only are the legal solutions arrived at in a democracy "consented to," but the democratic process itself involves all citizens in the participation of decision-making, thus allowing each to bring her moral sense to bear in a rational and informed way on the problems of the day. This gives the system a sort of political legitimacy that nondemocratic systems lack.[40]

Edmond Cahn (1906–1964), a professor at New York University,[41] offered a theory similar to Hall's in a book published in the same year as Hall's *Living Law of Democratic Society*. This was *The Sense of Injustice*,[42] a work constructed partly from previous articles by the author.[43] Cahn posited as the moral basis of the legal system a "sense of injustice" that was, for all intents and purposes, a sort of intuition, although Cahn seemed to think of it more as a psychological or biological phenomenon like "instinct." Like Hall, and for the same reasons, Cahn rejected elaborate ethical theories and broad moral principles, but he recognized the need for a moral basis to justify the law's exercise of coercive power. In particular, Cahn seemed to feel a need to justify the punishment of the Nazi leaders after World War II.[44]

40. One reviewer of Hall's book considered it "special pleading for the legal system . . . of the United States." Baldwin, Book Review, 25 N.Y.U.L.Q. Rev. 937 (1949).

41. Cahn was educated at Tulane University. He practiced law in New York as a tax attorney, joining the faculty of New York University in 1946. His main jurisprudential works are E. Cahn, *The Sense of Injustice* (1949), and E. Cahn, *The Moral Decision* (1955).

42. E. Cahn, *The Sense of Injustice: An Anthropocentric View of Law* (1949).

43. Cahn, Justice and Power, 55 Yale L. J. 336 (1946); Cahn, Freedom and Order, 23 N.Y.U.L.Q. 20 (1948).

44. See Cahn, note 42, 30.

The uniqueness of Cahn's position lies in seizing upon the negative side of justice as the basic intuitive device. He thinks that ideas of justice tend to vagueness and generality and vary greatly from one culture to another and from one moral theory to another. But injustice, as experienced in the concrete instance, is very real, understandable, and universal. " 'Justice' has been so beclouded by natural-law writings that it almost inevitably brings to mind some ideal relation or static condition or set of preceptual standards, while we are concerned, on the contrary, with what is active, vital, and experiential in the reactions of human beings."[45] The use of the term "reaction" is significant. For Cahn the sense of injustice is activated or triggered by concrete situations in which we perceive ourselves or others with whom we identify as being treated unjustly. "Its incidences show how justice arises and what biologic purpose it serves in human affairs." It is like the reaction of an animal threatened by another beast. "It denotes that sympathetic reaction of outrage, horror, shock, resentment, and anger, those affections of the viscera and abnormal secretions of the adrenals that prepare the human animal to resist attack. Nature has thus equipped all men to regard injustice to another as personal agression."[46]

Experience teaches us that we can identify or classify situations in which the sense of injustice is felt. Cahn claims that the main classifications, not intended to be exhaustive, are the demands for equality, desert (or merit), human dignity, conscientious adjudication, confinement of government to its proper functions, and fulfillment of common expectations. He gives illustrations of each of these situations.

By using the basic sense of injustice and formulating categories of injustice, one can form a theory of justice, or at least provide a moral basis for evaluating the positive law. Cahn spends much of his book explaining how his theory can explain and resolve what he considers the traditonal antinomies or contradictions between freedom and order, security and change, and justice and power, although it is not made entirely clear why this is important. His style is pleasantly literary, and his arguments depend more on metaphor than on analysis.[47] While not devoid of footnotes, Cahn's book does not attribute many of his ideas to others.

Both Cahn and Hall present the same basic difficulty to scholars skepti-

45. Ibid., 13.
46. Ibid., 24.
47. In a review of Cahn's book Felix S. Cohen said it was "half-prose and half-poetry." Cohen, Book Review, 63 Harv. L. Rev. 1481 (1949). Cahn's second book, dealing with law and morality, The Moral Decision (1955), is aimed at the lay reader and does not further develop his theory of "justice through injustice."

cal of intuition as the basis of morality. If one does not seem to find a "moral sense" or a "sense of injustice" in himself, he is simply not convinced. If one believes that these "senses" are not more than run-of-the-mill emotions dictated by acceptance of the common morality of one's culture, again he is unconvinced. Such a sense may be no more or less important than the sense of lust, the sense of competitiveness, the sense of accomplishment, the sense of power, and so forth, and therefore cannot serve as a basis for critical evaluation any more than the other "senses." They are completely subjective.

F.S.C. Northrop and First-Order Facts

F.S.C. Northrop (1893–   ) joined the Yale Law School faculty in 1947 as Sterling Professor of Philosophy and Law.[48] He taught a joint seminar with Underhill Moore in the last two years of Moore's tenure. Before joining the law faculty he had taught in the philosophy department at Yale for twenty-four years. Greatly influenced by Alfred North Whitehead, Bertrand Russell, and Albert Einstein, he was an expert in the philosophy of science. He became fascinated with the idea of the direct perception of empirical reality, or the phenomenon of raw sense data. By some twist, this inquiry led him to study eastern religions and philosophy, which also incorporated the notion of the direct perception of reality through contemplation. This in turn led him to an interest in the differences in understanding between cultures and how those differences might be overcome. When he turned his talents to jurisprudence after World War II, he brought a very unusual background to bear on the subject.

Northrop published several books and contributed numerous articles to periodicals and to scholarly collections.[49] He collected and edited one group of his essays, published as *The Logic of the Sciences and the Humanities* in 1947. Another set of his articles, together with new material, was published in 1959 under the title *The Complexity of Legal and Ethical Experience*. These two works deal most directly with jurisprudential subjects. In the following discussion we are concerned primarily with his contribution to natural-law thought.

Northrop was very motivated by the moral and political crises brought

48. Northrop earned degrees from Beloit College, Yale, and Harvard. He also attended Freiburg and Cambridge universities.

49. For Northrop's works, see the bibliography.

about by the end of World War II.[50] He recognized that the threat of human annihilation by atomic weapons was very real and that this fact mandated that his age develop international controls on violence. He also saw a personal mandate that shaped his own mission in working out a responsive jurisprudence. Relying on his expertise in far-eastern culture and philosophy, he thought that intellectual and cultural leadership as well as political power would gradually shift toward the Asian countries, especially China. This meant that westerners must become acquainted with eastern culture, and, more immediately important for him, that a system of universal standards of morality and law would have to be worked out. These standards would have to supersede mere cultural values, since the cultural values in East and West were quite different. The great differences in ideology between the Soviet bloc and the West also called for a common point of departure. A true natural law was needed, and it should be articulated by someone knowledgable about both East and West.

Northrop could not accept Thomistic natural law, which he thought was based on certain "errors" of epistemology. He was oriented toward natural science, particularly mathematical physics and its supporting philosophy. He was convinced that the truths of natural science were as close to The Truth as humanity would ever get, and any normative system of do's and don't's would have to be based on the epistemological methods so successfully pursued by physical science.

Northrop described a relationship between positive law, "living law," and natural law that provided the framework for his theory. He adopted the program of sociological jurisprudence as far as it would take him, and then he added to it. In good Poundian fashion he viewed positive law, the law that was typically taught in the law schools, as fragmentary, ambiguous, and, most important, fossilized. This formal law was the concrete enactment of the policies favored by society in times past; it often, but not always, lagged behind changing cultural patterns. Therefore, one of the characteristics of the legal process was continually to change the existing positive law, through legislation or court decision, to conform to what lawmakers thought was the right policy, that is, consistent with current moral and political values. Not only was this characteristic of a healthy society, but also it needed to be done to make the legal system viable. Thus, the relationship between formal law and the currently prevailing

---

50. See F. Northrop, *The Complexity of Legal and Ethical Experience*, 8–19 (1959). The following discussion is based primarily on this text.

cultural norms—what Northrop calls "living law" after Eugen Ehrlich—is one in which the living law is morally superior to the positive law and can serve as a guide to critique and reform. The positive law is the subject of study for legal scholars, and the living law is the subject of study for anthropologists and sociologists of law.

This is all consistent with the Poundian paradigm, but for Northrop it is not enough. What is regarded as good in certain primitive societies is thought to be bad in industrialized societies. Values held as very important in the West are considered insignificant in the East. Anthropologists have established that what people hold to be right and just is relative to their own culture. To promote the ultimate cultural values and the social interests of one's own society will not suffice for a world community because different groups have different ultimate cultural values. Indeed, the generalized ends or interests of a society will not provide an adequate ideal even for a single community as long as that community has a pluralistic makeup reflecting different values.

Northrop gives full credence to the discovery of the cultural relativity of morals and ethics found by anthropologists and sociologists. He is willing to go farther; the very way in which we envision the world about us is also culturally relative. He accepts the idea that there can be a sociology of knowledge. This means that what we know and accept as truth, for the most part, is a product of our culture. Hence, truth itself is relative, but only up to a point. At this juncture we must examine Northrop's epistemology in order to understand why all knowledge is not relative.

Northrop tells us that our knowledge of what is, or what exists, is a combination of two things: pure sense perception and the conceptual relationships that we create (postulate) in order to understand and use those sense perceptions. He calls these two components radical empiricism and epistemic correlation. The color blue is an irreducible sense datum. When we sense blue, we know it immediately and intuitively (not of course the linguistic label for it). If that were the only kind of knowledge we had, it would be personal, and communication with others would be impossible. But we can conceptualize sense data, generalize from them, and form logical relationships between different kinds of data. Such concepts can be communicated, and other persons can test the communications against their own conceptions and ultimately their own sense data. Thus, through trial and error knowledge becomes public. We can build a body of public knowledge through communication about things that are ultimately subject to testing through the senses. Truth lies in the correspondence between concept or postulate and empirical verification. The ordinary knowledge that we hold as common sense is of this nature. Northrop does not envision a direct correspondence between truth and fact; rather, truth relates as much to the logical validity of the postulates that we establish as to the sense data that we experience. The method we use to generalize and theorize about facts, our epistemology, can be valid or faulty. Both an adequate epistemology and factual verification are necessary for true knowledge.

Northrop's idea of science, or the kind of knowledge that natural science provides, is a systematized version of the same thing. It is often called the hypothetico-deductive model of science, although Northrop does not use that term. In this view science consists of general propositions about the natural world that can be verified ultimately through sense data. The truth of scientific propositions depends on their logical integrity and their empirical verification. Natural science uses many unproven and probably unprovable assumptions, like the concept of cause and effect or the idea that time moves in one direction or that the same scientific laws prevail in all parts of the world; but this is no barrier to the development of knowledge. Any scientific theory or law is subject to rejection in favor of one that explains more phenomena or fits better with other scientific theories.

Knowledge obtained by the method of natural science is not culturally relative. The mechanical laws that govern the movement of a star through space are not dependent on any knowledge that the star has or on the peculiar world view of an astronomical observer or on the culture of the discoverers of these mechanical laws. While it is true that ancient sages may have thought that the stars were holes in the tent of the sky and medieval observers thought that stars were bodies revolving around the earth, modern physics can demonstrate that those views fail to account for certain phenomena and that they are not confirmed through experiment. They are false postulates. This is not to say, of course, that Einstein's revision of Newton's mechanics might not be repeated some day in the future. But if a new theory is forthcoming, it will ultimately have to stand the empirical test of sense data.

Knowledge obtained by the social sciences, in contrast, is usually culturally based.[51] The social sciences, at least those most relevant to law, sociology, and anthropology, are enmeshed in concepts that themselves spring from a particular culture. This can be most easily seen when an

---

51. In Northrop's view certain aspects of social science, like physical anthropology, physiological aspects of psychology, and parts of economics, are not culturally relative.

anthropologist attempts to describe objectively the legal system of a primitive tribe by using the concepts of right, duty, liability, property, and others taken from western legal culture. The result is confusion and mistake. A culture understands its social institutions in terms of its own concepts; a whole matrix of ideas and values is combined in a particular world view. The truth or falsity, rightness or wrongness of any statement that can be made about a culture must be relative to that culture to be meaningful. Our own culture is no different.

This difference between the kind of knowledge we have of "nature" as given by natural science and the kind of knowledge we have about human activity as given by the social sciences leads Northrop to a classification of the subject matter of these two categories of disciplines. The propositions of natural science are verified by resort to first-order facts; the propositions of social science by second-order facts. First-order facts are raw sense data (blue, pain, cold) unconditioned by any concepts or knowledge that we may have. Second-order facts (bank deposits, suicide, overtime parking) are those shaped by our intellectual apparatus conditioned by our cultural view of the world.

Northrop is cognizant of the naturalistic fallacy first articulated by Hume: that it is logically impossible to derive a deontological (ought) proposition or statement from premises that contain only ontological (is) propositions. Indeed, this is the basis of his criticism of traditional sociological jurisprudence. That theory equates the "is," in terms of what society seeks or prefers, to the "ought," or what it should seek. Because this is a non sequitur, the values that a particular culture favors cannot serve as the basis for evaluation of those same values. The goodness or badness of any rules or norms must be found in standards outside those norms. Are there any such standards against which the accepted norms of a particular culture can be measured? Is our only resort to religious or metaphysical standards?

This brings us to the presentation of the Northropian two-step, or how to get Right from Truth without leaving Mother Nature. His reasoning is along the following lines. Normative argument uses descriptive statements, statements of fact, as minor premises. In addition, normative propositions, the kind of ought statements or rules that are found in ethics and law, contain empirically verifiable components. For example, the proposition "the speed limit is forty miles per hour" contains a reference to "forty miles per hour," a term which can, with appropriate definition and specification, have an empirical referent in the nature of first-order facts. In other words, by use of appropriate terminology and logic (epistemic correlation), together with appropriate measuring equipment, the speed of an object can be determined to be a fact or not apart from cultural differences. To put the matter differently, the speed at which an object moves can be objectively measured apart from the human culture in which such movement takes place. It is a fact of nature, not of culture. Of course, normative propositions more often contain references to second-order facts. For example, "competition must not be restricted." Here "competition" refers to a complex notion of business activity that may exist or not—may be ultimately referable to empirically observable phenomena, but those phenomena are conceived in terms of a particular cultural view of the social world. Business competition has no meaning in a simple hunting-and-gathering society. It is a fact of culture, not of nature.

Since ethical and legal propositions refer to facts and to our understanding or theory of those facts (epistemology), they may be true or false in the sense that the theory of knowledge is wrong or the facts in question do not support it. In simpler terms, normative discourse assumes knowledge of the world. If that knowledge is faulty, then the normative discourse is also faulty. If the knowledge is of second-order facts, that is, culturally limited knowledge, its truth is restricted to that culture. If the knowledge is of first-order facts, its truth is universal. Northrop maintains that moral and legal judgments are good or bad to the degree that they are based on universally true knowledge.[52] Since knowledge of nature, scientific knowledge, is not culturally relative, a normative system of values based on such knowledge would be universally good.

> This is why Adam and Eve had to eat of the tree of human knowledge and guide their behavior, in creating second-order artifacts, by this knowledge before there was any meaning for them to be, or know, good or evil. This meaning is that the second-order artifacts of human behavior are good or bad if the human theory guiding this behavior is true or false as tested empirically by appeal to the first-order facts of anyone's experience.[53]

52. Northrop says, "The thesis of natural law ethics and jurisprudence, therefore, is . . . (1) that there are certain natural entities, namely human beings, whose judgments and behavior are in part at least the expression of what they think all first-order facts are *qua* theory, and (2) that such judgments and behavior are good when the theory in question is true as tested empirically by reference solely to first-order facts *qua* facts." Northrop, note 50, 256–57.

53. Ibid., 257–58. Northrop also finds in eastern religious philosophies a similar basis for universal agreement. The undifferentiated immediate, direct experience of the

Northrop recognizes that more than one normative theory can incorporate a true theory of first-order facts. In this case the normative theory that incorporates the scientific theory that accounts for more first-order facts is the better one.

Northrop views a normative theory that incorporates the best scientific knowledge, knowledge of nature, as a natural-law theory. Such a theory would serve as a guide to providing for or criticizing the fundamental law of a society. Other laws, the living law and the positive laws of the society, would then be judged against the fundamental law.

In the last two chapters of *The Complexity of Legal and Ethical Experience* Northrop introduces an idea previously absent from his writings on this subject. He says:

> As man in his theories of natural science comes to think of first-order facts about himself and nature . . . the possibility is open to the human mind and to its normative imagination of ordering human relations normatively by such conceptual means. Since, moreover, such normative proposals are axiomatically introduced, and in this sense utopian, consent is of the essence so far as obligation to be measured by them is concerned, . . . and with respect to consent to any hypothetically constructed contract, all parties are born free and equal.[54]

This amazing cryptic passage and a few others like it in his last chapter suggest that Northrop is trying to bridge the is/ought gap with a Lockian social contract and, further, to postulate a complete equality among all persons as the first principle of the legal order. He does not, however, even discuss the myriad jurisprudential issues that a social-contract theory raises. If we are to take this contractarian suggestion seriously, it seems to undermine, or at least make irrelevant, the entire theory that he has previously constructed. However, Northrop does not come back to discuss this problem in his later work, so we may be justified in regarding it as an anomaly.

If we disregard Northrop's contractarian suggestion, it remains unclear how, as a practical matter, the incorporation of good scientific theory into a normative system of values will make a better system. Northrop gives a

---

world, like the sensation of blue, is extended into a stream of consciousness that is timeless, called nirvana by the Buddhists. This undifferentiated direct experience cannot be stated in language, but it provides a universal truth from which a concept of human dignity can be inferred. This idea, as yet, has not caught on in twentieth-century jurisprudence.

54. Ibid., 271–72.

few examples that might be instructive. He suggests that Hitler's knowledge of racial characteristics was based on unsound theory; hence, Hitler's regime was worse than others that had true biological views on race. Northrop suggests that some primitive tribes whose understanding of the world includes magic and superstition have legal and ethical systems that are inferior to societies that follow the dictates of modern science. He maintains that the United States Supreme Court's landmark decision on school desegregation was good because it was based on more scientific views of race and ethnicity than the formerly prevailing system of segregation. These examples and others not much more convincing,[55] instead of confirming Northrop's theory, raise doubts about it.

Indeed, Northrop was given fine marks for effort by critics, but not much for results.[56] At least four shortcomings in his theory have been pointed out. First, and most important, in spite of his own cautions Northrop committed the naturalist fallacy, albeit in a convoluted way. We may accept his point that the method of natural science will provide objective and universal truth and that it is desirable that the descriptive propositions and empirical referents used in normative argument be true and accurate. Nevertheless, this in no way affects the rightness or wrongness, goodness or badness of the normative propositions used in such argumentation. Northrop's position boils down to the assertion that well-informed judgments are good judgments and that the better informed they are, the better the judgment. Put this way, it seems clear that a legislator or judge can be very well informed, especially about the latest theories of natural science, and yet make a bad judgment based on bad normative propositions. The best knowledge of what is is not equivalent to an evaluation of what ought to be.[57]

55. For instance, Northrop says that the legal dominance of males in certain ancient societies can be attributed to an erroneous theory that genetic traits are passed from male to male, the female adding nothing. A true scientific view would recognize that both male and female contribute genetically to the offspring; hence, the law would require equality of treatment!

56. See, for example, Cohen, Book Review, 13 J. Leg. Ed. 95 (1960); Bodenheimer, Book Review, 108 U. Pa. L. Rev. 930 (1960).

57. Consider two alternative propositions of constitutional law: (1) the democratically elected parliament shall have complete governmental power; (2) governmental power shall be divided by function into a legislature, an executive, and a judiciary. One of these propositions is right and one is wrong, or at least one is better than the other. Why? Whatever justification is given, it will have to be in terms of other normative propositions; it cannot be justified by a descriptive statement, even if based on good scientific theory. The failure to join the normative with the descriptive may have led Northrop to make the "hypothetical contract" suggestion noted above; however, as

Second, many legal systems exist and many more could be conceived that are compatible with or incorporate the latest scientific theories in establishing their knowledge of the universe. Yet they may observe quite diverse ethical and legal policies that conflict with one another at many points. Who is to say today whether the Americans, the Japanese, the Soviets, or someone else is most scientific in outlook? Are less-developed countries that have few scientists and poor educational systems doomed to have bad ethics and law? While it is undisputed that ethical and legal judgment should be based on the best knowledge that can be mustered, knowledge, especially the theories of physical science, is only part of the picture. Indeed, the value of understanding the theory of gravity or an adequate understanding of subatomic particles is not terribly useful in resolving most ethical and legal problems.

Third, there is a problem with Northrop's neat relationship between positive law, living law, and natural law. He asserts that positive law must be constantly modified to bring it in line with living law, and the latter must be made to conform to natural law. This does not account for the widely recognized phenomenon that positive law has an impact on living law; it is often thought that positive law should be used to bring about changes in deeply ingrained cultural attitudes and patterns. If this is true, Northrop's analysis does not account for an important part of the legal process. This reverse effect also suggests two possibilities that do not fit Northrop's theory well. First, the problem of diverse cultures with their different living laws may be resolved by eliminating the diversity through the enactment of positive law (for example, Japan westernizing), and, second, in some way the living law may modify the natural law (shifting of means and ends).

Finally, the somewhat theoretical point is made that Northrop does not consider his favorite scientific epistemology, the hypothetico-deductive explanation of science, as a product of our culture. It has been argued that, unlike the facts of raw sense data, the method or theory of science is very much a product of western culture. If this is so, why are the fruits of this method not culturally relative? Could it not be that the Buddhist, about whom Northrop has much to say, would find our scientific theories pointless if not incomprehensible?

While Northrop's natural-law theory was found to be interesting by contemporaries, it did not generate further discussion and development. This may have been partly because few scholars interested in jurispru-

---

pointed out in the text, a social-contract theory needs bolstering from entirely different directions than are given in his main argument.

dence had any interest or competency in the philosophy of physical science. Northrop's theory was responsive to the demands of the time to provide a moral basis for an international legal system, but it failed to convince. Northrop's work in explaining the problem of cross-cultural understanding, on the other hand, was well received and constituted a substantial contribution to the philosophy of anthropology and sociology.[58]

The Eunomics of Lon Fuller

Professor Lon L. Fuller (1902–1978) was initially an adherent of the Poundian paradigm.[59] He achieved academic fame with the publication in 1931 of an exhaustive article on legal fictions, still the definitive work on that subject.[60] While sympathetic to much of the research being done by the legal realists in the 1930s, he nevertheless critiqued some of the more extreme philosophical positions of realism in a widely acclaimed article in 1934.[61] This was the first indication of his mounting concern for consideration of moral values in legal scholarship. As almost all of his writings indicate, he was an admirer of traditional German scholarship and regarded the policies of the Nazis, both before and during World War II, as barbaric, a great blow to the integrity of academic institutions and their tradition, and a subversion of the western idea of law. He viewed the legal order created by the Nazis as a bizarre distortion of what a legal system should be.

Called upon to give the prestigious Rosenthal lectures at Northwestern University in 1940, he engaged in extended research and much soul-searching to produce a ground-breaking thesis that was responsive to the political mood of the times. The lectures were published under the title *The Law in Quest of Itself*.[62] The themes set out in these lectures were pursued by Fuller in almost all of his subsequent jurisprudential work.[63]

58. See F. Northrop, *Philosophical Anthropology and Practical Politics* (1960); F. Northrop, *Cross-cultural Understanding: Epistemology in Anthropology* (1964).

59. For background on Fuller and his thinking, see K. Winston, ed., *The Principles of Social Order: Selected Essays of Lon L. Fuller* (1981); R. Summers, *Lon L. Fuller* (1984). Fuller was also known as a leading thinker in the field of contracts.

60. Fuller, Legal Fictions (3 pts.), 25 Ill. L. Rev. 363, 513, 877 (1931).

61. Fuller, American Legal Realism, 82 U. Pa. L. Rev. 429 (1934).

62. L. Fuller, *The Law in Quest of Itself* (1940).

63. Fuller's scholarly efforts were temporarily interrupted during World War II when he entered private practice in Boston, teaching only part-time at Harvard. After the war

Fuller's *Quest* delivered a two-part message. First, he maintained that both legal realism, in its extreme form as radical empiricism, and analytic jurisprudence, in its extreme form as exemplified by the work of Austrian Hans Kelsen, were inadequate and unacceptable theories of law because of their failure to account for values or purposes. Second, he insisted that the commonly accepted dichotomy between fact and value was a mistake and had led legal theory into blind alleys.

Fuller accomplished two important things in advancing his first thesis. Through his ingenious characterization of the analytic and empiricist modes of legal thinking, he identified these quite disparate types of jurisprudence (both historically and philosophically) as two developments of a single theme. Taking this new point of view, he suggested a common label for the two perspectives that would become standard usage for the next three decades. He denominated both of them "legal positivism," thus combining the Comteian and Austinian meanings of positivism. Whether this joinder of originally different concepts of "positivism" was a confusion on his part or a clever creative stroke, it was picked up and used in much of the jurisprudential discussion that followed.

In the most persuasive passages of *The Law in Quest of Itself* Fuller asserts that insistence on the separation of law and morals led Austin and the analysts down the road to a logical theory of definitions and terminology that was entirely divorced from reality. Starting with such abstract concepts as sovereignty, commands, rights, duties, and so on, the ultimate science of law became a science of initial assumptions, definitions, and theorems that had no necessary relationship to the actual law of any jurisdiction and very little relationship by way of coincidence. Kelsen's "pure theory of law," the ultimate extension of the expository paradigm, was in Fuller's mind a pure theory of initial assumptions and definitions, uncontaminated, to its author's delight, by any notions of public policy, morality, or politics. It was, indeed, pure theory.

The radical empiricists among the Poundians, misled by Holmes and Bingham, had erred in the other direction. They rejected "artificial" notions of rights, duties, or anything that smacked of conceptualism, doctrine, principles, or rules. They were committed to pure facts. The behavior of legal officials was the only legitimate object of the scientific study of law. Raw data, hopefully reduced to certain patterns of conduct, were the sole focus of attention of legal scholars as scholars.

---

he returned to fulltime teaching and writing, producing several important jurisprudential articles and three significant books. See the bibliography.

The common denominator found by Fuller in both radical legal empiricism and analytic jurisprudence is the rigid separation of the *is* from the *ought*. Under either view, the law is what the law is, apart from any extraneous considerations of what might be prudent, moral, or politically expedient. What the law should be is a matter for the concern of other academic disciplines, for religion, for politics, or for personal preference. Positivism in either form demands the clear and hardheaded separation of what is from what ought to be. To Fuller this view is the source of great error.

Fuller's primary thesis in the *Quest*, of course, is that law and morality cannot be separated.[64] Unfortunately for Fuller this thesis is perhaps not so persuasively demonstrated as is his illuminating critique of the newly defined positivism. The theme of inseparability of fact-value is asserted and reasserted throughout Fuller's subsequent writings, and it is challenged at every point.[65] We should, therefore, explore just what Fuller means by the inseparability or merger of fact and value in the law.

Fuller maintains that our perception of "facts" in the area of purposive human activity always has an element of value within it. The objective observer, scientist, or legal scholar does not understand what the facts are in relation to human actions unless she imputes certain values to the human subjects observed. This is further complicated in that the facts, as the observer understands them, may be true only if the person observed shares some or most of the same values or "purposes" of the observer. Fuller's favorite example is the observation of a boy at the beach trying to open a clam.[66]

64. Despite his later criticism of Fuller, Morris Cohen intimated in earlier writings that the separation of the law that is and the law that ought to be is not a simple matter. See Cohen, Law and Scientific Method, 6 Am. L. S. Rev. 231 (1928), reprinted in Assoc. Bar City N.Y., *Jurisprudence in Action*, 120 (1953); Cohen, Positivism and the Limits of Idealism in the Law, 27 Colum. L. Rev. 237, 238 (1927).

65. An excellent "debate" between Fuller and Columbia University philosopher Ernest Nagel over this thesis can be found in the following sources: Fuller, Human Purpose and Natural Law, 3 Nat. L. Forum 68 (1958); Nagel, On the Fusion of Law and Fact: A Reply to Professor Fuller, 3 Nat. L. Forum 77 (1958); Fuller, A Rejoinder to Professor Nagel, 3 Nat. L. Forum 83 (1958); Witherspoon, Comment: The Relation of Philosophy to Jurisprudence, 3 Nat. L. Forum 105 (1958); Nagel, Fact, Value and Human Purpose, 4 Nat. L. Forum 26 (1959).

66. An observer at the beach watches a small boy at some distance. The boy is poking around at the sand with something in his hand. His activity is meaningless until the observer sees enough to determine that the boy is trying to open clams. A purpose imputed by the observer to the boy gives meaning to the "facts." See Fuller, Human

Facts found in empirical legal studies are almost always laden with values. An extension of this idea Fuller believed illustrates the same point—that any rule of law is partly that which it is and partly that which it is becoming or ought to be.[67] Another illustration might be helpful. In a combination of several clauses and phrases the United States Constitution provides that the Congress may establish an army and a navy. Can the Congress establish an air force? Yes. The rule (an empowering rule in this case) that *is* is the same as the rule that *ought to be*. Fuller claims that this is because all legal rules have purposes, some of which are in the mind of the lawmaker at the time the law is made and some of which become clear as new situations arise to which the law appears to be applicable. Without taking into account purposes and the values implicit in seeking to accomplish those purposes, it is impossible for the law to "work itself out" as new cases arise and impossible for lawyers and judges to use the law intelligently.

Fuller concludes that normative behavior by human beings, including all behavior within the compass of the law, cannot adequately be understood purely as a matter of fact or purely as a matter of abstract legal rule. A jurisprudence must account for the normative or moral dimension necessary for an adequate understanding of what the participants in the legal process are doing. He suggests that traditional natural-law theory attempted to account for the moral dimension but had to be discarded in modern times because of the medieval metaphysics or the later "state of nature" theory that seemed inevitably to accompany it. One of Fuller's main objectives was to develop a legal theory that would fully disclose and account for the moral element shorn of the old anachronistic trappings. This theory would be called "eunomics" to avoid any illicit implications from the terminology of natural law.[68]

It was thought by many that Fuller would become the standard-bearer of a new secular natural-law theory. But the promise of eunomics did not materialize. Fuller did work out some of his earlier ideas in three areas: the "collaborative articulation of shared purposes," or the interaction of

---

Purpose and Natural Law, 3 Nat. L. Forum 68–71 (1958); Fuller, A Rejoinder to Professor Nagel, 3 Nat. L. Forum 83, 88 (1958).

67. See L. Fuller, *The Law in Quest of Itself*, 7–10 (1940). For a careful analysis of Fuller's idea, see Winston, Is/Ought Redux: The Pragmatist Context of Lon Fuller's Conception, 8 Ox. J. L. Stud. 329 (1988). See also Fuller's perceptive discussion of "implicit law" in *The Anatomy of the Law* (1968).

68. This term is first introduced in Fuller, Legal Philosophy at Mid-Century, 6 J. Leg. Ed. 457, 473 (1954).

means and ends; the "evaluation of different institutional arrangements for legal ordering"; and the "inner morality" of law.

The collaborative articulation of shared purposes was Fuller's favorite characterization of the process of working out means and ends through a rational dialectic involving several thinkers over a period of time. The development of legal rules and doctrine by common-law court decision over many decades is perhaps the greatest example of this idea. In arriving at decisions, and thereby creating a legal ordering of human relationships, the courts fashion means to achieve what appear to be the ends of the legal system. But these ends themselves change as new situations arise, and rules and doctrine must be restated to bring them in line with what now appear to be their purposes. Thus, ends and means interact in a process that permits a type of rational decision incorporating moral values even though the process does not postulate ultimate ends or purposes.

The second of Fuller's topics, the evaluation of institutional arrange-ments for legal ordering,[69] apparently interested him partly because of his experience as a labor arbitrator and mediator and partly because of his interest in far-eastern philosophy. Fuller suggested that jurisprudential efforts should be directed toward study of the different kinds of social ordering, including adjudication, mediation, consent (contract), legisla-tion, and managerial direction. Each of these processes results in establish-ing a legal and ethical order, that is, a set of rules and guidelines for human activity. Yet each process differs greatly from the others and appears to be well suited to certain areas of human activity but not to others. Some processes seem more congenial to certain types of culture than others as well. Fuller thought that careful study of the features of each of the processes, their context, and their consequences might lead to a better understanding of the ordering of human affairs generally, perhaps to some "natural laws" of a peculiar type. He did not pursue this project far enough himself to come close to such natural laws.

The development of the idea of the inner morality of law resulted from a series of exchanges with Professor H.L.A. Hart of Oxford, sometimes known as the Hart-Fuller debates, culminating in the publication in 1964 of Fuller's *The Morality of Law*.[70] The term "debates" is not quite appro-

69. This is first stated in chapter 6 of his book, *The Problems of Jurisprudence* (1949). This book also contains the famous hypothetical "Case of the Speluncean Explorers" used as a teaching device by Fuller.

70. For further discussion of these "debates" see chapter 11. The texts can be found in: Hart, Positivism and the Separation of Law and Morals, 71 Harv. L. Rev. 593

priate, however, since the two proponents did not come to issue on very many points. Hart defended the cause of the expository paradigm, giving that paradigm a new and more effective characterization. Fuller advanced the idea that there was an "inner morality" of law: certain canons or norms to which all lawmaking activity must conform at the risk of failing to make law. In an elaborate hypothetical involving good King Rex, Fuller demonstrates that a lawmaker will fail to make law unless that law is (1) general, (2) promulgated, (3) nonretroactive, (4) clear, (5) not self-contradictory, (6) capable of being followed, (7) enduring through time, and (8) administered as enacted.

The result of failing to live up to any of these canons of lawmaking is not bad law, but failure to make any law. Curiously, compliance with the canons can in fact result in bad law if the lawmaker's policy is faulty or, indeed, if he is malevolent. In what sense, then, is Fuller speaking of a morality? It is a use of the term in a very broad sense, but in a sense familiar to students of natural law. A carpenter must follow certain rules of thumb in order to do his work successfully. A piano tuner must tune the piano in certain ways in order to get the piano to play properly. A gardener must follow certain rules for planting, weeding, fertilizing, and harvesting his plants. The rules are dictated by the nature of the enterprise, and may, at least metaphorically, be called the morality of carpentry or of piano tuning or of gardening.

So what did Fuller prove in his entertaining exercise with King Rex?[71] He did not demonstrate the existence of any natural law in the traditional meaning of the term; and, as I have suggested, whether or not his canons of lawmaking should be called a morality is itself open to question. What he did show is that our concept of law—the meanings we import to the word "law"—imply an entire set of institutional arrangements. These constraining arrangements might be called the presuppositions of western legal systems. To the extent that scholars, judges, and lawyers operate within the confines of those presuppositions without questioning them, their choices are limited by the canons of the enterprise; they are obligated to follow the "inner morality" of the institution.[72]

(1958); Fuller, Positivism and Fidelity to Law—A Reply to Professor Hart, 71 Harv. L. Rev. 593 (1958); H. Hart, The Concept of Law (1961); L. Fuller, The Morality of Law (1964).

71. There were forty-six reviews of Fuller's book, and the common assessment among reviewers was that they could not understand what Fuller was trying to do or what he had done.

72. See Dworkin, Philosophy, Morality, and Law—Observations Prompted by Professor Fuller's Novel Claim, 113 U. Pa. L. Rev. 668 (1965).

Fuller was a very intelligent scholar, well read in fields outside the law and in German, French, and Italian legal materials as well as English, and he advanced innovative ideas and insights. Many of his contemporaries thought that he would put together the new moral paradigm they felt was so needed. A few thought he had accomplished that. For most, however, in spite of his admitted brilliant intellectual pathfinding, the path he followed led nowhere.

Most criticized was Fuller's contention that fact and value, or human action and human purpose, could not be separated. Among others Morris Cohen suggested that Fuller was an advocate for fuzzy thinking and had set back jurisprudence more than a century for suggesting that we should confuse what the law is with what it ought to be.[73] It can be argued, however, that Fuller was well ahead of his contemporaries in this matter. His argument might be interpreted as a statement of the thesis later advanced by philosopher Peter Winch to the effect that our knowledge of human actions is essentially different from our knowledge of inanimate matter and that there can be no social science that follows the methods of the physical and biological sciences, which assume deterministic cause and effect.[74] Winch advanced his view in 1958, much later than Fuller's *Quest*, but contemporaneous with some of Fuller's other writings. Winch in turn derived his ideas mainly from the work of the German sociologist Max Weber, the later work of the Austrian linguistic philosopher Ludwig Wittgenstein, and the historian R.G. Collingwood. While there are references to Wittgenstein and Weber in some of Fuller's later writings,[75] there is no evidence of any early connection between him and any of these thinkers.

Fuller's notion of the inseparability of the *is* and the *ought* as specifically related to legal rules can be traced to John Chipman Gray's treatise, a work with which Fuller was quite familiar. Gray thought that judges were under an obligation to follow and apply a rule of law that was clearly applicable, whether originating in legislation or precedent. This judicial

73. Cohen, Should Legal Thought Abandon Clear Distinctions?, 36 Ill. L. Rev. 239 (1941). See also Winston, note 67.

74. P. Winch, *The Idea of a Social Science and its Relation to Philosophy* (1958). This view has greatly influenced the philosophy of social science. See V. Pratt, *The Philosophy of the Social Sciences* (1978); see also Herget, The Scientific Study of Law: A Critique, 24 Jurim. J. 99 (1984).

75. See the Fuller-Nagel debate, note 65. Fuller spent a year in Germany in the early 1930s, and he may have become familiar with Weber's work at that time. His idea of the inseparability of fact and value bears close resemblance to what Weber discusses under the concepts of *Sinn* and *Verstehen*.

obligation meant that a judge would be required to apply "bad" rules, contrary to his own notions of morality or public policy, if their applicability was clear. On the other hand, where choices had to be made between competing rules, the judge should decide in favor of what the law ought to be. Thus, Gray concluded that the practical study of the law would necessarily involve a deontic element.[76] Fuller's position can be seen as an extension of this view: he would regard adjudication as a much looser process in which any rule in any case was in principle subject to reevaluation and restatement (or in some cases, rejection). Indeed, this seems to be the very activity that he liked to call "the collaborative articulation of shared purposes."

The main difficulty with Fuller's theory, is, however, that it consists of a number of important insights largely unconnected and undeveloped. System is entirely lacking, and he left unanswered many of the jurisprudential questions that his approach raised. Like Pound, Fuller failed to write the definitive treatise in which everything came together into a coherent whole. But unlike Pound, Fuller did not write enough to provide material for others to piece together the whole.[77] And, while he used the terms "morality" and "natural law" liberally in his writings, and he stressed the normative aspects of the legal process, he devised a relatively weak moral justification for the coercive power of law. Indeed, in retrospect Fuller's "purposes" that are collaboratively articulated by lawyers, judges, and scholars in the law's development look suspiciously similar to the "ends" of law discussed by Pound,[78] or even to the latter's "social interests."[79] One might conclude that Fuller never really escaped the pragmatic side of Poundian jurisprudence despite his brave efforts.[80]

If Fuller failed to get out from under the Poundian paradigm entirely, he advanced the normative side of it to a point that Pound would hardly

76. J. Gray, *The Nature and Sources of the Law*, 133–38 (1909). See the discussion of Gray in chapter 6.

77. See, however, the extended introduction in K. Winston, ed., *The Principles of Social Order: Selected Essays of Lon L. Fuller* (1981). Winston makes a good effort at putting together a coherent philosophy out of Fuller's writing, but there may be as much of Winston in this as of Fuller.

78. See Pound, The End of Law as Developed in Legal Rules and Doctrines, 27 Harv. L. Rev. 195 (1914); Pound, The End of Law as Developed in Juristic Thought (pts. 1–2), 27 Harv. L. Rev. 605 (1914), 30 Harv. L. Rev. 201 (1917).

79. Pound, A Theory of Social Interests, 26 Inter. J. Ethics 92 (1916). See generally chapter 6.

80. According to Kenneth Winston, Fuller's thinking was greatly influenced by Roscoe Pound, François Geny, and Morris R. Cohen. Winston, note 67, 331.

recognize. Fuller's insight into the judicial process and the other "legal processes" that he brought to attention and his explanation of the relationship of decision to intermediate means and ends set the stage for further development. His effective critique of "legal positivism" also prepared the ground for an even more devastating attack on the expository paradigm by his student Ronald Dworkin.

This does not exhaust the story of scholars seeking to establish the role and sometimes the priority of morality in the explanation and justification of law before 1970. However, developments beyond Fuller tend to draw upon his insights to forge new lines of battle that extend well beyond 1970. These new trends and ideas will be discussed in chapter 11.

THE CONTRIBUTIONS OF
THE MIGRANT SCHOLARS
1940 – 70

The United States received an injection of new jurisprudential blood in the period beginning around 1940 when scholars migrated from the totalitarian regimes of continental Europe. Many academics, most of them Jewish, fled Hitler's Germany when his regime came to power in 1933. Some came directly to America, while others arrived in a more roundabout fashion. The refugees included scientists, humanists, social scientists, and lawyers. They brought with them strong scholarly traditions in their disciplines; in the legal field the tradition was in many ways quite different from the Anglo-Saxon heritage that had dominated American thinking for so long. It was difficult to mesh the concepts and terminology of Continental thinking into Anglo-American discussion, but the migrants brought ideas and perspectives that were novel and insightful where they could be fitted in. In jurisprudence the input of a handful of scholars helped move American legal theory along, or at least stir it up. They also transmitted through their writings the ideas of other European scholars who were not well known in America.

Edgar Bodenheimer, Friedrich Hayek, and Hans Kelsen are the three jurisprudential scholars who had the most significant impact on American thinking. In addition, two groups of theorists added their expertise to the American melting pot: the natural-law thinkers associated for the most part with Thomistic philosophy, discussed in chapter 8, and the "Frankfurt School," a band of neo-Marxists who made a special contribution that was to bear fruit in later years.

It should be noted at the outset that the migrants all shared a strong distaste for the Nazi regime and for what was vaguely called "fascism." In varying degrees their writings reflect this strong orientation. They differed, however, in their theoretical responses to the Nazi phenomenon.

Bodenheimer: A Wider View of Jurisprudence

Edgar Bodenheimer (1908–   ) was educated in Germany, receiving his doctorate in law from the University of Heidelberg in 1932. He migrated to the United States shortly thereafter and earned an LL.B. degree from the University of Washington in 1937. He was an attorney for the government during the war and assisted the prosecution in the Nürnberg war trials. His academic career has been divided between the law schools of the University of Utah (1946–66) and the University of California at Davis (since 1966).[1]

Bodenheimer burst onto the jurisprudential scene in 1940 with the publication of *Jurisprudence*,[2] a 350-page text written "to give aid to the student of law and politics. . . ." This was the second American text devoted exclusively to jurisprudence since Pound's works in the early twenties.[3] While it did not present much that was original, it did provide a readable discussion of previous jurisprudential theories.[4] Perhaps more important, it presented a Continental view of the subject that was markedly different from the views prevalent in America at the time. The text was noteworthy in that it did not discuss how judges decide cases or how empirical work might be done in law or how rights and duties should be analyzed. Instead, Bodenheimer took an overtly political approach, emphasizing the need for the grounding of law on a firm political-moral basis.[5]

Bodenheimer's original contribution consisted of a definition or anal-

1. See Festschrift in Honor of Edgar Bodenheimer, 21 U. C. Davis L. Rev. 465 (1988).

2. E. Bodenheimer, *Jurisprudence* (1940).

3. The first was the Thomistic work of Father LeBuffe discussed in chapter 9. F. LeBuffe, *Outlines of Pure Jurisprudence* (1924); F. LeBuffe and J. Haynes, *Jurisprudence: With Cases to Illustrate Principles* (3d ed. 1938); Jerome Hall had produced a collection of readings in 1938 (see chapter 9).

4. Perhaps reflecting an American skepticism toward grand theory, one reviewer said, however, "The whole discussion is in the realm of doctrinaire theorizing, the views of various jurists being set out like so many dead insects stuck on pins." Levy, Book Review, 51 Yale L. J. 187 (1941).

5. Another migrant who also took a broad view of jurisprudence as a part of political theory was Arnold Brecht (1884–1977). See Brecht, The Myth of *Is* and *Ought*, 54 Harv. L. Rev. 811 (1941); Brecht, The Impossible in Political and Legal Philosophy, 29 Calif. L. Rev. 312 (1941); A. Brecht, *Political Theory* (1959); Mearns, Scientific Legal Theory and Arnold Brecht, 47 Va. L. Rev. 264 (1961). See also the work of Friedrich Kessler (1901–   ): Theoretic Bases of Law, 9 U. Chi. L. Rev. 98 (1941); Natural Law, Justice, and Democracy: Some Reflections on Three Types of Thinking about Law and Justice, 19 Tul. L. Rev. 32 (1944).

ysis of law as a compromise between despotism and anarchy. Despotism exists when the rulers have complete political power to control the people in a society; in contrast, anarchy is the complete freedom of the people in a society to pursue their own interests and thus, for some, to control other people. Bodenheimer sees law as the middle ground. Emphasizing the widely accepted Continental distinction between public law and private law, he sees public law as a protection from the usurpation of power by government (despotism) and private law as a protection against coercion by other private persons (anarchy). Thus, law is defined in terms of limitations on political power.

While a political approach to the understanding of law was promising and refreshing for the times, Bodenheimer's definition of law standing alone is clearly inadequate to carry a jurisprudence very far. It fails to treat such questions as who fashions the limitations, how they are fashioned, what structure of government is best, and how the law is to be identified and critiqued. Bodenheimer unfortunately did not see fit to supply his own answers to these questions by relating them to his definition; rather, he lapsed into a historical treatment of various legal philosophies, which, of course, deal with jurisprudential issues in their own terms. Apparently Bodenheimer recognized the inutility of his definition of law, since he discarded it in subsequent editions of the book.[6]

The real merit of the book is in Bodenheimer's discussion of European jurisprudential views, since only Pound among the Americans had been able until then to deal comfortably with them.[7] Bodenheimer's discussion of Marxist legal philosophy, Nazi legal philosophy, and what he calls "classic" natural-law theory is especially informative. But in the 1940 edition of his book Bodenheimer was not clear about what he was trying to do—analyze philosophies of others or present his own views. The historical discussion is not presented historically, that is, it contains a

6. E. Bodenheimer, *Jurisprudence: The Philosophy and Method of the Law* (2d ed. 1962, 3d rev. ed. 1974). In this work the author sees law as a means of achieving an appropriate balance between "order" and "justice." Unfortunately, these ideas are not nailed down well enough to provide a workable theory of law, justice, or order.

7. Another migrant who also did yeoman work in bringing to America an understanding of European jurisprudence was Wolfgang Gaston Friedmann (1907–1972). After earning a doctorate from Berlin, Friedmann fled Germany in 1937. He held academic posts in England, Australia, Canada, and eventually the United States, where he was a professor of law at Columbia until his death. Friedmann published *Legal Theory* in 1944, a work that describes all of the legal theories in western history from classical times to the twentieth century. This book became a standard reference work for jurisprudence, along with Bodenheimer's, and saw five editions, the last in 1967.

mixture of history and Bodenheimer's own ideas, and it is not related chronologically. In the second and third editions of the work this difficulty is mostly overcome by placing the historical exposition into its own section.[8]

Although Bodenheimer did contribute to the ongoing dialogue in jurisprudence (see chapter 11), it is impossible to piece together a coherent legal philosophy from his many articles and books.[9] Subscribing to ideas of very diverse theorists, which are incompatible with each other, his own approach is simply eclectic. He should be credited, however, as the first to direct jurisprudential discussion toward some of the larger unraised and unresolved questions of justice and political power and with transmitting to an American audience the views of German, French, and Italian legal theorists.

Hayek: The Spontaneous Order of Law

Friedrich August von Hayek (1899–   ) was born and educated in Vienna, Austria, receiving degrees in law, political science, and economics from the University of Vienna.[10] After a brief sojourn at New York University, he taught in Vienna until 1931. He then took a post at the London School of Economics as professor of economic science and statistics, becoming a British subject in 1938. In 1950 he joined the University of Chicago, where he served as professor of moral and social science until 1962, at which time he moved to Freiburg University in Germany as professor of economics. Hayek was awarded the Nobel Prize for economics in 1974.

Mostly in the field of economics, Hayek's list of publications in both

8. Bodenheimer also wrote *Treatise on Justice* in 1967 that elaborated his views on that subject. One reviewer called the work an out-of-date, unorganized presentation of diffuse utilitarianism, sufficiently imprecise to have any hard edges. Ladd, Book Review, 68 Colum. L. Rev. 1218 (1968).

9. For a plea by Bodenheimer for broader theory, especially in the natural-law direction, see Bodenheimer, The Province of Jurisprudence, 36 Corn. L. Rev. 1 (1960). He also published another book in the same general vein as his earlier works, *Power, Law and Society* (1973).

10. For a discussion of Hayek's intellectual development and his system of thought, see J. Gray, *Hayek on Liberty* (1984). Gray suggests that Hayek's thinking was most influenced first by Kant and then by Ernst Mach, Karl Popper, Ludwig Wittgenstein (a cousin), and Michael Polanyi. Ibid., 8–21. See also C. Nishiyama and K Leube, eds., *The Essence of Hayek* (1984).

English and German is long and impressive.[11] Of greatest renown is a small book written in 1944 called *The Road to Serfdom*, which extolled the virtues of the market economy and condemned the vices of planned economies.[12] More important for jurisprudence, however, are *The Constitution of Liberty* (1960), *Studies in Philosophy, Politics and Economics* (1967), and his later, three-volume work advancing many of the same ideas.[13]

Hayek, son of a professor of botany, was extremely well educated. He is a product of the Menger, or "Austrian," school of economics that flourished in the 1920s, but his work is not confined to economic matters. He has developed his own philosophy of science, his own political theory, and his own jurisprudence. Each of these fields is part of a larger, total system of thinking, and they reinforce each other. He acknowledges that he owes much to the Scottish moral philosophers of the eighteenth century, particularly David Hume, to Carl Menger, the Austrian economist, and to his contemporary in England, Karl Popper.

Hayek's jurisprudential theory is a variation on the evolutionary paradigm with some important additions and qualifications.[14] His starting point is the proposition that the human being is a rule-following animal. Every individual is socialized by learning through trial and error, imitation, and sometimes deliberate training to follow certain patterns of behavior.[15] These patterns of normative behavior can be described in terms of rules, even though the individual may not be able to articulate or describe the rules that she, nevertheless, intuitively follows. A prime example is the phenomenon of language. Individuals can speak a language without knowing the rules of grammar, syntax, and definition that they follow. Yet they have an important kind of knowledge in their grasp of the language, a knowledge that helps them cope with life.

11. For an extensive bibliography of Hayek's writings and of writings about Hayek and his theories, see ibid., 143–209.

12. F. Hayek, *The Road to Serfdom* (1944). This was published simultaneously in England and the United States.

13. F. Hayek, *Law, Legislation and Liberty* (vol. 1, 1973, vol. 2, 1976, vol. 3, 1979). While this work was published out of the time frame of this history, it develops more fully the ideas of earlier works. Therefore, in considering Hayek's theory as related to law, we will not be blind to his later, more polished views of the 1970s.

14. On the evolutionary paradigm, see chapters 1 and 5. The evolutionary paradigm has its origins with the Scottish moral philosophers of the eighteenth century. See P. Stein, *Legal Evolution* (1980).

15. See F. Hayek, *Studies in Philosophy, Politics and Economics*, 43–56 (1967). (This chapter originally appeared as an article in 1962.) The discussion that follows is drawn from this book and from F. Hayek, *The Constitution of Liberty* (1960).

When the people of a given society develop and follow "rules" of this kind relating to particular activities, the result of their collective rule-following is to establish an order. In the case of language a communicative order is established. Since no one has designed this order and no one can change it other than incrementally, Hayek calls it a "spontaneous" order. The market economy, a common morality, the institution of money, and technologies of various sorts are also examples of spontaneous orders. In contrast are "made" orders, specifically designed by someone for a purpose. The order of names in a telephone book is so designed; the allocation of powers provided for in a written constitution is another example of a made order.

In Hayek's view law originated historically as a spontaneous order, and it retains much of that character even today. People do not normally "obey" the law because they know and are trying to comply with formal written statutes and precedents. Rather, they follow rules of just conduct that they have learned in childhood, adolescence, and even adulthood, rules they may not be able to state in words. By each following such rules, individuals collectively create an order through which conflict is avoided and expectations are upheld. The written law of private conduct—the law of tort, crime, contract, property—is an articulation of the rules of this spontaneous order. The written law of codes or judicial opinions may more or less accurately reflect the underlying order in any given society; usually the ambiguities of language will permit the formal law to be shaped to fit the rules of the spontaneous order in any particular case.

One of the most important and dangerous things that people have learned to do over the course of history is to legislate: to make additional rules of conduct on top of the spontaneous legal order. According to Hayek, this has occurred primarily in the field of public law. The prescription of the functions and limits of units of government has become a matter of deliberate design. Private law, too, has been modified by legislation. More often than not, however, such legislation can be viewed as "corrective," that is, as modifying previous formal law to bring it into line with the demands of the spontaneous order, or as "declarative," that is, as reducing the felt norms to explicit rules. One of the difficulties with modifying the spontaneous legal order is that we do not know what many of the consequences of such a modification will be, because our knowledge of the entire spontaneous legal order is not organized and complete but intuitive and psychological. Thus, according to Hayek, well-intentioned reforms of private law often produce unforeseen negative results. Nevertheless, modern legal systems are a combination of "grown" law and "made" law.

Hayek thinks there is a strong analogy between law and the market economy. In both institutions individuals follow the dictates of their own minds, yet the overall result for society is a system or order. The order produced by free economic activity is the extant scheme of production and distribution of goods and services. The order produced by following the rules of just conduct is the totality of legal relationships—rights, duties, and so forth—that constitute the legal system. In both cases government "intervention" in the natural order is often convenient or even necessary to alleviate certain problems. However, Hayek cautions that intervention in both cases can cause as much trouble as it can cure because we cannot foresee many of the consequences of disturbing a highly complex system of relationships that was not itself designed.

In human society spontaneous orders do not remain static. Changes in one part of a culture will often produce changes in other parts. A change in economic patterns, religious views, technology, or geographical circumstances and even natural disasters like the Black Plague can have an impact on the spontaneous order of the law. What was fair and just yesterday may appear arbitrary or biased today. A rule of conduct long unchallenged might be brought into question by new circumstances. When these changes occur, the rules are also changed and the resulting order is modified. Normally such change is incremental and slow, and while small parts of the order are changing, others remain static. This gradual transformation of a legal order Hayek calls evolution. Spontaneous orders evolve to meet the needs of the time.

Hayek draws an important conclusion from the phenomenon of legal evolution. Because the rules of just conduct and the spontaneous order that they create help a society to survive and prosper, there is a sort of built-in presumption in favor of the perpetuation of such rules and order. A given rule of conduct cannot be justified in terms of the "purpose" it serves because it serves no purpose. It was not invented or designed. The rule has evolved as a part of the entire order. But the order as a whole is conducive, and indeed some such order is necessary, to the successful pursuit of life's goals by individuals in the society. Therefore, the rules of just conduct that make up the order have a legitimacy, a value conferred by virtue of having been evolved as a part of the whole.[16]

Hayek takes pains to point out that reformers and revolutionists alike often labor under the fallacy of "constructivism," an assumption that all

16. Note the similarity to traditional natural-law theory, which holds that rules of the system, although neutral in themselves as to ethical value, have a claim to be obeyed simply because the system as a whole is necessary. See chapter 9.

human institutions are the result of deliberate design. From this view it follows that any human institution, including a rule of law, must be justified in terms of the purpose or purposes that it serves or fails to serve. Failure to establish a rational justification means that the institution must be modified or discarded. According to Hayek, this fallacious view fails to take into account the evolutionary character of most human institutions. They have become what they are because in their complex relation to other social institutions they fill a niche; they serve a function, even though we may not understand what that function is. The corollary to the constructivist fallacy is that we know enough to make new institutions and new laws that will do a better job than the old. Hayek maintains that our knowledge of society is so imperfect that a particular reform will more likely lead to bad than to good overall consequences, hence, the danger of legislation.

The foregoing discussion suggests that Hayek supports a very individualistic, laissez-faire conception of the good society; but this does not always mean that he champions the status quo. Hayek recognizes the need for deliberate social change, and he offers an analysis of how rational deliberation proceeds toward that end. This is the process of "immanent criticism."[17] Any moral principle, political program, legal regime, or social policy can be evaluated from the standpoint of other normative propositions taken to be true for the sake of argument. This is the way normative argumentation usually proceeds. We take certain principles as given or accepted, and we demonstrate that the normative proposition in question is either logically inconsistent or incompatible in application with those accepted principles. Or we may argue to justify a new position that is most consistent with other accepted principles. The important point is that critique must be undertaken from within an overall normative structure (including spontaneous orders). In making legal or moral judgments we always operate within the normative framework that our culture provides. Indeed, we cannot escape these constraints. This does not mean, of course, that we cannot turn our critique toward any particular phase of law, politics, or morality when we wish. Hayek's concept of immanent criticism bears close resemblance to the earlier ideas of Morris R. Cohen (see chapter 7).

Although assessment of Hayek's views continues, it is clear that he was

17. This is best developed in Hayek's later work, *Law, Legislation and Liberty: The Mirage of Social Justice*, 25ff. (vol. 2, 1976). According to Hayek's intellectual biographer, John Gray, this notion is derived from Kant's critical philosophy. See J. Gray, *Hayek on Liberty*, 4–6 (1984).

able to revive the evolutionary paradigm from its apparent premature death in the 1920s. What is most significant is Hayek's demonstration that what he calls spontaneous orders, accepted in the social sciences, can exist in normative orders like morality and law. His whole effort seems to be to remove classic liberal political and legal theory from a base of naive rationalism and place it on a base of evolutionary institutionalism. He has made "invisible hand" explanations applicable to law as well as to the economy.[18]

Hayek's views are subject to many of the objections leveled at Savigny's school and at Americans William G. Hammond and James C. Carter at the turn of the century. The bias toward the status quo on the basis of evolution is an indirect but real relic of social Darwinism. Like Hammond and Carter, Hayek also fails to distinguish clearly between community morality and law, *the* cardinal sin in the eyes of supporters of the expository paradigm. His jurisprudence also suggests ethical relativity, since any normative critique must be grounded upon other normative principles accepted by the culture, and these may vary from culture to culture; hence, natural-law adherents would reject this aspect of his philosophy. In spite of these criticisms, Hayek has made American theorists rethink the problem of explaining long-term change in the law.

Kelsen: The Pure Theory of Law

Hans Kelsen (1881–1973) was born in Prague, Czechoslovakia (then Austria-Hungary). He attended Heidelberg, Berlin, and Vienna universities, receiving an LL.D. degree from the latter institution in 1906. He taught at Vienna and Cologne until 1933, when he moved to the University of Geneva, Switzerland. From 1940 to 1942 he visited at Harvard; he then became a member of the political science faculty at the University of California, Berkeley, the institution with which he was associated for the remainder of his career.

Kelsen produced many articles and books in both German and English over the course of his long life.[19] He was a scholar of international law,

18. For a brief discussion of invisible hand explanations see R. Nozick, *Anarchy, State and Utopia*, 18–22 (1974).

19. His principal jurisprudential works are *Hauptprobleme der Staatsrechtslehre* (1911), *Allgemeine Staatslehre* (1925), and *Reine Rechtslehre* (1934). The latter two works have been translated and expanded as *General Theory of Law and State* (trans.

but his principal pursuit was jurisprudence. Continuously refining his work, he developed what he called the "pure theory of law." His effort carried the expository paradigm to its most comprehensive and advanced form.

Most of Kelsen's jurisprudential thinking was done between 1906 and 1934, although he continued to elaborate on his favorite themes for many years thereafter. His work received great attention in Europe, Japan, and Latin America, but it became known in the United States only gradually in political-science circles in the 1930s.[20] Publication of Kelsen's English-language articles in American legal journals began in 1941,[21] when the author was sixty years old, and the translation of his main work into English was accomplished in 1945.[22] This accident of chronology, primarily because of his migration to the United States late in his career, placed Kelsen's work out of sequence in the development of American jurisprudence.

By 1940 the defenders of the old Austinian analytic jurisprudence had been largely routed by the Poundians. While it was true that the restatement project still flourished, attempts to refurbish the command theory, to analyze rights and duties, and to worry about who the sovereign was had almost disappeared. The skeptical realists were emphasizing the illusion of the formal legal system, and the legal social scientists were bent upon rejecting formal law and pursuing empirical investigation of legal behavior. On the other side the natural-law advocates were castigating the immorality of "positivism" in both its empirical form and its analytic form. Much of the critique and polemic of each group was aimed at the

---

Wedberg 1945), and *The Pure Theory of Law* (trans. Knight, rev. ed. 1967). For a complete bibliography of Kelsen's works and the work of others treating the pure theory of law through 1945, see the appendix to the Wedberg translation.

20. See Voegelin, Kelsen's Pure Theory of Law, 42 Pol. Sci. Q. Rev. 268 (1927); Janzen, Kelsen's Theory of Law, 31 Am. Pol. Sci. Rev. 205 (1937); Husik, The Legal Philosophy of Hans Kelsen, 3 J. Soc. Phil. 297 (1938). Kelsen did publish in a British legal journal in 1935. Kelsen, The Pure Theory of Law (pts. 1–2), 50 L.Q. Rev. 474 (1934), 51 L.Q. Rev. 517 (1935).

21. The Pure Theory of Law and Analytical Jurisprudence, 55 Harv. L. Rev. 44 (1941); The Law as a Specific Social Technique, 7 U. Chi. L. Rev. 75 (1941). Kelsen earlier contributed an essay to a book honoring the one-hundredth anniversary of the New York University law school: The Function of the Pure Theory of Law, in *Law: A Century of Progress, 1835–1935*, 231 (vol. 2, 1937). See also note 20. Some American scholars, like Fuller, read the original German works published much earlier.

22. H. Kelsen, *General Theory of Law and State* (Wedberg trans. 1945). For a good review of this work see Kunz, Book Review, 13 U. Chi. L. Rev. 221 (1946).

expository paradigm, but there was no contemporary exponent of that paradigm in America. Then, just off the boat from Europe, stepped Hans Kelsen with his pure theory of law.

For Americans Kelsen was an anachronism. It should be kept in mind that Kelsen was a contemporary of Henry T. Terry, Albert Kocourek, Wesley N. Hohfeld, and John Salmond. Like them but unlike many of his German contemporaries, Kelsen was enamored of the expository paradigm. His theory carried to the extreme everything that the current American jurisprudential theory of 1940 rejected. As a result he was a convenient object of attack, and he served as intellectual whipping boy for realists, social scientists, and natural-law thinkers.[23]

Kelsen's theory is extremely positivistic, and he deliberately avoids any ethical connection with pure law. This may seem strange in view of the fact that Kelsen was a refugee from the Nazis, and the great revival of natural-law thinking in the forties and fifties was partly a reaction against the totalitarianism of that regime.[24] Why was Kelsen not in step? Why did he not press for the necessity of a moral and humane law? Part of the answer is that Kelsen had formulated the main features of his theory long before the Nazi era, and he stuck with it. His own comment on this question suggests that a value-free rational science of law is preferable to a political approach.[25] Distinguishing between his scientific method and a jurisprudence of ideology (which could include natural law or Nazi theory), he says:

> It is precisely by its anti-ideological character that the pure theory of law proves itself a true science of law. Science as cognition has always the immanent tendency to unveil its object. But political ideology veils reality either by transfiguring reality in order to conserve and defend it, or by disfiguring reality in order to attack, to destroy, or to replace it by another reality. Every political ideology has its root in volition, not in cognition; in the emotional, not in the rational, element of our consciousness; it arises from certain interests, or, rather, from interests other than the interest in truth.[26]

23. For example, Rooney, Law without Justice? The Kelsen and Hall Theories Compared, 23 Notre Dame Lawyer 140 (1948).

24. Gustav Radbruch, another German positivist, radically changed his jurisprudence as a result of the Nazi experience. See Fuller, Legal Philosophy at Mid-Century, 6 J. Leg. Ed. 457, 483–85 (1954).

25. Kelsen, note 22 xvii. The following discussion is based primarily on Kelsen's General Theory.

26. Ibid., xvi.

Thus, in Kelsen's view the pure theory, free from passing notions of justice and politics, advances the cause of truth.

What is the pure theory? Like Austin and his Anglo-American followers of an earlier time, Kelsen is determined to develop a science of law that is neither transcendental (ideal or metaphysically based) nor empirical (sociologically based). This science must be kept pure from contamination by either of those two seductive alternatives. A conception of law based on natural law, political ideology, or similar ethical imperatives is for Kelsen a pseudoscience in which he finds no merit; it is in the last resort an exercise in politics. An empirical science of law based on the study of actual human behavior is, on the other hand, legitimate, but that science is sociology. The pure theory of law considers as its object the study of positive legal norms stripped of their emotive, political, and behavioral connotations.[27] The theory itself is a general conceptual scheme, in more modern parlance a "model," that allows one to understand all legal systems.[28]

It is beyond the scope of this book to trace the origins of Kelsen's theory in German legal philosophy. Presumably he did not originally borrow his main theses from John Austin. However, the parallel between Austin's and Kelsen's works is obvious, and American critics of the pure theory usually saw the connection and regarded Kelsen's efforts as an extension of the older analytic jurisprudence. In fact, much of the value of his version of the expository paradigm can fruitfully be viewed as a corrective of Austin's work.

Kelsen defines law in the broad sense as a coercive order. This order is made up of norms (ought propositions), and any given ought proposition is a law if it is a part of the legal order. The coercive aspect distinguishes the legal order from other orders in society that do not carry necessary sanctions. He thus rejects the Austinian view of law as a command of the sovereign or in other versions as the will of the legislator. To Kelsen these

27. "The Pure Theory of Law undertakes to delimit the cognition of law against these disciplines [psychology, sociology, ethics, and political theory], not because it ignores or denies the connection, but because it wishes to avoid the uncritical mixture of methodologically different disciplines (methodological syncretism) which obscures the essence of the science of law and obliterates the limits imposed upon it by the nature of its subject matter." H. Kelsen, *The Pure Theory of Law*, 1 (Knight trans. 1967).

28. "The subject matter of a general theory of law is the legal norms, their elements, their interrelation, the legal order as a whole, its structure, the relationship between different legal orders, and, finally, the unity of the law in the plurality of positive legal orders." Kelsen, note 22, xiii.

definitions unnecessarily incorporate psychological or political notions that are foreign to the pure conception of law. *A* law is an impersonal norm that is a part of the legal order. *The* law is that order.

The law cannot be a collection of unrelated "laws" or norms carrying sanctions for two reasons. First, since specific laws are ought propositions applicable to the people in any given society, they must be consistent. One law may not require "X," and another require "not X." Otherwise one or both cannot be complied with or enforced (sanctioned); hence, one or both cannot be a law. The necessity of consistency itself thus creates system. Second, the legal order is structured so that the existence of any law must be determined from other laws in the system. A legal order is hierarchical in the sense that the basic constitutional law validates further lawmaking by legislature, court, or agency by prescribing the procedures for valid lawmaking. This lawmaking further validates the laws that are so made, and these laws further validate the decisions of courts in specific cases, which further validate the actions of sheriffs, marshals, and other officials of the system in carrying out court orders and judgments. To answer the question of whether any particular law, judgment, or official action is legal is to point to the higher norm that authorizes the norm or action in question.

The existence of any law is thus equivalent to its validity, and this in turn is determined by higher norms in the pyramid of authority. If an infinite regression is to be avoided, eventually the highest norms of the system must be validated by a basic norm (the famous *Grundnorm*). These highest norms are usually referred to as the constitution of the particular legal order; however, the constitution itself is not the basic norm. Rather, the basic norm is a postulate, or presupposition, that underlies any legal system, namely, that the rules of the constitution shall serve as the highest norms in the legal order. Put another way, legal science presupposes that every society accepts and observes the fundamental proposition that its constitution is the highest norm or complex of norms in the legal order.

The pure theory itself is not empirically derived, but it necessarily allows for an empirical input in its application to any given legal system. This means that the scholar of law must find in law books the actual rules, decisions, and orders that the particular system validates. Whether or not a particular law is observed in practice, is followed, or is invoked by courts—in short, whether it is efficacious—is not a concern of the legal scholar, although it may be of interest to the sociologist. Efficacy becomes a significant consideration only when we ask whether a particular legal system exists in a particular society. Kelsen maintains that a particular legal system exists in a society when it is generally efficacious: not all rules of law must be followed, but the system as a whole must be observed. It is, of course, possible to discuss and analyze legal systems that do not exist in this sense, the obvious example being present-day discussion of Roman law. The rules of Roman law exist even today in the sense that they have validity as a part of a particular legal order.

Kelsen analyzes rights, duties, persons, competence, sanctions, and other general legal concepts. Regarding sanctions Kelsen reverses Austin's distinction between primary and secondary duties. A norm or rule of law imposes a duty upon an individual to do or refrain from doing some act; but this duty is derivative in Kelsen's view. The primary duty is imposed on the official (sheriff, bailiff) charged with enforcing the sanction. All of law can ultimately be reduced to such orders to legal officials. Kelsen also distinguishes between substantive law and adjective law, called by Kelsen material and formal law respectively. In the application of any law by an organ of the state, two kinds of norms are always involved: "(1) the formal norms which determine the creation of this organ and the procedure it has to follow, and (2) the material norms which determine the contents of its judicial or administrative act."[29] In making this distinction it would appear that Kelsen anticipates the later division of legal rules by H. L. A. Hart into "primary" and "secondary."[30]

It might appear superficially that Kelsen's model of a legal system is somewhat wooden and mechanical, as was Austin's. He says, however, that there is much room for creativity built into the system. In fact he contends that the difference between creation and application of law is one of degree, not of kind. In every act of legislation there is some element of application, and in every act of application there is some element of legislation. When a legislature enacts a statute, it does so pursuant to general constitutional provisions conferring such power. It "individuates" the general power by confining it to a specific subject. When a court interprets the statute, it further individuates the law by determining that a specific situation does or does not come within the meaning of the general language of the legislation. Although there are differences of degree, in each case of individuation there is an applying aspect and a creating aspect. We should, therefore, not be surprised that judicial decision-making often entails some obvious legislating.

29. Ibid., 129.
30. See H. Hart, *The Concept of Law*, 77ff. (1961).

Kelsen criticizes the Poundians for failure to distinguish between the methods and assumptions of normative and empirical sciences. No amount of empirical investigation alone can determine what the law is, because law is normative. Conversely, knowledge of the content of the normative propositions of law cannot lead to precise predictions of what judges or other legal officials will do. The cognitive object of the science of law, of the pure theory, is a body of norms, a system of "oughts." What judges do, if it can be generalized at all, is a matter of fact of concern to the sociologist. To mix these two fundamentally different kinds of thinking, for Kelsen, is to invite confusion.

Kelsen is equally uncompromising in his critique of natural law and related doctrines that try to make law an appendage of ethical theory. Reflecting the attitudes of the Vienna Circle of logical positivists to which he was long exposed, Kelsen considers all questions of justice, ethics, and natural law as essentially irrational and emotional.[31] He regards jurisprudence that attempts to establish a moral foundation for law as misguided and confused. His famous critique of natural law, first published in 1929 in German, is translated and contained as an appendix to *General Theory of Law and State*.[32]

Kelsen also offers a theory of the state as well as a theory of law. The former has not received much attention in the legal literature, and the reason seems fairly obvious. The state in traditional Anglo-American thinking is equivalent to government, and it does not carry the metaphysical connotations of German philosophical idealism; as such, it is a subject almost exclusively dealt with in the United States by the discipline of political science. This, of course, shows a significant difference in the traditions of jurisprudence in America and continental Europe. There is no necessary connection between Kelsen's theory of the state and the pure theory of law other than his contention that the state is simply the legal order seen from a different perspective.

The Frankfurt School and Critical Theory

A group of German scholars escaped the Hitler regime in 1933 and came to the United States en masse via stopovers for some in Switzer-

31. For a description of the Vienna Circle see Kunz, The Vienna School and International Law, 11 N. Y. U. L. Q. Rev. 370 (1934).

32. See Kelsen, note 22, 389.

land, England, and France.[33] They were members and associates of the Institute for Social Research, an organization affiliated with the University of Frankfurt. Upon arriving in the United States, some of the scholars established a base at the New School for Social Research at Columbia University, and others found affiliations elsewhere. In 1950 three core members of the group, Horkheimer, Adorno, and Pollock, returned to Frankfurt and reestablished the Institute there; however, most of the group remained in the United States. When the Institute was founded in 1923, its only philosophic orientation was a general Marxist approach to social questions, but as time went by a specific brand of social philosophy, called critical theory, became characteristic of the works of these scholars, and they became known as the Frankfurt School.[34] A former student of the restored Institute and an inheritor of the critical tradition in Germany is Jürgen Habermas (1929–), whose own advanced version of critical theory has recently commanded attention in Europe, America, and elsewhere.[35]

The intellectual tradition that the critical scholars inherited and extended was as far from the mainline tradition in America as could be imagined. These thinkers were strongly influenced by the philosophies of Friedrich Nietzsche and Wilhelm Dilthey, by the sociology of Max Weber, and by the general philosophical current known as *Lebensphilosophie*, or existentialism. Most of all, they were influenced by Marx.

Initially they accepted the general orientation and terminology of the Marxist tradition. Important to them was the proposition that society be studied holistically; the division of social study into watertight compart-

33. In addition to Max Horkheimer, director of the Institute, who was a philosopher and sociologist, this group of migrants included Theodore Adorno, musicologist, sociologist, and philosopher; Walter Benjamin, literary critic; Erich Fromm, psychologist; Henryk Grossmann, economist; A. R. L. Gurland, economist and sociologist; Otto Kirchheimer, lawyer and political scientist; Leo Lowenthal, literary and cultural critic; Herbert Marcuse, philosopher; Franz Neumann, political scientist; and Friedrich Pollock, economist.

34. For discussions of the work of the Frankfurt School see T. Bottomore, *The Frankfurt School* (1984); D. Held, *Introduction to Critical Theory: Horkheimer to Habermas* (1980); M. Jay, *The Dialectical Imagination: A History of the Frankfurt School and the Institute of Social Research, 1923–1950* (1973).

35. See Bottomore and Held, note 34; see also T. McCarthy, *The Critical Theory of Jürgen Habermas* (1978). Habermas' principal works translated into English are *Towards a Rational Society* (1970); *Knowledge and Human Interests* (1971); *Legitimation Crisis* (1976); *Communication and the Evolution of Society* (1979); *Theory of Communicative Action* (1984).

ments like psychology, political science, legal science, sociology, and economics was part of a scientistic false ideology called positivism. Other Marxist concepts originally accepted include the idea of the class struggle, the idea that the ruling class in capitalist society exploits the proletariat, the idea that the means of production determines the features of a culture in a given historical era, the idea that the working class will develop a class-consciousness that enables it to perceive and understand the struggle, and the idea that alienated workers will lead in the eventual revolution. Perhaps most important was the idea that social reality was distorted by ideology so that what are really contingent and repressive relationships between people appear to be necessary and unavoidable.

Over time critical scholars began to discard many of the classical Marxist notions and to develop their thought in other directions. Much of the older Marxist dogma had been challenged by historical events: the failure of workers' movements in Europe following World War I to bring about the expected transformation; the Soviet example of potential transformation turned to totalitarianism; the opportunism of the Stalin-Hitler pact in 1939; and the relative prosperity and complete lack of revolutionary consciousness among workers in the United States. Faith in the inevitability of revolution was lost. The class struggle became less and less significant or was qualified into extinction. The complete determination of cultural features like law, religion, music, and literature by the "means of production" was rejected, and more complex relationships were acknowledged. What was left intact was the general conception that most individuals in capitalist society are exploited and repressed by the political-economic-social system; that this oppression is masked by ideology; that liberation from this condition requires a transformation in social institutions and ways of thinking; and, finally, that it is the function of the scholar to point out the ways in which unjust dominance of some by others pervades society. The scholar becomes the instrument through which consciousness of true social reality is awakened.

Although increasingly pessimistic, the Frankfurterians hoped for a future utopian "emancipation" of individuals from various forms of "dominance." They recognized that relationships of dominance and hierarchy had changed greatly from Marx's simple paradigm of worker and capitalist. Therefore, they devoted much effort to the study of the problem of individual autonomy (or freedom from dominance) in contemporary social relationships. They were also interested in popular culture, particularly the way mass entertainment and advertising promoted a false social reality and at the same time stifled dissent. A third theme prominent in their work was the critique of what they called "positivism," which included "empiricism." By this term was vaguely meant a crude Comteian doctrine or unsophisticated empiricism which they took to be the view of science widely prevailing in the United States. They maintained that scientific objectivity was impossible, and worse, a deceptive myth. They sought to expose scientism, the false ideology of technology, and the bureaucratic rationalization and patterns of dominance and hierarchy that science and technology bring to society.

Most scholars of the Frankfurt School were not law-trained and did not devote attention to traditional jurisprudential subjects. However, there is a jurisprudence implied in their theory of how society can be understood, a jurisprudence unlike anything in the traditional American mold. By the 1970s and 1980s this view had become known as "critical legal scholarship"; but that development is beyond the scope of this book.[36]

One member of the Frankfurt group, Otto Kirchheimer (1905–1965), was law-trained, and his contributions to jurisprudence should be noted. Kirchheimer earned his doctorate in law from Bonn University in 1928.[37] His early writings were in both German and French; after migrating to the United States in 1937, he began to publish in English. An early work, coauthored with George Rusche, was *Punishment and Social Structure* (1939). His magnum opus, published in 1961, was *Political Justice: The Use of Legal Procedure for Political Ends*. A collection of earlier essays, mostly written in the forties and fifties, was published posthumously in 1969 under the title *Politics, Law, and Social Change*. At the time he died, Kirchheimer was professor of public law and government at Columbia University.

Kirchheimer did not attempt to put together a complete legal philosophy; indeed, he subscribed to the view that understanding society was a holistic undertaking; and, in common with most other Continental scholars, he found no clear line of demarcation between political and legal

36. Critical legal scholarship seems to have grown in part out of the student protest movements of the late 1960s and early 1970s. The influence of Herbert Marcuse on these movements has been noted. See Bottomore, note 34, 39. Marcuse's most influential works are *Eros and Civilization: A Philosophical Inquiry into Freud* (1951); *Reason and Revolution: Hegel and the Rise of Social Theory* (1941), reprinted in paperback (1960); *One Dimensional Man* (1964); *Negations: Essays in Critical Theory* (1968), a collection of older essays.

37. For biographical information on Kirchheimer, see the Introduction by Herz and Hula to Kirchheimer, *Politics, Law, and Social Change*, ix (1969). This volume also contains a bibliography of Kirchheimer's writings.

thought. As he saw it, his function was to analyze and critique social institutions to expose the social reality hidden by false consciousness. We can briefly examine how this perspective works by considering some aspects of *Political Justice*.[38]

This book analyzes the phenomenon of using legal machinery to accomplish political objectives, that is, the use of legislation or adjudication by one political group to assert power over another. In an attenuated sense, all trials, appeals, and acts of legislation further or retard a political position, but Kirchheimer has in mind the more blatant attempts to discredit or eliminate political opposition, whether by majority government against minorities or by minority government against majority political groups. The author uses historical examples from various societies, from the trial of Socrates to the trial of Adolf Eichmann; mostly he uses twentieth-century European and American illustrations.

Kirchheimer analyzes the process involved in political trials in terms of a number of variables like the choices open to participants, the tactics available, the roles to be played, the possible outcomes in terms of publicity, credit, or discredit to the cause, credit or discredit to the government, the implication of other defendants, and the sentence received by the principal defendant. For example, Kirchheimer points out that the defense counsel might be fully associated with the opposing cause as a member or advocate; or, he might be a defender of "neutral" constitutional principles like an attorney for the American Civil Liberties Union who has come to champion the rights of the accused without supporting the particular cause. Each of these models of defense counsel will carry with it its own tactical advantages. Thus, the attorney associated with the cause will be in a good position to turn the trial into a propaganda vehicle for the cause. On the other hand, the neutral attorney will be in the best position to mute the political aspects of the trial and possibly win the case for the individual defendant.

Similarly, Kirchheimer points out some of the strategies that defense counsel can employ. Anticipating the actual practice of counsel in such celebrated cases as the "Chicago Seven"[39] some years later, he suggests that the judge himself may be attacked as an instrument of a repressive

38. As commentators on the Frankfurt School have pointed out, Kirchheimer and others became less and less radical as they stayed on in America after the war, although they never lost their Marxist orientation. *Political Justice* (1961) was written toward the end of Kirchheimer's career; as a result, his views therein are somewhat moderate compared to earlier times and to some of the other critical theorists.

39. See Niederhoffer and Smith, Power and Personality in the Courtroom: The Trial of the Chicago 7, 3 Conn. L. Rev. 233 (1970), and newspaper accounts cited therein.

regime, a "part of the official apparatus, discounting the judgment from the outset, and fitting its result in advance into their own propaganda line." Or, counsel may take a different tack and emphasize ameliorating circumstances and avoid antagonizing the court. Kirchheimer notes that officials of the established regime, including those of the court system, also have means of eliminating politically troublesome lawyers through the contempt process, through political tests for admission to the bar, and through the bar's disciplinary procedures.

Kirchheimer's approach is for the most part sympathetic with the premises of American legal realism. He endorses the notion that judges use "hunches," rationalize their decisions, and act on their own political views, their "legal consciousness." However, judges belong "inextricably to the dominant minority," and their decisions will over the long run reflect the legal consciousness of that minority. This does not mean that a judge may not occasionally interpret laws in favor of victims of the system: "In doing so he will carefully avoid taking issue with the purposes of the legislators. Positivism, keeping to an exegesis of the meaning of the texts and harmonizing them among each other, may in this instance serve as a means to take an occasional stab at the widening gap between the legal consciousness of the majority and the dominant minority."[40]

Kirchheimer's perspective, rejecting all tenets of positivism of either the Austinian-Kelsenian type or of the empirical variety, sees the legal process as inherently flexible, as a political process with peculiar judicial trappings. It is a game played for political stakes, and the outcome of the game depends on the skill of the participants, the available resources, and the degree of motivation. In political trials at least, what "the law" is has very little to do with outcomes.[41] The most powerful determinants are the establishment's governmental apparatus and public opinion as molded by the institutions of mass culture.

While Kirchheimer's approach can be described as both objective and Machiavellian, he makes a few concessions, perhaps slips, to a transcendental notion of justice. Of the Nürnberg trials he says: "In spite of the Nürnberg trial's infirmities, the feeble beginning of transnational control of the crime against the human condition raises the Nürnberg judgment a

40. O. Kirchheimer, *Political Justice: The Use of Legal Procedure for Political Ends*, 211 (1961). See Murphy, Book Review, 35 Temp. L. J. 444 (1962).

41. Kirchheimer offers as an example of this point the prosecutions of American Communists under the Smith Act. The Supreme Court opinions in these cases seem to support Kirchheimer's view. See *Dennis v. United States*, 341 U.S. 494 (1951); *Yates v. United States*, 354 U.S. 298 (1957); *Scales v. United States*, 367 U.S. 203 (1961).

notch above the level of political justice. . . ." Kirchheimer's dedication of the book to "the past, present, and future victims of political justice" conveys the idea, as does his conclusion, that the use of legal machinery for political ends is here to stay and that this practice has mixed consequences in relation to political power. However, his occasional references to absolute values raise a problem that pervades all of the works of the critical theorists. While the critical theorist sees the values of everyone in society as shaped by ideology and hence false, how do his own values escape this taint? Why is his consciousness true while that of others is false? On what basis does his understanding of "the human condition" or the "basic rules of human conduct" become objective and absolute? Kirchheimer does not give us answers.

The holistic approach taken by the critical theorists made their work appear to be confined to philosophy or sociology. Their publications, mostly books, monographs, and articles in philosophical and sociological journals, also did not attract the attention of American legal scholars. Even Kirchheimer published only three pieces in legal periodicals.[42] The ultimate impact of critical theory was to resound in the future.

The contributions of the European migrant scholars have been aptly captured in a simple metaphor:

> We [American] lawyers too often regard the law as a mechanic regards an automobile: we confine our attention to an understanding of its elements and to the development of skills necessary to make it work. . . . The automobile is, to be sure, a machine, and the mechanic's function is to see that it operates properly. But the automobile is also a social artifact, and economic product, an historical incident and an object of aesthetic judgment. Likewise, our law is more than a system of legal rights and duties which is studied and manipulated by its mechanics. It is also, among other things, a mechanism for the distribution of wealth, an embodiment of a system of morality, and an area for the resolution of individual and social conflict and a vehicle or medium of political action.[43]

42. Kirchheimer, The Administration of Justice and the Concept of Legality in East Germany, 68 Yale L. J. 705 (1959); Kirchheimer, Parteistruktur und Massendemokratie in Europa, 79 Archiv des öffentliche Rechts 301 (1954); Kirchheimer, The Act, The Offense and Double Jeopardy, 58 Yale L. J. 513 (1949). Most of his English-language materials appeared in political science periodicals.

43. Bloustein, Book Review of Kirchheimer, *Political Justice*, 48 Corn. L. Rev. 208 (1962).

The European influence in broadening American views has no doubt been beneficial. The migrant scholars also brought expertise from philosophy, sociology, and political science to bear on jurisprudential questions, thus showing the value of interdisciplinary inquiry. It can safely be said that they opened some American eyes and that the consequences of their migration are still being felt in American jurisprudence.

11

NEW CORN FROM

OLD FIELDS

1945–70

In the period from the end of World War II to 1970 some old trends in jurisprudence continued, others died out, and some fresh ideas were articulated. "Jurimetrics" appeared on the scene with new possibilities for legal theory. The study of legal phenomena through behavioral science was pursued using sophisticated methods, producing fruitful results. The expository paradigm was revived, prompting an informative debate involving many scholars. Finally, the moral paradigm was extended and focused on new problems.[1]

The New Science: Jurimetrics

The influence of science on legal scholars took a new form following World War II. Specifically, four developments invited application to legal theory: the improvement of the computer; the creation of systems analysis, sometimes called cybernetics; new developments in scientific logic and communications theory, including the development of

1. What has come to be called "law and economics" also got its start in this period. In 1958 the University of Chicago began publication of the *Journal of Law and Economics*, devoted to economic analysis of legal problems. One article in particular by Ronald Coase, The Problem of Social Cost, 3 J. Law and Econ. 1 (1960), showed how public policy expressed in ordinary rules of tort and property law could be assessed in terms of economic costs and benefits. Coase's analysis opened the way for similar analyses in all field of law. See also, Calabresi, *The Cost of Accidents* (1970). However, the pre-1970 law-and-economics work did not amount to a new jurisprudence, if it ever did. It was, in fact, the logical extension of the Poundian paradigm through the use of economics. It analyzed the economic consequences of judicial decisions, legal doctrine, and legislation.

symbolic logic; and new philosophical approaches to linguistics. These four movements were interrelated and generally flourished under the banner of "jurimetrics."

The computer seemed to offer great potential for the law, from simply retrieving legal data to replacing judges to decide cases. In the early postwar period, in addition to better and cheaper hardware, the computer needed programming and software. Computers could not be talked to in natural languages; they needed an absolutely precise language. If legal data were to be used in computers, it would have to be in a symbolic or mathematical form. Hence, it was suggested that symbolic logic and new theories of communication should be applied to the legal field. Systems analysis, the study and control of systems of all kinds, likewise favored expression in precise symbolic terms, and the computer seemed an ideal instrument to manipulate the many variables involved in systems. New ideas about language could also be directly applied to the law since law itself was a peculiar form of communication. Decision-making processes in military and business management had benefited both from symbolic representations, or models, and from systems analysis. Why shouldn't judicial decision-making be subjected to the same kinds of analysis? In the legal periodicals in the early 1950s the message was: let's apply science to law. Some of this literature appeared to have serious implications for jurisprudence; most of it simply advocated the application of new technologies to law practice and teaching.

Before World War II the computer was regarded primarily as an intellectual curiosity. Early designs depended on mechanical devices, as opposed to electronic, and were cumbersome, unreliable, and slow. During the war the army and navy made considerable progress in developing workable computers. Partly because of these advances Norbert Wiener suggested in 1948 that a science dealing with the control of animals and machines was about to come into existence; he called it cybernetics.[2] At the same time strides were being made in the field of symbolic logic. On the other side of the Atlantic, with beginnings in the 1930s but coming into fruition in the forties and early fifties, was a British movement in the philosophy of language. One of its offspring was an influential article published in 1945 by Englishman Glanville Williams (1911–   ) entitled "Language and the

---

2. N. Wiener, *Cybernetics, or Control and Communication in the Animal and the Machine* (1948); see also N. Wiener, *The Human Use of Human Beings: Cybernetics and Society* (1950). Wiener's work stemmed from the successful military project to control antiaircraft gunfire with radar.

Law."[3] Williams introduced legal scholars to many of the recent advances in linguistics. He maintained that thought was inextricably bound to language, and the study of language as a subcategory of symbols and signs could eliminate many of the law's puzzles. He recognized that words have core and fringe meanings, and, therefore, judicial decision-making will often necessarily be creative. His comments on interpretation and the meaning of legal texts are also enlightening.

One of the first Americans to see the importance of all these developments to law was Lee Loevinger (1913–   ), Minneapolis practitioner and later commissioner of the Federal Communications Commission. In a crusading article advocating the application of science to law, Loevinger coined the term "jurimetrics."[4] Reviewing the history of legal philosophy in this article, he concludes that jurisprudence has been a waste of time and has directed attention away from more fruitful pursuits. Now, however, the time for science has come.[5] He anticipates adverse reaction: "The suggestion that science be introduced into law and other social fields is a threat to all those with a vested interest in a viewpoint, and so it is met with indignant objection." Reviewing recent progress in behavioral studies, logic, semantics, and other areas of "science," he concludes, "The next step forward in the long path of man's progress must be from jurisprudence (which is mere speculation about law) to *jurimetrics*—which is the scientific investigation of legal problems." As a tentative start Loevinger lists nine more or less unconnected problem areas of the law that he deems suitable for scientific treatment.[6] Further writings by Loevinger advocating the use of science and scientific techniques appeared in the next decade.[7]

Others joined Loevinger in the effort to apply science to law. Ilmar Tammelo (1917–   ), a legal scholar originally from Estonia, concen-

3. Williams, Language and the Law (5 pts.), 61 L.Q. Rev.71, 179, 293, 384 (1945), 62 L.Q. Rev. 387 (1946). Williams drew his inspiration from C. K. Ogden and I. A. Richards, *The Meaning of Meaning* (1923).

4. Loevinger, Jurimetrics, The Next Step Forward, 33 Minn. L. Rev. 455 (1949).

5. Loevinger obviously did not realize that much previous work in jurisprudence had as its object to make law "scientific."

6. These are behavior of witnesses, behavior of judges, behavior of legislators, legal language and communication, legal procedure and recordation, nonaberrant personal maladjustment, aberrations of behavior, unintentional personal injury, and macrolegal techniques of investigation.

7. An Introduction to Legal Logic, 27 Ind. L. J. 471 (1952); Dogmatism and Skepticism in Law, 38 Minn. L. Rev. 191 (1954); *Jurimetrics: Science and Prediction in the Field of Law* (1961); Science and Legal Thinking, 25 Fed. B. J. 153 (1965).

trated on the application of symbolic logic to law. He analyzed legal terms, showed how legal arguments could be transposed into symbolic notation, and categorized various fallacies common to legal argument.[8] A British author, influenced by the new philosophy of language, contributed a good discussion of the logical status of legal statements and the role of definition in law.[9] Walter Probert (1925–) contributed several articles explaining the application of communications theory to law.[10] Layman Allen (1927–) added an analysis of law in terms of modern logic and predicted important uses for the computer.[11] A committee on jurimetrics was established within the Association of American Law Schools, and conferences were held at the University of California, Los Angeles, in 1960 and 1962 and at Yale in 1963.[12]

In the early sixties a committee was formed within the American Bar Association on electronic data retrieval. This committee began to publish a quarterly newsletter in 1966 called *Modern Uses of Logic in Law* (MULL), which proved to be an important vehicle for the new legal scientists. Articles appeared dealing with a wide variety of topics from the mechanization of the tax code to the use of punched cards for title searches to automatic referencing of citations (shepardizing). Anything having a bearing on "science" was fair game, from programmed learning

8. Tammelo, Sketch for a Symbolic Juristic Logic, 8 J. Leg. Ed. 277 (1956); Tammelo, On the Logical Openness of Legal Orders, 8 Am. J. Comp. L. 187 (1959); Tammelo and Prott, Legal and Extra-Legal Justification, 17 J. Leg. Ed. 412 (1965). See also Clark, On Mr. Tammelo's Conception of Juristic Logic, 8 J. Leg. Ed. 491 (1956).

9. Stoljar, The Logical Status of Legal Principles, 20 Univ. Chi. L. Rev. 181 (1953).

10. Law and Persuasion: The Language Behavior of Lawyers, 108 Univ. Pa. L. Rev. 35 (1959); The Psycho-Semantics of the Judicial Process, 33 Temp. L. Rev. 235 (1961); Law Through the Looking Glass of Language and Communicative Behavior, 20 J. Leg. Ed. 253 (1968); Law, Science and Communications: Some New Facets to Empiricism, 10 Jurimetrics J. 51 (1969).

11. Symbolic Logic: A Razor-Edged Tool for Drafting and Interpreting Legal Documents , 66 Yale L. J. 833 (1957); Logic, Law and Dreams, 52 Law Lib. J. 131 (1959); Beyond Document Retrieval Toward Information Retrieval, 47 Minn. L. Rev. 713 (1963). See also L. Allen, R. Brooks, P. James, *Automatic Retrieval of Legal Literature: Why and How* (1962). For further scholarship of the 1960s in the general jurimetrics framework see H. Jones, ed., *Law and the Social Role of Science* (1967); Symposium, Jurimetrics, 28 Law and Contemp. Prob. 1 (1963); Symposium, Jurisprudence and the Lawyer, 19 Fla. L. Rev. 395 (1967); Kaplan, Decision Theory and the Factfinding Process, 20 Stan. L. Rev. 1065 (1968); also many short articles in M.U.L.L.

12. The papers read at the 1963 conference were published in L. Allen and M. Caldwell, eds., *Communication Sciences and Law: Reflections from the Jurimetrics Conference* (1965).

to the evaluation of the West Publishing Company's "key number system" for computer use. Among regular contributors to MULL were Lee Loevinger, Layman Allen, and Walter Probert. MULL changed its name to the *Jurimetics Journal* in 1967, becoming the organ of the ABA committee on science and technology.

The connection between legal language, symbolic logic, and computers can best be seen in some articles on jurimetrics published in the sixties. Because precision in legal language was so necessary for computer use, attempts were made to translate legal materials into symbolic notation. One of the difficulties was in phrasing the legal language to avoid ambiguity. Yale philosopher and logician Alan Anderson (1925–   ) seized upon the idea of using the Hohfeldian analysis as a basis for clarification,[13] which led to a revival of Hohfeld's wondrous schema.[14]

Cybernetics, or systems analysis, also received its share of attention in the legal periodicals. Jay Sigler (1933–   ), writing in the *Temple Law Journal*, suggests that political scientists have worked out the application of the new science to political decision-making.[15] The next step is, therefore, to apply it to law. Sigler is optimistic; he thinks that this development will have important repercussions for jurisprudence, possibly changing our entire conception of law.

Did all of the cheering for science bring about a new jurisprudence? In spite of the excitement and the disparagement of traditional jurisprudence, it did not. It did have an effect on the practice and teaching of law and on legal scholarship. Ovid Lewis (1932–   ), writing in 1970, sees four areas of intersection between science and law: scientific evidence and methods of investigation; technological and scientific advances that require modification of legal doctrine; creation of new hazards through technology that must be regulated by law; and allocation of scarce resources through law toward or away from scientific enterprise.[16] To these we might add that electronic word-processing has significantly changed

13. Logic, Norms and Roles, 4 Ratio 36 (1962); The Logic of Norms, 2 Logique et Analyse 84 (1958), reprinted in L. Allen and M. Caldwell, note 12, 69.

14. See Stone, Analysis of Hohfeld, 48 Minn. L. Rev. 313 (1963); Cullison, An Orientation for Formalized Hohfeldian Analysis, M.U.L.L. 58 (June 1966); Cullison, Review of Hohfeld's Fundamental Legal Concepts, 16 Cleve. Marsh. L. Rev. 559 (1967); Cullison, Logical Analysis of Legal Doctrine, 53 Iowa L. Rev. 1209 (1968). For a description of the "Wondrous Schema" of Wesley Newcomb Hohfeld see chapter 4.

15. Sigler, A Cybernetics Model of the Judicial System, 41 Temp. L. J. 398 (1968); see also Raab, Suggestions for a Cybernetic Approach to Sociological Jurisprudence, 17 J. Leg. Ed. 397 (1965); Lewis, Systems Theory and Judicial Behavioralism, 21 Case-West. Res. L. Rev. 361 (1970).

16. Lewis, note 15, 362–63.

law practice and court-records management. However, the promise of symbolic logic and systems analysis for law has simply not materialized. With the benefit of hindsight it is clear the new applications of science to law that went under the banner of jurimetrics had no conceptual unity, nor was any one of them theoretically broad enough to suggest a new jurisprudence.

Behavioral Science and Law

As described in chapter 8, skepticism about the value of a social-science approach to law remained high among legal academics into the 1950s.[17] But this began to change as more studies by social scientists, some in cooperation with lawyers, began to demonstrate that empirical methods could contribute worthwhile knowledge about legal institutions.[18] In addition, many of the champions of systems analysis, computer technology, and symbolic logic endorsed behavioral research in law as still another way to submit law to scientific investigation.

Social scientists themselves showed increasing interest in legal phenomena as an appropriate subject for study. Much of their interest focused on the activist decision-making of the Warren court.[19] Indeed, the

17. See, for example, Rostow, The Study of Economics in Relation to Education in Law, 2 J. Leg. Ed. 335 (1950); Llewellyn, On What Makes Legal Research Worthwhile, 8 J. Leg. Ed. 399, (1956); Cohen, Factors of Resistance to the Resources of the Behavioral Sciences, 12 J. Leg. Ed. 67 (1959); Wiener, Decision Prediction by Computer: Nonsense Cubed—and Worse, 48 A.B.A.J. 1023 (1962); Spengler, Machine Made Justice: Some Implications, 28 L. and Contemp. Prob. 36 (1963).

18. See, for example, Schwartz, Social Factors in the Development of Legal Control: A Case Study of Two Israeli Settlements, 63 Yale L. J. 471 (1954); P. Bohannan, *Justice and Judgment Among the Tiv* (1957); J. Cohen, R. Robson, and A. Bates, *Parental Authority: The Community and the Law* (1958); J. Carlin, *Lawyers on Their Own: A Study of Individual Practitioners in Chicago* (1962); Macaulay, Non-Contractual Relations in Business: A Preliminary Study, 28 Am. Soc. Rev. 55 (1963); A. Conard, *Automobile Accident Costs and Payments* (1964); W. LaFave, *Arrest: The Decision to Take a Suspect into Custody* (1965); H. Kalven and H. Zeisel, *The American Jury* (1966).

19. See, for example, Kort, Predicting Supreme Court Decision Mathematically: A Quantitative Analysis of the "Right to Counsel" Cases, 51 Am. Pol. Sci. Rev. 1 (1957); Mavrinac, From Lochner to Brown v. Topeka: The Court and Conflicting Concepts of the Political Process, 52 Am. Pol. Sci. Rev. 641 (1958); Ulmer, An Empirical Analysis of Selected Aspects of Law-Making on the United States Supreme Court, 8 J. Pub. L. 414 (1959); Krislov, Constituency Versus Constitutionalism: The Desegregation Issue and Tensions and Aspirations of Southern Attorneys General, 3 Mid. J. Pol. Sci. 75 (1959);

Warren court's relatively open policy-making supported the thesis that court decision was simply another type of political decision and, therefore, the proper subject of study by political scientists, social psychologists, and sociologists. Within the field of law generally, judicial behavior was a major but not exclusive focus of empirical studies in the late fifties and sixties.[20]

An enthusiasm for a social-science approach to legal questions prompted the formation of the Law and Society Association, an organization devoted to the study of law in its broad societal context. The association, organized at the annual meeting of the American Sociological Association in 1964, initiated the publication of a journal in 1966 with the assistance of funding from the Russell Sage Foundation. This journal, the *Law and Society Review*, has continued to publish a wide variety of articles dealing with all aspects of the law and social science relationship. The quality of its material gained the respect of many of the most traditional of legal academics.

Did these efforts lead to any kind of new jurisprudence? Martin Shapiro (1933–   ), writing in 1964, thought that he could see a new theory emerging, something he called "political jurisprudence."[21]

> This new movement is essentially an extension of certain elements of sociological jurisprudence and judicial realism, combined with the substantive knowledge and methodology of political science. Its foundation is the sociological jurist's premise that law must be understood not as an independent organism but an integral part of the social system. Political jurisprudence is in one sense an attempt to advance sociological jurisprudence by greater specialization.[22]

Shapiro recognizes that the new jurisprudence is incomplete. It has "so far failed to provide itself a theoretical rationale that grapples with the

---

Ulmer, The Analysis of Behavior Patterns on the United States Supreme Court, 22 J. Politics 629 (1960); Bachrach, The Supreme Court, Civil Liberties, and the Balance of Interests Doctrine, 14 West. Pol. Q. 391 (1961); Hamilton, Southern Judges and Negro Voting Rights: The Judicial Approach to the Solution of Controversial Social Problems, 1965 Wis. L. Rev. 1.

20. The leader of studies in judicial behavior was political scientist Glendon Schubert. See G. Schubert, *Quantitative Analysis of Judicial Behavior* (1959); G. Schubert, ed., *Judicial Decisionmaking* (1963); G. Schubert, ed., *Judicial Behavior: A Reader in Theory and Research* (1964); G. Schubert, *The Judicial Mind: Attitudes and Ideologies of Supreme Court Justices 1946–1963* (1965). Further discussion of Schubert's work follows.

21. Shapiro, Political Jurisprudence, 52 Ky. L. J. 294 (1964).

22. Ibid., 201–202.

problems of twentieth-century legal philosophy." Because it uses social-science methodology, it can deal with values only in terms of the values it finds expressed in society; there is no bridge to any higher evaluation. But, Shapiro maintains, political jurisprudence is not in any worse position than competing theories. "Indeed since the admittedly subphilosophical jural postulates of Roscoe Pound, nearly all talk has been of the need for and means of finding moral principles rather than the substance of those principles. The reason for this failure is quite obviously the failure of post-Marxian political philosophy to provide any acceptable "truths" about the nature and ends of government. . . ."[23] As Shapiro acknowledged, the new political jurisprudence was simply an extension of the Poundian paradigm, a welcome extension in that it successfully integrated the practices and current knowledge of political science and sociology into the overall scheme.

A more ambitious claim was made for "behavioral jurisprudence" by Glendon Schubert (1918–   ) in a 1968 article which, incidentally, exhibits that same hostility to traditional jurisprudence that many jurimetrics advocates were also expressing.[24] After tracing the early but unsuccessful efforts of the realist-scientists in the thirties, Schubert announces that the new behavioral jurisprudence is now ready to provide a scientific understanding of judicial decision-making. He identifies four features of the new approach that contrast with older views: (1) relating how persons behave in adjudicatory roles to the general body of knowledge of human decision-making; (2) observing the factors that influence adjudicatory decisions, assessing the preferred values and observing the effect on other people; (3) focusing on judges as people (with personality, cultural traits, and so on); and (4) explaining the effect that cultural differences have on adjudicatory behavior.

Schubert provides a model in schematic form for inquiry under the new behavioral jurisprudence. The model describes a system of judicial behavior composed of four subsystems: physiological, cultural, social, and psychological (or personality). These subsystems presumably identify the classes or types of factors that influence judicial behavior. Since decision-making is viewed as a system, it must have input, output, and feedback. Schubert provides a chart classifying the types of input functions, input structures, and conversion functions that lead to choice. He also provides a chart of output functions. Schubert then shows how applying the system

23. Ibid., 218. Shapiro is particularly critical of "self-satisfied" Catholic neoscholastic legal philosophy. Ibid., 219.

24. Schubert, Behavioral Jurisprudence, 2 Law and Soc. Rev. 407 (1968).

of inputs and outputs to the original four subsystems results in three types of rationality in adjudicative decision-making: logical, psychological, and nonlogical. Judicial decision can be analyzed and explained in any of the three modes; presumably a complete explanation that would lead to prediction must account for all three types of rationality. The various concepts and their interrelationships introduced by Schubert are intended to establish components of the judicial process in a way that will identify the empirical data needed to explain the process and to show how different data must be plugged in to understand the whole. Of most importance for political scientists, research under the Schubert system should lead to results related to other established theory in the discipline of political science.

Schubert's jurisprudence presupposes the whole body of epistemology underlying social science generally and does not purport to discuss it. His elaborate system should be contrasted to the paucity of theoretical structure that accompanied the early work of Underhill Moore and the "scientists" of the Johns Hopkins Law Institute (see chapter 7). The older social science assumed that all the investigator was required to do was to pursue the facts, and the relevant facts were indentified in simplistic terms. Although the new approach is sophisticated, like the work of Moore and his generation, Schubert's approach does not provide any guidance to judge or legislator. It has no normative dimension. It is a strategy for empirical investigation by an outside observer and therefore can lead only to descriptive generalization. As such, it is a mini-jurisprudence, capable of being subsumed under the umbrella of the Poundian paradigm.

Hart and the Resurgence of the Expository Paradigm

Herbert Lionel Adolphus Hart (1907–   ) was appointed professor of jurisprudence at Oxford University in 1952, bringing to this position a dual background as practicing lawyer and teacher of philosophy. Hart was very much in the British tradition of both law and philosophy, and, as such, would not ordinarily merit much attention in a history of American jurisprudence. However, his work drew its greatest critical reaction in the United States, not in Great Britain. The debates involved several American scholars and took place mainly on this side of the Atlantic, since many of his works were published in America; hence, he is a key figure in the development of American legal theory.

Hart was greatly influenced by the linguistic movement in contemporary English philosophy. Chief among the scholars that made up this movement were G.E. Moore, Ludwig Wittgenstein, and Hart's colleagues at Oxford, J.L. Austin and Gilbert Ryle. Hart absorbed the teachings of the movement and applied them to the field of jurisprudence. Since jurisprudence in England at this time still consisted in the study of the expository paradigm as expounded by Austin, Salmond, and others,[25] Hart directed his efforts toward examining the old expository tradition in the light of new linguistic theory.[26] The end result was a new and persuasive statement of the expository paradigm,[27] a descendant of the theories of Austin, Hohfeld, and (by adoption) Kelsen. As might have been expected, this new theory would come under attack in America, where realists, natural lawyers, and social scientists populated the academic halls in large numbers.[28]

In Hart's inaugural address at Oxford he maintained that analytic jurisprudence had foundered on the rocks of an inadequate understanding of linguistics.[29] The earlier analysts had attempted to build their theories upon definitions of key concepts. These definitions, said Hart, were at fault. Definitions are appropriate to explain the meaning of a term to someone who does not know it. However, simple definition can easily fail if it is used as the basis of a theory that attempts to clarify poorly understood complex relationships. Following the lead of Wittgenstein, Hart illustrates his thesis by analogizing to games. Asking "What is law?" or "What is a right?" is analogous to asking "What is an out?" in a baseball game or "What is a trick?" in bridge. An ordinary definition will not fully explain the matter. The adequate explanation will take into account the fact that a game is being played, that certain rules apply, and that the meaning of "out" or "trick" consists in showing the relationship of certain facts to the applicable rules. "Though theory is to be welcomed, the growth of theory on the back of definition is not." The meaning of "X

25. Hart himself explains this in Hart, Philosophy of Law and Jurisprudence in Britain (1945–1952), 2 Am. J. Comp. L. 355 (1953).

26. "[When] I became Professor of Jurisprudence at Oxford, I formed the view that analytical inquiries into the nature of law and legal concepts had come to a premature standstill." Hart, Analytical Jurisprudence in Mid-Twentieth Century: A Reply to Professor Bodenheimer, 105 U. Pa. L. Rev. 953, 957 (1957).

27. The theory is fully stated in H. Hart, The Concept of Law (1961).

28. Hart was also active on another jurisprudential front; he sought to clarify the meaning of criminal responsibility. See H. Hart, Punishment and the Elimination of Responsibility (1962); H. Hart, The Morality of the Criminal Law (1964).

29. Hart, Definition and Theory in Jurisprudence, 70 L.Q. Rev. 37 (1954); the address was given in May 1953.

has a right to payment of $10" cannot be successfully demonstrated by beginning with a definition of "right." Instead, this statement can be shown to be a deduction from a complex "game" called a legal system, which entails the operation of certain rules and the presence of certain facts. Our understanding of legal terms and concepts is thus a more complex thing than the simple correspondence between word and object that a standard definition suggests.

Edgar Bodenheimer challenged Hart's approach as too narrow and sterile.[30] He also mistakenly thought that Hart, by rejecting the starting point of simple definition, was making "a sort of swan song of analytical jurisprudence." While Bodenheimer's suggestions about the value of interdisciplinary study and the study of judicial behavior were sound, he apparently misunderstood Hart's basic thesis.

Another American critic of Hart was Carl Auerbach (1915–), a confirmed Poundian. Auerbach argued that legal analysis was one of the least fruitful ways to approach the law.[31] He maintained that lawyers and judges, as well as legal academics, could gain a better grasp of what the law was and how it worked by studying its history and its purposes. It appears that Auerbach may not have fully understood Hart, or, on the other hand, that he regarded the linguistic subtleties that Hart introduced as trivial.

Hart responded in the legal literature with a vigorous defense of legal analysis.[32] Indeed, his argument in this article may be the best justification of the expository paradigm ever given. He also restates why he thinks the earlier analysts went astray and how a more sophisticated understanding of legal language will permit the resolution of many jurisprudential puzzles. He convincingly shows how Bodenheimer's and Auerbach's arguments do not join issue with his own thesis, which he further elaborates.

Hart's exposition was followed by a reply from Bodenheimer that came much closer to hitting the mark.[33] Bodenheimer challenges Hart's description of the traditional aims of analytical jurisprudence by showing that Austin's own language (supported by the interpretation of Pound) supports the proposition that the expository paradigm necessarily postulates

30. Bodenheimer, Modern Analytical Jurisprudence and its Usefulness, 104 U. Pa. L. Rev. 1080 (1956).

31. Auerbach, On Professor Hart's Definition and Theory in Jurisprudence, 9 J. Leg. Ed. 39 (1956).

32. Hart, note 26.

33. Bodenheimer, Analytical Positivism, Legal Realism, and the Future of Legal Method, 44 Va. L. Rev. 365 (1958).

an autonomous system of self-consistent rules. He says, "Austin considered it the function of analytical jurisprudence to hammer out a science of law uncontaminated by social, ethical, or policy judgments."

More to the point, Bodenheimer argues that positivism confronts a dilemma from which it cannot escape. Legal rules and principles have "normative ambiguity," that is, their meaning is often indeterminate in any specific context. If the positivists do not admit this ambiguity, then their theory is contradicted by a reality of which every lawyer is aware. If they admit this ambiguity, then they will have to include in their theory some explanation of how such ambiguity is resolved and consequently of how the courts resort to extralegal sources. Thus, admitting the ambiguity will force the positivist to go outside the autonomous system, which will "inevitably become diluted by a dash of sociological or historical jurisprudence." The expository paradigm thus fails to explain law because it does not "provide the judiciary with a well-considered theory of the nonformal (that is, nonpositive) sources of the law."[34]

While visiting for a year at Harvard, Hart was asked to give the Oliver Wendell Holmes lecture in the spring of 1957, before Bodenheimer's rejoinder to Hart was published. This lecture was published in 1958 in the *Harvard Law Review*.[35] Therefore, it was not directly responsive to Bodenheimer's criticisms; however, in the course of his observations Hart did address some of the same issues. Hart's thesis in the Holmes lecture was that the tradition of the expository paradigm consisted of three doctrines: (1) that law is defined as the command of the sovereign, (2) that law and morality must be carefully distinguished, and (3) that the logical analysis of terms and concepts is vital to our understanding of the law. Hart further maintains that discrediting the first of these doctrines, the command theory, has mistakenly been thought by some to have discredited them all.

In particular Hart is concerned to demonstrate that the separation of law and morals is sound doctrine. He admits that the imperative theory (that law is the command of the sovereign) advanced by Bentham and Austin is unworkable; in fact, he points out, it was rejected by two of the early champions of the expository paradigm, John Salmond and John

34. While admitting the value of the insights of realism, Bodenheimer also finds this view to be too negative. Instead of emphasizing the admittedly irrational factors that go into judicial decision-making, the realists, he thinks, should work on constructing a positive theory of the elements, formal and nonformal, that affect decision.

35. Hart, Positivism and the Separation of Law and Morals, 71 Harv. L. Rev. 593 (1958).

Chipman Gray, as well as by Kelsen. In his view, however, this does not affect the validity of distinguishing between the law that is and the law that ought to be. He advances several arguments that show how a failure to make this fundamental distinction can lead to confusion.

Hart responds to Poundian or realist criticisms of the kind made by Bodenheimer by pointing out a linguistic feature of legal rules, namely, that they have a core of clear meaning and a fringe or penumbra of ambiguity. The core meaning fits most situations in daily life, and disputes over the application of the rule to specific facts are rare. Except for possible factual disputes, there is not much sense in litigating cases involving the core meaning of a legal rule; hence, litigated cases are likely to involve penumbral applications of a rule.[36] Appealed cases, those studied so carefully by American lawyers, are even more likely to involve situations at the penumbra. The fault of the realists is in mistaking these highly self-selected examples as characteristic of the operation of the law. Hart says, "Preoccupation with the penumbra is, if I may say so, as rich a source of confusion in the American legal tradition as formalism in the English."

Devoting exclusive attention to the decision-making of judges on appellate benches also leads to another false inference. Since the law in these cases, almost by definition, is ambiguous to some degree, the judge must adopt a new rule or extend an old rule or elect not to extend a rule; in short, he must legislate within the confines of the case. When he does, he will seek justification by invoking standards taken from outside the positive law. They may be moral standards, although usually they are propositions thought to be consistent with the public policy reflected in other areas of the law. The fact that moral standards are sometimes invoked to justify judicial legislation has been, according to Hart, wrongly seen as a demonstration of a kind of necessary link between morality and law. Such a link is weak and certainly not necessary.

Hart characterizes the challenges to positivism made by Poundians as an invitation to revise our conception of what a legal rule is. "We are invited to include in the 'rule' the various aims and policies in the light of which its penumbral cases are decided on the ground that these aims have, because of their importance, as much right to be called law as the core of legal rules whose meaning is settled."[37] Hart declines this invitation for two reasons; it would distort the use of legal language and cause confu-

36. Note the basically similar argument made by William G. Hammond in 1890, discussed in chapter 2.

37. Hart, note 35, 614.

sion, and it would provide a distorted account of the actual operation of the law by assuming that all legal questions are fundamentally like those of the penumbra. "It is to assert that there is no central element of actual law to be seen in the core of central meaning which rules have, that there is nothing in the nature of a legal rule inconsistent with *all* questions being open to reconsideration in the light of social policy."[38]

Finally, Hart takes aim directly at the thesis of his temporary colleague at Harvard, Lon Fuller, to suggest that *Is* and *Ought* cannot be separated in law.[39] First, Fuller's thesis applies only to cases at the penumbra. Second, Fuller's contention that "purpose" guides judicial decision-making in the penumbra is clever but misleading. It suggests that judges "find" the purposes of the law and are driven to decide accordingly. All this really means, says Hart, is that judges do not act arbitrarily when they legislate. But the idea of finding and following purpose hides the important factor of deliberate choice between alternatives.

> To use in the description of the interpretation of laws the suggested terminology of a fusion or inability to separate what is law and ought to be will serve (like earlier stories that judges only find, never make, law) only to conceal the facts, that here if anywhere we live among uncertainties between which we have to choose, and that the existing law imposes only limits on our choice and not the choice itself.[40]

Fuller immediately replied to Hart's arguments in an article published in the same issue of the *Harvard Law Review*.[41] He took issue with Hart's main thesis that the failure of Austin's command theory did not invalidate the proposition that law and morality must be separated. Fuller pointed out that Austinian positivism separated law from morality and other norms by providing a system of identification that would authoritatively determine what counted as law and what did not. This identifying mechanism was the command of the sovereign. If the idea of authoritative commands is eliminated from the theory, there is no method of distinguishing the legal from the nonlegal. Attempts to substitute some other identifying mechanism to tag properly the legal rules, such as a constitution or Kelsen's Grundnorm, assume an empirical proposition that the

38. Ibid., 615.

39. Hart specifically refers to Fuller, Human Purpose and Natural Law, 3 Nat. L. Forum 68 (1958).

40. Hart, note 35, 629.

41. Fuller, Positivism and Fidelity to Law—A Reply to Professor Hart, 71 Harv. L. Rev. 630 (1958). For further discussion of Fuller's views, see chapter 9.

people in a society accept the legitimacy of the system. Law thus becomes grounded upon public morality.

Fuller also says that the positivist approach fails to assist a judge in interpreting the law, a point made earlier and perhaps better by Bodenheimer. Finally, Fuller challenges the core-penumbra analysis of legal terms. He maintains that understanding the law entails understanding the context in which terms are used and the purposes that law seeks to achieve. Single words do not have "standard instances" and "penumbral meanings"; rather, they take on meaning from the rules in which they are used construed against a background of factual context and legislative purpose. Fuller illustrates with Hart's own example of "vehicle" as used in an ordinance prohibiting vehicles in a park. Does a tricycle or an engine-driven model airplane qualify as a vehicle? The proper interpretation of the ordinance, in Fuller's view, does not lie in ascertaining the standard and variant meanings of the word "vehicle." Rather, the solution lies in ascertaining the purpose of the ordinance. Is it intended to prevent noise and insure quietude, or is it intended to assure that pedestrians are not physically injured by moving machines? A noisy automobile would be prohibited under either interpretation, a tricycle under neither, and a model airplane under only one.

Fuller also begins development of his theory of the "inner morality of law," discussed in chapter 9. He analyzes some of the laws of the Nazi regime and the practice of postwar German courts in ignoring those laws. His conclusions differ from Hart's; however, the differences may be more verbal than substantive.

Hart restated and supplemented his views in a highly acclaimed work, *The Concept of Law*, published in 1961. The most notable additions to his theory offered in this book are the notion of the "rule of recognition" and the distinction between primary and secondary rules. The rule of recognition is the mechanism that identifies those rules that count as law in any legal system and is thus a substitute for Austin's sovereign and a functional equivalent to Kelsen's Grundnorm. Of most significance, it is not a person or a legislative body or a "presupposition," but a rule or complex of rules that are accepted by the people who operate the legal system in any society. This formulation of the indentifying or authoritative mechanism in terms of a rule avoids many of the puzzles that Austin's idea of a sovereign created.[42] For Hart, like Kelsen, the "existence" of a

---

42. Such as: Who is the sovereign? How can sovereignty be "legally" passed on? How can a law of one sovereign have effect in the reign of another sovereign?

legal rule is equivalent to its "validity" as a part of the system. This validity is ultimately determined by resort to the rule of recognition, which cannot itself be valid but can "exist" or not as an empirical matter. The apparent mystery surrounding this ultimate rule is dissipated by a clever analogy to the meter. We may question whether any particular meter bar (yardstick) is exactly one meter in length. We may measure it by another meter bar, of course, but ultimately any meter bar must be measured by the standard meter bar in Paris that is the accepted test of the correctness of all measurements in meters. To ask if this meter bar is exactly one meter is like asking if the rule of recognition is valid in a legal system. This is the wrong question because both the ultimate meter bar and the rule of recognition are the measure of all others.

The distinction between primary and secondary rules is an important feature of Hart's theory.[43] Primary rules directly apply to the behavior of persons in the society and include among others the rules forbidding various crimes and the rules of liability in tort. Secondary rules, or empowering rules, determine how and when the primary rules are to be applied. They include among others rules of legal procedure, rules authorizing the formation of contracts and wills, and rules providing for the exercise of various governmental powers, including legislation. These kinds of rules obviously cannot be forced into the mold of a command, and earlier attempts to do so in the literature of the expository paradigm created serious conceptual problems. Hart maintains that the union of primary and secondary rules is the key to understanding a legal system.[44]

Hart's book immediately became a new affirmation of faith for those of the positivist persuasion and an object of attack from scholars inclined toward other views. Professor John T. Noonan (1926–) addressed the shortcomings of *The Concept of Law* from the natural-law perspective.[45] Noting that Hart is forced to concede in his analysis of what a rule is that rules are "accepted" by the people in a society (the internal point of view),

43. This distinction was noted by Kelsen, but he did not make much of it. See H. Kelsen, *General Theory of Law and State*, 129 (Wedberg trans. 1945).

44. Hart's book also contains many significant insights that space limitations do not permit us to discuss in full. He analyzes the idea of a rule and recognizes the "internal" and "external" point of view toward law, a matter of perspective first elaborated fully by Lasswell and McDougal. He sees a kernel of truth in the idea of natural law, but finds it unfruitful. He illuminatingly contrasts the differences between rules of law and rules of morality, and he defends the expository paradigm against the charges of the realists on the same grounds stated in his earlier articles. If we equate rules with norms, Hart's overall model is not substantially different from Kelsen's.

45. Noonan, Book Review, 7 Nat. L. Forum 169 (1962).

Noonan questions why Hart does not explore the distinction between just and unjust laws in connection with such acceptance. He concludes that Hart's jurisprudence is much too limited, foreclosing considerations of values and the ends of law, considerations that Noonan finds very important.

Noonan also attacks Hart's modest concession to natural law. Hart had stipulated that survival was a goal common to all of humanity; once that goal was stipulated and certain conditions of human nature were taken into account like approximate equality, vulnerability, limited altruism, and limited resources, then one could infer certain principles that human beings must observe in order to achieve the goal of survival. This was Hart's "minimum content of natural law." Noonan scolds Hart for taking such a limited view. "Once one embarks on an enumeration of the minimum moral ingredients of law, is one not led, perhaps inexorably, to an enumeration of what one believes to be the maximum requirement of justice? 'Survival won't do the job.' Other more complex notions, recognizing more human needs, reflecting a richer range of human capacities, are [needed]. . . ."[46] Noonan argues that an analysis of law in terms of these human needs, the natural-law perspective, will yield much more fruitful results than the model of rules Hart suggests. Noonan also points out that such a natural-law approach requires an accompanying psychology and epistemology.[47]

Philosopher Herbert Morris (1928–) offered a generally favorable appraisal of Hart's book, but he had some serious reservations about certain problems presented by Hart's analysis.[48] One difficulty in particular was spotlighted. According to Morris, Hart uses the term "standard" in several contradictory ways. This minor error obscures a more fundamental flaw in Hart's model. "It is clear that we employ language in speaking about standards that reveals a conceptual framework quite different from that associated with rules, for we do not 'live up to' rules nor are they ever 'high' or 'low.' " Standards can be disregarded, but rules are violated.

When we critically appraise conduct using a mandatory rule and conclude that there has been a violation, the crucial critical concept

46. Ibid., 175.

47. For further arguments in this direction, but based more on Fuller's notion of legal obligation, see Lewis, Moral Obligation and the Concept of Law, 23 Rutgers L. Rev. 68 (1968).

48. Morris, Book Review, 75 Harv. L. Rev. 1452 (1962).

appears to be "subsumption." In the case of precise standards, such as those governing weights and measures, we put whatever is in question alongside the standard and the crucial critical concept appears that of "comparison." If the standard is a vague one, as most legal standards are, the crucial critical concept seems to be that of "weighing"....[49]

Morris points out that courts regularly use standards like "due care," "public interest," "fair price," and "substantial evidence." But the standards themselves as measuring devices do not make any specific conduct mandatory; they do not require action, although they may, of course, be incorporated into a rule that requires action. Since standards do not require action, they cannot be violated.

[Another] important difference between rules and standards is that many standards, perhaps all, involve what I shall label "an order to attainment." We talk of "barely failing to meet the standard," and "striving to reach it," and "not coming up to it," and "falling below it." This suggests that we can partially satisfy standards and that there are levels of attainment. In the case of a mandatory rule, one either violates or does not violate it. It is not a concept that admits of half-way houses.[50]

Morris also maintains that Hart's notion of "acceptance of a rule" is inadequate; this in turn affects Hart's characterization of the "internal" and "external" aspects of rules. Finally, Morris suggests that some rules may not fit within Hart's category of either primary or secondary rules.

Morris' review was followed by an article published in 1963 by Ronald Dworkin (1931–   ) that challenged the model of rules set forth in *The Concept of Law*.[51] First, Dworkin developed Fuller's earlier criticism of the "core-penumbra" idea. Hart would have us believe, according to Dworkin, that when the meaning of a legal rule was in the penumbra, the judge was required to legislate, that is, she was free to decide as she saw fit. She had discretion. But Dworkin says that she does not have discretion, even where positive legal rules provide no guidance. The belief that judges do have such discretion is the source of much confusion both in jurisprudence and in practical application of the law by courts.

The judge has no real discretion because the decision is dictated by

49. Ibid., 1456.
50. Ibid.
51. Dworkin, Judicial Discretion, 60 J. Phil. 624 (1963).

standards that take the form of principles or policies. To fulfill the duties of her judicial office the judge is required to apply these standards, and hence does not have discretion. Dworkin offers an analogy to games to illustrate his point. Hart had compared the game of baseball to the game of "scorer's discretion" to show that the realist thesis, "law is what courts do," misses the point. Baseball is played by the rules of baseball even though the umpire or scorer has the last word on scoring. The realists failed to recognize that the scorer as well as the players are bound by the rules. If he were not, we would have a different game, scorer's discretion. Dworkin suggests two games that fall between the extremes of baseball and scorer's discretion. He calls them "limited scorer's discretion" and "policies." In limited scorer's discretion the rules of baseball apply except that the umpire is allowed complete discretion within one specific area, say, calling balls and strikes. He can call any pitch a strike or ball as his fancy permits, regardless of its proximity to the strike zone. Neither batter nor pitcher can complain of "bad calls."

In contrast to limited scorers discretion the game of policies employs all of the rules of baseball but adds a requirement that the umpire apply these rules so as to further certain policies like making the game exciting or avoiding injury to players. Thus, since a player runs a risk of hurting himself when running toward the fence, the umpire might call a fly ball hitter safe, even though the ball was caught, because the fielder ran too close to the fence. This call would encourage fielders not to run close to fences. The rules might be modified by this policy in other dangerous situations like a runner sliding into a base or players running together to catch a fly ball.

Dworkin asks his readers which of the two games, limited scorer's discretion or policies, is more analogous to the operation of a legal system. Hart's position favors limited scorer's discretion; Dworkin believes the answer is clearly policies. A judge never has the complete albeit limited discretion suggested by the first game. She cannot arbitrarily make decisions, nor can she deliberately follow her own personal desires. She must follow the standards of the system as a whole because the players are entitled to decisions in conformity with both rules and standards. An adequate account of the process of judicial decision-making must explain the operation of standards and their relation to positive rules.

In 1967 Dworkin again took on Hart's theory, with many of the same arguments but expressed more persuasively and more fully.[52] This frontal

52. Dworkin, The Model of Rules, 35 Univ. Chi. L. Rev. 14 (1967).

assault dealt more than a casual blow to the expository paradigm. Dworkin convincingly demonstrates that Hart's earlier refusal of the invitation to broaden the meaning of law results in a theory that fails to explain the most pressing problems of jurisprudence.[53] Making the same distinction expressed earlier by Herbert Morris between rules on the one hand and standards, or principles and policies, on the other, Dworkin maintains that courts apply both kinds of norms in deciding cases. In most litigation, which is what mainly concerns the lawyer, more than rules must be taken into account in order to determine what the law is. Courts will rely on principles, and sometimes policies, to ground their decisions. Dworkin points out that in landmark cases courts often apply a principle in direct contradiction to the formal rules of the system. But principles are not within the authoritative positivist scheme, hence are not "law."

This does not mean that judges are free to ignore clearly authoritative rules or to apply principles and policies willy nilly as they see fit. In many cases judging may be difficult, but courts are obligated to seek the right answer. Their decisions are determined by law, not merely the formal law of positivist rules but also those standards that compose the political and moral normative structure of society. These principles and policies stand in the background behind the formalized rules to be invoked when the occasion requires. This may occur when applicable formal rules are ambiguous or absent, or it may occur when formal rules are clear but would lead to a result so out of harmony with the more general norms of society that they must be rejected. The suitors in any litigation are entitled to a decision that conforms to the whole of the law.

Nor can Hart's model of rules be modified to take into account those standards called principles and policies. This is because of the different nature of rules and standards pointed out initially by Morris.[54] Standards cannot be valid or invalid; they cannot be violated. The rules of a system cannot be in conflict, but the standards, principles, and policies often are diametrically opposed to one another. Finally, because their origin is not in authoritative legislation, they cannot be cataloged to be included within the official body of precepts blessed by the rule of recognition. Thus, from Dworkin's perspective the model of rules cannot adequately account for the operation of a legal system or the concept of law.[55] Dworkin subse-

53. See the quotations from Hart on pp. 296–97.

54. See Morris, note 48.

55. For a critique of Dworkin's article that misses the mark, see Christie, The Model of Principles, 1968 Duke L. J. 649.

quently used his critique of Hart as the basis for construction of a theory of his own, resulting in three significant books.[56]

An equally incisive critique of Hart's theory along similar lines was provided by Graham Hughes (1928–), a transplanted Englishman teaching at the law school of New York University.[57] Hughes' thesis is that a jurisprudence should be an intellectual guide to scholarship and practice. Hart's theory, as well as Kelsen's, dwells on the structure of a legal system as determined by rules. This emphasis is misdirected. While an understanding of the structure of a legal system and its relation to other social phenomena is necessary, it is not sufficient. The difficult intellectual tasks of the legal scholar and practitioner lie in the area of understanding legal reasoning—the process of argumentation that judges, advocates, and legal advisers undertake. This process must take into account policies and maxims of the law as well as rules.

What Hughes calls policies can be found in some instances enunciated in prior judicial decisions. In other cases policy requirements are actually legislated in statutes. More often, policy considerations can easily be implied from the language of legislation or case law—what Fuller calls "purpose."

> The first step in any discussion of how issues of policy enter into decision-making should be an examination of how these issues are often very much imbedded in these different layers of material used in legal reasoning. When is a recourse to considerations of policy in applying a rule a reference to extralegal materials and when is it, at least in part, a reference to a more general legal notion in the form of another rule or principle or maxim?[58]

The positivist's rigid distinction between rules that are of the system and rules that are not thus undermines any attempt to understand legal reasoning, which necessarily involves consideration of policy.

> Hart's rule-centered model of law therefore does not seem to account for all the materials which we would want to call law; it certainly does not include all the materials actually employed in legal reason-

56. *Taking Rights Seriously* (1977), *A Matter of Principle* (1985), and *Law's Empire* (1986).

57. Hughes, Rules, Policy and Decisionmaking, 77 Yale L. J. 411 (1968). Although this article appeared in the January 1968 issue of the *Yale Law Journal*, it was apparently written before Hughes had the opportunity to read Dworkin's critique, which appeared in the Autumn 1967 issue of the *University of Chicago Law Review*.

58. Ibid., 419–20.

ing and judicial decision. And most important, it diverts attention from a study of the part played by principles and maxims of policy in the decision-making process which produces the final text of the law.[59]

Hughes concludes that the American tradition in jurisprudence, following Holmes, Pound, and the realists (the Poundian paradigm), is more fruitful than the sterile analytical jurisprudence of Hart and Kelsen because it directs attention to the more significant problems of the law.

Besides pointing out some of the deficiencies of Hart's theory, Hughes' article raises the broader question of what a legal theory or jurisprudence should attempt to do. We may well ask what Hart accomplished by setting forth his concept of law. He has, of course, provided a general model of a legal system, and within that system he has shown the relationship between social rules, legal rules, moral rules, lawmaking, application of law, and other features of the system. However, he has not resorted to empirical data, although occasionally and anecdotally Hart refers to certain facts. On what basis, then, are we asked to accept this model? Does it describe reality better than alternatives do? Presumably the answer would require empirical verification. Does it prescribe an ideal to which actual legal systems should aspire? Clearly not; both good and evil legal systems are compatible with Hart's general model. Does the Hart model explain puzzling features of the law better than other views do? Arguably it does explain some puzzling aspects of the law, but it fails to deal adequately with many other issues.[60]

This broad question of the purpose of legal theory was addressed in an article by philosopher William L. McBride (1938–   ) that uses the theories of Hart and Kelsen as examples for analysis.[61] McBride sees the phenomenon of law as a complex of facts that need interpretation. Legal theory or jurisprudence provides an intellectual structure through which the complexity of fact can be arranged, related, and absorbed. Without theory even the lawyer "sees" legal phenomena as bits and pieces only roughly integrated into a whole. "The central task of jurisprudence is to enable us to look at legal phenomena themselves . . . through new eyes."

---

59. Ibid., 424. Hughes also carefully analyzes the reasons why the analogy of legal rules to the rules of games is misleading.

60. Such as how the obligation to obey the law is justified, or how law undergoes nondeliberate change over time, or how judges should decide difficult cases.

61. McBride, The Essential Role of Models and Analogies in the Philosophy of Law, 43 N.Y.U.L. Rev. 53 (1968).

How does jurisprudence accomplish its task? It uses definition, analogy, metaphor, and models. McBride demonstrates how analogy, metaphor, and models are used in the jurisprudence of Hart and Kelsen. For example, Hart uses the analogy of pathology to resolve the positivist conundrum of revolution.[62] Where there is political instability, the "existence" of a legal system may be brought into question. Is this a question of fact or validity? In these unusual situations Hart suggests that the legal system may be compared to a sick organism, one that might either die or recover, thus offering a certain insight into this phenomenon. At many points in his discussion Hart also uses the analogy of the rules of games to the rules of a legal system. Although this provides insight, it may also mislead in the sense that the analogy emphasizes certain aspects of legal phenomena and rejects other aspects. McBride shows how the game analogy fails in several ways to compare with legal systems (an analysis basically similar to that given by Hughes).

How legitimate are such analogies and their counterparts, metaphors and models? They obviously can provide insight, but they should not be carried too far. McBride tells us that there can be no general standard of legitimacy: "It is possible to debate rationally the merits of any particular analogy in legal theory, and some proposed analogies will generally be found to be relatively poor (i.e., of little explanatory value, often because too remote from the phenomenon to be explained); others, relatively strong. But no *absolute* standards for measuring their respective strengths and weaknesses will ever be found."[63]

McBride maintains that the only true test of theory is to ask how well it accomplishes the purposes that its author had in mind. The purposes of various scholars can be quite different: the analyst wishes to clarify; the natural lawyer attempts to justify; the evolutionist tries to explain historical change; and the social scientist seeks the truth of scientific principles. Since the purposes of theorists can vary considerably, this means that no jurisprudential theory can claim primacy by any a priori standards (save the hypothetical theory that accomplishes all purposes).

Internally, the use of devices like analogy is useful, and, indeed, inevitable, although to be effective such devices must maintain some plausible

62. When a coup or revolution topples the leaders of a government, the sovereign (or Grundnorm) has changed. According to the expository paradigm, a new legal system therefore comes into existence. If the rebels are later forced out, another legal system suddenly emerges. What law is the law under these circumstances? Must it be either one system or the other?

63. McBride, note 61, 76.

connection with the complexity of facts that we call law or a legal system. "The selection of these devices is not a totally arbitrary one, since the complex phenomena that together constitute 'the law' are, in certain obvious senses, *known* to begin with. Yet the range of choices is indefinitely large, and the writers in the history of legal theory can be located at widely scattered places within this range."[64]

McBride's thesis is in a sense an argument in support of an eclectic approach to jurisprudence, provided that each of the theories in itself is rationally defensible; indeed, McBride sees diversity in jurisprudence as potential complementarity. Perhaps more important, he implies that legal theorists should pay more attention to their own purposes and should take pains to make them more explicit.

A final contribution to jurisprudence related to the work of H.L.A. Hart and the expository paradigm generally is *Legalism* by political scientist Judith Shklar (1928–   ).[65] Shklar's work is not a critique of Hart per se, but is a critique of a larger ideology that includes the work of Hart, Kelsen, and the natural lawyers. It owes a debt to Hart and Kelsen in the same way that Bentham's work is indebted to Blackstone; by producing clear and comprehensive jurisprudential models, both Hart and Kelsen have exposed their thinking to criticism from a much broader perspective.

Shklar maintains that both positivism and natural law attempt to deal with the phenomenon of law from the standpoint of a certain ideology she calls "legalism." In other disciplines dealing with social theory, however, scholars have rejected or transcended the ideology of legalism; their thinking takes place within a framework incompatible with legalism. This incompatibility results in a failure of communication between jurisprudential scholars and other social theorists like moralists and political scientists. Jurisprudence is thus isolated; lawyers talk to themselves and fail to seek or receive stimulation and assistance from other intellectual sources.

What Shklar calls legalism is roughly equivalent to what Max Weber called rationality in law. It is a way of approaching moral and legal questions that assumes that they are matters of rules. Conversely it excludes the possibility of approaching normative human behavior from different standpoints like harmonization, mediation, and socialization. Social theory that stresses intuition (morality of the heart) or the consequences of acts or self-realization—all as opposed to a morality of

64. Ibid., 87.
65. J. Shklar, *Legalism* (1964).

rules—is systematically excluded in legal discourse by operation of the "ethic of legalism." Being litigious, individualistic, and rights-conscious, Americans are perhaps the prime examples of legalists, although the tradition of legalism is strong in all of western society. The legalistic ethic or mentality "expresses itself not only in personal behavior but also in philosophical thought, in political ideologies, and in social institutions." The thrust of Shklar's book is to explain legalism in all of its ramifications and to suggest other ways of thinking about law.

One of the interesting consequences of legalism, according to Shklar, is that we tend to assume that the legal system is "there"—that there exists, in some sense, an autonomous or semi-autonomous system of rules that somehow operate. Related to this assumption is an acceptance of the notion of the "rule of law," which implies that this autonomous body of rules should or does override all other factors in the determination of human activity. Legalism, at least in its positivist manifestation, also requires that we believe that politics and law are distinct phenomena, a concept rejected by Shklar. She also argues that natural law, while admitting the connection between law and a specific kind of rule-oriented morality, is necessarily repressive because it insists on agreement about basic moral principles in a world populated by people of diverse views.

Shklar points out that our society's obsession with viewing the world from a legalistic perspective has often obscured or made difficult the analysis of problems that, from another perspective, would not be nearly so troublesome. The futile and pointless Hart-Fuller debate over whether the Nazi laws were "legal" is an example. A similar example is the conduct of the Nürnberg and Tokyo "trials" under legalistic trappings when there was no applicable legal system.[66]

Shklar raises some provocative questions in her work.[67] She certainly places her finger on similarities in the positivist and natural-law theories that had previously gone unnoticed. Two criticisms of her work should be noted, however. Even if we assume the truth of Shklar's thesis that jurisprudence would benefit from being liberated from the straitjacket of legalism, she does not take into account the fact that jurisprudence must deal to a large extent with legal institutions as they are. Since these institutions incorporate legalism in their structures and practices, at-

66. In discussing these political trials Shklar acknowledges her reliance on the work of Kirchheimer. See the discussion of Kirchheimer in chapter 10.

67. For a thoughtful review of Shklar's book see Weinreb, Book Review, 78 Harv. L. Rev. 1494 (1965).

tempts to move jurisprudence away from this ethic would amount to moving toward ideals and utopias having little to do with the real world. Perhaps this is why utopian theory has traditionally been the province of political philosophers and not jurisprudential theorists. Second, Shklar fails to present any clear picture of what jurisprudence would be like if it abandoned a legalistic stance. The alternative picture that she sets out to paint is simply not painted. This shortcoming of her work very much resembles the same deficiency in the later work of critical legal scholars like Roberto Unger.[68]

New Directions for the Moral Paradigm

While the debate over the merits of Hart's new version of the expository paradigm continued, some scholars were concerned with re-developing the moral paradigm. A significant article appeared in the *Vanderbilt Law Review* in 1962 that reviewed all of the current ethical theory in England and the United States and assessed its value for jurisprudence.[69] This extensive review included theories of utilitarianism, intuitionism, emotivism, and others as well as the ethical side of Roscoe Pound's theory. It also discussed the value of the "neutral principles" concept in constitutional law for the light it shed on jurisprudence.[70] This review gave the legal scholars a good look at what the philosophers were doing.

The natural lawyers were also still busy. Although the *Natural Law Forum* changed its name to the *American Journal of Jurisprudence* in the 1960s, it continued to publish many analytic, historical, and critical

68. See R. Unger, *Law in Modern Society* (1976); R. Unger, *Critical Legal Studies* (1983).

69. Rose, Ethical Theory and Legal Philosophy, 15 Vand. L. Rev. 327 (1962).

70. The "neutral principles" concept is associated with the work of Herbert Wechsler. See Wechsler, Toward Neutral Principles of Constitutional Law, 73 Harv. L. Rev. 1 (1959). Neutral principles and what has been called "legal process theory," attributable to the work of H. Hart and A. Sacks, *The Legal Process* (tent. ed. 1958), have both been regarded as types of jurisprudence. In my opinion these works do not purport to offer any substantial new legal theory; their concern is at a much lower level of generality than "jurisprudence" as that idea has been used in this book. Wechsler proposed a constitutional-law theory to meet the problem of result-oriented Supreme Court decisions, and Hart and Sacks proposed a new strategy for teaching law. Neither attempted to create a general legal theory. It is true that jurisprudential implications can be drawn from these works, but that is true of almost any legal scholarship.

articles dealing with Thomistic natural law. Expositions of the scholastic doctrine could be found in other publications, too.[71] Some scholars sought to expand upon some of Fuller's ideas in an effort to promote the moral paradigm as well.[72] Many were content to rely on a Poundian balancing of interests or a practical utilitarianism traceable to Bentham. The economists in particular assumed as a part of their work that individual persons were rational maximizers of economic goods, and so a sort of utilitarianism stood over the work of these scholars.

A subtle change in the attitude of writers concerned with the relationship of morality and law was taking place. When natural law was revived in 1940 scholars were attempting to provide a rational argumentative structure that would justify the law and accepted political morality (see chapter 9). Specifically they sought to justify American democracy against totalitarian claims on one side and against the ethical relativism associated with legal realism on the other. Some were concerned about justifying the "higher law" imposed at Nürnberg and Tokyo. Their efforts were not critical but justificatory of the existing legal and political systems. During the 1950s, however, the civil-rights movement made great strides, and white America gradually became aware of the plight of blacks in a system of segregation. A few victories on behalf of civil rights were achieved in the courts and occasionally in the legislatures, the most widely known being the school desegregation decision of the Supreme Court in 1954.[73] Many legal scholars began to regard the American legal system, with its support of segregation and inequality, as flawed at the very least. Increasingly, their ethical and political concerns were to rectify the evils of the domestic system. The growing unpopularity of the war in Viet Nam in the late sixties, with its connection to racial discrimination, aggravated the situation. For a theorist inclined toward the moral paradigm the problem became how to justify human rights that would override the positive law. While Thomistic theory could be turned in that direction, a natural-rights rationale akin to those of the seventeenth and eighteenth centuries seemed to have more possibilities.

71. See, for example, C. Wu, *Fountain of Justice: A Study in Natural Law* (1955); R. Begin, *Natural Law and Positive Law* (1959); S. Buchanan, *Rediscovering Natural Law* (1962); D. O'Connor, *Aquinas and Natural Law* (1968); Symposium, Natural Law and Modern Thought, 13 Ohio St. L. Rev. 121 (1952); Symposium, Law and Morals, 31 Tulane L. Rev. 437 (1957).

72. See, for example, Symposium, The Morality of Law, 10 Vill. L. Rev. 624 (1965); Summers, Professor Fuller on Morality and Law, 18 J. Leg. Ed. 1 (1965); Lewis, Moral Obligation and the Concept of Law, 23 Rutgers L. Rev. 68 (1968).

73. *Brown v. Board of Education*, 347 U.S. 483 (1954).

The work of one scholar in particular illustrates the changing motivations that occurred in this period. Richard Wasserstrom (1936–) wrote *The Judicial Decision* in 1961, an exellent contribution aimed at solving the puzzle, especially in the context of the Poundian paradigm, of how judges use deductive logic in their decision-making yet are free in some sense to decide a hard case either way.[74] Wasserstrom distinguished between two processes involved in judicial decision-making: the process of discovery and the process of justification.[75] It is the latter process in which deductive arguments play a prominent role. Wasserstrom goes on to argue for a particular model of decision-making that combines the advantages of both strict precedent and a looser equity.[76]

By 1963 Wasserstrom's concerns had changed radically. This was a time of lunch counter sit-ins and mass demonstrations in the civil-rights movement. Wasserstrom struggled valiantly, but perhaps unpersuasively, to explain why one was not under a legal obligation to obey the law in all circumstances.[77] He attempted to justify civil disobedience in the context of unjust laws. In doing so, however, he did not formulate a general theory. Others were wrestling with the same problem.[78] Finally, in 1969 Wasserstrom took on the difficult question of the morality of war.[79] While some of his arguments are cogent, he again fails to provide a general theory that would support human or natural rights against positive law.

A more dispassionate, prolonged, and successful effort to create a new theory within the moral paradigm was undertaken by philosopher John Rawls (1921–). Rawls' early writings were published in the philosophy literature, where they were not likely to attract the attention of legal

---

74. R. Wasserstrom, *The Judicial Decision* (1961).

75. The distinction had previously been suggested by Herman Kantorowicz, Some Rationalism about Realism, 43 Yale L. J. 1240 (1934), and Max Radin, The Method of Law, 1950 Wash. U. L. Q. 471.

76. For a critique of this view see Dworkin, Does Law Have a Function: A Comment on the Two-Tier Level Theory of Decision, 74 Yale L. J. 640 (1965).

77. Wasserstrom, The Obligation to Obey the Law, 10 U.C.L.A.L. Rev. 780 (1963). Wasserstrom, Rights, Human Rights, and Racial Discrimination, 61 J. Phil. 628 (1964).

78. See DeBoisblanc, Dilemma of the Disobedient: A Solution, 42 Ind. L. J. 521 (1967); Blackstone, Civil Disobedience: Is It Justified?, 3 Ga. L. Rev. 679 (1969). Ronald Dworkin was similarly motivated in fashioning his "rights thesis." See R. Dworkin, *Taking Rights Seriously* (1977). This work was drawn in part from previous articles.

79. Wasserstrom, On the Morality of War: A Preliminary Inquiry, 21 Stan. L. Rev. 1627 (1969).

theorists.[80] However, Charles Fried (1935–), a law professor at Harvard, became interested in Rawls' work and used it as the basis for some theorizing of his own.[81] When word of Rawls' work diffused throughout the world of legal scholarship, he was invited to give the *Natural Law Forum* lecture at Notre Dame in 1968. This lecture anticipated his final version of *A Theory of Justice*;[82] it appeared in the *Forum* in that year.[83]

Both Fried and Rawls take what might be called a Kantian approach. They recognize the principle that each person must be considered as an end in himself and not merely as a means. The actions taken by people are to be morally judged on the basis of whether they are right or wrong, not merely on their consequences. Both Rawls and Fried are opposed to the utilitarian approach and take great pains to distinguish how their own principles work out differently than the utilitarian's in specific instances. Fried's work is not as broad in scope as Rawls'. He is concerned with the moral basis of choice in such Kantian dilemmas as trapped miners, starving sailors in a lifeboat, and preventing the killing of a hostage. Fried also builds a moral justification for a right of privacy.

Rawls is concerned with the larger questions of justice. In fact he has worked out two principles that provide the basis for a just society. These principles are standards to which the basic structure of society, its constitution, must conform in order to be just. His two principles are: (1) each person is to have an equal right to the most extensive basic liberty compatible with a similar liberty for others; and (2) social and economic inequalities are to be arranged so that they are both (a) to the advantage of the least well-off person, and (b) attached to positions and offices equally open to all. Under the first principle are basic rights such as the right to participate in the political process, the right of free speech, freedom of religion, and so forth. The second principle applies primarily to the distribution of social and economic goods. How do we know that Rawls'

80. See Rawls, Two Concepts of Rules, 64 Phil. Rev. 3 (1955); Rawls, Justice as Fairness, 67 Phil. Rev. 164 (1958); Rawls, Constitutional Liberty and the Concept of Justice, 6 Nomos 98 (1963); Rawls, Legal Obligation and the Duty of Fair Play, in S. Hook, ed., *Law and Philosophy*, 3 (1964); Rawls, Distributive Justice, in P. Laslett and W. Runciman, eds., *Philosophy, Politics and Society*, 58 (1967).

81. See Fried, Moral Causation, 77 Harv. L. Rev. 1258 (1964); Fried, Reason and Action, 11 Nat. L. Forum 13 (1966); Fried, Privacy, 77 Yale L. J. 475 (1968); Fried, The Value of Life, 82 Harv. L. Rev. 1415 (1969). See also C. Fried, *An Anatomy of Values: Problems of Personal and Social Choice* (1970); C. Fried, *Right and Wrong* (1978).

82. J. Rawls, *A Theory of Justice* (1971).

83. Rawls, Distributive Justice: Some Addenda, 13 Nat. L. Forum 51 (1968).

principles of justice are the right ones? Here a peculiar type of social contract is offered to justify the choice. Rawls envisions a hypothetical "original position" in which all of the people in the society are given an opportunity to review various proposed principles of justice. They have general knowledge about all aspects of life, but they do not have specific knowledge about themselves, that is, they do not know whether they will be one of the poor or the rich, the talented or the untalented, or what their specific likes and dislikes will be. This Rawls calls the "veil of ignorance." It is necessary to insure disinterested and fair deliberation and choice by the people in the original position.

Once the original position has been established the participants are given a list of possible principles by which their ideal society is to be modeled. This list consists of the standard theoretical schemes of justice that have been debated in philosophy like utilitarianism, anarchy, pure equality, aristocracy of merit, and others. Rawls then argues convincingly why his two principles would be chosen. The fact that his principles would be chosen proves that they are, therefore, the best of all practical alternatives. The hypothetical social contract adds to the intrinsic merit of his principles the value of procedural justice.

Rawls' presentation of his theory through a series of disconnected articles left a great many questions open. This problem was remedied in part by the publication of his comprehensive book, A Theory of Justice, in 1971. Still, debate over his theory has continued for two decades. It is interesting to note that in spite of the formality of Rawls' system and in spite of the elaborate philosophical arguments underpinning it, the theory shows that special concern for racial equality, equality of opportunity, and fair treatment of the disadvantaged characteristic of thought within the moral paradigm in the 1960s. Of course, the merits of Rawls' theory would be a focus of debate in the 1970s.

At the end of the 1960s we find jurisprudence in flux, as it would be found at most times in history. The force of the jurimetrics movement had largely been spent. The social-science approach to law had been taken over by the social scientists, and the jurisprudence of that enterprise became the province of philosophers of science. Thomistic natural-law theory continued to be spun, but the spinners were isolated and outside the mainstream. The expository paradigm seemed to have been confined mainly to the British Isles, where it flourished vigorously. Hayek remained the only advocate for the evolutionary paradigm. The work of John Rawls and Ronald Dworkin had moved to center stage. On the periphery was the influence of German critical philosophy earlier reflected in the works of

Shklar and Kirchheimer. The Poundian paradigm did not disappear; it survived in the forms of legal realism and law and economics as well as a more diffuse pragmatic attitude toward law. No one view dominated jurisprudence in 1970. There was plenty of room for diverse perspectives and for new ideas. New corn was being harvested from old fields.

SELECTED BIBLIOGRAPHY

The most important original works on the subject of jurisprudence published in the United States in the period from 1870 to 1970 are listed under primary sources. Works that discuss, criticize, or explain the primary works are listed under secondary sources. In a few cases works have both original and secondary significance; these have been included in both lists. Some British and Canadian works have been included when they have a direct bearing upon academic discourse in the United States. The two lists are broken down into subcategories of "Books and Monographs" and "Articles," the latter including independent works of chapter size or smaller contained in collections. In addition, two series of works on jurisprudence, the Modern Legal Philosophy Series and the Twentieth-Century Legal Philosophy Series, are included in the list of primary sources and appear separately at the end of the bibliography.

PRIMARY SOURCES 1870–1970

Books and Monographs

Adler, M. *St. Thomas and the Gentiles* (1938).
———. *Scholasticism and Politics* (1940).
———. *A Dialectic of Morals* (1941).
Allen, C. *Law in the Making* (1927).
Allen, L., and Caldwell, M., eds. *Communication Sciences and Law: Reflections from the Jurimetrics Conference* (1965).
Amos, S. *A Systematic View of the Science of Jurisprudence* (1872).
———. *The Science of Law* (1874).
Andrews, J. *American Law: A Treatise on the Jurisprudence, Constitution and Laws of the United States* (1900).
Arens, R., and Lasswell, H. *In Defense of Public Order* (1960).
Arnold, T. *The Symbols of Government* (1935).
———. *The Folklore of Capitalism* (1937).
Association of American Law Schools, Various Authors. *The Science of Legal Method* (trans. Register and Bruncken, 1917), vol. 9, MLPS.
Austin, J. *The Province of Jurisprudence Determined* (1832).
———. *Lectures on Jurisprudence* (1861–63).
Bayne, D. *Conscience, Obligation and the Law* (1966).
Beard, C. *An Economic Interpretation of the Constitution* (1913).
Begin, R. *Natural Law and Positive Law* (1959).
Bentley, A. *The Process of Government* (1908, reprinted 1967).

Berolzheimer, F. *The World's Legal Philosophies* (trans. Jastrow, 1912), vol. 2, MLPS.

Beutel, F. *Some Potentialities of Experimental Jurisprudence as a New Branch of Social Science* (1957).

———. *Democracy and Scientific Method in Law* (1965).

Bigelow, M., ed. *Centralization and the Law: Scientific Legal Legal Education* (1906).

Bodenheimer, E. *Jurisprudence: The Philosophy and Method of the Law* (1940, 2d ed. 1962, 3d rev. ed. 1974).

———. *Treatise on Justice* (1967).

Brecht, A. *Political Theory* (1959).

Broderick, A., ed. *French Institutionalists: Maurice Hariou Georges Renard, Joseph Delos* (trans. Wellington, 1970), vol. 7, TCLPS.

Brookings Institution, ed. *Essays on Research in the Social Sciences* (1931).

Brown, A. *The Austinian Theory of Law* (1906).

Bryce, J. *Studies in History and Jurisprudence* (1901).

Buchanan, S. *Rediscovering Natural Law* (1962).

Cahn, E. *The Sense of Injustice* (1949).

———. *The Moral Decision* (1955).

Cairns, H. *Law and the Social Sciences* (1935).

———. *The Theory of Legal Science* (1941).

———. *Law and its Premises* (1962).

———. *What is Law?* (1970).

Calabresi, G. *The Cost of Accidents* (1970).

Campbell, E. *The Science of Law, According to the American Theory of Government* (1897).

Cardozo, B. *The Nature of the Judicial Process* (1921).

———. *The Growth of the Law* (1924).

———. *The Paradoxes of Legal Science* (1928).

Carter, J. *A Communication to the Special Committee* (Assn. Bar City N.Y., 1883).

———. *The Proposed Codification of Our Common Law* (Proc. Assn. Bar City of N.Y., 1884).

———. *Argument in Opposition to the Bill to Establish a Civil Code* (1887).

———. *The Provinces of the Written and Unwritten Law* (1889).

———. *President's Address to American Bar Association* (1895).

———. *Law: Its Origin, Growth and Function* (1907).

Clark, E. *Practical Jurisprudence: A Comment on Austin* (1883).

Clark, R. *The Science of Law and Lawmaking* (1898).

Cohen, F. *Ethical Systems and Legal Ideals* (1933).

Cohen, M. *Reason and Nature* (1931).

———. *Law and the Social Order* (1933).

———. *Reason and Law* (1950).

Cohn, G. *Existentialism and Legal Science* (trans. Kendal, 1967).

Commons, J. *Legal Foundations of Capitalism* (1924).

———. *Anglo-American Law and Economics* (1926).

Davitt, T. *The Elements of Law* (1959).

Dawson, J. *The Oracles of the Law* (1959, reprinted 1968).

DelVecchio, G. *The Formal Bases of Law* (trans. Lisle, 1914), vol. 10, MLPS.

D'Entreves, A. *Natural Law: An Introduction to Legal Philosophy* (1951).

Devlin, P. *The Enforcement of Morals* (1965).

Dillon, J. *The Laws and Jurisprudence of England and America* (1894).

Ehrlich, E. *Fundamental Principles of the Sociology of Law* (trans. Moll, 1936).

Fouillee, A., Charmont, J., Duguit, L., and Demogue, R. *Modern French Legal Philosophy* (trans. Chamberlain and Scott, 1916), vol. 7, MLPS.

Fowler, R. *Codification in the State of New York* (1884).

Frank, J. *Law and the Modern Mind* (1930).

———. *Fate and Freedom* (1945).

Fried, C. *An Anatomy of Values: Problems of Personal and Social Choice* (1970).

Fuller, L. *The Law in Quest of Itself* (1940).

———. *The Problems of Jurisprudence* (1949).

———. *The Morality of Law* (1964).

———. *The Anatomy of the Law* (1968).

Gareis, K. *Science of Law* (trans. Kocourek, 1911), vol. 1, MLPS.

Geny, F. *Method of Interpretation and Sources of Law* (1899, 2d ed. 1921, 2d ed. Eng. trans. Mayda, 1954).

Gerhart, E. *American Liberty and Natural Law* (1953).

Ginsburg, M. *On Justice in Society* (1965).

Gottlieb, G. *The Logic of Choice: An Investigation of the Concepts of Rule and Rationality* (1968).

Gray, J. *The Nature and Sources of the Law* (1909, 2d ed. 1919).

Haines, C. *The Revival of Natural Law Concepts* (1930).

Hall, J. *Readings in Jurisprudence* (1938).

———. *Living Law in a Democratic Society* (1949).

———. *Studies in Jurisprudence and Criminal Theory* (1958).

———. *Comparative Law and Social Theory* (1963).

Hammond, W. *Hammond's Blackstone* (1890).

Hart, H., and Honore, A. *Causation in the Law* (1959).

———. *The Concept of Law* (1961).

———. *Punishment and the Elimination of Responsibility* (1962).

———. *Law, Liberty and Morality* (1963).

———. *The Morality of the Criminal Law* (1964).

———. *Punishment and Responsibility* (1968).

Hayek, F. *The Constitution of Liberty* (1960).

———. *Studies in Philosophy, Politics and Economics* (1967).

————. *Law, Legislation and Liberty* (vol. 1, 1973, vol. 2, 1976, vol. 3, 1979).

Hearn, W. *The Theory of Legal Duties and Rights, An Introduction to Analytical Jurisprudence* (1883).

Holaind, R. *Natural Law and Legal Practice* (1899).

Holland, T. *Essays on the Form of the Law* (1870).

————. *Elements of Jurisprudence* (1880, 12th ed. 1917).

Holmes, O. *The Common Law* (1881, Howe ed. 1963).

Howard, C., and Summers, R. *Law: Its Nature, Functions and Limits* (1965).

Jhering, R. *Law as a Means to an End* (1877–82, trans. Husik, 1913), vol. 5, MLPS.

Jones, H., ed. *Law and the Social Role of Science* (1967).

Kantorowicz, H. *The Definition of Law* (1958).

Keller, A. *Societal Evolution* (1915).

Kelsen, H. *General Theory of Law and State* (trans. Wedberg, 1945), vol. 1, TCLPS.

————. *The Pure Theory of Law* (trans. Knight, rev. ed. 1967).

Kinkead, E. *Jurisprudence: Law and Ethics* (1905).

Kirchheimer, O. *Political Justice: The Use of Legal Procedure for Political Ends* (1961).

————. *Politics, Law, and Social Change* (1969).

Kocourek, A., and Wigmore, J. *Sources of Ancient and Primitive Law*, vol. 1 of *Evolution of Law: Select Readings on the Origin and Development of Legal Institutions* (1915).

————. *Primitive and Ancient Legal Institutions*, vol. 2 of *Evolution of Law: Select Readings on the Origin and Development of Legal Institutions* (1915).

————. *Formative Influences of Legal Development*, vol. 3 of *Evolution of Law: Select Readings on the Origin and Development of Legal Institutions* (1918).

————. *Jural Relations* (1927, 2d ed. 1928).

————. *An Introduction to the Science of Law* (1930).

Kohler, J. *Philosophy of Law* (trans. Albrecht, 1914), vol. 12, MLPS.

Korkunov, N. *General Theory of Law* (trans. Hastings, 1909), vol. 4, MLPS.

Kreilkamp, K. *The Metaphysical Foundations of Thomistic Jurisprudence* (1939).

Langdell, C. *A Selection of Cases on the Law of Contract* (1871, 2d ed. 1880).

————. *A Brief Survey of Equity Jurisdiction* (1906).

Lask, E. *The Legal Philosophies of Lask, Radbruch and Dabin* (trans. Wilk, 1950), vol. 4, TCLPS.

Lasswell, H. *Politics: Who Gets What, When, How* (1936).

————. *The Analysis of Political Behaviour* (1949).

————, and Kaplan, A. *Power and Society: A Framework for Political Inquiry* (1950).

LeBoutillier, C. *American Democracy and Natural Law* (1950).

LeBuffe, F. *Outlines of Pure Jurisprudence* (1924).

———, and Haynes, J. *Jurisprudence: With Cases to Illustrate Principles* (3d ed. 1938).

———. *The American Philosophy of Law: With Cases to Illustrate Principles* (rev. ed. 1947).

Lee, G. *Historical Jurisprudence* (1900).

Lenin, V. *Soviet Legal Philosophy* (trans. Bubb, 1951), vol. 5, TCLPS.

Lieber, F. *Legal and Political Hermeneutics* (3rd ed. 1880).

Lightwood, J. *The Nature of Positive Law* (1883).

Llewellyn, K. *The Bramble Bush: On Our Law and Its Study* (1930).

———, and Hoebel, A. *The Cheyenne Way* (1941).

Llewellyn, K. *The Common Law Tradition: Deciding Appeals* (1960).

Lloyd, D. *The Idea of Law* (1964).

Loevinger, L. *An Introduction to Legal Logic* (1952).

London School of Economics, ed. *Modern Theories of Law* (1933).

Maine, H. *Ancient Law* (1861, American ed. 1864, reprinted 1986).

———. *Village Communities in the East and West* (1871, 7th ed. 1895).

———. *Early History of Institutions* (1875, 7th ed. 1897).

———. *Dissertations on Early Law and Custom* (1883).

Maritain, J. *The Rights of Man and Natural Law* (1944).

———. *Man and the State* (1951).

Markby, W. *Elements of Law Considered with Reference to Principles of General Jurisprudence* (1871, 6th ed. 1905).

McClennan, J. *Primitive Marriage* (1865).

McDougal, M., and Associates. *Studies in World Public Order* (1960).

———, and Feliciano, F. *Law and Minimum World Public Order: The Legal Regulation of International Coercion* (1961).

Mellinkoff, D. *The Language of the Law* (1963).

Miller, W. *Lectures on the Philosophy of Law* (1884).

———. *The Data of Jurisprudence* (1903).

Miraglia, L. *Comparative Legal Philosophy* (trans. Lisle, 1912), vol. 3, MLPS.

Myers, G. *History of the Supreme Court of the United States* (1912).

Nagel, S. *The Legal Process from a Behavioral Perspective* (1969).

Newman, R., ed. *Essays in Jurisprudence in Honor of Roscoe Pound* (1962).

Northrop, F. *The Meeting of East and West: An Inquiry Concerning World Understanding* (1946).

———. *The Logic of the Sciences and the Humanities* (1947).

———. *The Complexity of Legal and Ethical Experience* (1959).

———. *Philosophical Anthropology and Practical Politics* (1960).

———. *Man, Nature and God: A Quest for Life's Meaning* (1962).

———. *Ideological Differences and World Order* (1963).

———. *Cross-cultural Understanding: Epistemology in Anthropology* (1964).

Northwestern Univ., ed. *My Philosophy of Law: Credos of Sixteen American Scholars* (1941).

O'Connor, D. *Aquinas and Natural Law* (1968).

Parsons, F. *Legal Doctrine and Social Progress* (1911).

Paton, G. *A Textbook of Jurisprudence* (1951, 4th ed. 1972).

Pattee, W. *The Essential Nature of Law* (1909).

Patten, S. *The Theory of Social Forces* (1896).

Patterson, E. *Jurisprudence: Men and Ideas of the Law* (1953, mimeographed editions 1940, 1946, 1949, 1951).

Perelman, C. *The Idea of Justice and the Problem of Argument* (1963).

Petrahitskii, L. *Law and Morality* (trans. Bubb, 1955), vol. 7, TCLPS.

Pollock, F. *Essays in Jurisprudence and Ethics* (1882).

―――. *Oxford Lectures and Other Discourses* (1890).

Pound, R. *Introduction to the Study of Law* (1912).

―――. *Outlines of Lectures on Jurisprudence* (1913, 5th ed. 1943).

―――. *The Spirit of the Common Law* (1921).

―――. *An Introduction to the Philosophy of Law* (1922).

―――. *Interpretations of Legal History* (1923).

―――. *Law and Morals* (1926).

―――. *Contemporary Juristic Theory* (1940).

―――. *Social Control through Law* (1942).

―――. *Jurisprudence* (5 vols. 1959).

Raymond, G. *Ethics and Natural Law* (2d ed. 1920).

Recasens-Siches, L. *Latin American Legal Philosophy* (trans. Ireland, 1948), vol. 3, TCLPS.

Reuff, J. *From the Physical to the Social Sciences* (trans. Green, 1929).

Rheinstein, M., ed. *Max Weber on Law in Economy and Society* (trans. Shils, 1954), vol. 6, TCLPS.

Ritchie, D. *Natural Rights, A Criticism of Some Political and Ethical Conceptions* (1895).

Robinson, E. *Law and Lawyers* (1935).

Robson, W. *Civilization and the Growth of the Law* (1935).

Rodell, F. *Woe Unto You, Lawyers* (1939).

Rommen, H. *The State in Catholic Thought* (1945).

―――. *The Natural Law: A Study in Legal and Social History and Philosophy* (trans. Hanley, 1947).

Rooney, M., *Lawlessness, Law and Sanction* (1937, reprinted 1982).

Ross, E. *Social Control* (1901).

Rümelin, M. *The Jurisprudence of Interests* (trans. Schoch, 1948), vol. 2, TCLPS.

Salmond, J. *Essays in Jurisprudence and Legal History* (1891).

―――. *First Principles of Jurisprudence* (1893).

―――. *Jurisprudence, or Theory of Law* (1902, 12th ed. 1966).

Sayre, P., ed. *Interpretations of Modern Legal Philosophies: Essays in Honor of Roscoe Pound* (1947).

Schubert, G. *Quantitative Analysis of Judicial Behavior* (1959).

―――, ed. *Judicial Decision-making* (1963).

————, ed. *Judicial Behavior: A Reader in Theory and Research* (1964).

————. *Judicial Policy-Making* (1965).

————. *The Judicial Mind* (1965).

Scott, H. *The Evolution of Law: A Historical Review* (1908).

Shklar, J. *Legalism* (1964).

Simon, R., ed. *The Sociology of Law* (1968).

Smith, G. *The Elements of Right and of the Law* (1886, 2d ed. 1887).

————. *The Law of Private Right* (1890).

————. *A Critical History of Modern English Jurisprudence: A Study in Logic, Politics and Morality* (1893).

————. *Logic; or, the Analytic of Explicit Reasoning* (1901).

Smith, J. *Spirit of American Government* (1907).

Smith, M. *Jurisprudence* (1919).

Snyder, O. *Preface to Jurisprudence: Text and Cases* (1954).

Spooner, L. *Natural Law or the Science of Justice* (1882).

Stammler, R. *The Theory of Justice* (trans. Husik, 1925), vol. 8, MLPS.

Stapleton, L. *Justice and World Society* (1944).

Stone, J. *The Province and Function of Law* (1946, 2d ed. 1950).

————. *Legal System and Lawyers' Reasoning* (1964).

————. *The Social Dimensions of Law and Justice* (1966).

Strauss, L. *Natural Right and History* (1953).

Stumpf, S. *Morality and Law* (1966).

Sumner, W. *Folkways* (1906).

Taylor, F. *The Law of Nature* (1891).

Taylor, H. *The Science of Jurisprudence* (1908).

Terry, H. *Some Leading Principles of Anglo American Law, Expounded with a View to its Arrangement and Codification* (1884).

Timasheff, N. *Introduction to the Sociology of Law* (1941).

Tourtoulon, P. *Philosophy in the Development of Law* (trans. Read, 1922), vol. 13, MLPS.

Tylor, E. *Anahuac* (1861).

————. *Primitive Culture* (1871).

Vinogradoff, P. *Historical Jurisprudence* (1920).

Ward, L. *Dynamic Sociology* (1883).

Wasserstrom, R. *The Judicial Decision: Toward a Theory of Legal Justification* (1961).

Wigmore, J. *Select Cases on the Law of Tort* (2 vols. 1911–12).

————, and Kocourek, A. *The Rational Basis of Legal Institutions* (1923).

Wild, J. *Plato's Modern Enemies and the Theory of Natural Law* (1953).

Wright, B. *American Interpretations of Natural Law* (1931).

Wu, C. *Fountain of Justice* (1955).

————. *Cases and Materials on Jurisprudence* (1958).

Articles

A.B.A. Committee on Classification of the Law, Report, 14 Reports, A.B.A. 379 (1891).

A.B.A. Committee on Classification of the Law, Report, 25 Reports, A.B.A. 21, 425 (1902).

A.B.A. Committee on Legal Education, Report, 15 Reports, A.B.A. 317 (1892); same as Hammond, The Proper Course of Study for Law Schools, 26 Am. L. Rev. 705 (1892).

Adams, The Nature of Law: Methods and Aims of Legal Education, in *Centralization and the Law: Scientific Legal Education* 20 (1906).

———, Law under Inequality: Monopoly, in *Centralization and the Law: Scientific Legal Education* 63 (1906).

———, The Modern Conception of Animus, 19 Green Bag 12 (1907).

Adler, Legal Certainty, 31 Colum. L. Rev. 91 (1931).

Albertsworth, The Changing Conception of Law, 8 A.B.A.J. 673 (1922).

———, The Program of Sociological Jurisprudence, 8 A.B.A.J. 393 (1922).

———, Is there a Legal Cycle?, 11 Calif. L. Rev. 381 (1923).

Alexander, Memorandum *in re Corpus Juris*, 22 Green Bag 59 (1910).

Ames, Law and Morals, 22 Harv. L. Rev. 97 (1908).

Anderson, Logic, Norms and Roles, 4 Ratio 36 (1962).

Andrews, The Next Great Step in Jurisprudence, 19 Yale L.J. 485 (1910), summarized in Andrews, The Next Great Step in Jurisprudence, 22 Green Bag 405 (1910).

———, The Classification of Law, 22 Green Bag 556 (1910).

———, Jurisprudence: Development and Practical Vocation, 25 Yale L.J. 306 (1915).

———, Classification and Restatement of the Law, 14 Ill. L. Rev. 465, 622 (1920).

Auerbach, On Professor Hart's Definition and Theory in Jurisprudence, 9 J. Leg. Ed. 39 (1956).

Babb, Petrazhitskii: Science of Legal Policy and Theory of Law, 17 Bost. U. L. Rev. 793 (1937).

Barrett, The Natural Law and the Lawyer's Search for a Philosophy of Law, 1 Cath. Law. 128 (1955).

Beutel, Some Implications of Experimental Jurisprudence, 48 Harv. L. Rev. 169 (1934).

———, The Impossible in Political and Legal Philosophy, 29 Calif. L. Rev. 312 (1941).

———, Crisis in Legal Education, 25 Neb. L. Rev. 46 (1946).

———, Outline of the Nature and Methods of Experimental Jurisprudence, 51 Colum. L. Rev. 415 (1951).

————, Traffic Control as Experimental Jurisprudence in Action, 31 Neb. L. Rev. 349 (1952).

————, The Lag between Scientific Discovery and Legal Procedures, 33 Neb. L. Rev. 349 (1953).

————, Elementary Semantics: Criticisms of Realism and Experimental Jurisprudence, 13 J. Leg. Ed. 67 (1960).

Bienenfeld, Prolegomena to a Psychoanalysis of Law and Justice, 53 Calif. L. Rev. 754 (1965).

Bigelow, Definition of Law, 5 Colum. L. Rev. 1 (1905); reprinted in *Centralization and the Law: Scientific Legal Education* 135 (1906).

————, A Scientific School of Legal Thought, 17 Green Bag 1 (1905); reprinted in *Centralization and the Law: Scientific Legal Education* 165 (1906).

————, Theory and Doctrine of Tort, 18 Green Bag 64, 132 (1906).

————, Economic Forces and Municipal Law, 41 Am. L. Rev. 27 (1907).

Bingham, Some Suggestions Concerning "Legal Cause" at Common Law, 9 Col. L. Rev. 16, 136 (1909).

————, What Is the Law?, 11 Mich L. Rev. 1, 109 (1912).

————, Science and the Law, 25 Green Bag 162 (1913).

————, The Nature of Legal Rights and Duties, 12 Mich. L. Rev. 1 (1913).

————, Legal Philosophy and the Law, 9 Ill. L. Rev. 98 (1914).

Bizzell, A Critique of the Austinian Theory of Sovereignty, 22 Green Bag 514 (1910).

Blackshield, The Importance of Being: Some Reflections on Existentialism in Relation to Law, 10 Nat. L. Forum 67 (1965).

Blatt, The Effect of the Imitative Instinct on the Common Law, 37 Am. L. Rev. 892 (1903).

————, Some Principles of Legal Evolution, 23 Yale L.J. 168 (1913).

————, The Law Making Forces, 47 Am. L. Rev. 641 (1913).

Bodenheimer, Modern Analytic Jurisprudence and Its Usefulness, 104 U. Pa. L. Rev. 1080 (1956).

————, Law as Order and Justice, 6 J. Pub. L. 194 (1957).

————, Analytical Positivism, Legal Realism, and the Future of Legal Method, 44 Va. L. Rev. 365 (1958).

————, A Decade of Jurisprudence in the United States of America, 3 Nat. L. Forum 44 (1958).

————, The Province of Jurisprudence, 46 Corn. L.Q. 1 (1960).

————, Reflections on the Rule of Law, 8 Utah L. Rev. 1 (1962).

————, The Case against Natural Law Reassessed, 17 Stan. L. Rev. 39 (1964).

————, A Neglected Theory of Legal Reasoning, 21 J. Leg. Ed. 373 (1969).

Bohlen, The Rule in Rylands v. Fletcher, 59 Univ. Pa. L. Rev. 298, 373, 423 (1911).

Borchard, Jurisprudence in Germany, 12 Colum. L. Rev. 301 (1912).

Brandeis, Living Law, 10 Ill. L. Rev. 461 (1916).

Brecht, The Myth of *Is* and *Ought,* 54 Harv. L. Rev. 811 (1941).

Britt, Social Psychology of Law, 34 Ill. L. Rev. 802, 919 (1940).

Brown, B. Natural Law and the Law Making Function in American Jurisprudence, 15 Notre Dame Lawyer 9 (1939).

———, Natural Law: Dynamic Basis of Law and Morals in the Twentieth Century, 31 Tulane L. Rev. 491 (1957).

Brown, W. The Purpose and Method of a Law School, 18 L.Q. Rev. 78, 192 (1902).

———, The American Law School, 21 L.Q. Rev. 69 (1905).

———, Sovereignty, 18 Jurid. Rev. 1 (1906).

———, Law Schools and the Legal Profession, 6 Com. L. Rev. 3 (1908).

———, Jurisprudence and Legal Education, 9 Colum. L. Rev. 238 (1909).

———, Austin, Korkunov, and Mr. Hastings—A Reply, 11 Colum. L. Rev. 348 (1911).

———, The Jurisprudence of M. Duguit, 32 L.Q. Rev. 168 (1916).

———, Law and Evolution, 29 Yale L.J. 394 (1920).

———, Re-analysis of a Theory of Rights, 34 Yale L.J. 765 (1925).

Bryce, The Interpretation of National Character and Historical Environment on the Development of the Common Law, 24 L.Q. Rev. 9 (1908).

Buckland, Difficulties of Abstract Jurisprudence, 6 L.Q. Rev. 436 (1890).

Burdick, Is Law the Expression of Class Legislation?, 25 Harv. L. Rev. 349 (1912).

Cahn, Justice, Power and Law, 55 Yale L.J. 336 (1946).

———, Freedom, Order and Law, 23 N.Y.U.Q. Rev. 20 (1948).

———, Authority and Responsibility, 51 Colum. L. Rev. 838 (1951).

Cairns, Law and Anthropology, 31 Colum. L. Rev. 32 (1931).

———, The Valuation of Legal Science, 40 Colum. L. Rev. 1 (1940).

Cantor, Law and the Social Sciences, 16 A.B.A.J. 385 (1930).

Carter, The Ideal and the Actual in the Law, 24 Am. L. Rev. 752 (1890), also in 13 Reports Ann. Meeting, A.B.A. 217 (1890).

Cavers, Science, Research and the Law: Beutel's "Experimental" Jurisprudence, 10 J. Leg. Ed. 162 (1957).

Chase, Methods of Legal Study, 1 Colum. Jurist 69, 77 (1885).

Christie, Vagueness and Legal Language, 48 Minn. L. Rev. 885 (1964).

———, The Model of Principles, 1968 Duke L. Rev. 649.

———, Objectivity in the Law, 78 Yale L.J. 1311 (1969).

Chroust, The Jus Gentium in the Philosophy of St. Thomas Aquinas, 17 Notre Dame Lawyer 22 (1941).

——— and Collins, Basic Ideas in the Philosophy of Law of St. Thomas Aquinas, 26 Marq. L. Rev. 11 (1941).

——— and Osborn, Aristotle's Conception of Justice, 17 Notre Dame Lawyer 129 (1942).

Chroust, Law and the Administrative Process: An Epistemological Approach to Jurisprudence, 58 Harv. L. Rev. 573 (1945).

———, The Managerial Function of Law, 34 Bost. U. L. Rev. 261 (1954).

———, A Proposal for a New Definition of Law, 31 Tulane L. Rev. 437 (1957).

Clark, C., Relations Legal and Otherwise, 5 Ill. L.Q. 26 (1922).

Clark, E., Jurisprudence: Its Use and its Place in Legal Education, 1 L.Q. Rev. 201 (1885).

Clark, R., On Mr. Tammelo's Conception of Juristic Logic, 8 J. Leg. Ed. 491 (1956).

Coase, The Problem of Social Cost, 3 J. Law and Econ. 1 (1960).

Cohen, F., The Ethical Basis of Legal Criticism, 41 Yale L.J. 201 (1931).

———, Transcendental Nonsense and the Functional Approach, 35 Colum. L. Rev. 809 (1935).

———, Letter to the Editor, 5 Ford. L. Rev. 548 (1936).

———, The Problem of a Functional Jurisprudence, 1 Modern L. Rev. 5 (1937).

———, Field Theory and Judicial Logic, 59 Yale L.J. 238 (1950).

Cohen, Marshall, Law, Morality and Purpose, 10 Vill. L. Rev. 640 (1965).

Cohen, Morris, Jurisprudence as a Philosophical Discipline, 10 J. Phil. Psy. and Sci. Methods 228 (1913).

———, History versus Value, 11 J. Phil. Psy. and Sci. Methods 701 (1914).

———, The Process of Judicial Legislation, 48 Am. L. Rev. 161 (1914).

———, The Place of Logic in the Law, 29 Harv. L. Rev. 622 (1916).

———, Jus Naturale Redivivum, 25 Phil. Rev. 761 (1916).

———, Positivism and the Limits of Idealism in the Law, 27 Colum. L. Rev. 237 (1927).

———, Law and Scientific Method, 6 Am. L. S. Rev. 231 (1928).

———, Justice Holmes and the Nature of Law, 31 Colum. L. Rev. 352 (1931).

———, Philosophy and Legal Science, 32 Colum. L. Rev. 1103 (1932).

———, On Absolutisms in Legal Thought, 84 Univ. Pa. L. Rev. 691 (1936).

———, Book Review of T. Arnold, The Symbols of Government [1935], 31 Ill. L. Rev. 411 (1936).

———, Book Review of E. Robinson, Law and Lawyers [1935], 22 Corn. L.Q. 171 (1937).

———, Should Legal Thought Abandon Clear Distinctions?, 36 Ill. L. Rev. 239 (1941).

Comment, The Philosophy of Law, 6 Alb. L.J. 179 (1872).

Comment, The Scientific Basis of Law, 7 Alb. L.J. 321 (1873).

Comment, Case-Law and Inductive Science, 10 Alb. L.J. 301 (1874).

Comment, Law as a Science and as an Art, 10 Alb. L.J. 365 (1874).

Comment, Is the Law a Philosophy, a Science, or an Art?, 10 Alb. L.J. 371 (1874).

Comment, Legal Education in England, 11 Alb. L.J. 72 (1875).

Comment, Natural Law, 11 Alb. L.J. 97 (1875).

Comment, What Shall be Done with the Reports?, 15 Cent. L.J. 41 (1882).

Comment, Survey of Editorial Comment on the Corpus Juris Proposal, 22 Green Bag 457 (1910).

Comment, Jurisprudence and the Nature of Language: Contrasting Views of Hart and Chomsky, 42 Wash. L. Rev. 847 (1967).

Commons, Law and Economics, 34 Yale L.J. 371 (1925).

——, The Problem of Correlating Law, Economics and Ethics, 8 Wis. L. Rev. 3 (1932).

Cook, Hohfeld's Contribution to the Science of Law, 28 Yale L.J. 721 (1919).

——, Scientific Method and the Law, 13 A.B.A.J. 303 (1927).

——, Legal Logic, 31 Colum. L. Rev. 108 (1931).

——, "Facts" and "Statements of Fact," 4 U. Chi. L. Rev. 233 (1937).

Cooley, The Uncertainty of the Law, 4 Repts. Ga. Bar Assn. 109, 116 (1887).

Corbin, The Law and the Judges, 3 Yale Rev. 234 (1914).

——, Legal Analysis and Terminology, 29 Yale L.J. 163 (1919).

——, Jural Relations and their Classification, 30 Yale L.J. 226 (1921).

——, What is a Legal Relation?, 5 Ill. L.Q. 50 (1922).

——, The American Law Institute, 15 Iowa L. Rev. 19 (1929).

Corwin, The "Higher Law" Background of American Constitutional Law, 42 Harv. L. Rev. 149, 365 (1929).

Cossio, Jurisprudence and the Sociology of Law, 52 Colum. L. Rev. 356 (1952).

Cowan, The Relation of Law to Experimental Social Science, 96 U. Pa. L. Rev. 484 (1948).

——, Postulates for Experimental Jurisprudence, 9 Rutgers L. Rev. 404 (1954).

——, Group Interests, 44 Va. L. Rev. 331 (1958).

——, Law, Morality and Scientific Method, 38 Neb. L. Rev. 1039 (1959).

——, Studies in Legal Philosophy: Nietzsche, 14 Vand. L. Rev. 151 (1960).

——, Decision Theory in Law, Science, and Technology, 17 Rut. L. Rev. 499 (1963).

——, Some Problems Common to Jurisprudence and Technology, 33 Geo. W. L. Rev. 3 (1964).

Crane, Natural Law in the United States, 15 Notre Dame Lawyer 195 (1940).

Cullison, A Review of Hohfeld's Fundamental Legal Concepts, 16 Cleve. Mar. L. Rev. 559 (1967).

——, Logical Analysis of Legal Doctrine, 53 Iowa L. Rev. 1209 (1968).

Curtis, A Better Theory of Interpretation, 3 Vand. L. Rev. 407 (1950).

DeSloovere, Analytical Jurisprudence as Related to Modern Legal Methods, 7 N.Y.U.Q. Rev. 88 (1929).

Desvernine, Philosophy and Order in Law, 17 Proc. Am. Cath. Phil. Assoc. 135 (1941).

Devlin, Mill on Liberty and Morals, 32 U. Chi. L. Rev. 215 (1965).

Dewey, Logical Method and Law, 10 Corn. L.Q. 17 (1924).

Dickerson, Statutory Interpretation: Core Meaning and Marginal Uncertainty, 29 Mo. L. Rev. 1 (1964).

Dickinson, The Law Behind Law, 29 Col. L. Rev. 113, 285 (1929).

———, Legal Rules—Their Function in the Process of Decision, 79 U. Pa. L. Rev. 833 (1931).

———, Legal Rules—Their Application and Elaboration, 79 U. Pa. L. Rev. 1052 (1931).

———, Legal Change and the Rule of Law, 44 Dick. L. Rev. 149 (1940).

Dowdall, The Present State of Analytical Jurisprudence, 42 L.Q. Rev. 451 (1926).

Drake, Jurisprudence: A Formal Science, 13 Mich. L. Rev. 34 (1914).

———, The Sociological Interpretation of Law, 12 Mich. L. Rev. 599 (1918).

———, Juristic Idealism and Legal Practice, 25 Mich. L. Rev. 571, 752 (1927).

Duguit, The Law and the State, 31 Harv. L. Rev. 1 (1917).

Dworkin, Judicial Discretion, 60 J. Phil. 624 (1963).

———, Does Law Have a Function: A Comment on the Two-Tier Level Theory of Decision, 74 Yale L.J. 640 (1965). Also printed in 75 Ethics 47 (1964).

———, The Elusive Morality of Law, 10 Vill. L. Rev. 631 (1965).

———, Philosophy, Morality, and Law—Observations Prompted by Professor Fuller's Novel Claim, 113 U. Pa. L. Rev. 668 (1965).

———, Lord Devlin and the Enforcement of Morals, 75 Yale L.J. 986 (1966).

———, The Case for Law: A Critique, 1 Val. L. Rev. 201 (1967).

———, The Model of Rules, 35 U. Chi. L. Rev. 14 (1967).

Ehrlich, Montesquieu and Sociological Jurisprudence, 29 Harv. L. Rev. 582 (1916).

———, The Sociology of Law, 36 Harv. L. Rev. 130 (1922).

Ellwood, The Sociological Foundations of Law, 22 Green Bag 576 (1910).

Feibleman, Institutions, Law and Morals, 31 Tulane L. Rev. 503 (1957).

Ferson, The Nature of Law and Rights, 1 U. Cinn. L. Rev. 154 (1927).

———, Factors of Legal Reasoning, 12 U. Cinn. L. Rev. 318 (1938).

Field, Dalhousie Convocation Address, 19 Am. L. Rev. 616 (1885).

Ford, The Fundamentals of Holmes' Juristic Philosophy, 11 Ford. L. Rev. 255 (1942).

———, The Totalitarian Justice Holmes, 159 Cath. World 115 (1944).

Foulke, Definition and the Nature of Law, 19 Colum. L. Rev. 351 (1919).

Fowler, Holland's Elements of Jurisprudence, 27 Alb. L.J. 206 (1883).

———, The Future of the Common Law, 13 Colum. L. Rev. 595 (1913).

———, The New Philosophies of Law, 27 Harv. L. Rev. 718 (1914).

Fox, Law and Fact, 12 Harv. L. Rev. 545 (1899).

———, Law and Logic, 14 Harv. L. Rev. 39 (1900).

Frank, J., Are Judges Human?, 80 U. Pa. L. Rev. 17 (1931).

———, Mr. Justice Holmes and NonEuclidean Legal Thinking, 17 Corn. L.Q. 568 (1932).

————, What Courts Do in Fact, 24 Ill. L. Rev. 645, 761 (1932).

————, A Plea for Lawyer-Schools, 56 Yale L.J. 1303 (1947).

————, "Short of Sickness and Death": A Study of Moral Responsibility in Legal Criticism, 26 N.Y.U.L. Rev. 545 (1951).

Frank, L., An Institutional Analysis of the Law, 24 Colum. L. Rev. 480 (1924).

Frankfurter, The Conditions for and the Aims and Methods of Legal Research, 15 Iowa L. Rev. 129 (1930).

Franklin, Law, Morals and Social Life, 31 Tulane L. Rev. 465 (1957).

Freund, Historical Jurisprudence in Germany, 5 Pol. Sci. Q. 468 (1890).

Fried, Moral Causation, 77 Harv. L. Rev. 1258 (1964).

————, Reason and Action, 11 Nat. L. Forum 13 (1966).

————, Privacy, 77 Yale L.J. 475 (1968).

————, The Value of Life, 82 Harv. L. Rev. 1415 (1969).

Fuchs, The Newer Social Scientists Look at Law, 13 St. Louis L. Rev. 33 (1927).

Fuller, Legal Fictions (pts. 1–3), 25 Ill. L. Rev. 363, 513, 877 (1931).

————, American Legal Realism, 82 Pa. L. Rev. 429 (1934).

————, Reason and Fiat in Case Law, 59 Harv. L. Rev. 376 (1946).

————, The Case of the Speluncean Explorers, 62 Harv. L. Rev. 616 (1949).

————, Legal Philosophy at Mid-Century, 6 J. Leg. Ed. 457 (1954).

————, Freedom—A Suggested Analysis, 68 Harv. L. Rev. 1305 (1955).

————, Human Purpose and Natural Law, 53 J. Phil. 697 (1956); same as Fuller, Human Purpose and Natural Law, 3 Nat. L. Forum 68 (1958).

————, A Rejoinder to Professor Nagel, 3 Nat. L. Forum 83 (1958).

————, Positivism and Fidelity to Law—A Reply to Professor Hart, 71 Harv. L. Rev. 593 (1958).

————, Adjudication and the Rule of Law, 1 Proc. Am. Soc. Int. Law 8 (1960).

————, Irrigation and Tyranny, 17 Stan. L. Rev. 1021 (1965).

————, A Reply to Professors Cohen and Dworkin, 10 Vill. L. Rev. 655 (1965).

Gager, Book Review, 28 Yale L.J. 617 (1919).

Gannon, What Are We Really Fighting For?, 11 Ford. L. Rev. 161 (1942).

Gareis, Systematic Classification of the Law, 23 Green Bag 180 (1911).

Gavet, Individualism and Realism, 29 Yale L.J. 523, 643 (1920).

Gibbs, Definitions of Law and Empirical Questions, 2 L. and Soc. Rev. 429 (1968).

Gilmore, Law, Logic and Experience, 3 How. L.J. 26 (1957).

————, Legal Realism: Its Cause and Cure, 70 Yale L.J. 1037 (1961).

Goble, Affirmative and Negative Legal Relations, 4 Ill. L.Q. 94 (1922).

————, Negative Legal Relations Re-examined, 5 Ill. L.Q. 36 (1922).

————, Terms for Restating the Law, 10 A.B.A.J. 58 (1924).

————, The Sanction of a Duty, 37 Yale L.J. 426 (1928).

————, A Redefinition of Basic Legal Terms, 35 Colum. L. Rev. 535 (1935).

Goodhart, Law and the State, 47 L.Q. Rev. 118 (1931).

————, The Ratio Decidendi of a Case, 22 Mod. L. Rev. 117 (1959).

Gray, Some Definitions and Questions in Jurisprudence, 6 Harv. L. Rev. 21 (1892).

————, Judicial Precedent—A Short Study of Comparative Jurisprudence, 9 Harv. L. Rev. 27 (1895).

Green, The Relativity of Legal Relations, 5 Ill. L.Q. 187 (1923).

————, The Duty Problem in Negligence Cases, 28 Colum. L. Rev. 1014 (1928).

Gregg, The Pragmatism of Mr. Justice Holmes, 31 Geo. L.J. 294 (1943).

Gupta, The Method of Jurisprudence, 33 L.Q. Rev. 154 (1917).

Gurvitch, Major Problems of the Sociology of Law, 6 J. Soc. Phil. 197 (1941).

Haines, The Law of Nature in State and Federal Judicial Decisions, 25 Yale L.J. 617 (1916).

————, General Observations on the Effects of Personal, Political, and Economic Influences in the Decisions of Judges, 17 Ill. L. Rev. 96 (1922).

Hall, Nulla Poene sine Lege, 47 Yale L.J. 189 (1937).

————, Integrative Jurisprudence, in *Interpretations of Modern Legal Philosophy* 312 (1947).

————, Concerning the Nature of Positive Law, 58 Yale L.J. 545 (1949).

————, The Challenge of Jurisprudence, 37 A.B.A.J. 23, 85 (1951).

————, Unification of Political and Legal Theory, 69 Pol. Sci. Q. 15 (1954).

————, The Present Position of Jurisprudence in the United States, 44 Va. L. Rev. 321 (1958).

————, From Legal Theory to Integrative Jurisprudence, 33 U. Cinn. L. Rev. 153 (1964).

Hammond, The Proper Course of Study for Law Schools, 26 Am. L. Rev. 705 (1892).

Harno, Theory, Experience, Experimentation and the Logical Method, 17 A.B.A.J. 659 (1931).

Harper, Forms of Law and Moral Content, 22 Ill. L. Rev. 259 (1927).

————, Some Implications of Juristic Pragmatism, 39 Int. J. Ethics 269 (1929).

Harris, Idealism Emergent in Jurisprudence, 10 Tulane L. Rev. 174 (1936).

Hart, The Ascription of Responsibility and Rights, in Flew, ed., *Logic and Language* (1951).

————, Philosophy of Law and Jurisprudence in Britain (1945–1952), 2 Am. J. Comp. L. 355 (1953).

————, Definition and Theory in Jurisprudence, 70 L.Q. Rev. 37 (1954).

————, Analytical Jurisprudence in Mid-Twentieth Century: A Reply to Professor Bodenheimer, 104 U. Pa. L. Rev. 953 (1957).

————, Positivism and the Separation of Law and Morals, 71 Harv. L. Rev. 593 (1958).

————, Kelsen Visited, 10 U.C.L.A.L. Rev. 709 (1963).

————, Varieties of Responsibility, 83 L.Q. Rev. 346 (1967).

————, Social Solidarity and the Enforcement of Morality, 35 Univ. Chi. L. Rev. 1 (1967).

Heilman, The Correlation Between the Sciences of Law and Economics, 20 Calif. L. Rev. 379 (1932).

————, The Bases of Construction of Systems of Legal Analysis, 26 Ill. L. Rev. 841 (1932).

Henson, A Criticism of Criticism: In re Meaning, 29 Ford. L. Rev. 553 (1961).

Herman, Economic Predeliction and the Law, 31 Am. Pol. Sci. Rev. 821 (1937).

Hildebrand, The Dethronement of Truth, 18 Proc. Am. Cath. Phil. Assn. 9 (1942).

Hill, The Natural Law, 13 Geo. L.J. 367 (1925).

Hoebel, Fundamental Concepts as Applied in the Study of Primitive Law, 51 Yale L.J. 951 (1942).

Hohfeld, Relations between Law and Equity, 11 Mich. L. Rev. 537 (1913).

————, Some Fundamental Legal Conceptions as Applied in Judicial Reasoning, 23 Yale L.J. 16 (1913).

————, A Vital School of Jurisprudence and Law, 14 Proc. Assoc. Am. L. Schools 76 (1914).

————, Fundamental Conceptions as Applied in Judicial Reasoning, 26 Yale L.J. 710 (1917).

Holmes, Codes, And the Arrangement of the Law, 5 Am. L. Rev. 1 (1870).

————, Review of Holland, Essays upon the Form of the Law, 5 Am. L. Rev. 114 (1870).

————, Review of Dicey, A Treatise on the Rules for the Selection of the Parties to an Action, 5 Am. L. Rev. 534 (1871).

————, Review of Langdell, A Selection of Cases on the Law of Contracts, 5 Am. L. Rev. 539 (1871).

————, Misunderstandings of the Civil Law, 6 Am. L. Rev. 37 (1871).

————, Review of Langdell, A Selection of Cases on the Law of Contracts, 6 Am. L. Rev. 353 (1872).

————, The Law Magazine and Review, 6 Am. L. Rev. 723 (1872).

————, The Arrangement of the Law—Privity, 7 Am. L. Rev. 46 (1872).

————, The Theory of Torts, 7 Am. L. Rev. 652 (1873).

————, Primitive Notions in Modern Law (pts. 1–2), 10 Am. L. Rev. 422 (1876), 11 Am. L. Rev. 641 (1877).

————, Possession, 12 Am. L. Rev. 688 (1878).

————, Trespass and Negligence, 1 Am. L. Rev. (n.s.) 1 (1880).

————, Review of Langdell, A Selection of Cases on the Law of Contract, 2d edition, 14 Am. L. Rev. 233 (1880).

———— and Langdell, Harvard Celebration Speeches, 3 L.Q. Rev. 118 (1887).

Holmes, The Path of the Law, 10 Harv. L. Rev. 469 (1897).

————, Law in Science and Science in Law, 12 Harv. L. Rev. 443 (1899).

————, Natural Law, 32 Harv. L. Rev. 40 (1918).

Howell, The Search for Jurispolitical Philosophy, 44 Va. L. Rev. 409 (1958).

Hughes, The Existence of a Legal System, 35 N.Y.U.L. Rev. 1001 (1960).

———, Rules, Policy and Decisionmaking, 77 Yale L.J. 411 (1968).

Hull, Moore and Callahan's "Law and Learning Theory"; A Psychologist's Impressions, 53 Yale L.J. 330 (1944).

Husick, Hohfeld's Jurisprudence, 72 U. Pa. L. Rev. 263 (1924).

Hutcheson, The Judgment Intuitive: The Function of the "Hunch" in Judicial Decision, 14 Corn. L.Q. 274 (1929).

Isaacs, "The Law" and the Law of Change, 65 U. Pa. L. Rev. 665, 748 (1917).

———, The Schools of Jurisprudence, 31 Harv. L. Rev. 373 (1918).

Jacoby, Some Realism about Judicial Statistics, 25 Va. L. Rev. 528 (1939).

Jaffe, Natural Law and the Nürnberg Trials, 26 Neb. L. Rev. 90 (1946).

Jones, Modern Discussions of the Aims and Methods of Legal Science, 47 L.Q. Rev. 62 (1931).

Joslyn, Philosophy of Law, 12 Green Bag 142 (1900).

Kantorowicz and Patterson, Legal Science—A Summary of its Methodology, 28 Colum. L. Rev. 679 (1928).

Kantorowicz, Some Rationalism about Realism, 43 Yale L.J. 1240 (1934).

Kaplan, Decision Theory and the Factfinding Process, 20 Stan. L. Rev. 1065 (1968).

Keller, Law in Evolution, 28 Yale L.J. 769 (1919).

Kelsen, The Pure Theory of Law: Its Method and Fundamental Concepts (pts. 1–2), 50 L.Q. Rev. 474 (1934), 51 L.Q. Rev. 517 (1935).

———, Pure Theory of Law and Analytic Jurisprudence, 55 Harv. L. Rev. 44 (1941).

———, Law as a Specific Social Technique, 9 U. Chi. L. Rev. 75 (1941).

———, On the Basic Norm, 47 Calif. L. Rev. 107 (1959).

———, Professor Stone and the Pure Theory of Law, 17 Stan. L. Rev. 1128 (1965).

Kennedy, Pragmatism as a Philosophy of Law, 9 Marq. L. Rev. 63 (1925).

———, Principles or Facts?, 4 Ford. L. Rev. 53 (1935).

———, Functional Nonsense and the Transcendental Approach, 5 Ford. L. Rev. 272 (1936).

———, More Functional Nonsense: A Reply to Felix S. Cohen, 6 Ford. L. Rev. 75 (1937).

———, Legal Realism, What Next?, 8 Ford. L. Rev. 45 (1939).

———, A Review of Legal Realism, 9 Ford. L. Rev. 362 (1940).

———, A Required Course in Jurisprudence, 9 Am. L. Sch. Rev. 593 (1940).

———, Psychologism in the Law, 29 Geo. L.J. 139 (1940).

Kessler, Theoretic Bases of Law, 9 U. Chi. L. Rev. 98 (1941).

———, Natural Law, Justice and Democracy: Some Reflections on Three Types of Thinking about Law and Justice, 19 Tul. L. Rev. 32 (1944).

Ketcham, Law as a Body of Subjective Rules, 23 Ill. L. Rev. 360 (1928).

Keyser, On the Study of Legal Science, 38 Yale L.J. 413 (1929).

———, The Nature of the Doctrinal Function and its Role in Rational Thought, 41 Yale L.J. 713 (1932).

Kocourek, Review of Bingham, 8 Ill. L. Rev. 138 (1913).

———, The Formal Relation between Law and Discretion, 9 Ill. L. Rev. 225 (1914).

———, Various Definitions of Jural Relation, 20 Colum. L. Rev. 394 (1920).

———, The Plurality of Advantages and Disadvantages in Jural Relations, 19 Mich. L. Rev. 47 (1920).

———, Hohfeld's System of Fundamental Legal Concepts, 15 Ill. L. Rev. 24 (1920).

———, Rights in Rem, 68 U. Pa. L. Rev. 322 (1920).

———, Tabulae Minores Jurisprudentiae, 30 Yale L.J. 215 (1921).

———, The Classification of Jural Relations, 1 Boston U. L. Rev. 208 (1921).

———, Nomic and Anomic Relations, 7 Cornell L.Q. 11 (1921).

———, Non-Legal–Content Relations, 4 Ill. L. Rev. 233 (1922).

———, Non-Legal–Content Relations Recombated, 5 Ill. L.Q. 150 (1923).

———, Juristic Knots and Nots; A Reconsideration of Juristic Terminology, 19 Ill. L. Rev. 285 (1923).

———, The Alphabet of Legal Relations, 9 A.B.A.J. 237 (1923).

———, Sanctions and Remedies, 72 U. Pa. L. Rev. 91 (1924).

———, Acts, 73 U. Pa. L. Rev. 335 (1925).

———, Attribution of Physical Qualities to Legal Relations, 19 Ill. L. Rev. 435, 542 (1925).

———, Subjective and Objective Elements in Law, 21 Ill. L. Rev. 489 (1927).

———, Classification of the Law, 11 N.Y.U.L.Q. 319 (1934).

Kohler, The Mission and Objects of the Philosophy of Law, 5 Ill. L. Rev. 423 (1911).

Kramer, The "Uneasy Case" in Jurisprudence, 44 Va. L. Rev. 379 (1958).

Kreilkamp, Dean Pound and the End of Law, 9 Fordham L. Rev. 196 (1940).

———, Dean Pound and the Immutable Natural Law, 18 Ford. L. Rev. 173 (1949).

Landman, Primitive Law, Evolution and Sir Henry Sumner Maine, 28 Mich L. Rev. 404 (1930).

Langdell, A Brief Survey of Equity Jurisdiction, 1 Harv. L. Rev. 55 (1887).

———, Classification of Rights and Wrongs, 13 Harv. L. Rev. 537, 659 (1900).

Laserson, The Work of Leon Patrazhitskii, 51 Colum. L. Rev. 59 (1951).

Lashly, Evolution and the Law, 11 St. Louis L. Rev. 107 (1926).

Lasswell and McDougal, Legal Education and Public Policy: Professional Training in the Public Interest, 52 Yale L.J. 203 (1943).

Lasswell, The Interrelations of World Organization and Society, 55 Yale L.J. 870 (1946).

———, The Impact of Psychiatry on Jurisprudence, 21 Ohio St. L.J. 17 (1960).

————, The Interplay of Economics, Political and Social Criteria in a Legal Policy, 14 Vand. L. Rev. 451 (1961).

————, A Brief Discourse about Method in the Current Madness, 57 Proc. Am. Soc. Int. L. 72 (1963).

———— and McDougal, Jurisprudence in Policy Oriented Perspective, 19 U. Fla. L. Rev. 486 (1967).

Lee, Is a Bad Law a Real Law?, 31 Tulane L. Rev. 479 (1957).

LeFroy, Jurisprudence: Derivation and Definition, 27 L.Q. Rev. 180 (1911).

Leonhard, Methods Followed in Germany by the Historical School of Law, 7 Colum. L. Rev. 573 (1907).

Lepaulle, The Function of Comparative Law with a Critique of Sociological Jurisprudence, 35 Harv. L. Rev. 838 (1922).

Lerner, The Shadow World of Thurman Arnold, 47 Yale L.J. 687 (1938).

Levi, Natural Law, Precedent and Thurman Arnold, 24 Va. L. Rev. 587 (1938).

————, An Introduction to Legal Reasoning, 15 U. Chi. L. Rev. 501 (1948).

Lewis, J., Moral Obligation and the Concept of Law, 23 Rut. L. Rev. 68 (1968).

Lewis, O., Systems Theory and Judicial Behavioralism, 21 Case West. L. Rev. 361 (1970).

Lewis, W., The Social Sciences as the Basis of Legal Education, 61 Univ. Pa. L. Rev. 531 (1913).

Lindsey, The Development of a Scientific View of Law, 45 Am. L. Rev. 513 (1911).

Litchman, Economics the Basis of Law, 61 Am. L. Rev. 357 (1927).

————, Four Modern Philosophies and their Relation to Law, 5 Temple L.Q. 215 (1931).

————, The Application of the Theory of Relativity to Law, 6 Temple L.Q. 211, 515 (1932).

Llewellyn, The Effect of Legal Institutions Upon Economics, 15 Am. Econ. Rev. 665 (1925).

————, A Realistic Jurisprudence—The Next Step, 30 Colum. L. Rev. 431 (1930).

————, Law and the Modern Mind—Legal Illusion, 31 Colum. L. Rev. 82 (1931).

————, Some Realism about Realism—Responding to Dean Pound, 44 Harv. L. Rev. 1222 (1931).

————, The Constitution as an Institution, 34 Colum. L. Rev. 1 (1934).

————, One Realist's View of Natural Law for Judges, 15 Notre Dame Lawyer 3 (1939).

————, The Normative, The Legal, and the Law Jobs: The Problem of Juristic Method, 49 Yale L.J. 1355 (1940).

————, On Reading and Using the Newer Jurisprudence, 40 Colum. L. Rev. 593 (1940).

————, On the Good, The True, the Beautiful, in Law, 9 Univ. Chi. L. Rev. 247 (1942).

———, Law and the Social Sciences—Especially Sociology, 62 Harv. L. Rev. 1286 (1949).

———, Remarks on the Theory of Appellate Decision and the Rules or Canons about How Statutes Are To Be Construed, 3 Vand. L. Rev. 395 (1950).

———, On What Makes Legal Research Worthwhile, 8 J. Leg. Ed. 399 (1956).

Loevinger, Jurimetrics—the Next Step Forward, 33 Minn. L. Rev. 355 (1947).

———, An Introduction to Legal Logic, 27 Ind. L.J. 471 (1952).

———, Dogmatism and Skepticism in Law, 38 Minn. L. Rev. 191 (1954).

———, Jurimetrics: Science and Prediction in the Field of Law, 46 Minn. L. Rev. 255 (1961).

———, Science and Legal Thinking, 25 Fed. B. J. 153 (1965).

Lucey, Jurisprudence and the Future Social Order, 16 Social Sci. 213 (1941).

———, Natural Law and American Legal Realism, 30 Geo. L. Rev. 498 (1942).

Malan, The Behavioristic Basis of the Science of Law (2 pts.), 8 A.B.A.J. 737 (1922), 9 A.B.A.J. 43 (1923).

Manion, The American Metaphysics in Law, 18 Proc. Am. Cath. Phil. Assn. 132 (1942).

———, The Founding Fathers and the Natural Law, 35 A.B.A.J. 461 (1949).

Marceau, A Descriptive Theory of Justice, 6 La. L. Rev. 350 (1945).

McBride, The Essential Role of Models and Analogies in the Philosophy of Law, 43 N.Y.U.L. Rev. 53 (1968).

McDougal, Fuller v. The American Legal Realists: An Intervention, 50 Yale L.J. 827 (1941).

———, The Law School of the Future: From Legal Realism to Policy Science in the World Community, 56 Yale L.J. 1345 (1947).

———, The Role of the Law in World Politics, 20 Miss. L.J. 253 (1949).

———, Law and Power, 46 Am. J. Int. L. 102 (1952).

———, Law as a Process of Decision: A Policy Oriented Approach to Legal Study, 1 Nat. L. Forum 53 (1956).

——— and Reisman, The Changing Structure of International Law: Unchanging Theory for Inquiry, 65 Colum. L. Rev. 810 (1965).

McDougal, Jurisprudence for a Free Society, 1 Georg. L. Rev. 1 (1966).

McKinnon, Higher Law: Reaction has Permeated our Legal Thinking, 33 A.B.A.J. 106, 202 (1947).

Mechem, The Jurisprudence of Despair, 21 Iowa 669 (1936).

Milner, Restatement: The Failure of a Legal Experiment, 20 U. Pitt. L. Rev. 795 (1959).

Moore, The Rational Basis of Legal Institutions, 23 Colum. L. Rev. 609 (1923).

———, An Institutional Approach to the Law of Commercial Banking, 38 Yale L.J. 703 (1929).

——— and Sussman, Legal and Institutional Methods Applied to the Debiting of Direct Discounts (pts. 1–6), 40 Yale L.J. 381, 555, 752, 928, 1055, 1219 (1931).

—— and Sussman, The Lawyer's Law, 41 Yale L.J. 566 (1932).

—— and Callahan, Law and Learning Theory, 53 Yale L.J. 1 (1943).

Morris, C., Law and Fact, 55 Harv. L. Rev. 1303 (1942).

——, Law, Reason and Sociology, 107 U. Pa. L. Rev. 147 (1958).

——, Justice and the Scientific Method, 60 Colum. L. Rev. 936 (1960).

Morris, H., Book Review of Hart's *Concept of Law* [1961], 75 Harv. L. Rev. 1452 (1962).

Nagel, On the Fusion of Law and Fact: A Reply to Professor Fuller, 3 Nat. L. Forum 77 (1958).

——, Fact, Value and Human Purpose, 4 Nat. L. Forum 26 (1959).

Niemeyer, Significance of Function in Legal Theory, 18 N.Y.U.Q. Rev. 1 (1940).

Noonan, Natural Law, 3 Marquette L. Rev. 91 (1919).

Northrop, Underhill Moore's Legal Science: Its Nature and Significance, 59 Yale L.J. 196 (1950).

——, Ethical Relativism in the Light of Recent Legal Science, 52 J. Phil. 649 (1955).

——, Petrazycki's Psychological Jurisprudence, 104 U. Pa. L. Rev. 651 (1956).

——, Philosophical Issues in Contemporary Law, 2 Nat. L. Forum 41 (1957).

——, The Mediational Approval Theory of Law in American Legal Realism, 44 Va. L. Rev. 347 (1958).

——, Comparative Philosophy of Comparative Law, 45 Corn. L.Q. 617 (1960).

——, Law, Language and Morals, 71 Yale L.J. 1017 (1962).

——, The Epistemology of Legal Judgments, 58 N.W.U.L. Rev. 734 (1963).

Noyes, Law and the Scientific Method, 55 Pol. Sci. Q. 496 (1940).

Nozick, Moral Complications and Moral Structures, 13 Nat. L. Forum 1 (1968).

Nussbaum, Fact Research in Law, 40 Colum. L. Rev. 189 (1940).

Oikawa, Application of Beutel's Experimental Jurisprudence to Japanese Sociology of Law, 39 Neb. L. Rev. 629 (1950).

Oliphant, Current Discussions of Legal Methodology, 7 A.B.A.J. 241 (1921).

——, Study of the Operation of the Rules of Law, 9 A.B.A.J. 497 (1923).

——, A Return to Stare Decisis, 14 A.B.A.J. 71, 159 (1928).

——, Facts, Opinions, and Value-Judgments, 10 Tex. L. Rev. 127 (1932).

Page, Professor Ehrlich's Czernowitz Seminar of Living Law, 14 Proc. Assoc. Am. L. Schools 46 (1914).

Palmer, Hobbes, Holmes, and Hitler, 31 A.B.A.J. 569 (1945).

——, Natural Law and Pragmatism, 23 Notre Dame Lawyer 313 (1948).

——, Groping for a Creative Legal Philosophy: Natural Law in a Creative and Dynamic Age, 35 A.B.A.J. 3 (1949).

Patten, The New Jurisprudence, 62 U. Pa. L. Rev. 1 (1913).

Patterson, Can Law be Scientific?, 25 Ill. L. Rev. 121 (1930).

————, Some Reflections on Sociological Jurisprudence, 44 Va. L. Rev. 395 (1958).

Platt, The Proposed Civil Code of New York, 20 Am. L. Rev. 713 (1886).

Pollock, Oxford Law Studies, 8 L.Q. Rev. 453 (1886).

————, History of the Law of Nature: A Preliminary Study (pts. 1–2), 1 Colum. L. Rev. 11 (1901), 2 Colum. L. Rev. 131 (1902).

————, Notes on Maine's Ancient Law (pts. 1–3), 21 L.Q. Rev. 165, 273 (1905), 22 L.Q. Rev. 73 (1906).

————, A Plea for Historical Interpretation, 39 L.Q. Rev. 163 (1923).

Pound, A New School of Jurists, 4 Univ. Neb. Studies 249 (1904).

————, The Decadence of Equity, 5 Colum. L. Rev. 20 (1905).

————, Do We Need a Philosophy of Law?, 5 Colum. L. Rev. 339 (1905).

————, The Causes of Popular Dissatisfaction with the Administration of Justice, 29 A.B.A. Rep. 395 (1906).

————, The Spirit of the Common Law, 18 Green Bag 17 (1906).

————, Spurious Interpretation, 7 Colum. L. Rev. 379 (1907).

————, The Need for a Sociological Jurisprudence, 19 Green Bag 607 (1907).

————, The German Movement for Reform in Legal Administration and Procedure, 1 Bull. Comp. L. Bureau A.B.A. 32 (1908).

————, Enforcement of the Law, 20 Green Bag 401 (1908).

————, Mechanical Jurisprudence, 8 Colum. L. Rev. 605 (1908).

————, Common Law and Legislation, 21 Harv. L. Rev. 383 (1908).

————, Law in Books and Law in Action, 44 Am. L. Rev. 12 (1910).

————, The Scope and Purpose of Sociological Jurisprudence (pts. 1–3), 24 Harv. L. Rev. 591 (1911), 25 Harv. L. Rev. 140, 489 (1912).

————, Theories of Law, 22 Yale L.J. 114 (1912).

————, Legislation as a Social Function, 18 Am. J. Sociol. 755 (1913).

————, Courts and Legislation, 7 Am. Pol. Sci. Rev. 696 (1913), reprinted in *Science of Legal Method* 202 (1917).

————, Justice According to Law (pts. 1–3), 13 Colum. L. Rev. 696 (1913), 14 Colum. L. Rev. 1, 103 (1914).

————, The End of Law as Developed in Legal Rules and Doctrines, 27 Harv. L. Rev. 195 (1914).

————, The End of Law as Developed in Juristic Thought (pts. 1–2), 27 Harv. L. Rev. 605 (1914), 30 Harv. L. Rev. 201 (1917).

————, Making and Finding the Law, 82 Cent. L.J. 351 (1916).

————, Legal Rights, 26 Inter. J. Ethics 92 (1916).

————, Juristic Science and Law, 31 Harv. L. Rev. 1047 (1918).

————, A Theory of Social Interests, 15 Proc. Am. Sociol. Soc. 16 (1921).

————, The Theory of Judicial Decision (pts. 1–3), 36 Harv. L. Rev. 640, 802, 940 (1923).

————, Classification of the Law, 37 Harv. L. Rev. 933 (1924).

————, Jurisprudence, in H. Barnes, ed., *The History and Prospects of the Social Sciences* 444 (1925).

———, The Progress of the Law: Analytical Jurisprudence, 1914–1927, 41 Harv. L. Rev. 174 (1928).

———, The Call for a Realist Jurisprudence, 44 Harv. L. Rev. 697 (1931).

———, Law and the Science of Law in Recent Theories, 43 Yale L.J. 525 (1933).

———, Fifty Years of Jurisprudence, 50 Harv. L. Rev. 557 (1937), 51 Harv. L. Rev. 444, 777 (1938).

Probert, Law and Persuasion: The Language Behavior of Lawyers, 108 U. Pa. L. Rev. 35 (1959).

———, The Psycho-Semantics of the Judicial Process, 33 Temp. L. Rev. 235 (1961).

———, Law Through the Looking Glass of Language and Communicative Behavior, 20 J. Leg. Ed. 253 (1968).

———, Law, Science and Communications: Some New Facets to Empiricism, 10 Jurim. J. 51 (1969).

Raab, Suggestions for a Cybernetic Approach to Sociological Jurisprudence, 17 J. Leg. Ed. 397 (1965).

Radin, The Theory of Judicial Decision: Or How Judges Think, 11 A.B.A.J. 357 (1925).

———, The Permanent Problems of the Law, 15 Corn. L.Q. 1 (1929).

———, Scientific Method and the Law, 19 Calif. L. Rev. 164 (1931).

———, Legal Realism, 31 Colum. L. Rev. 824 (1931).

———, The Education of a Lawyer, 25 Calif. L. Rev. 688 (1937).

———, A Restatement of Hohfeld, 51 Harv. L. Rev. 1141 (1938).

———, The Method of Law, 1950 Wash. U.L.Q. 471.

Radbruch, Anglo-American Jurisprudence through Continental Eyes, 52 L.Q. Rev. 530 (1936).

Randall, Hohfeld on Jurisprudence, 41 L.Q. Rev. 86 (1925).

Rawls, Two Concepts of Rules, 64 Phil. Rev. 3 (1955).

———, Justice as Fairness, 67 Phil. Rev. 164 (1958).

———, Constitutional Liberty and the Concept of Justice, 6 Nomos 98 (1963).

———, Legal Obligation and the Duty of Fair Play, in S. Hook, ed., *Law and Philosophy* (1964).

———, Distributive Justice, in P. Laslett and W. Runciman, eds., *Philosophy, Politics and Society* (1967).

———, Distributive Justice: Some Addenda, 13 Nat. L. Forum 51 (1968).

Riesman, Law and Social Science, 50 Yale L.J. 636 (1940).

Robinson, Law and Economics, 2 Mod. L. Rev. 257 (1939).

Rooney, Law and the New Logic, 16 Proc. Am. Cath. Phil. Assn. 217 (1940).

———, The Movement for a Neo-Scholastic Philosophy of Law in America, 18 Proc. Am. Cath. Phil. Assn. 185 (1942).

———, Law without Justice? The Kelsen and Hall Theories Compared, 23 N.D. Lawyer 140 (1948).

Rose, Ethical Theory and Legal Philosophy, 15 Vand. L. Rev. 327 (1962).

Rottschaefer, Jurisprudence: Philosophy or Science?, 11 Minn. L. Rev. 293 (1927).

Sabine, Political Science and the Juristic Point of View, 22 Am. Pol. Sci. Rev. 553 (1928).

Salmond, The Law of Nature, 11 L.Q. Rev. 121 (1895).

———, Names and the Nature of the Law, 15 L.Q. Rev. 367 (1899).

Schmidt, An Approach to the Natural Law, 19 Ford. L. Rev. 1 (1950).

Schroeder, The Psychologic Study of Judicial Opinions, 6 Calif. L. Rev. 89 (1918).

Schubert, Behavioral Jurisprudence, 2 Law and Soc. Rev. 407 (1968).

Shapiro, Political Jurisprudence, 52 Ky. L.J. 294 (1964).

Sigler, A Cybernetics Model of the Judicial System, 41 Temp. L. Rev. 398 (1968).

Simms, A Dissent from Greatness, 28 Va. L. Rev. 467 (1940).

Simonton, Austin's Classification of Proprietary Rights, 11 Corn. L.Q. 277 (1926).

Simpson and Field, Social Engineering through Law, 22 N.Y.U.Q. Rev. 145 (1947).

Smith, The English Analytical Jurists, 21 Am. L. Rev. 270 (1887).

———, The Certainty of the Law and the Uncertainty of Judicial Decisions, 23 Am. L. Rev. 699 (1889).

———, The True Method of Legal Education, 24 Am. L. Rev. 211 (1890).

———, Hammond's Blackstone, 25 Am. L. Rev. 376 (1891).

———, Of the Nature of Jurisprudence and of the Law, 38 Am. L. Rev. 68 (1904).

———, Of the Historical Development of the Law, 38 Am. L. Rev. 801 (1904).

———, Of Actions Old and New, 39 Am. L. Rev. 223 (1905).

———, Of the Subject Matter of Jurisprudence, 39 Am. L. Rev. 531 (1905).

———, Of the Nature of Rights: And of the Principles of Right or Jurisprudence, 40 Am. L. Rev. 58 (1906).

———, Logic, Jurisprudence and the Law, 48 Am. L. Rev. 801 (1914).

Spencer, Professor Gareis' Introduction to the Science of Law, 23 Green Bag 191 (1911).

———, Jurisprudence Not an Objective Science, 25 Green Bag 74 (1913).

———, Neo-Hegelianism in Jurisprudence, 25 Green Bag 112 (1913).

Stammler, The Idea of Justice, 71 U. Pa. L. Rev. 303 (1923).

———, Fundamental Tendencies in Modern Jurisprudence (pts. 1–3), 21 Mich. L. Rev. 623, 765, 862 (1923).

———, Legislation and Judicial Decision, 23 Mich. L. Rev. 362 (1925).

Sternberg, Natural Law in American Jurisprudence, 13 Notre Dame Lawyer 89 (1938).

———, The Adequacy of Scholastic Idealism, 20 Neb. L. Rev. 317 (1941).

Stoljar, Logical Status of Legal Principles, 20 U. Chi. L. Rev. 181 (1953).

Stone, H., Some Aspects of the Problem of Law Simplification, 23 Colum. L. Rev. 319 (1923).

Stone, R., Analysis of Hohfeld, 48 Minn. L. Rev. 313 (1963).

——, The Complete Wrangler, 50 Minn. L. Rev. 1001 (1966).

——, Logic and Law: The Precedence of Precedents, 51 Minn. L. Rev. 655 (1967).

——, Metaphysics and Law, 1969 Duke L.J. 897.

Sullivan, The Speculation of Thurman W. Arnold, 1 Polamerican L.J. 3 (1938).

Summers, The New Analytical Jurists, 41 N.Y.U.L. Rev. 861 (1966).

Symposium, Ethical Values and the Law in Action, 12 Ohio St. L.J. 1 (1951).

Symposium, Fuller's *The Morality of Law*, 10 Vill. L. Rev. 624 (1965).

Symposium, Integrating Law and other Learned Professions, 32 Va. L. Rev. 695 (1946).

Symposium, Jurimetrics, 28 L. and Contemp. Prob. 1 (1963).

Symposium, Jurisprudence, 10 U.C.L.A.L. Rev. 709 (1963).

Symposium, Jurisprudence and the Lawyer, 19 Fla. L. Rev. 395 (1967).

Symposium, Language of the Law, 9 West. Res. L. Rev. 115 (1958).

Symposium, Law and Morals, 31 Tulane L. Rev. 437 (1957).

Symposium, Law and Social Science, 5 Vill. L. Rev. 247 (1960).

Symposium, Legal Philosophy, 44 Va. L. Rev. 315 (1958).

Symposium, Natural Law, 15 Notre Dame Lawyer 1 (1940).

Symposium, Natural Law, Science and Modern Thought, 13 Ohio St. L.J. 121 (1952).

Symposium, Science Challenges the Law, 19 Case West. L. Rev. 5 (1967).

Symposium, Stability and Change through Law, 17 Vand. L. Rev. 1 (1963).

Symposium, The Morality of Law, 10 Vill. L. Rev. 624 (1965).

Symposium, The Relation of Law and Morals, 1 J. Pub. L. 259 (1952).

Symposium, To the Memory of Felix S. Cohen, 9 Rut. L Rev. 355 (1954).

Symposium, The Philosophy of H.L.A. Hart, 35 U. Chi. L. Rev. 1 (1967).

Tammelo, Sketch for a Symbolic Juristic Logic, 8 J. Leg. Ed. 277 (1956).

——, On the Logical Openness of Legal Orders, 8 Am. J. Comp. L. 187 (1959).

—— and Prott, Legal and Extra-Legal Justification, 17 J. Leg. Ed. 412 (1965).

Taylor, The Science of Jurisprudence, 22 Harv. L. Rev. 241 (1909).

Terry, Letter to American Bar Association, 12 Reports, A.B.A. 327 (1889).

——, The Arrangement of the Law, 22 Green Bag 499 (1910).

——, Proximate Consequences in the Law of Torts, 28 Harv. L. Rev. 10 (1914).

——, The Correspondence of Duties and Rights, 25 Yale L.J. 171 (1916).

——, The Arrangement of the Law, 17 Colum. L. Rev. 291, 365 (1917).

——, Arrangement of the Law, 15 Ill. L. Rev. 61 (1920).

——, Duties, Rights and Wrongs, 10 A.B.A.J. 123 (1924).

Thayer, A., Natural Law, 21 L.Q. Rev. 60 (1905).

Thayer, E., Judicial Legislation: Its Legitimate Function in the Development of the Common Law, 5 Harv. L. Rev. 172 (1891).

Thayer, J., Law and Logic, 14 Harv. L. Rev. 139 (1900).

Thorne, Concerning the Scope of Jurisprudence, 35 Am. L. Rev. 546, 1 Can. L. Rev. 28 (1901).

Timasheff, Crisis in the Marxian Theory of Law, 16 N.Y.U.L.Q. 519 (1930).

Vinogradoff, The Crisis of Modern Jurisprudence, 29 Yale L.J. 312 (1920).

———, The Aims and Methods of Jurisprudence, 24 Colum. L. Rev. 1 (1924).

———, The Foundations of a Theory of Rights, 10 Va. L. Reg. n.s. 549 (1924), same as Vinogradoff, The Foundations of a Theory of Rights, 34 Yale L.J. 60 (1924).

Wade, The Concept of Legal Certainty: A Preliminary Skirmish, 4 Modern L. Rev. 183 (1941).

Watkins, Jurisprudence and Contemporary Psychology, 18 Notre Dame Lawyer 1 (1942).

Wasserstrom, The Obligation to Obey the Law, 10 U.C.L.A.L. Rev. 780 (1963).

———, Rights, Human Rights, and Racial Discrimination, 61 J. Phil. 628 (1964).

———, On the Morality of War: A Preliminary Inquiry, 21 Stan. L. Rev. 1627 (1969).

Wigmore, Responsibility for Tortious Acts: Its History, 7 Harv. L. Rev. 315 (1894).

———, The Tripartite Division of Torts, 8 Harv. L. Rev. 200 (1894).

———, A General Analysis of Tort Relations, 8 Harv. L. Rev. 377 (1895).

———, The Pledge Idea: A Study in Comparative Legal Ideas (pts. 1–3), 10 Harv. L. Rev. 321, 389 (1897), 11 Harv. L. Rev. 18 (1897).

———, The Terminology of Legal Science with a Plea for the Science of Nomothetics, 28 Harv. L. Rev. 1 (1914).

———, Nova Methodus Discendae Docendaeque Jurisprudentiae, 30 Harv. L. Rev. 812 (1917).

———, Problems of the Law's Evolution, 4 Va. L. Rev. 247 (1917).

———, Problems of the Law's Mechanism in America, 4 Va. L. Rev. 337 (1917).

———, Problems of World Legislation and America's Share Therein, 4 Va. L. Rev. 423 (1917).

Wilkin, Natural Law: Its Robust Revival Defies the Positivists, 35 A.B.A.J. 192 (1949).

Williams, Language and the Law (pts. 1–5), 61 L.Q. Rev.71, 179, 293, 384 (1945), 62 L.Q. Rev. 387 (1946).

———, The Concept of Legal Liberty, 56 Colum. L. Rev. 1129 (1956).

Willis, Some Fundamental Legal Concepts, 1 Ind. L.J. 18 (1926).

Wilson, The Inter-relation of Sociology, Politics, and Jurisprudence, 5 Am. Pol. Sci. Rev. 1 (1911).

Witherspoon, The Relation of Philosophy to Jurisprudence, 3 Nat. L. Forum 105 (1958).

Wormser, Sociology and the Law, 1 N.Y.U.L. Rev. 8 (1924).

Wright, American Interpretations of Natural Law, 20 Am. Pol. Sci. Rev. 524 (1926).

Yntema, The Hornbook Method and the Conflict of Laws, 37 Yale L.J. 468 (1928).

———, The Rational Basis of Legal Science, 31 Colum. L. Rev. 925 (1931).

———, Mr. Justice Holmes' View of Legal Science, 40 Yale L.J. 696 (1931).

———, The Purview of Research in the Administration of Justice, 16 Iowa L. Rev. 337 (1931).

———, Implications of Legal Science, 10 N.Y.U.Q.L. Rev. 279 (1933).

———, The American Law Institute, 12 Can. B. R. 319 (1934).

———, Legal Science and Reform, 34 Colum. L. Rev. 207 (1934).

———, Jurisprudence on Parade, 39 Mich. L. Rev. 1154 (1941).

———, "Law and Learning Theory" Through the Looking Glass of Legal Theory, 53 Yale L.J. 338 (1944).

———, Jurisprudence and Metaphysics—Triangular Correspondence, 59 Yale L.J. 273 (1950).

Zane, German Legal Philosophy, 16 Mich. L. Rev. 287 (1918).

SECONDARY SOURCES

Books and Monographs

Aichele, G. O.W. Holmes, Jr., Soldier, Scholar, Judge (1989).

Baade, H., ed. Jurimetrics (1963).

Bechtler, T., ed. Law in a Social Context: Liber Amicorum Honouring Prof. Lon L. Fuller (1978).

Bodenheimer, E. Jurisprudence: The Philosophy and Method of the Law (1940, 2d ed. 1962, rev ed. 1974).

Brown, B. The Natural Law Reader (1960).

Buckland, W. Some Reflections on Jurisprudence (1945).

Burrow, J. Evolution and Society: A Study in Victorian Social Theory (1966).

Cairns, H. Legal Philosophy from Plato to Hegel (1949).

Carpenter, W. Foundations of Modern Jurisprudence (1958).

Christie, G. Jurisprudence: Text and Readings in Jurisprudence and Legal Philosophy (1973).

Cohen, F., and Cohen, M., eds. Readings in Jurisprudence and Legal Philosophy (1951).

Cohen, M., ed. Ronald Dworkin and Contemporary Jurisprudence (1984).

Columbia Law Review, ed. *Essays on Jurisprudence from the Columbia Law Review* (1963).

Cowan, T. *The American Jurisprudence Reader* (1967).

Dawson, J. *The Oracles of the Law* (1959, reprinted 1968).

Dias, R. *Bibliography of Jurisprudence* (1970).

———, and Hughes, G. *Jurisprudence* (1957, 3rd ed. 1970).

Friedmann, W. *Legal Theory* (1944, 5th ed. 1967).

Friedrich, C. *The Philosophy of Law in Historical Perspective* (1963).

Garlan, E. *Legal Realism and Justice* (1941).

Golding, M., ed. *The Nature of Law: Readings in Legal Philosophy* (1966).

Gray, J. *Hayek on Liberty* (1984).

Hacker, P., and Raz, J. *Law, Morality and Society: Essays in Honor of H.L.A. Hart* (1977).

Haines, C. *The Revival of Natural Law Concepts* (1930).

Hall, J. *Foundations of Jurisprudence* (1973).

Harding, A., ed. *Origins of the Natural Law Tradition* (1955).

———, ed. *Natural Law and Natural Rights* (1955).

Harris, J. *Introduction to Legal Philosophies* (1980).

Henson, R. *Landmarks of Law* (1960).

Hollinger, D. *Morris R. Cohen and the Scientific Ideal* (1975).

Hommes, H. *Major Trends in the History of Legal Philosophy* (1979).

Honnold, J. *The Life of the Law* (1964).

Hook, S., ed. *Law and Philosophy* (1964).

Hughes, G., ed. *Law, Reason and Justice* (1969).

Hunt, A. *The Sociological Movement in Law* (1978).

Johnson, J. *American Legal Culture, 1908–1940* (1981).

Jones, H., ed. *Law and the Social Role of Science* (1967).

Jones, J. *Historical Introduction to the Theory of Law* (1940).

Kalman, L. *Legal Realism at Yale: 1927–1960* (1986).

Keeton, G. *The Elementary Principles of Jurisprudence* (1930).

Kellogg, F. *The Formative Essays of Justice Holmes: The Making of an American Legal Philosophy* (1984).

Kent, E. *Law and Philosophy: Readings in Legal Philosophy* (1970).

Lasswell, H., and Lerner, D. *The Policy Sciences: Recent Developments in Scope and Method* (1951).

LeBuffe, F. *Outlines of Pure Jurisprudence* (1924).

———, and Haynes, J. *Jurisprudence: With Cases to Illustrate Principles* (3d ed. 1938).

———. *The American Philosophy of Law: With Cases to Illustrate Principles* (rev. ed. 1947).

Lewis, W. *Eight Great American Lawyers* (1909).

Lloyd, D., and Freeman, M. *Lloyd's Introduction to Jurisprudence* (1959, 5th ed. 1987).

London School of Economics, ed. *Modern Theories of Law* (1933).

MacCormick, N. *H.L.A. Hart* (1981).

MacGuigan, M. *Jurisprudence: Readings and Cases* (1966).

Mayda, J. *François Geny and Modern Jurisprudence* (1978).

Morison, W. *John Austin* (1982).

Morris, C. *The Great Legal Philosophers* (1959).

Murphy, C. *Modern Legal Philosophy: The Tension between Experimental and Abstract Thought* (1978).

Murphy, J., and Coleman, J. *The Philosophy of Law: An Introduction to Jurisprudence* (1984).

Nishiyama, C., and Leube, K., eds. *The Essence of Hayek* (1984).

Novick, S. *Honorable Justice: The Life of Oliver Wendell Holmes* (1989).

O'Connor, D. *Aquinas and Natural Law* (1967).

Paton, G. *A Textbook of Jurisprudence* (1946, 4th ed. 1972).

Patterson, E. *Jurisprudence: Men and Ideas of the Law* (1953).

Pohlman, H. *Justice Oliver Wendell Holmes and Utilitarian Jurisprudence* (1984).

Pollack, E. *Jurisprudence: Principles and Applications* (1979).

Presser, S., and Zainaldin, J. *Law and Jurisprudence in American History: Cases and Materials* (1980, 2d ed. 1989).

Purcell, E. *The Crisis of Democratic Theory: Scientific Naturalism and the Problem of Value* (1973).

Reisman, W., and Schreiber, A. *Jurisprudence, Understanding and Shaping Law: Cases, Readings, Commentary* (1987).

Reuschlein, H. *Jurisprudence: Its American Prophets: A Survey of Taught Jurisprudence* (1951).

Rosen, P. *The Supreme Court and Social Science* (1972).

Rosenberg, J. *Jerome Frank: Jurist and Philosopher* (1970).

Rumble, W. *American Legal Realism: Skepticism, Reform and the Judicial Process* (1968).

———. *The Thought of John Austin: Jurisprudence, Colonial Reform, and the British Constitution* (1985).

Sayre, P. *The Life of Roscoe Pound* (1948).

Schubert, G., ed. *Judicial Behavior: A Reader in Theory and Research* (1964).

———. *Judicial Decisionmaking* (1963).

Schuchman, P. *Cohen and Cohen's Readings in Jurisprudence and Legal Philosophy* (1979).

Setaro, F. *A Bibliography of the Writings of Roscoe Pound* (1942).

Simon, Y. *The Tradition of Natural Law* (1965).

Stein, P. *Legal Evolution* (1980).

Snyder, O. *Preface to Jurisprudence* (1954).

Strait, G. *A Bibliography of the Writings of Roscoe Pound, 1940–1960* (1960).

Stumpf, S. *Morality and Law* (1966).

Summers, R., ed. *Essays in Legal Philosophy* (1968).
———. *Instrumentalism and American Legal Theory* (1982).
———. *Lon L. Fuller* (1984).
Twining, W. *Karl Llewellyn and the Realist Movement* (1973).
———, ed. *Legal Theory and Common Law* (1986).
White, G. *Patterns of American Legal Thought* (1978).
White, M. *Social Thought in America: The Revolt against Formalism* (1949).
Wiener, P. *Evolution and the Founders of Pragmatism* (1949).
Wigdor, D. *Roscoe Pound: Philosopher of Law* (1974).
Winston, K. *The Principles of Social Order: Selected Essays of Lon L. Fuller* (1981).
Wortley, B. *Jurisprudence* (1967).
Wu, C. *Cases and Material on Jurisprudence* (1958).

ARTICLES

Amos, Roscoe Pound, in *Modern Theories of Law* 86 (1933).
Arnold, Professor Hart's Theology, 73 Harv. L. Rev. 1298 (1960).
Aronson, Roscoe Pound and the Resurgence of Juristic Idealism, 6 Jour. Soc. Phil. 47 (1940).
———, Tendencies in American Jurisprudence, 4 Univ. Toronto L.J. 90 (1941).
———, The Juridical Evolution of James Coolidge Carter, 10 Univ. Toronto L.J. 1 (1953).
Atiyah, The Legacy of Holmes through English Eyes, 63 Bost. U. L. Rev. 341 (1983).
Ayer, In Quest of Efficiency: The Ideological Journey of Thurman Arnold in the Interwar Period, 23 Stan. L. Rev. 1049 (1971).
Babb, Petrazhitskii: Science of Legal Policy and Theory of Law, 17 Bost. U. L. Rev. 793 (1937).
Baybrooke, The Sociological Jurisprudence of Roscoe Pound, 5 U. W. Aust. L. Rev. 288 (1961).
Beatty, On Legal Realism—Some Basic Ideas of Jerome Frank, 11 Ala. L. Rev. 239 (1959).
Bloustein, Logic and Realism: The Realist as a Frustrated Idealist, 50 Corn. L. Q. 24 (1964).
———, Holmes: His First Amendment Theory and His Pragmatist Bent, 40 Rutgers L. Rev. 283 (1988).
Bodenheimer, Significant Developments in German Legal Philosophy since 1945, 3 Am. J. Comp. L. 379 (1954).
———, Cardozo's Views on Law and Adjudication Revisited, 22 U.C. Davis L. Rev. 1095 (1989).
Brody, The Pragmatic Naturalism of Mr. Justice Holmes, 46 Chi.-Kent L. Rev. 9 (1969).

Brown, Jerome Frank and the Natural Law, 5 Cath. Lawyer 133 (1959).

Brownell, Robert Maynard Hutchins, 1899–1977, 86 Yale L.J. 1547 (1977).

Burton, Justice Holmes and the Jesuits, 27 Am. J. Juris. 32 (1982).

Cairns, The Legal Philosophy of Morris R. Cohen, 14 Vand. L. Rev. 239 (1960).

Campbell, German Influences on English Legal Education Jurisprudence in the 19th Century, 4 U. West. Aust. L. Rev. 357 (1959).

Casebeer, Escape from Liberalism: Fact and Value in Karl Llewellyn, 1977 Duke L.J. 671.

Cassels, Lon Fuller: Liberalism and the Limits of Law, 36 U. Toronto L.J. 318 (1986).

Cassidy, Roscoe Pound: The Scope of His Life and Work, 7 N.Y.U.Q L. Rev. 897 (1930).

Cavers, Science, Research and the Law: Beutel's "Experimental Jurisprudence," 10 J. Leg. Ed. 162 (1957).

Chase, The Birth of the American Law School, 23 Am. J. Leg. Hist. 329 (1979).

Chroust, German Definitions of Law and Legal Philosophy from Kant to Kelsen, 22 Notre Dame Lawyer 365 (1947).

Clark, D., Tracing the Roots of American Legal Education—A Nineteenth-Century German Connection, 51 Rabels Zeitschrift 313 (1987).

Clark, R., Hans Kelsen's Pure Theory of Law, 22 J. Leg. Ed. 170 (1970).

Cohen, M., A Critical Sketch of Legal Philosophy in America, in *Law: A Century of Progress* 266 (1937).

Comment, The Proposed Restatement of the Law, 1 N.Y.U.L. Rev. 204 (1923).

Comment, Legal Theory and Legal Education, 79 Yale L.J. 1153 (1970).

Comment, Liberalism and Legal Science: The Jurisprudence of Morris Raphael Cohen, 52 Notre Dame Lawyer 653 (1977).

Comment, Dworkin and Subjectivity in Legal Interpretation, 40 Stan. L. Rev. 1517 (1988).

Comment, Karl Llewellyn and the Intellectual Foundations of Enterprise Liability Theory, 97 Yale L.J. 1131 (1988).

Cowan, Legal Pragmatism and Beyond, in Sayre, ed., *Interpretations of Modern Legal Philosophies* 130 (1947).

———, Report on the Status of Philosophy of Law in the United States, 50 Colum. L. Rev. 1086 (1950).

Crystal, Codification and the Rise of the Restatement Movement, 54 Wash. L. Rev. 239 (1979).

D'Amato, Lon Fuller and Substantive Natural Law, 26 Am. J. Juris. 202 (1981).

Dudziak, Oliver Wendell Holmes as a Eugenic Reformer, 71 Iowa L. Rev. 833 (1986).

Elison, Kohler's Philosophy of Law, 10 J. Pub. L. 408 (1961).

Elliott, Holmes and Evolution: Legal Process as Artificial Intelligence, 13 J. Leg. Stud. 113 (1984).

————, The Evolutionary Tradition in Jurisprudence, 85 Colum. L. Rev. 38
    (1985).
Farnum, Dean Roscoe Pound: His Significance in American Legal Thought, 14
    Bost. U. L. Rev. 715 (1934).
Ferguson, Holmes and the Judicial Figure, 55 U. Chi. L. Rev. 506 (1988).
Fisch, Justice Holmes, The Prediction Theory of Law and Pragmatism, 39 J.
    Phil. 85 (1942).
Frank, A Conflict with Oblivion: Some Observations on the Founders of Legal
    Pragmatism, 9 Rutgers L. Rev. 425 (1954).
Franklin, Philosophy and Legal Philosophy of Chaim Perelman, 19 Buff. L. Rev.
    261 (1970).
Freund, Historical Jurisprudence in Germany, 5 Pol. Sci. Q. 468 (1890).
Geis, Sociology and Sociological Jurisprudence: Admixture of Lore and Law, 52
    Ky. L.J. 267 (1964).
Golding, Jurisprudence and Legal Philosophy in Twentieth-Century America—
    Major Themes and Developments, 36 J. Leg. Ed. 441 (1986).
Goldring, Julius Stone and the Study of Law and Society in Australia, 2 Austl. J.
    L. and Soc. 4 (1985).
Goodhart, Some American Interpretations of Law, in Modern Theories of Law
    1 (1933).
Gordon, Holmes' Common Law as Legal and Social Science, 10 Hofstra L. Rev.
    719 (1982).
Grey, Langdell's Orthodoxy, 45 U. Pitt. L. Rev. 1 (1983).
————, Holmes and Legal Pragmatism, 41 Stan. L. Rev. 787 (1989).
Grossman, The Legal Philosophy of Roscoe Pound, 44 Yale L.J. 605 (1935).
Hadley, Historic Background of the Plan for the Restatement of the Law, 9
    A.B.A.J. 203 (1923).
Hall, The Present Position of Jurisprudence in the United States, 44 Va. L. Rev.
    322 (1958).
Hantzis, Legal Innovation within the Wider Intellectual Tradition: The
    Pragmatism of Oliver Wendell Holmes, Jr., 82 N.W. L. Rev. 541 (1988).
Harris, Kelsen's Concept of Authority, 36 Camb. L.J. 353 (1977).
Hart, Philosophy of Law and Jurisprudence in Britain (1945–52), 2 Am. J.
    Comp. L. 355 (1953).
Herget and Wallace, The German Free Law Movement as the Source of
    American Legal Realism, 73 Va. L. Rev. 399 (1987).
Herman, Llewellyn the Civilian: Speculation on the Contribution of Continental
    Experience to the Uniform Commercial Code, 56 Tulane L. Rev. 1125 (1982).
Hoeflich, Law and Geometry: Legal Science from Leibnitz to Langdell, 30 Am.
    J. Leg. Hist. 95 (1986).
Hoffheimer, Holmes, L.Q.C. Lamar and Natural Law, 58 Miss. L.J. 71 (1988).
————, The Early Critical and Philosophical Writings of Justice Holmes, 30
    Bost. Coll. L. Rev. 1221 (1989).
Hovenkamp, Evolutionary Models in Jurisprudence, 64 Tex. L. Rev. 645 (1985).

————, Social Science and Segregation before *Brown*, 1985 Duke L.J. 624.

Hull, Some Realism about the Llewellyn-Pound Exchange on Realism: The Newly Uncovered Private Correspondence, 1927–1931, 1987 Wis. L. Rev. 921.

————, Reconstructing the Origins of Realistic Jurisprudence: A Prequel to the Llewellyn-Pound Exchange over Legal Realism, 1989 Duke L. J. 1302.

Husik, The Legal Philosophy of Hans Kelsen, 3 J. Soc. Phil. 297 (1938).

Isaacs, The Schools of Jurisprudence, 31 Harv. L. Rev. 373 (1918).

Janzen, Kelsen's Theory of Law, 31 Am. Pol. Sci. Rev. 205 (1937).

Jones, Law and Morality in the Perspective of Legal Realism, 61 Colum. L. Rev. 799 (1961).

Kaplan, Encounters with O. W. Holmes, 96 Harv. L. Rev. 1828 (1983).

Kocourek, A Critique of Pound's Theory of Justice, 20 Iowa L. Rev. 531 (1935).

————, A Century of Analytic Jurisprudence since John Austin, in *Law: A Century of Progress* 195 (1937).

————, Roscoe Pound as a Former Colleague Knew Him, in Sayre, ed., *Interpretations of Modern Legal Philosophies* 419 (1947).

Konefsky, Mensch, and Schlegel, In Memoriam: The Intellectual Legacy of Lon Fuller, 30 Buff. L. Rev. 263 (1981).

Kreilkamp, Dean Pound and the End of Law, 9 Ford. L. Rev. 196 (1940).

————, Dean Pound and the Immutable Natural Law, 18 Ford. L. Rev. 173 (1949).

Landman, Primitive Law, Evolution and Sir Henry Sumner Maine, 28 Mich. L. Rev. 404 (1930).

LaPiana, Victorian from Beacon Hill: Oliver Wendell Holmes' Early Legal Scholarship, 90 Colum. L. Rev. 809 (1990).

Laserson, The Work of Leon Petrazhitskii, 51 Colum. L. Rev. 59 (1951).

Laski, Morris Cohen's Approach to Legal Philosophy, 15 U. Chi. L. Rev. 575 (1948).

Leonhard, Methods Followed in Germany by the Historical School of Law, 7 Colum. L. Rev. 573 (1907).

Lewis, O., Synergistic Jurisprudence and Eugen Ehrlich, 4 N. Ky. L. Rev. 21 (1977).

Lewis, W., The Plan to Establish the American Law Institute, 9 A.B.A.J. 77 (1923).

————, The Restatement of the Law, 3 Wis. L. Rev. 1 (1924).

Lucey, Natural Law and American Legal Realism: Their Respective Contributions to a Theory of Law in a Democratic Society, 30 Geo. L.J. 493 (1942).

March, Sociological Jurisprudence Revisited: A Review (More or Less) of Max Gluckman, 8 Stan. L. Rev. 531 (1966).

McDougal and Reisman, Harold Dwight Lasswell, 73 Am. J. Int. L. 655 (1979).

McManaman, Social Engineering: The Legal Philosophy of Roscoe Pound, 33 St. John's L. Rev. 1 (1958).

McWhinney, Wolfgang Friedmann and Eclectic Legal Philosophy, 6 Ind. L.J. 169 (1972).

Mearns, Scientific Legal Theory and Arnold Brecht, 47 Va. L. Rev. 264 (1961).

Mellen, Ralph Waldo Emerson, Mr. Justice Holmes and the Idea of Organic Form in American Law, 14 New Eng. L. Rev. 147 (1978).

Mermin, Computers, Law and Justice: An Introductory Lecture, 1967 Wis. L. Rev. 43.

Moore, Prolegomenon to the Jurisprudence of Myres McDougal and Harold Lasswell, 54 Va. L. Rev. 662 (1968).

Morison, Some Myth about Positivism, 68 Yale L.J. 212 (1958).

Morris, Verbal Disputes and the Legal Philosophy of John Austin, 7 U.C.L.A.L. Rev. 27 (1960).

Moskowitz, The American Legal Realists and an Empirical Science of Law, 11 Vill. L. Rev. 480 (1966).

———, The Prediction Theory of Law, 39 Temp. L.Q. 413 (1966).

Nys, Francis Lieber—His Life and his Work, 5 Am. J. Int. L. 84, 355 (1911).

O'Toole, The Jurisprudence of François Geny, 3 Vill. L. Rev. 455 (1958).

Page, Professor Ehrlich's Czernowitz Seminar of Living Law, 14 Proc. Assoc. Am. L. Schools 46 (1914). Reprinted in 4 N. Ky. L. Rev. 37 (1977).

Pannam, Professor Hart and Analytical Jurisprudence, 16 J. Leg. Ed. 379 (1964).

Patterson, Pound's Theory of Social Interests, in Sayre, ed., *Interpretations of Modern Legal Philosophies* 558 (1947).

———, Historical and Evolutionary Theories of Law, 51 Colum. L. Rev. 681 (1951).

———, Hans Kelsen and His Pure Theory of Law, 40 Calif. L. Rev. 5 (1952).

Paulson, Constraints on Legal Norms: Kelsen's View in the Essays, 42 Univ. Chi. L. Rev. 768 (1975).

Peller, Neutral Principles in the 1950s, 21 J. Law Reform 561 (1988).

Pollok, Roscoe Pound and Sociological Jurisprudence, 47 So. Afr. L.J. 247, 374 (1930).

Pound, The Progress of the Law: Analytical Jurisprudence, 1914–1927, 41 Harv. L. Rev. 174 (1927).

———, The Ideal and the Actual in the Law—Forty Years After, 1 Geo. Wash. L. Rev. 431 (1930).

———, Fifty Years of Jurisprudence, 50 Harv. L. Rev. 557 (1937).

———, The Revival of Natural Law, 17 Notre Dame Lawyer 287 (1942).

Powers, Some Reflections on Pound's Jurisprudence of Interests, 3 Cath. U. L. Rev. 10 (1953).

Radbruch, Anglo-American Jurisprudence through Continental Eyes, 52 L.Q. Rev. 530 (1936).

Raleigh, Legal Education in London, 23 L.Q. Rev. 258 (1907).

Raz, Kelsen's Theory of the Basic Norm, 19 Am. J. Juris. 94 (1974).

Reck, The Philosophical Context of F.S.C. Northrop's Legal Theory, 34 Tulane L. Rev. 505 (1960).

Reimann, The Historical School Against Codification: Savigny, Carter, and the Defeat of the New York Civil Code, 37 Am. J. Comp. L. 95 (1989).

Roberts, Justice Cardozo Revisited: Phenomenological Contributions to Jurisprudence, 12 Cath. U. L. Rev. 92 (1963).

Robertson, The Legal Philosophy of Leon Green, 56 Tex. L. Rev. 393 (1978).

Rogat, Mr. Justice Holmes: A Dissenting Opinion, 15 Stan. L. Rev. 254 (1963).

Rosenblatt, Holmes, Pierce and Legal Pragmatism, 84 Yale L.J. 1123 (1975).

Rosenfield, Morris R. Cohen: A Philosopher's Influence on the Law, 26 Cath. Lawyer 52 (1980).

Rumble, Rule-Skepticism and the Role of the Judge: A Study of American Realism, 15 J. Pub. L. 251 (1966).

———, Jerome Frank and His Critics: Certainty and Fantasy in the Judicial Process, 10 Pub. L. 125 (1961).

———, John Austin and His Nineteenth Century Critics: The Case of Sir Henry Sumner Maine, 39 No. Ireland L.Q. 119 (1988).

Sabine, Rudolf Stammler's Critical Philosophy of Law, 18 Corn. L.Q. 321 (1933).

Sadurska, The Jurisprudence of Leon Petrazycki, 32 Am. J. Juris. 63 (1987).

Schechter, Paul Vinogradoff: The Pontiff of Comparative Jurisprudence, 24 Ill. L. Rev. 528 (1930).

Schlegel, American Legal Realism and Empirical Social Science: From the Yale Experience, 28 Buffalo L. Rev. 459 (1979).

———, American Legal Realism and Empirical Social Science: The Singular Case of Underhill Moore, 29 Buff. L. Rev. 195 (1980).

Sinclair, The Use of Evolution Theory in Law, 64 Univ. Detroit L. Rev. 451 (1987).

Soper, Legal Theory and the Obligation of the Judge: The Hart/Dworkin Dispute, 75 Mich. L. Rev. 473 (1977).

Speziale, By Their Fruits You Shall Know Them: Pragmatism and the Prediction Theory of Law, 9 Manitoba L.J. 29 (1978).

———, Langdell's Concept of Law as a Science, 5 Vt. L. Rev. 1 (1980).

———, Oliver Wendell Holmes, Jr., William James, Theodore Roosevelt and the Strenuous Life, 13 Conn. L. Rev. 663 (1981).

———, The Experimental Logic of Benjamin Nathan Cardozo, 77 Ky. L. Rev. 821 (1989).

Starke, Fundamental Views and Ideas of Hans Kelsen, 48 Aust. L.J. 388 (1974).

Starr, Law and Morality in H.L.A. Hart's Legal Philosophy, 67 Marq. L. Rev. 673 (1984).

Stone, A Critique of Pound's Theory of Justice, 20 Iowa L. Rev. 531 (1935).

———, Roscoe Pound and Sociological Jurisprudence, 78 Harv. L. Rev. 1578 (1965).

——— and Moens, Ilmar Tammelo—A Personal Appreciation, 10 Sydney L. Rev. 128 (1983).

Stumpf, Austin's Theory of the Separation of Law and Morals, 14 Vand. L. Rev. 117 (1960).

Summers, Professor Fuller on Morality and Law, 18 J. Leg. Ed. 1 (1965).

———, The New Analytical Jurists, 41 N.Y.U.L. Rev. 861 (1966).

Swygert and Bruce, The Historical Origins, Founding, and Early Development of Student-Edited Law Reviews, 36 Hastings L.J. 739 (1985).

Symposium, Cardozo and the Judicial Process, 71 Yale L.J. 195 (1961).

Symposium, Chaim Perelman, 12 N. Ky. L. Rev. 391 (1985).

Symposium, Chaim Perelman, 5 Law and Phil. 281 (1986).

Symposium, Charles A. Beard, 56 Geo. Wash. L. Rev. 1 (1987).

Symposium, Charles Sanders Pierce, 7 J. Pub. L. 1 (1958).

Symposium, Edmond Cahn, 40 N.Y.U.L. Rev. 207 (1964).

Symposium, Felix S. Cohen, 9 Rutgers L. Rev. 355 (1954).

Symposium, Festschrift for Leon Green, 56 Tex. L. Rev. 381 (1978).

Symposium, Festschrift in Honor of Edgar Bodenheimer, 21 U. C. Davis L. Rev. 465 (1988).

Symposium, John Henry Wigmore, 75 Nw. U. L. Rev. 130 (1981).

Symposium, Julius Stone, 9 U.N.S.W.L.J. 1 (1986).

Symposium, Mr. Justice Holmes, 31 Univ. Chi. L. Rev. 213 (1964).

Symposium, Mr. Justice Holmes, 28 Fla. L. Rev. 365 (1976).

Symposium, Science Challenges the Law, 19 Case-West. Res. L. Rev. 5 (1967).

Symposium, Studies in Legal Philosophy, 14 Vand. L. Rev. 1 (1960).

Symposium, To the Memory of Felix S. Cohen, 9 Rut. L. Rev. 355 (1954).

Symposium, Tribute to Hans Kelsen, 59 Calif. L. Rev. 617 (1971).

Symposium, Wolfgang Friedmann, 10 Colum. J. Trans. L. 1 (1971).

Touster, Holmes: The Years of the Common Law, 64 Colum. L. Rev. 230 (1964).

———, In Search of Holmes from Within, 18 Vand. L. Rev. 437 (1965).

———, Holmes a Hundred Years Ago: The Common Law and Legal Theory, 10 Hofstra L. Rev. 673 (1982).

Tushnet, The Logic of Experience: Oliver Wendell Holmes, Jr., on the Supreme Judicial Court, 63 Va. L. Rev. 975 (1977).

Veilleux, The Scientific Model in Law, 75 Geo. L.J. 1967 (1987).

Verdun-Jones, The Jurisprudence of Karl Llewellyn, 1 Dalhousie L.J. 441 (1974).

———, Jerome N. Frank: A Study in American Legal Realism, 7 Sydney L. Rev. 180 (1974).

———, Jurisprudence Washed with Cynical Acid: Thurman Arnold and the Psychological Bases of Scientific Jurisprudence, 3 Dalhousie L.J. 470 (1976).

——— and Cousineau, The Voice Crying in the Wilderness: Underhill Moore as a Pioneer in the Establishment of an Interdisciplinary Jurisprudence, 1 Int. J. Law and Psychiatry 375 (1978).

Vetter, Postwar Legal Scholarship on Judicial Decisionmaking, 33 J. Leg. Ed. 412 (1983).

———, The Evolution of Holmes, Holmes and Evolution, 72 Calif. L. Rev. 343 (1984).

Voegelin, Kelsen's Pure Theory of Law, 42 Pol. Sci. Q. Rev. 268 (1927).

Volkomer, Judge Jerome Frank: The Legal Realist as Jurist, 60 N.Y. St. Bar J. 38 (1988).

Walter, The Legal Ecology of Roscoe Pound, 4 Miami L.Q. 178 (1950).

Wellman, Dworkin and the Legal Process Tradition: The Legacy of Hart and Sacks, 29 Ariz. L. Rev. 413 (1987).

White, The Rise and Fall of Justice Holmes, 39 Univ. Chi. L. Rev. 51 (1971).

————, From Sociological Jurisprudence to Realism: Jurisprudence and Social Change in Early Twentieth-Century America, 58 Va. L. Rev. 999 (1972).

————, The Integrity of Holmes' Jurisprudence, 10 Hofstra L. Rev. 633 (1982).

————, From Realism to Critical Legal Studies: A Truncated Intellectual History, 40 S.W.L.J. 819 (1986).

————, Chief Justice Marshall, Justice Holmes, and the Discourse of Constitutional Adjudication, 30 Wm. and Mary L. Rev. 131 (1988).

Whitman, Commercial Law and the American *Volk*: A Note on Llewellyn's German Sources for the Uniform Commercial Code, 97 Yale L.J. 156 (1987).

Winston, Is/Ought Redux: The Pragmatist Context of Lon Fuller's Conception, 8 Ox. J. L. Stud. 329 (1988).

Woodard, The Limits of Legal Realism: An Historical Perspective, 54 Va. L. Rev. 689 (1968).

Wu, The Juristic Philosophy of Roscoe Pound, 18 Ill. L. Rev. 288 (1924).

————, Justice Holmes and the Common Law Tradition, 14 Vand. L. Rev. 221 (1960).

Yntema, American Legal Realism in Retrospect, 14 Vand. L. Rev. 317 (1960).

Zane, German Legal Philosophy, 16 Mich. L. Rev. 287 (1918).

The Modern Legal Philosophy Series

Vol. 1 Gareis, K. *Science of Law* (trans. Kocourek, 1911).

Vol. 2 Berolzheimer, F. *The World's Legal Philosophies* (trans. Jastrow, 1912).

Vol. 3 Miraglia, L. *Comparative Legal Philosophy* (trans. Lisle, 1912).

Vol. 4 Korkunov, N. *General Theory of Law* (trans. Hastings, 1909).

Vol. 5 Jhering, R. *Law as a Means to an End* (1877–82, trans. Husik, 1913).

Vol. 6 Not published.

Vol. 7 Fouillee, A., Charmont, J., Duguit, L., and Demogue, R. *Modern French Legal Philosophy* (trans. Chamberlain and Scott, 1916).

Vol. 8 Stammler, R. *The Theory of Justice* (trans. Husik, 1925).

Vol. 9 Association of American Law Schools, Various Authors, *The Science of Legal Method* (trans. Register and Bruncken, 1917).

Vol. 10 DelVecchio, G. *The Formal Bases of Law* (trans. Lisle, 1914).

Vol. 11 Not published.

Vol. 12 Kohler, J. *Philosophy of Law* (trans. Albrecht, 1914).

Vol. 13 Tourtoulon, P. *Philosophy in the Development of Law* (trans. Read, 1922).

Twentieth-Century Legal Philosophy Series

Vol. 1 Kelsen, H. *General Theory of Law and State* (trans. Wedberg, 1945).

Vol. 2 Ruemelin, M., et al. *The Jurisprudence of Interests* (trans. Schoch, 1948).

Vol. 3 Recasen-Siches, L. *Latin American Legal Philosophy* (trans. Ireland, 1948).

Vol. 4 Lask, E., et al. *The Legal Philosophies of Lask, Radbruch and Dabin* ·(trans. Wilk, 1950).

Vol. 5 Lenin, V. *Soviet Legal Philosophy* (trans. Bubb, 1951).

Vol. 6 Rheinstein, M., ed. *Max Weber on Law in Economy and Society* (trans. Shils, 1954).

Vol. 7 Petrazhitskii, L. *Law and Morality* (trans. Bubb, 1955).

Vol. 8 Broderick, A., ed. *French Institutionalists: Maurice Hariou, George Renard, Joseph T. Delos* (trans. Wellington, 1970).

APPENDIX A
HOLMES' CLASSIFICATION
OF DUTIES

A. DUTIES TO ALL THE WORLD

1. To the sovereign
   - a. Law of prize
   - b. Military service
   - c. Criminal law

2. To all the world
   - a. Law of libel and slander (civil actions)
   - b. Injuries to the person—false imprisonment, etc.
   - c. Some nuisances?
   - d. Fraud independent of contract or special relations

3. To persons in particular situations or relations (some of these are only special applications of the class A-2)
   - a. Law of offices—corporations
   - b. Monopolies, such as patent rights
   - c. Possession
   - d. Ownership. Easement. Rent? etc.
   - e. Contract?
   - f. Domestic relations

B. DUTIES OF PERSONS IN PARTICULAR SITUATIONS OR RELATIONS

1. To the sovereign (perhaps for reasons of convenience to follow duties of all the world to the sovereign)
   - a. Duties of officers—impeachment, etc.
   - b. Eminent domain
   - c. Taxes on property

2. To all the world (perhaps to be put with duties of all the world to persons in the same situations. Some of these are special applications of A-2)
   - a. Corporations?
   - b. Duties of landowners to not make nuisances on their land, etc.

3. To persons in particular situations or relations (including more special applications of A-2 and A-3)
   - a. Members of corporation to each other
   - b. Landlord and tenant, etc.
   - c. Trustee and *cestue que trust*
   - d. Contractor and contractee
   - e. Master and servant
   - f. Guardian and ward, etc.

Source: 7 Am. L. Rev. 48 (1872)

APPENDIX B
HOLMES' CLASSIFICATION OF
PROPERTY TRANSFER

SUCCESSIONS

A. UNIVERSAL, or successions to the entire PERSONA of another, subject to greater or less exceptions
1. By will or death (executors and administrators)
2. By act inter vivos:
    a. By assignments in bankruptcy (assignees)?
    b. By marriage (husband to wife)?

B. PARTIAL, or successions to a special PERSONA, or group of rights and duties, severable from the other rights and duties of the party first sustaining it
1. By descent (lands)
2. By will (lands, chattels)
3. By act inter vivos:
    a. By voluntary change of possession (feoffment, delivery of chattels out of market overt, either with or without consideration)
    b. By deed (land or chattels)
    c. By other formalities, irrespective of consideration, such as transfer of shares on the books of a corporation
    d. By conveyance, either oral or in writing not under seal, for a consideration but without change of possession (chattels)
    e. By simple agreement or mutual assent without consideration or change of possession (certain gifts in equity)

To which may be added SUBDIVISIONS of a persona. Joint Administration Joint tenancy, etc. Particular estates

REPRESENTATIONS

Or introduction of one individual under a *persona* sustained by another.
1. For purposes indefinite in number and kind—slaves, servants, wives, some general agents
2. For definite purposes—agents

Source: 7 Am. L. Rev. 67 (1872)

APPENDIX C
HOLMES' CLASSIFICATION OF TORTS

	Consciousness of Party an Element	Determined by Acts or Events Exactly Defined	Determined by Acts or Events Not Exactly Defined
Duties of All to All	Fraud Willful or malicious injuries Negligence *stricto sensu*	Assault and battery Extreme cases, shading into negligence *latiori sensu*, which are not left to the jury	Negligence *latiori sensu*
Duties of Persons in Particular Situations to All		Liability of master for servant Ferocious animals Cattle Other things having an active tendency to do damage, e.g., reservoirs	
Duties of All to Persons in Particular Situations	Maliciously causing breach of contract Domestic relations?	Franchise or monopoly Possession Property Easements exactly defined by deed, or by an arbitrary rule of law	Prescriptive easements not exactly defined

Source: 7 Am. L. Rev. 667 (1873)

APPENDIX D
FIELD'S CLASSIFICATION
OF THE LAW
(PROPOSED CODES)

A. Political Code (constitutional, administrative and local government law)
B. Criminal Code
C. Code of Criminal Procedure
D. Code of Civil Procedure
E. Civil Code
  I. Persons
     1. Persons (generally legal capacity)
     2. Personal Rights (including law of libel and slander)
     3. Personal Relations
       a. Marriage
       b. Parent and Child
       c. Guardian and Ward
       d. Master and Servant
  II. Property
     1. In General
     2. Real Property
     3. Personal Property
     4. Acquisition of Property (including wills and succession)
  III. Obligations
     1. In General
     2. Contracts
     3. Torts
     4. Obligations Arising from Particular Transactions (including trusts, commercial transactions, common carriers, insurance, agency, partnership)
  IV. General Provisions Applicable to Persons, Property, and Obligations
     1. Relief (including damages and specific relief)
     2. Debtor and Creditor
     3. Nuisance
     4. Maxims of Jurisprudence
     5. Definitions and General Provisions

Source: Report of the New York Commissioners (1865)

APPENDIX E
TERRY'S CLASSIFICATION OF
THE ANGLO-AMERICAN LAW

I. Public Law
   A. Boundaries, geographical divisions of the state
   B. Constitutional law
   C. Administrative law
   D. Military and naval law
   E. Ecclesiastical law
   F. Criminal law
   G. Conflict of laws
II. Private Law
   A. The Law of Normal Persons
      (1) Definitions and general principles
         1. Persons
         2. Things
         3. Conduct (including acts, omissions, and forbearances)
         4. Consequences
         5. Intention and motive
         6. Negligence and reasonableness
         7. Malice
         8. Fraud
         9. Duties and rights in general
         10. Dispositive facts
         11. Wrongs
         12. Possession
         13. Juristic acts (including contracts)
         14. Miscellaneous
      (2) Rights and Duties
         1. Rights *in rem*
         2. Duties corresponding to rights *in rem*
         3. Rights *in personam*
         4. Trusts
      (3) Remedies
         1. Remedial rights
         2. Adjective law (procedure)
   B. The Law of Abnormal Persons
      (1) Natural persons
      (2) Artificial persons

Source: H. Terry, *Leading Principles* 633–36 (1884)

357

APPENDIX F
ABA COMMITTEE'S
CLASSIFICATION OF
THE LAW

I. International
II. Internal or Municipal
   A. Public
      1. Constitutional
      2. Legislative
      3. Administrative
      4. Criminal law and procedure
   B. Private
      1. Substantive
         a. Normal, or the law of things, i.e., relating to rights and duties not dependent upon any peculiarity of the persons affected
           (1) Rights considered with reference to the objects thereof and their correlative wrongs; in general property rights
              (a) Specific property
                 1) Tangible (real and personal)
                 2) Intangible (patents, contract rights, etc.)
              (b) Nonspecific rights such as life, freedom, etc., the violation of which constitutes torts
           (2) Rights considered with reference to the person or persons against whom they are available, and their correlative wrongs
              (a) Rights *in rem* (property, personal rights)
              (b) Rights *in personam* (contract, quasi-contract)
         b. Abnormal, or the law of persons; i.e., relating to rights and duties dependent upon peculiarities of the persons affected
           (1) Natural persons
           (2) Artificial persons
      2. Adjective Law (procedure and remedies)

Source: 14 Reports, Pro. ABA 402 (1891)

APPENDIX G
ANDREWS' CLASSIFICATION
OF AMERICAN LAW

I. International Law
   A. Public
   B. Private
II. Municipal Law
   A. Persons
      1. Public
         a. The people
         b. Magistrates
            (1) National (legislative, executive, judicial, etc.)
            (2) State (legislative, etc.)
      2. Private
         a. Classes of persons (corporations, aliens, citizens, etc.)
         b. Civil rights
         c. Domestic relations (husband-wife, parent-child, etc.)
   B. Things
      1. Personal property
         a. Species
             (1) Chattels
             (2) Choses
         b. Modes of transfer
             (1) By contract
                (a) Elements of contract
                (b) Specific types of contract (sales, agency, partnership insurance, negotiable instruments, etc.)
             (2) By will or descent
      2. Real property
         a. Things real
         b. Ownership
         c. Estates in land
         d. Of title
   C. Actions
      1. Civil remedies and procedure
      2. Criminal law and procedure

Source: J. Andrews, American Law lxiv–lxv (1900)

APPENDIX H
POUND'S CLASSIFICATION
OF THE LAW

I. Public Law
II. Criminal Law
III. Private Law
    A. General Part
        1. Forms of law
           a. Construction of statutes
           b. Application of precedents
        2. Application of law—conflict of laws
    B. Special Part
        1. Subjects of law
           a. Normal and abnormal persons—capacity and disability
           b. Legal entities—corporations, partnerships, etc.
        2. Objects of Law—property, including succession & mortgages
        3. Liability
           a. Measure of liability—damages, etc.
           b. Liability as a result of acts
               (1) Contract
                  (a) Common law
                  (b) Commercial
                  (c) Special—insurance, suretyship, etc.
               (2) Torts
           c. Liability as a result of relations
               (1) Family law
               (2) Public service by private agencies
               (3) Agency
               (4) Trusts
           d. Equitable liabilities—quasi-contract
        4. Enforcement of law—procedure and evidence

Source: 2 Proceedings, ALI 423–25 (1924)

APPENDIX I
KOCOUREK'S CLASSIFICATION OF THE LAW

I. General Introduction
   A. Constitutional Law
   B. Sources of Law
   C. Methods of Interpretation

II. Private Law
   A. General Part

1. Personateness	12. Consent
2. Capacity	13. Estoppel
3. Acts	14. Waiver
4. Intention	15. Ratification
5. Negligence	16. Warranty
6. Malice	17. Repudiation
7. Fraud	18. Rescission
8. Accident	19. Condition
9. Mistake	20. Abandonment
10. Duress	21. Representation
11. Privilege	22. Etc.

   B. Special Part

1. Family law	5. Public callings
2. Succession	6. Negotiable instruments
3. Trusts	7. Trade relations
4. Corporations	8. Workmen's compensation, etc.

III. Public Law
   A. General Part (?)
   B. Special Part

1. Organization	6. Operation
2. Legislation	7. Administration
3. Adjudication	8. Military
4. Police	9. Representation
5. Revenue	

IV. Special Law (new extension of older law)
   A. Private
   B. Public

Source: 11 NYUQ 319 (1934)

INDEX

Adams, Brooks, 118, 131–34, 143, 145, 159, 175
Adler, Mortimer, 209, 235
Albertsworth, A.F., 143n
Allen, Layman, 287–88
American Academy of Jurisprudence, 76–81
American Bar Association, 67–80
American Law Institute, 77–81, 217
American legal realism, *see* Poundian paradigm
analysis of rights and duties, 38, 47–49, 53–62, 84–90, 95–99, 101–115, 274–75
analytic jurisprudence, *see* expository paradigm
Anderson, Alan, 288
Andrews, James Dewitt, 73, 75–81
anthropology, 183–85
Aquinas, Thomas, *see* Thomism
Arnold, Thurman, 181–88, 219
arrangement of law, *see* classification
Auerbach, Carl, 294
Austin, John, 12–22, 38–41, 43, 47–48, 55, 74, 79, 82–91, 116, 130, 149, 189, 194, 230–31, 273–74, 293–95, 298
autonomy of law, 20

bad man, Holmes', 151
balancing of interests, *see* jurisprudence of interests
basic norm, see *Grundnorm*
Beard, Charles A., 134
behavioral jurisprudence, 291–92
behaviorism, 154–55, 160–62, 173, 195, 198–200, 289–92
Bentham, Jeremy, 13–22, 43, 130, 149, 157, 175, 190, 229–31, 295, 310
Bentley, Arthur F., 160–62, 175, 177, 198
Beutel, Frederick K., 194, 201–204

Bigelow, Melville M., 133
Bingham, Joseph W., 154–55, 177, 198, 254
Blackstone, William, 13–22, 32, 33, 36, 50, 55, 69–70, 74
Blatt, William M., 135
Bodenheimer, Edgar, 262–65, 294–95
Bohlen, Francis H., 142
Brecht, Arnold, 263n
Brown, W. Jethro, 140–41
Buckland, W.W., 87, 91–92
Burdick, Francis M., 134

Cahn, Edmond, 239, 242–44
Cairns, Huntington, 213–16
Campbell, Edward L., 231
Cardozo, Benjamin N., 172
Carter, James Coolidge, 67, 74, 118, 120–30, 139, 143, 145, 149, 153, 270
Chroust, Anton, 235
Clark, Charles E., 111, 213
class struggle, *see* Marxist jurisprudence
classification of law, 38–39, 62–63, 69, 73–74, 78–81
codification, 33–34, 41, 63–65, 68, 121
Cohen, Felix S., 180, 188–90, 219
Cohen, Morris R., 175, 185–88, 194, 208–214, 217–19, 259, 269
Columbia curriculum study, 174–75, 206
command theory of law, 19, 48, 123, 131, 149, 273–74, 297–98
common law, 31, 50–52, 80, 123–24, 126
Commons, John R., 113
Compte, Auguste, 12, 254
Cook, Walter Wheeler, 107, 194, 206–207, 212
Corbin, Arthur L., 106–111, 142
Corpus Juris Project, 75–76

363